The Huguenot Struggle for Recognition

N. M. Sutherland

The Huguenot Struggle
for Recognition

New Haven and London
Yale University Press
1980

Copyright © 1980 by Yale University.
All rights reserved. This book may not be reproduced, in whole
or in part, in any form (beyond that copying permitted by Sec-
tions 107 and 108 of the U.S. Copyright Law and except by
reviewers for the public press), without written permission from
the publishers.

Designed by Thos. Whitridge and set in VIP Janson type.
Printed in the United States of America by Vail-Ballou Press,
Binghamton, N.Y.

Published in Great Britain, Europe, Africa, and Asia (except
Japan) by Yale University Press, Ltd., London. Distributed in
Australia and New Zealand by Book & Film Services, Artar-
mon, N.S.W., Australia; and in Japan by Harper & Row, Publishers, Tokyo Office.

Library of Congress Cataloging in Publication Data

Sutherland, Nicola Mary.
  The Huguenot struggle for recognition.

  Bibliography: p.
  Includes index.
  1. Huguenots—France—History. 2. Persecution—
France—History. 3. France—Church History—16th
century. I. Title.
BX9454.2S9   272'.4   79-64070
ISBN 0-300-02328-6

For C. V. Wedgwood

Contents

Preface

THIS BOOK EXAMINES THE RELATIONS between the Protestants, the Catholics, and the crown in sixteenth-century France. The first two chapters, on the origins and development of the religious persecution, are introductory to the Huguenot struggle for recognition.

The author is aware that such a work is never "finished": much more extensive research could be done on the national level alone; also that the full story of the Huguenot struggle for survival and recognition requires numerous provincial studies. If this study provokes others to pursue the subject further, it will have served a useful purpose.

If this is not a complete study of the Huguenot struggle, still less is it a history of France. The criterion of what to include or omit has been the material necessary to explain the nature and content of each successive "religious" edict, as well as the manner in which, one after the other, they were frustrated. The edicts therefore form the structure and backbone of the work; hence their extensive analysis in the appendix. These important documents have never been treated as a single corpus of material; consequently they have not been interpreted either in relation to each other or in relation to the circumstances from which each one arose. Both approaches are essential if they are to yield their meaning.

The introduction was first published, in an annotated version, in the *Proceedings of the Huguenot Society of London*, xxiii, 1978. Chapter 3 was first published in *History*, June 1962, and chapter 9 in *Annali*, ii (i), 1968 (Milan). Both chapters have been slightly altered and amended.

I would especially like to record my thanks and gratitude to Dame Veronica Wedgwood for her unfailing help, advice, and encouragement over the years.

I would also like to express my thanks to the following friends and colleagues who have helped me with information, advice, corrections, and references; also a number of transcriptions which I was unable to make for myself: Dr. J. Bergin; Dr. Joan M. Davies; Mr. Alastair Duke; Mr. R. J. Knecht; the late Dr. Hélène Michaud; Dr. A. Soman and Dr. J. J. Woltjer.

London, April 1978

Introduction

THE FRENCH HUGUENOTS WERE CALVINISTS, whether from conviction, policy or varying proportions of both. But, while there were probably Calvinists in France from some time in the 1540s, the epithet Huguenot was not used before 1560. It then denoted a party, whose fortunes therefore became political. This development arose from the crisis which followed the death of Henry II, on 10 July 1559, after a jousting accident. The Protestants at first mistook this catastrophe for a merciful dispensation of providence because Henry had been poised to exterminate his heretic subjects.

The savage edict of Compiègne, 24 July 1557, had outlawed all Protestants and imposed the death penalty, not only for heresy but also for a number of ancillary offenses. This edict bore the same date as letters patent confirming the papal appointment of three cardinal inquisitors—Lorraine, Bourbon and Châtillon. As Bourbon was a feeble individual and Châtillon was shortly to become a married, Protestant cardinal, this virtually amounted to the appointment of Charles de Guise, cardinal of Lorraine, as a grand inquisitor—with legatine powers. Lorraine was also one of the ablest and richest men in France. It is therefore easy to see why he should have become the Huguenots' most dangerous and implacable enemy. The edict of Compiègne was intended to fulfill the king's undertaking to support the newly decreed inquisition with all the might of his secular arm. Consequently it contained an explicit declaration of war on the heretics. This had the effect of cementing the already close affiliation of the Guises with the crown, a relationship which they frantically struggled to preserve under Henry's youthful successor, Francis II. The pro-

posed inquisition did not materialize, largely owing to the Gallican opposition of the *parlement*, without whose cooperation it
could not have been enforced.

Henry, nevertheless, made it unequivocally clear that he still
meant to proceed with force against the Protestants, once the
peace of Cateau-Cambrésis, in April 1559, had terminated the
war with Spain. He had in fact already ordered an army into,
Normandy, and others were ready to move southward. At the
same time, he also meant to prosecute the claim of Mary queen of
Scots, wife of the dauphin Francis, to the throne of Protestant
England. Thus, from the very beginning, the Huguenot struggle
had international ramifications, and was closely involved with
England. By the same token it was also to become disastrously
entangled with the Netherlands. It is vitally important to
understand this inquisitorial background to the conflict which
followed Henry's death. Although it is widely known that he was
a persecutor, it is not generally realized that the extermination of
Calvinists, by force of arms, had already begun. This explains a
great deal. It accounts for the significance of the monopolization
of the government by the Guises, Henry's lieutenants, who
were already in situ. By assuming control, they excluded the
rightful claims of the princes of the blood, Antoine de Bourbon,
king of Navarre and his brother Louis, prince de Condé, to whom
Calvin and the churches had already turned for princely protection.

Consequently, Henry's policy of extermination could not be
executed by the Guises, in the name of Francis II, or Charles IX,
without provoking violent opposition. Thus, by 1559 power and
religion had become inseparably linked. The fight for the one was
a fight for the other. The danger of civil war was always implicit
in this situation, which turned the French Calvinists into the
Huguenot faction, at least on the national level. From being a
persecuted religious minority, they became a party in the State.
A war initiated by Henry, as defender of the faith, could be
euphemistically described, and limited in extent to the king's own
objectives. But hostilities initiated by ministers, under a de facto
regency, necessarily became uncontrollable civil war between
rival politico-religious factions, each with its foreign affiliations.

The first clash between these factions occurred in the conspiracy of Amboise in March 1560. This was an instance of tumultuous petitioning on the part of the Huguenot gentry. They were trying to break the Guise stranglehold on the court and council, and attempting to end their Henrician policy of persecution. The conspiracy failed; but the Guises were so shaken, both by the event itself and by its implications, that it enabled the queen mother, Catherine de Medici, to inaugurate a policy of greater moderation. This had clearly become essential in the interests of peace. In these circumstances, Catherine began to compete with the Guises for the control of royal policy—which was largely a matter of dominating the council. Catherine prevailed, if only just, in the sense that policy was actually modified. But the Catholics prevailed in the sense that the execution of this modified policy was effectively frustrated.

While Francis I had evaded the long-term implications of heresy, Henry II would definitely have gone to war for the sake of religion—more especially since this also offered dynastic advantages. But Henry's death and the conspiracy of Amboise caused a radical change in French politics. Thus, in spite of everything that happened from 1560 to 1598, the consistent policy of the crown was the maintenance of peace. That this policy was submerged in eight civil wars is both a measure of the weakness of the crown and a testimony to the power of the Catholics. The essential struggle in sixteenth-century France was not—as has commonly been thought—between the Huguenots and the crown, but rather between the crown and the Catholic extremists. These extremists, led by successive members of the Guise family (together with a number of Italian immigrants), were the Huguenots' principal enemies. It is essential to understand this point because the first civil war, which began in June 1562, has often been represented as a Protestant rebellion; in fact it stemmed from a breach between royal and extremist Catholic policy.

The period March 1560–January 1562 witnessed the first phase of the Huguenot struggle for recognition. This was obtained through a series of eight so-called religious edicts and, by the edict of January 1562, the Huguenots received a measure of limited, supervised toleration. This series of edicts, which contained contradictions and absurdities, uniquely reflects the intensity of the struggle at court for control of the council. None of these edicts, except for that of January 1562, was primarily concerned with religion itself, but with the disorders arising from religious dissent or, in other words, with peace, law and order.

Thus there was on the one hand the extreme Catholic policy of extermination and, on the other, the royal policy of moderation and civil containment. In the circumstances, this was virtually bound to lead, as it did in 1562, to some measure of toleration. Consequently, the difference between the moderate Catholic policy of the crown and that of the Protestants was reduced to a matter of degree. Given a little goodwill, this was far from insurmountable. From 1561 to 1598, however, the Catholic extremists steadily obstructed any and every accommodation between the crown and the Huguenots. Because they were unable to sustain the wars, they could not prevent the conclusion of successive treaties of peace and edicts of religion. But it was relatively easy to sabotage and to destroy them. This became a cyclical process which was repeated over and over again in evolving circumstances. Ultimately the Catholics had to be conquered in the field by Henry IV before anything like civil and religious peace could be established. Previously, the crown had always been too weak to enforce its policy against that of the Catholic extremists. The main reason for this remarkable degree of Catholic success was that they had behind them the power of Spain and the Papacy. They were steadily supported by the Spanish ambassadors, and papal nuncios and legates—sometimes two or three of them simultaneously.

In April 1561 the Catholic leaders formed a cabal, called the Triumvirate, which looked to Philip II for leadership. The timing is probably explained by Catherine's incorporation of Navarre into the regency for Charles IX, and her admission of his brother Condé to the council. The Guises no longer controlled the court, and the Protestants seemed likely to obtain satisfaction. The overt purpose of the Triumvirate was the destruction of Navarre—who was held to be a corrupting influence on the young king—the extinction of the Bourbon "family," and the extermination of

Protestantism in France. This was to be followed by its suppression elsewhere. While Germany and Geneva were the original targets, attention was rapidly switched to the Netherlands and England. Thus, even before the civil wars began, Huguenot affairs were thoroughly entangled.

There is no doubt whatever that the Triumvirate fully intended to make war—contrary to the policy of the crown—but what they had outlined was a general program, not a specific project. Thus they did not, in the event, begin with an assault on Navarre because he was too easily duped into supporting them. At the same time as they obtained his allegiance, in February 1562, the Spanish ambassador and papal nuncio, through unremitting efforts, procured the expulsion of the Protestant leaders, the admiral Coligny and his brothers d'Andelot and Châtillon, from the council. Not until June 1572 was Coligny again suffered to take his place in the council without violent intervention from the Guises; and he was dead less than three months later. Lorraine understood very well that control of the council was fundamental to success; and, after 1561, the Huguenots had no hope of achieving this. The edict of January 1562 was only obtained in the absence of the Catholics, who had quit the court—without license to depart—in October 1561. Consequently, this was the first of the important edicts which they undertook to nullify. At this point the Triumvirate took up arms and, in March 1562, Guise advanced on Paris to obstruct the registration of the edict.

The duc de Guise was murdered during the first civil war and, as an operational unit, the Triumvirate was destroyed. But its policy was continuously adapted to changing circumstances by Lorraine and other members of the Guise family, by successive popes, Spain, and Philip's governors in the Netherlands. It was, more than anything else, the sturdy and protracted revolt of the Netherlands which distorted the Catholics' original extirpation plans for France, Geneva and Germany. This—apart from economic and geographical factors—is why the Netherlands became the hub and focus of European affairs, their fortunes closely affecting those of the Huguenots and of England. Consequently, the second and third civil wars (1567–68 and 1568–70) were both to some extent joint French and Netherlands enterprises. In August 1568 an offensive/defensive treaty was drafted between William of Orange in the Netherlands and Condé and Coligny in France.

Here we have the basic pattern of the Huguenot struggle. The Catholics were trying to exclude Protestant leaders from court, council and office; to prevent any religious settlement, no matter how moderate, and to destroy the settlements which were concluded despite them. Finally, from 1563 on, the Catholics—who were not required to keep faith with heretics—constantly plotted to catch and to kill the Huguenot leaders. Although the Huguenots could never defeat the Catholics who, at least in time of war, availed themselves of the power of the crown, they were capable of waging a war of attrition in the south and west where they were strongest.

This situation contained all the ingredients of deadlock, which was probably one reason—though not explicitly—why the Catholics tried, with such dogged persistence, to murder the Huguenot leaders. But as one Englishman put it, they went about "well fenced." By the time that most of the original leaders were dead, a new generation was almost ready to assume command— in particular Henry of Navarre. It was hoped to avert this new command by means of Henry's marriage to the king's sister, Marguerite. In the event, it simply delayed his assumption of effective leadership for about three years.

It is the deadlock situation which accounts for the violent oscillations of Huguenot fortunes from 1570 to 1598. With the peace of Saint-Germain, it looked, in 1570, as though the Huguenots might, at last, have secured their recognition, together with adequate religious liberties, civil liberties and, for the leaders, four *places de sûreté*. These afforded a measure of *personal* safety. Furthermore, in August 1570, Lorraine and the Guises were themselves excluded from the council. Thus the treaty of Saint-Germain represented the zenith of Huguenot achievement. The carefully drafted edict influenced all its successors because it had provided for the Protestants' basic needs. There was, just possibly, an outside chance that it might have afforded a measure of stability, had it not been for the Huguenots' involvement with the Netherlands. But any support of Philip II's "rebels and heretics" could be expected to entail the opposition of Catholic extremists and probably war between France and Spain. The murder of Coligny in August 1572 and the subsequent massacre of St. Bartholomew both proceeded, at least in the short term, from a determination to avert an invasion of the Netherlands and war with Spain. While the king was, as usual, little more than a helpless adjunct, he was burdened with the responsibility for the massacre. Thus the massacre not only completely destroyed the Protestant achievements of three civil wars, and the excellent edict of Saint-Germain, but it also poisoned Huguenot relations with the crown. This, in spite of the wars, had not previously been the case, and it was not the crown which had effectively excluded the Huguenots from the council.

This new hostility between the crown and the Huguenots was gravely exacerbated by the accession of Henry III because, as heir presumptive, he had been a Catholic extremist and an enemy of England. Not only was he believed to have been implicated in the massacre, but with him returned the Huguenots' worst enemy: the abominated cardinal of Lorraine. Thus, in the summer of 1574, the Huguenots appeared to be almost back to where they had started in 1559. They had nothing but freedom of conscience and three fortified towns. They were virtually without recognition, once again in opposition to the crown, and in considerable danger.

In the contest which inevitably followed—first diplomatic and then military—there was consequently a new element of resistance to the crown. Indeed, the next peace, that of Monsieur in May 1576, was extorted by means of a Protestant military pincer movement, and it was the only edict to grant general toleration. Whether or not Henry himself would have been inclined to honor that capitulation, the Catholics did not suffer him to do so. His extremist affiliations as heir presumptive had fashioned a fatal noose for his own royal neck. For it was to be the Catholics, rather than the now highly organized Huguenots, who prevented him from imposing his policy of peace, and who caused his ruin. But although the Catholics destroyed the peace of Monsieur, they were powerless to prevent its modification—after renewed hostilities—in the peace of Bergerac, September 1577. This was subsequently extended in the treaty of Nérac, 1579, and the treaty of Fleix, 1580. Like the peace of Saint-Germain, these edicts of pacification—as they were called collectively—just might have brought to France a degree of stability, and to Henry the peace that he desired, were it not—once again—for the French involvement in the affairs of the Netherlands.

The murder of William of Orange in July 1584 precipitated a crisis in the Netherlands, which closely affected both France and England. This caused Philip II to make a formal alliance with the French Catholic League in December 1584. The Guises had already begun to organize the League when the death of the king's brother Anjou, in June 1584, left the Protestant Navarre heir to the throne. Philip's purpose, however, was not so much the obstruction of a Protestant succession as the resuscitation of strife in France. This was designed to keep the Huguenots out of the Netherlands, and to prevent any Anglo-French cooperation against Spain. As a direct result of their alliance with Spain, the Guises, in July 1585, were able to impose the treaty of Nemours on the hapless king. Where the Catholics had failed in 1576, owing to the military strength of the Huguenots, the League now succeeded. The edicts of pacification were all revoked, and the Protestant cult prohibited. This was followed in September by a papal bull excluding Navarre from the succession. On 30 November 1585 he declared war. This was exactly what Philip required, while he concentrated on the problem of England.

The stranglehold of the League on Henry III was to lead to his murder of the duc de Guise, in December 1588. His death enabled Henry and Navarre to suspend their religious quarrel in order to oppose their common enemies who violated the king's authority and disturbed his state. With their "traité de la trève," in April 1589, came at least the hope and theoretical possibility of a permanent settlement, because the conflict was no longer triangular. For the next few months, until Henry himself was murdered by a priest in August 1589, there were only two combatant parties. Only in these circumstances could France be released from the recurrent Catholic tyranny which had afflicted her since 1561. But, when Navarre succeeded to the throne, his impatient Huguenot followers became intransigent. Like his predecessors, Henry IV was isolated, and confronted by a renewal of the triangular struggle, together with foreign war. As king, Navarre's first need was to conquer the League and finally shatter the power of the Catholic extremists, before attempting to satisfy the Huguenots. In the meanwhile, he restored to the Protestants the terms they had enjoyed under the peace of Amboise, 1563, and the peace of Bergerac, 1577. In 1591 he reissued the edicts of pacification. But the disappointed Huguenots, or more precisely their factious noble leaders, turned against the king; which is why the triangular situation recurred. By this foolish perversity, the Protestants almost betrayed their sovereign into the hands of Spain. This only prolonged the wars and delayed their new edict, for the sake of which they had stooped to blackmail the king. But Henry IV was not to be coerced. He stood his ground and risked the possible consequences of Huguenot treachery. Sick and discouraged, he was prepared for death in battle; instead, he triumphed. Not until he had defeated both the Catholic League and, significantly, the king of Spain, was Henry prepared to conclude the new edict—of Nantes—because only then was he in a position to enforce it.

I

The Beginning of the Protestant Persecution, 1521–1547

THE HUGUENOTS WERE CALVINISTS, and the Reformation in France in its principal and most durable form was essentially Calvinist. This final phase was well under way by the time of the catastrophic death of Henry II in July 1559, which led swiftly to the formation of the Huguenot faction within the State.[1] Nevertheless, the French Reformation necessarily had an extensive pre-Calvinist background, dating from approximately the second decade of the century. There is even a sense in which the Protestant Reformation might actually be said to have originated in France since, as early as 1512, after translating the Epistles of St. Paul,[2] Lefèvre d'Etaples derived from them the doctrine of justification by faith alone. This doctrine emphasized interior spirituality more than outward observance. Taken a little further, as it was by Martin Luther, this was held to rock the papal throne by rendering an ecclesiastical hierarchy potentially superfluous. This was not, however, an inevitable interpretation and, in practice, the major reformers did not attempt to dispense with a Church Visible. Nor was the quest for a deeper, purer spirituality in itself heretical, in spite of the impending fragmentation of Christendom. This quest for a purer spirituality was in fact a European

1. This is not intended to imply that they would not otherwise have emerged, but only to state the circumstances in which they did. The term Huguenot was not used until about 1560.
2. This work was reprinted in 1516, still without attracting censure. Imbart de la Tour, *Les Origines de la Réforme*, iii, 217.

movement, whose occult roots lie beyond the frontiers of scholarship and whose external forms were most directly derived from two great supranational forces: the printing press and Erasmian humanism. In its historic form, the Protestant upheaval is comprehensibly dated from Luther's Wittenberg challenge in 1517, but it might equally well have erupted in Zurich, or even in France, which was no less receptive, although everywhere different political and external conditions determined different effects.

When, propagated by the printed word, Lutheranism is first known to have reached Paris early in 1519, Lefèvre, professor of philosophy and mathematics at the Collège du Cardinal Lemoine, was working on his translation of the Bible. Two years later he became one of the celebrated group of reformers, which included Gérard Roussel and Guillaume Farel, who served Guillaume Briçonnet in his bishopric of Meaux. In the current atmosphere of intense intellectual ferment, Lutheranism was bound to arouse curiosity and attract attention, and it is said to have spread with great rapidity. Inevitably it also attracted the attention of the Sorbonne. In May 1520 that austere bastion of theological orthodoxy was invited by Frederick of Saxony to examine Luther's opinions. This investigation was principally entrusted to Jacques Barthélémi, and Noel Bédier whom Erasmus contemptuously dismissed as "une souche plutôt qu'un homme." On 15 April 1521 the Sorbonne pronounced Luther a pernicious enemy of the church of Christ, who had "vomi une doctrine de pestilence" which was "remplie d'erreurs exécrables."[3] This was followed on 13 June by a prohibition of the *parlement* of Paris against the publication of any religious books without consent of the Sorbonne. Thus began the censorship of Protestant works, through the dual action of the Sorbonne and the *parlement*. It had the effect of endangering the genuinely Catholic reformers like Briçonnet, and Lefèvre who was accused of heresy in 1521, by rendering them all suspect. Thus, although it was to be a long time before heresy was adequately disentangled from humanism, a miscellany of advanced opinions, and a great deal of fluctuating

3. Viénot, *Histoire de la Réforme*, i, 50–52, 51, n. 1.

confusion of thought and mind, Protestant persecution may be said to have begun in France about 1521.

For a fuller understanding of its form and nature and the reactions of those primarily concerned—the Sorbonne, the *parlement*, the Church and the crown—the development of the persecution in France ought, properly, to be studied against the background of the residual Inquisition. This, however, could not be explored without deflecting attention from the relation of the developing persecution to the growth of Calvinism, in order to explain the origins and juridical position of the Huguenots who emerged in 1560. A study of the Inquisition would, however, help to explain why the persecution of Protestants began with the Sorbonne. It would also throw light on the major and, in effect, legislative role of the *parlement* in religious affairs, and on the attitude of the crown. This, in the case of Francis I, has been much misunderstood.[4]

Francis I could and did encourage humanistic learning and so, unavoidably, various degrees and combinations of advanced opinions. His court and conduct could not be described as canonical, and he was necessarily less intemperate than the Sorbonne, which was unencumbered by the needs of diplomacy. This did not mean that the king of France condoned heresy, if and when it could be identified, or that he was content to permit its growth when he might have prevented it. But in theory at least, his intervention was not necessary. That royal intervention ultimately became necessary was largely a matter of scale—the growing dimensions of the problem, and for such intervention there were good historical precedents.[5]

Meanwhile, there is no doubt that the king's mind was primarily on other matters. He certainly had more reason to fear the ever-present dangers of a turbulent nobility than the still remote threat of a minority opinion. There was no reason to suppose, about 1521, that this could ever endanger the monolithic French

4. This statement is sufficiently substantiated by the variety of conflicting opinions about not only the king's attitude to heresy, but also his actions.

5. The most obvious precedent is the Albigensian crusade of 1209.

monarchy, which was quite different from the two-tier political structure of princes and emperor in Germany. Lutheranism in the Empire was very soon to serve the interests of France by creating division and distracting the emperor from other problems and enemies. But it was still far from equally clear that Protestantism in any form might ever serve the Hapsburg cause by creating havoc in France. On the other hand, anything which might threaten to disrupt the Church would have domestic repercussions on the fundamentally important matters of patronage and finance, and abroad on diplomatic relations with the Papacy. Experience had already shown, since the inception of the Italian wars in 1494, that France was unlikely to retain any Italian conquest at the expense of the emperor without the cooperation of the pope. In other words, as the Protestant movement developed in France, far more was involved than purely religious problems. It will be seen that originally the crown sought to assist and support ecclesiastical and other authorities in these matters, while *specifically royal* action may be correlated, if not exclusively, with politics and, in particular, with the exigencies of foreign policy. This correlation is extremely important, especially towards the end of the reign of Henry II, if we are to understand the Huguenots' predicament and the nature of their struggle for survival.

When the specifically Protestant problem first arose in France in 1520, the king was deeply involved in foreign affairs. Fifteen twenty was the year of the Field of Cloth of Gold; in 1521 Francis I was driven from Milan; in 1523 the constable duc de Bourbon defected to the emperor and laid siege to Marseilles; and, on 24 February 1525, Francis I was defeated at the battle of Pavia and sent to Madrid as a prisoner of war.

During this time the religious ferment in France had steadily increased. The condemnation of Luther's works by the Sorbonne, in 1521, did nothing to suppress them. On the contrary, other works appeared defending them, including an apology by his lieutenant, Melancthon. Following its prohibition of June 1521 against the publication of religious works, the *parlement* decided to expel from Paris the four mendicant orders which lodged many of the students and scholars who passed freely between

Germany, Switzerland and France. Later the *parlement* settled for
merely curtailing their activities, because their expulsion would
annoy the Swiss cantons whose goodwill and mercenary forces
were essential to the king. Besides, it was to this "haine aveugle
contre tout esprit de libre examin" and the circumscription of
humane studies that Francis I objected.[6] It had become dangerous even to read the Bible in the vernacular. Indeed the *parlement*,
which had already accused Lefèvre of heresy in 1521, condemned
his translations—the Old Testament in 1522 and the New Testament in 1523—as being "de périleuse conséquence,"[7] although
the king had permitted at court translations of forbidden works
by the young Louis de Berquin. On 1 August 1523, however,
while the king was engaged in war, the *parlement* arrested Berquin. Francis ordered his release, but his works were burnt
nonetheless. The general clamor, repression and persecution
mounted considerably during the king's absence at war in 1523,
the year of the death of the first French martyr, Jean Vallière. In
this heated atmosphere Briçonnet lost his nerve and tried to arrest
the movement he had begun, thus the pioneer Meaux group began
to break up. This might be seen as a small-scale parallel to
Luther's rapid loss of control over the movement he had equally
unwittingly begun in Germany.[8]

From his prison in Madrid, the king tried in vain to restrain and
moderate what may have appeared to be mounting hysteria in
Paris. However, later in 1524 the new pope, Clement VII,[9] had
become an ally of France and the regent, Louise de Savoie, informed him of the disquieting spread of heresy and heretical
literature.[10] Her anxiety was doubtless considerably increased by
the attentions of the Swiss radical Zwingli. In March 1525, apparently at the instigation of French reformers, Zwingli dedicated
to the king his *Traité de la vrai et fausse religion*. This was the work
in which he developed his notably symbolic interpretation of the

6. Imbart de la Tour, iii, 211-12; Viénot, i, 89.
7. Viénot, i, 65-67.
8. Imbart de la Tour, iii, 230 seq; 247-51, 253.
9. 1523-34.
10. Imbart de la Tour, iii, 242.

Eucharist.[11] Whether or not this dedication had any effect on the *parlement* it is impossible to say. But on 20 March 1525 it resolved upon the institution of a special commission of two *conseillers*, Philippes Pot and André Verjus, together with two doctors of theology, Guillaume du Chesne and Nicole (also called Nicholas) Leclerc, to prosecute heretics and suspects. Their intention was that the bishop of Paris should appoint these nominees as his *vicaires* for this purpose.[12]

The *parlement* then took advantage of a request from Louise for advice, and presented a remonstrance with a long passage devoted to religion.[13] They maintained that "pour le jour d'huy, n'y a estat en ce royaulme qui n'en soit maculé et infect." They claimed to have been diligent in trying to eradicate these errors from the area of their jurisdiction, but their regulations were evaded. They were principally concerned about two points: appeals to other courts, and the immunity of the clergy—since they strongly suspected that there were heretics in high Church office. For this reason they said that it was necessary to appeal to the pope to appoint "aucuns bons et notables personnages pour proceder et informer contre archevesques, evesques et autres prelats exemptz qui pourroient estre trouvez coupables." Indeed, this was also to include abbots and lesser clergy. Where the bishop refused to empower the nominees of the *parlements* to prosecute heretics, they wished the queen regent to authorize them, by letters patent, to enforce this cooperation. As a result of these overtures, on 29 April Louise wrote to the pope asking him to sanction the requests of the *parlement* and to dispatch a "rescript contenant commission aux personnages qui ont este nommez... pour procedar à l'encontre de tous ceulx qui seront trouvé maculé et sectateurs des erreurs pour les punir... sans aucune acception de personnes de quelque estat, qualité et conditions qu'ils soient,

11.   Zwingli's doctrine of the Eucharist is generally understood to be commemorative and symbolic although, in reality, it was less crude than this and much more complex. See Potter, *Zwingli*, chaps. xii and xiii.

12.   Mayer, *La Religion de Marot*, 141–42.

13.   Ibid., 142–44. I am indebted to R. J. Knecht for drawing my attention to this work.

rejectées toutes appellations qui seront interjectées . . . et à se faire requeoir le bras seculier." All this was according to the memoir which the *parlement* addressed to the pope. This therefore covered what they felt to be the new needs and, on 17 May, the pope authorized the *parlement's* nominees to constitute themselves into this special commission. Within the jurisdiction of the *parlement*, they were to dispatch heresy cases without appeal. Except that Philippe Pot was replaced by Jacques de la Varde, the commissioners were the same as those to be appointed by the bishop of Paris. Their powers were therefore greatly extended. Three days later the pope also wrote to the *parlement* and the Sorbonne ordering them to take the most severe measures against heretics.[14] This underlines the role of the *parlement* and the Sorbonne in religious affairs, and the extent to which the pope was prepared to cooperate with them. On 10 June 1525 the regent issued letters patent ordering the registration of the bull.[15] Consequently, during the following summer quite a number of those who had been active at Meaux were accused of heresy. Late in September one of these, Gérard Roussel, wrote to Guillaume Farel—who had fled to Basle in 1524—that the king's captivity had "rendu tout-puissants ces docteurs bien éloignés du Christ."[16] In October Lefèvre fled to Strasbourg. Thus the king himself had been directly approached—and by a Swiss *sacramentaire*—and the regent, in his absence, had promoted the persecution to be carried out by inquisitors, the Church, the *parlement* and the Sorbonne. These authorities and the joint commission were now dealing not simply with an academic infiltration but with nascent evangelism of a Zwinglian complexion, deliberately aimed at France. This was potentially dangerous in a way that scattered groups of Lutheran scholars could never have been. Furthermore, persecution had begun to bring about dispersal, through which both more, and more radical influences began to play upon France from the Empire and from Switzerland.

14. Ibid.,144–48.
15. Isambert, *Recueil général*, xii, 232–37; *Catalogue des Actes*, i, 405, no. 2154; Imbart de la Tour, iii, 248–49.
16. Viénot, i, 96.

An *arrêt* of the *parlement* of 5 February 1526 forbade both the printing and possession of Luther's works; also the translation of St. Paul, the Apocalypse and other works, and all opposition to the decrees of the Church.[17] When the king returned from captivity in March 1526 it was to a considerable hue and cry, and Berquin had again been arrested for spreading evangelical propaganda in northern France. On 5 February 1526 the *parlement* prohibited, under pain of severe penalty, the possession or reading of any books of the Bible translated from Latin, the preaching or teaching of any doctrines of Luther, or the *contradiction, in any manner, of Catholic doctrines on the Sacrament*, the Virgin, saints, images, prayers for the dead, or fasting.[18] Francis I, whose orders from Madrid had been ignored, again exerted his moderating influence, and intervened a second time to save Louis de Berquin.[19] He also permitted the return of Roussel and Farel. He was not yet in a position to realize how influential and dangerous Farel was to become. For a while they sheltered in the service of the king's sister Marguerite who, in 1527, married Henry d'Albret, king of Navarre, thereby increasing her independence. This reaction of the king to events which occurred in his absence more accurately reflects his hostile relations with the *parlement* than the nature of his personal opinions.

While Francis was certainly still anxious to protect and foster the remarkable intellectual activity of his world center of learning, he nevertheless ordered the new papal *juges délégués* to proceed diligently against "quelque erreur touchant le sainct sacrement de l'autel."[20] A determination to permit no interference with the Sacrament of the Eucharist was then, and continued to be, Francis's definitive attitude towards heresy. This was quite clearly adopted and annunciated in, or by, April 1526. The confused and contradictory claims of historians that Francis I was

17. Ibid., 70–71.
18. Ibid., 97, gives 6 February; Imbart de la Tour, iii, 251–52. This prohibition, together with the death penalty, was incorporated into the edict of Coucy, 16 July 1535.
19. Imbart de la Tour, iii, 256.
20. Ibid., 255 seq., 1 April 1526.

lenient,[21] or indifferent, that he took little action until 1533,[22] that he became reactionary after the affair of the *placards* in 1534,[23] that he was clement in 1535 and 1536, that he only turned against the Protestants in 1538[24] and, finally, that he did nothing on a national scale until 1539,[25] are all disproved by authentic documentation. Referring to the summer of 1538, for instance, even the distinguished Imbart de la Tour wrote: "Désormais entre la royauté et la Réforme, la rupture décisive et violente est consommée. Le régime de tolérance établi en 1530, sanctionné par les édits de Coucy et de Lyon va prendre fin"; [26] an astonishing statement. Fifteen thirty was the date of the first royal edict against heresy, and that of Coucy introduced the death penalty.

In spite of the fact that Francis accepted the papal bull of 1525 and ordered the *juges délégués* to proceed diligently, which amounted to an inquisition, greater emphasis has been placed on his rescue of Louis de Berquin. According to Imbart de la Tour, the extreme pressure lifted for a while and the atmosphere seemed less stifling and alarming.[27] He appears to relate this less to the return of the king from Madrid than to the suppression by the pope, on 17 January 1527—which was already nine months later—of his *juges délégués*. They were replaced by an episcopal commission, together with three theologians appointed by the University as a whole. Two of the bishops, of Bayeux (Louis Canossa) and Langres (Michel de Boudet), are said to have been friends of Erasmus.[28] But if purely Erasmian reformists might possibly have breathed more freely, this was rather on account of the membership than the form of the commission. Little, if any-

21.   Ibid., 525.

22.   *Ordonnances*, vi, 135, no. 2. This refers to the publication, in August 1533, of two papal bulls relating to the suppression of heresy. *Catalogue des Actes*, ii, 497, no. 6194; 552, no. 6450; 579, no. 6584, 10 December 1533, lettres adressées au parlement de Paris.

23.   Viénot, i, 124.

24.   Imbart de la Tour, iii, 560, 597–98.

25.   Weiss, *Bull. Prot.*, xxxviii, 1889, p. 238.

26.   Imbart de la Tour, iii, 597.

27.   Ibid., 259.

28.   Ibid., 259 and n. 5; Mayer, *La Religion de Marot*, 149, 25 January 1527, papal bull.

thing, can be said to have changed for the more evangelical who were no longer Catholic at heart. An episcopal commission was certainly a more Gallican arrangement, but it is unlikely that it was really intended to temper the persecution which, in the long run, Francis was in no position to resist. This was partly because he needed money and partly because the features of heresy were gradually becoming more distinct. On the other hand, Francis was anxious not to alienate the Lutheran opponents of Charles V who, whether formally or fortuitously, were among his most valuable allies; and 1526, the year of his release from Madrid, was a critical moment in the Franco-Hapsburg struggle. Thus he preferred the religious dispensation in France to appear as inoffensive as possible.

After the defeat of Pavia and his ignoble incarceration, the king's attention was still primarily fixed on foreign affairs. Following the treaty of Madrid in January 1526, which secured his release, Francis concluded the League of Cognac with the pope, Venice, Florence and Milan in May 1526. It was therefore appropriate that he should have made, as he did, a clear pronouncement on heresy in the previous month of April. A year later, in May 1527, Rome was sacked by a mutinous Imperial army. This army apparently contained Lutheran bands from the duchy of Bourbon which had followed the renegade constable of Bourbon into the service of the emperor. The pope was captured and forced to pay a ransom and renounce the alliance of France. Francis I, who was anxious to recover this alliance, had rather pressing need not only for money, but also for the cooperation of the *parlement* to abrogate the treaty of Madrid. Upon his release Francis had informed the emperor that he could not observe the treaty, which was concluded under duress, but that he would pay the ransom. In order to liberate his two sons, the hostage princes, he had either to return to prison himself, to surrender the duchy of Burgundy, or else to pay a royal ransom of 2,000,000 *écus*. To assist him in making this decision, Francis held an assembly of notables in Paris in the summer of 1527.

Thus, on 24 July 1527 the *président* Guillart of the *parlement* of Paris exploited the king's political predicament in order to augment the religious persecution. He proclaimed that "l'integrité de la foi" was the sole foundation of spiritual life and public peace, and that those who entertained "mauvaises et reprouvées doctrines," in public or in private, should be persecuted and extirpated like counterfeiters of false coin. He therefore urged the king to assemble "conciles ou gens de bonne vie, élegante doctrine [sic] et longue expérience pour du tout mectre hors ceste mauvaise et supersticieuse doctrine luthérienne ... laquelle commance à entrer en alcuns lieux."[29] The attitude of the clergy was similar. Thus, on 20 December 1527, in a plenary session of the *parlement* held for the abrogation of the treaty of Madrid, the cardinal of Bourbon requested the king to "desraciner et du tout extirper la dampnable et insupportable secte luthérienne ... ensemble toutes les autres hérésies qui pulullent" [dans le royaume]. In return, they offered the king 1,300,000 *livres*, but they could not commit the rest of the Church.[30] The king immediately accepted the advice to summon provincial councils and to request of them four *décimes*.[31] Three days later every archbishop was required to summon a council in his province.[32] While the Church was primarily concerned with morals and heresy, the king was preoccupied with the problem of his ransom. This, however, was understandable, since the alternative cession of Burgundy, a frontier province, was a serious matter, and a voluntary return to prison was unthinkable. But, in order to raise this money from the Church, Francis was obliged to agree—during the time of peace which was subsequently expected—to extirpate heresy, "en quoy il tiendra la main, et se y emploira par tous moiens a luy possibles."[33]

Perhaps the most important of the diocesan councils was that held in Paris in February 1528, presided over by the chancellor,

29. Imbart de la Tour, iii, 260–61.
30. Idem. Part of the bargain was that the king must liberate the pope.
31. *Décime* or clerical tenth: in theory a tax of one tenth of the revenue of a benefice.
32. Mansi, *Sacrorum conciliorum*, xxxii, 1134–40, 23 December 1527, the king's instructions to the archbishop of Lyons.
33. Ibid., 1139, 23 December 1527, the king's instructions to the archbishop of Lyons.

Cardinal Duprat, who therein attempted to clarify the religious problem. The cardinal de Bourbon, in his original demand for the councils, had referred both to Lutheranism and *other heresies*, possibly on account of the mounting influence in France of Guillaume Farel and the Swiss *sacramentaires*. This point was taken up again by Duprat, who demonstrated the unedifying disunity within the reform movement—the disagreement of the Lutherans and the Zwinglians. He went on to propound sixteen articles defining Catholic orthodoxy on controversial issues and then enumerated thirty-one erroneous assertions.[34] Here, therefore, seventeen years before the opening of the council of Trent, were some specific criteria by which to define heresy. Finally, Duprat worked out a procedure to be used against different categories of religious offenders. Paradoxically enough, in attempting to complement the persecution of heresy by reform of Church discipline, the prelates themselves approached the position of some of the original Catholic reformers whose opinions had been regarded as suspect. Nevertheless, partly as a result of Duprat's Catholic definitions, and partly on account of the growth of sectarianism in Germany and Switzerland, it was becoming much easier to distinguish between harmless, if radical, erudition on the one hand and, on the other, dangerous heresy which had begun to penetrate France from abroad. This distinction was to be further facilitated by the colloquy of Marburg in October 1529, which rendered definitive the breach between Luther and the Swiss reformers, in particular Zwingli, because of their inability to agree upon the nature of the Real Presence.

We have seen that the king had not been prepared to sacrifice scholarship and learning in order to extinguish (if this could be done) miscellaneous elements of Lutheranism, which, in Germany, was one of his sharpest weapons against the emperor. But he was not prepared to tolerate, as he had already proclaimed, "quelque erreur touchant le sainct Sacrement." Erastian Lutheranism, not as yet fully organized in Germany, did not *of itself* pose any serious threat to France. Furthermore, some sort of

34. Ibid., 1161, 1181–83.

reconciliation was still envisaged by the optimistic, since Luther's doctrine of consubstantiation was not a "monstrous opinion"[35] and did not exclude the essential Catholic dogma of the Real Presence. For the sectarians, however, the Eucharist was closer to being commemorative.

It was on account of the German and Swiss sectarians that the French Reformation took a radical turn. The severity of the early persecution, and particularly the dispersal of the Meaux group around 1524, had precipitated the flight of the more articulate and energetic. These were the most strongly evangelical, who might otherwise have provided indigenous leadership and organization. Consequently, if there was to be a reformation in France at all, it could only be achieved through direction from abroad, which was necessarily more dangerous and more complex. Thus the Reformation in France became the gargantuan task of the French religious exiles. They ensured close and constant foreign contacts, with Strasbourg and Switzerland in particular, just when sectarianism was beginning to develop there. This led not only to the breach with Luther over the Eucharist controversy and the fatal cleavage within the Protestant movement, but also to the founding of new, independent, and therefore potentially seditious, ecclesiastical organizations.

Thus it was not the reformist predilections and partial Lutheranism of the Christian humanists which threatened the Church and State of France with religious revolution. It was originally the sectarianism of Zwingli—who was guilty of "quelque erreur touchant le sainct sacrement"—and, later, the organization of Calvin. But it was primarily through the relatively neglected, intermediate work of the exile Guillaume Farel that these influences took effect in France.

Guillaume Farel had worked under Lefèvre in Paris and was loosely attached to the Meaux group. He appears to have left France late in 1523; in February 1524 he went to Basle, where he openly attacked the saints and the pope. Shortly after, he rejected

35. This, at least in France, appears to have been a denial of the Trinity.

the mass and accepted the doctrines of Carlstadt and Zwingli.[36] Carlstadt was one of the first of Luther's breakaway colleagues. Radical, and indeed violent and destructive from the start, he was forced to flee from Wittenberg in 1524; he went to Strasbourg, where he denied the doctrine of the Real Presence. At the same time, Zwingli was developing his doctrine of the Eucharist in Zurich. There, in 1525, mass was abolished in favor of a more austere commemoration of the Last Supper in the upper room. This was the year in which Zwingli addressed his *Traité de la vraie et fausse religion* to Francis I.

Farel was therefore among the first of those to form a distinct and positive break from Luther. What they primarily retained of Lutheranism was the doctrine of justification by faith and the belief in the sole authority of the Bible. But, whereas Luther could admit of anything not prohibited by the scriptures, Zwingli and his follower Farel could only accept what the scriptures included.[37] Because the scriptures did not enjoin the veneration of images, this led to a primitive and aggressive severity, hence the iconoclastic and, in the civil sense, dangerous element in the new teaching. Theologically, their denial of the Real Presence proved more devastating than any of Luther's initial thunderbolts. It was round Farel that the French exiles tended to gather, and it was predominantly *his* radical, Zwinglian form of Protestantism that, over a long period of time, prepared the foundations for Calvinism in France. It is, however, interesting to note that Calvin, who equally upheld the sole authority of the scriptures, did not derive from them any doctrine of violence. If they did not *require* the veneration of images, neither did they command their destruction. He enjoined his followers to obedience, and sternly reproved them for disorders and iconoclasm. Much more conservative than the military Zwingli, his intentions were neither riotous nor revolutionary. But, through force of circumstance and the deviations of his followers, much that was evidently radical and Zwinglian in origin has customarily been debited to Calvin.

36. Imbart de la Tour, iii, 458–60.
37. Ibid., 485, and n. 1.

By about 1528 the works of Zwingli were not only known in Paris, but also in Alençon, Guyenne, Agenais, Toulouse and Provence; thus his mounting impact on France must have been becoming apparent.[38] This is suggested by the cardinal de Bourbon's reference to Lutheranism and "toutes les autres hérésies," by a request from the council of Lyons for additional help, [39] and by the first acts of iconoclasm. These occurred in Paris on 2 June 1528 and greatly angered the king. He ordered a solemn procession and replaced the smashed statue with a silver one.[40] Attacks on the mass and the Eucharist, which were also becoming fairly common, had been denounced by the provincial councils of 1528, in which Zwingli was mentioned by name. This evident consciousness of his growing influence would also account for renewed efforts to prevent the publication, diffusion and use of religious works, including the reading of the scriptures in the vernacular, and for the prohibition of assemblies and "conventicules."[41] These were dangerous new departures which could not be ignored. These new measures brought about a further exodus from France just when Farel, in Switzerland, was seeking to attract lieutenants.[42]

Whether or not Farel consciously endeavored to fuse the heterogeneous elements of the Reformation in France and provide it with some new principle of authority, is not yet clear. But while the works of Zwingli, like those of Luther before them, were steadily spreading in France, Farel multiplied his contacts and sought to establish himself close to the frontier. Expelled from Basle, he went to Berne in 1527, and in 1529 to Neuchâtel, where he wanted to found a French city of refuge. But, strategically, the finest center was undoubtedly Geneva, with its access to Lyons and the Rhône valley, and thence into Dauphiné, Provence and Languedoc. There, in Geneva, on 10 August 1535,

38. Ibid., 461, 471. This list probably ought to include Languedoc.
39. Ibid., 264.
40. Ibid., 268; Viénot, i, 100.
41. Imbart de la Tour, iii, 265–66.
42. Ibid., 479.

Farel and Pierre Viret[43] succeeded in having mass abolished. A year later, in July 1536, it was Farel's "awful thunderings" which detained the then reluctant Calvin.

By this time France was invested with Protestant communities from the Rhine to the Rhône, and Farel through some ten years' work had become "le chef d'une organisation occulte . . . le représentant le plus autorisé de la Réforme française." Through him France was beginning to receive "un centre de direction," [une] "croyance," "un gouvernement."[44] To achieve this Farel had, in his turn, to supply the indispensable literature, although he did so on an incomparably smaller and more practical scale than either Luther or Zwingli. Thus, as early as 1524, he produced two books of prayers in French—*L'Oraison dominicale* and *Le Symbole*—which were circulated in parts of France.[45] These were followed by two additional works: *La Manière et fasson qu'on tient ès lieux que Dieu de sa grâce a visités*, which outlined a new liturgy, and *Le Sommaire*, which comprised a simple confession of faith. The *Sommaire* adopted Zwingli's sacramentarian doctrine of the Eucharist and the absolute authority of the Bible.[46] It is thought to have been modeled on the *Traité de la vraie et fausse religion*, dedicated by Zwingli to Francis I in March 1525.

In order to survive, this faith would require some sort of organization, however simple. But, whereas Luther in the two-tier political structure of Germany, and Zwingli in the city of Zurich, had called in the State—albeit vastly different states—Farel could not do this with France. He therefore fell back on the basic conception of independent churches, common to all the reformers.

Farel returned to the primitive, biblical conception of the small group gathered together in the name of Christ to pray and to read the scriptures aloud, without ritual, properties or music. The

43. Pierre Viret became a "Calvinist" who openly preached resistance in the south of France, where little enough incitement was necessary.

44. Imbart de la Tour, iii, 478, 480.

45. Ibid., 481–82.

46. The dates of these works are not known for certain, but they did not appear in their definitive form until 1533 and 1534, respectively. Ibid., 482–84.

minister read from and expounded the scripture. Baptism, the use
of clear water on a child's head, and the Eucharist, a sharing of
the same bread and the same wine, were celebrated with equally
unceremonious simplicity. For these three services no priest was
necessary. The priest had become "le ministre de la parole." This
was descriptive of function, and whoever performed it thereby
became the minister. Nevertheless, Farel did proceed to found a
pastorate. This was clearly essential in practice, in order to maintain standards and unity of faith, as well as to obviate "les caprices
de la foule," and, at least in theory, dependence on the State.[47]
Thus, the church, or the churches, could exist independently of
the State where, as in France, this was necessary. This simple
doctrine therefore permitted both the formation of communities anywhere at any time and, in the absence of a pastor,
their survival until one became available. These provisions were
completed in 1535 by Olivétan's new translation of the Bible
which, though closely based on that of Lefèvre, eliminated terms
especially evocative of Catholicism. Farel had now initiated in
France what Imbart de la Tour called "la Réformation du saint
Évangile"; it had "ses idées directrices, son centre, [Geneva] sa
Bible."[48] It now needed a theological system in which its doctrines
were coordinated, together with some superior organization capable of unifying its separate groups. The way was therefore
prepared for the evangelical work of Calvin.

Well before the influence of Calvin, however, but when that of
Zwingli was spreading, both the *parlement* and the Church had
not only requested but, in 1528, had actually bargained with the
king for the intervention of the State in the suppression of heresy.
Intervention must soon have come, in any case, following the
greater clarification of heresy and, above all, with the beginning
of civil disturbances. But, in 1529, the king was occupied by the
peace of Cambrai, by which he renounced his claims in Italy.
Thus the first royal edict came on 29 December 1530.[49] This was

47. Ibid., 491.
48. Ibid., 494.
49. *Catalogue des Actes*, vi (supplement, 1527–47), 240, no. 20120.

very limited in scope, since it merely required the *parlements, baillis, sénéchaux, prévôts* "et autres officiers des justices royales d'avoir a prêter main forte aux juges délégues par Antoine Du Prat... pour procéder contre les Luthériens de concert avec les inquisiteurs de la foi (ou il s'en trouvera)." The prelates were also reminded of their duty in this respect, and the document indicates the appointment of four "savans personnaiges" for the jurisdiction of the *parlement* of Paris.[50] The role of the *parlement* in the persecution was therefore restored. Much stronger pressure on the king was soon to come from the pope.

By 1532 Francis was, politically, already looking again towards Rome, and negotiating for the marriage of Henri duc d'Orléans (later Henry II) to the pope's niece, Catherine de Medici. The union was solemnized at Marseilles in October 1533 by Clement VII himself. This was naturally the occasion of more than a marriage bargain. Having obtained an agreement that France would not support Henry VIII in his complex matrimonial quarrel with Rome,[51] Clement scandalously condoned Francis's (political) support of the German Lutherans in return for an assurance that this did not imply any authorization of heresy in France.[52] Doubtless with this in mind, both before and after the marriage, the pope prepared the bulls of 30 August and 10 November 1533. The former invited Francis "à travailler à l'extirpation de l'hérésie de Luther et rétablissant le tribunal de l'inquisition en France ou la poursuivre." The second bull related to the degradation of the heretical priests.[53]

While the king was still in the south on the occasion of the marriage, there occurred another resounding and now famous incident in Paris. According to custom, on All Saints' Day the

50.   Those delegated for the *parlement* of Paris were Jacques Mesnager, Jean Chauderon, Jean Lécuyer and Quélan. Idem; *Ordonnances,* vi, 135–36, no. 553.

51.   Francis's support was no longer needed, in this respect, as late as 1533.

52.   Imbart de la Tour, iii, 524. The pope arrived in Marseilles on 11 October.

53.   *Catalogue des Actes,* ii, 497, no. 6194; 552, no. 6450.

rector of the University, Nicholas Cop, delivered a sermon to the entire academic staff. It created an uproar, during which Cop fled to Basle and Calvin to Angoulême—where he is thought to have begun work on his *Institution Chrétienne*—while the *parlement* of Paris protested to the king. Replying from Lyons on 10 December, Francis forwarded for registration the two papal bulls of August and November.[54] At the same time he wrote to the *parlement* deploring the strength of heresy in Paris and declaring his wishes that "telle et si griefve punition en soit faicte," to be an example to others. He also commanded the *parlement* to appoint from its members several commissioners to pursue and prosecute heretics and suspects "curieusement et diligemment." The king was asking the bishop of Paris to authorize two *conseillers* to undertake the prosecution of heresy. This had spread as a result of negligence at the outset. Now he wished them to proceed "réellement et de fait par main forte et armée, si mestier est, et nous envoyer en diligence memoires necessaires pour avoir toutes les provisions requises."[55] It appears that the *parlement* had, once again, taken advantage of the king's absence to assert itself, exaggerating the gravity of the situation in Paris. The commission was not in fact constituted.[56] Nevertheless, Francis had been induced to restore, in effect, the papal commission of 1525. He had also authorized the use of armed force against the heretics. Whatever the outcome, it is impossible to maintain that it was only the notorious affair of the *placards* in October 1534 which definitively turned the king against heresy in France, although once he had become directly involved, his role was bound to increase.

During the night of 17 October broadsheets "contre l'honneur et la verité du saint Sacrement" were stuck up in Paris and other places including, apparently, Amboise, where Francis happened to be. These had been printed by a Lyonnais, Pierre Wingle, who had set up a printing press in Neuchâtel, where Farel and An-

54. Ibid., 579, no. 6548.
55. Mayer, *La Religion de Marot*, 150–51.
56. I am indebted to R. J. Knecht for this point.

toine Marcourt were then operating.[57] It was doubtless the Cop affair, together with the *placards*, which account for the edict of 29 January 1534/35 against those who harbored, concealed, and succored heretics, thereby saving them from being brought to justice.[58] This was reinforced by two far-reaching measures of 13 January and 23 February 1535 on the subject of printing. The former prohibited, during pleasure, the printing of "aucun livre nouveau dans le royaume." This was interpreted by the wording of the second measure to have meant a prohibition against the printing of anything at all ("prohibitions de n'imprimer *quoi que ce soit*, portée par l'ordonnance du 13 janvier"), until arrangements could be made to confine the right to print "à Paris seulement les livres approuvés et necessaires pour le bien de la chose publique." Whether "seulement" referred to "Paris" or to "books" is debatable but, to judge from the first measure, it probably referred to Paris.[59]

The need for these domestic measures against printing, and harboring Protestants, was politically embarrassing, just when the king was concluding an alliance (signed on 28 January 1535) with the princes of Saxony, Bavaria and Hesse against the emperor.[60] Imperialists, seeking to break the Franco-German alliance, made as much capital as possible from the outcry in France, the augmented persecution, and the imprisonment of Germans. On 1 February Guillaume du Bellay, seigneur de Landey, the king's representative in the Empire, had the king sign a memoir addressed to the German estates, in which he defended his various attitudes and gave his own version of the *placards*. This memoir attracted the attention of Calvin. During the summer du Bellay strove to restore the king's damaged relations in Germany,

57. Imbart de la Tour, iii, 475, 553. It appears that Marcourt was responsible for the *placards*. Berthoux, *Antoine Marcourt*, ch. vi.

58. *Catalogue des Actes*, iii, 8, no. 7486. This date has sometimes been incorrectly rendered in the old style as January 1534.

59. Ibid., 3, no. 7461, 13 January 1534/35; 23-24, no. 7559, 23 February 1535.

60. Ibid., 8, no. 7484, 28 January 1535. Saxony and Hesse were Protestant; Bavaria was Catholic.

but evidently felt that some further gesture of conciliation was needed. Thus, on 16 July 1535, the very day on which Barnabé de Voré departed for the Empire, bearing the king's apology,[61] Francis issued the much misinterpreted edict of Coucy.[62]

It was this diplomatic need for outward conciliation, not any change of religious policy from persecution to indulgence, which accounts for the edict of Coucy. This has generally been described as an edict of clemency because its drafting was slanted so as to serve the king's political purpose in Germany. The Protestant historian Haag coldly described it as a "declaration pour le retour des protestants fugitifs sous la condition qu'ils feront abjuration," which is correct. The preamble states—incorrectly—that heresy in France had ceased. Suspects and those charged with heresy would not be liable to proceedings; religious prisoners were to be released, confiscations restored, and exiles permitted to return, provided they abjured within six months; but any who relapsed would be severely punished. It is possible that a few relatively harmless individuals may thereby have escaped from prison, or that a few suspects may have had cautious second thoughts. But it is very unlikely that any significant number who had once ventured to place their faith above their security, home and property would change their minds and return, on the remarkably slender hope of actually obtaining their rights under the edict. The king, therefore, can hardly be said to have given much away,[63] more particularly since the supposed clemency clauses explicitly excluded not only recidivists but also the *sacramentaires*. These would have comprised both the majority of all those concerned, and everyone at all likely to have been seditious. Upon careful consideration, therefore, the "clement" edict of Coucy

61. The time lag between February and July seems excessively long.

62. *Catalogue des Actes*, iii, 109, no. 7900. Bourrilly, *Guillaume du Bellay*, 188–96. Bourrilly seems to have been deceived by this propaganda, and to have ignored the last paragraph of the edict, since he wrote: "c'était la fin des mésures de rigueur."

63. The editor of the *Ordonnances*, viii, 94, n. 1 points out that its effect was strictly limited. He cites two instances in which proceedings were taken for the confiscation of property, but does not say if the owners were sacramentarians.

detracted nothing from the stated purpose of the previous edict of January 1534/35 that the king intended to exterminate heresy. Coucy, furthermore, was the first edict to introduce the death penalty, for anyone who read, declared, translated, composed or printed, in public or in private, any doctrine contrary to the (Roman Catholic) Christian faith; in other words, for heretical matters, as such, as distinct from any civil disorders.

That the king had no intention of encouraging or tolerating heresy is further borne out by his letters patent of 30 May 1536 from Lyons, confirming Mathieu Ory in the office of inquisitor; an office which, by ancient papal delegation, was vested in the prior of the Friars Preachers in Paris.[64] Ory was thereby expressly authorized to act not only in Paris but "par tout nostredit royaume."[65]

The timing of Ory's succession was unfortunate for Francis,[66] who, deeply involved in war with the emperor, was just sending Guillaume du Bellay to soothe his German allies and to seek levies of troops in the Empire.[67] Du Bellay's letters of credence, like those confirming Ory's appointment, were also dated 31 May 1536, and on the following day the king reissued his supposedly clement edict of Coucy.[68] Whether or not this helped to reassure his German allies—which is doubtful—it certainly had the advantage of reaffirming the law against *sacramentaires*, and the prohibition, on pain of death, against reading, expounding, translating, composing or printing any doctrine contrary to the (Catholic) Christian faith. This was not without some topical point, since in March 1536 the radical first Helvetic confession appeared in

64. These were the Dominicans. Douais, *L'Inquisition*, 19; *Catalogue des Actes*, iii, 208-9, no. 8472.

65. *Ordonnances*, viii, 91 and n. 2; Weiss, *La Chambre ardente* (ed. 1970), p. xvii, n. 1; François, *Le Cardinal François de Tournon*, 458, n. 3, 511.

66. There is no significance in the date of this appointment. Ory merely succeeded his predecessor.

67. In 1536 Francis conquered Savoy and Piedmont, and Charles V invaded Provence.

68. *Catalogues des Actes*, iii, 209-10, no. 8476; Bourrilly, *Guillaume du Bellay*, 216-18.

Basle, and Calvin had published the first (Latin) edition of his *Institution Chrétienne*. Possibly with the earlier example of Zwingli in mind, he prefaced this with an address to the king, audaciously demanding justice for the Protestants. The work and its preface therefore served the purpose of defending the Protestants against the accusations of Francis I in his "memoir" of 1 February 1535 addressed to the Germans. This, in sixteenth-century terms, amounted to a public debate, in which Calvin had therefore joined issue with the king of France in a matter of high politics. Thus Calvin's influence was already boldly manifest even though, on account of his struggles in Geneva, it was to be another twenty years before Calvinist churches began to be formed in France.

For two more years Francis was primarily concerned with war until, in June 1538, he met the reformer-pope Paul III at Nice, and, in July, the emperor at Aigues-Mortes. The pope, who in 1542 was to establish the Congregation of the Inquisition in Rome, extracted a promise of firm measures against heresy, while Charles and Francis agreed "en premier lieu persuader aux devoyez... de se réduire et accorder amyablement" and, if they refused, to "tenir la main."[69] This sounds like an adumbration of the treaty of Cateau-Cambrésis, twenty-one years later in 1559. An interesting comparison could be made between these two dates, and there are some grounds for maintaining that the great politico-religious struggle of the sixteenth century was already under way. Whether or not it was yet apparent to Francis I, whose mind had been on the war, it is clear in the light of hindsight that Calvin had already joined with Farel in projecting something of an evangelical campaign in France. From this time on his influence was slowly, if steadily, mounting, and it was also from this time that Francis first marshaled *all* the forces of the State behind those of the Church.

Back in Paris from his meetings in the south, Francis first turned his attention to Languedoc, which had evidently been causing anxiety for some five years or more. In March 1533 Francis had ordered the bishops of Languedoc—a strategic province with twenty-three small dioceses—to reform and extirpate abuses

69.   Imbart de la Tour, iii, 596–97.

there.[70] Three years later, at the critical moment of March 1536 when the king was involved in the Savoy-Piedmont campaign, the Dominican Vidal de Becanis had been appointed inquisitor to the archdiocese of Toulouse, in which the absent incumbent was Odet de Coligny, cardinal de Châtillon, later to become a Calvinist. While not proving anything, this appointment tends to suggest that Calvinist influence was either feared or already operative in Languedoc.[71] Now, in December 1538, Toulouse merited a particular edict on the request of the *procureur général* of the *parlement*.[72] The purpose of the edict was therefore to authorize the *parlement* itself to proceed against heretics, those who in any way trafficked in or concealed "maudictz livres," and recedivists. This last item suggests that a few heretics may have returned under the "clemency" clauses of the edicts of 1535 and 1536 and then recommenced their activities. But the fact that this edict was not registered until the following April tends to suggest that there was some conflict within the *parlement* itself.

Turning from Languedoc, Francis next addressed himself to the kingdom in general. The principal purpose of the edict of Paris of 24 June 1539[73] was to extend jurisdiction against all heretics, of whatever condition, to all the royal courts, *baillis*, *sénéchaux* or their deputies. This was without appeal unless the *procureurs* of the *parlements* intended to increase the sentence. Why a further major edict was required a year later, on 1 June 1540,[74] is not entirely clear, except for the fact that the edict of 1539 had not been registered by the *parlement* of Paris, which probably objected to the absolute powers, in this respect, accorded to *all* the royal courts and provincial officials. While this interpretation is conjectural, it is sustained by the terms of the edict of 1540, which again permitted all the royal courts and officials including, this time, seigneurial courts, to initiate proceedings in heresy cases. But they were now required to submit their findings to the

70. Ibid., 530 and n. 1, 28 March 1533.
71. *Ordonnances*, viii, 91 n. 2.
72. *Catalogue des Actes*, iii, 660, no. 10534.
73. Ibid., iv, 14, no. 11072.
74. Ibid., iii, no. 11509.

parlements "pour par icelles [*cours souveraines*] estre jugés promptement à toute diligence, en la chambre criminelle dicelles."[75] Emphasis was placed on the absolute and immediate priority to be
given to heresy cases, of which the king wished to be informed by
the *parlements* every six months. The Protestant historian
Nathanael Weiss interprets this edict of 1540 in terms of the
complaint that "aucuns prelats et pasteurs de l'église n'estoient
pas assez songneux de pourvoir à si grand affaires concernans
l'honneur de Dieu et tranquillité de l'Estat de la République,"
or, in other words, "les lenteurs episcopales."[76] Apart from the
considerable extension of jurisdiction in heresy cases, the principal importance of this edict is its definition of heresy as being of
itself sedition: "tels erreurs [hérésie] et fausses doctrines *contiennent en soy* crime de lèze-majesté divine et humaine, sédition
du peuple, et perturbation de nostre estat et repos public." This
juridical definition was soon lost sight of, and the assertion that
heresy was seditious came to be regarded as merely opprobrious.
Years later, however, shortly before the first civil war, the
Calvinists were constantly accused of being seditious. Where they
had lived quietly this provoked indignant denials, more especially
since Calvin and their confession of faith imposed on them the
duty of obedience.

The drafting of this edict—which was confirmed on 30 August
1542—is obscure.[77] Contemporaries found it so, and the clergy
complained that it diminished their powers.[78] This in fact was
not true, since article nine explicitly stated otherwise. Thus the
further edict of 23 July 1543, itself no model of clarity, interpreted that of 1540 to have meant—and it shows no sign of having
stated this—that while any of the ecclesiastical or royal authorities could *initiate* proceedings in heresy cases, the Church
must judge of heresy, and the civil authorities must rule on the
related offenses of sedition and disorders. The *parlements*, how-

75. Article 3; the *chambre criminelle* had been instituted in 1515.
76. Weiss, *La Chambre ardente*, introd. p. xvi. He derived this, presumably, from the preamble to the edict of 19 November 1549.
77. *Catalogue des Actes*, iv, no. 12709.
78. This complaint was recorded in the preamble to the edict of 13
July 1543.

ever, were now no longer to judge these disorders, but only to be informed of them within two months. The expression "related offenses" meant anything which was manifest beyond the mere holding of heretical opinions.

The prosecution of heresy was therefore already thoroughly provided for when, towards the end of 1541, the first French edition of Calvin's *Institution Chrétienne*—based on the second Latin edition of 1539—burst upon France, provoking a series of regulations by the *parlement* relating to printed works. The *Institution* either produced a considerable impact within a matter of months, or else its potential influence was greatly feared, or both, since the first of these regulations, 1 July 1542, specifically forbade its possession, and commanded its surrender within twenty-four hours, *on pain of death*. The *arrêt* went on to impose the most rigorous controls on the sale and printing of books—which might be done only by master printers in specific places. Bookshops were subject to the inspection of four "libraires jurez" and every single work had to be censored by a suitable member of the University, according to its subject matter. This was because one ruse had been to insert religious works into books ostensibly on other subjects "mesme en alphabetz que l'on imprime pour les petitz enffans." This had presumably been adopted as a way, albeit dangerous, of circumventing the already stringent regulations of 13 January and 23 February 1535, not to mention the supposedly clement edict of 1535, reissued in 1536, which imposed the death penalty for such offenses.

The events of the years 1542–45 show that there really was very little more that could be done to arrest the spread of heresy or the mounting influence of Calvin, except in terms of detail. Thus the confirmative edict of 30 August 1542, addressed to all the *parlements* of France, was a reminder of their duty to enforce the heresy laws with the utmost rigor. At the same time special commissioners were appointed to sensitive areas. Three members of the *parlement* of Bordeaux were assigned to Guyenne and one, Jacques Le Roux from Paris, to the archbishopric of Sens, then under Louis cardinal de Bourbon.[79]

79. Viénot, i, 155.

The efforts of the king and the *parlements* were forcefully supplemented by the work of the Sorbonne: on 10 March 1543, it produced a set of twenty-five articles of faith which included the acceptance of transubstantiation, the Catholic (as opposed to Lutheran or Calvinist) version of the doctrine of the Real Presence.[80] At the request of the Sorbonne these articles were ratified by the crown on 23 July 1543, the date on which Francis "clarified" the complex, major edict of 1 June 1540 in a manner calculated to propitiate the clergy.[81] Enactment of the Sorbonne articles by the crown, the rejection of any one of which constituted heresy, would—juridically—strongly endorse the definition of heresy in the edict of 1 June 1540 as sedition against the State.[82]

The Sorbonne then set to work on a list of proscribed works, producing, in the following March 1544, a preliminary index of sixty-five items. Fourteen of them were condemned by the *parlement* to be publicly burnt. These included Calvin's *Institution*, Olivétan's Bible, and works of Erasmus and the Lutheran Melancthon. The fact that Calvin responded with a refutation of the Sorbonne articles shows that he was following events in France. On 5 April 1545 the king issued letters patent providing for the dispatch of five commissioners from the *parlement* of Paris "pour la recherche et la punition des hérétiques," to five areas under their jurisdiction: Anjou and Touraine, Sens, Meaux and Provins, the duché de Bourbonnais and Orléans, and the comté de Blois.[83] At the request of the "inquisiteur de la foi," probably Mathieu Ory, the *parlement* on 23 June 1545 prohibited the pos-

---

80. Ibid., 153.

81. The Sorbonne also issued forty articles which were specially condemned. Weiss points out that the decrees of Trent were drafted "presque dans les mesmes termes" as the Sorbonne articles of faith. Mansi, *Sacrorum Conciliorum*, xxxii, prints the articles of faith (in Latin), p. 1161, and the condemned articles, pp. 1181–83; Weiss, *La Chambre ardente*, introd. p. xxxvi, n. 1; Fontanon, *Les Édits et Ordonnances*, iv, 230–34.

82. *Catalogue des Actes*, iv, 473–74, no. 13224; 474, no. 13225.

83. *Bull. Prot.*, xxxiv, 1885, pp. 26–27. The commissioners were Claude des Asses, Jacques le Roux, Nicole Sanguin, Guillaume Bourgoing and Louis Gayant, in this order, for the areas listed.

session, as well as the sale of, books on the Index—which was reprinted on 20 July.[84] Whether, or to what extent, these events of 1545 were influenced by the appearance of the first complete edition of Luther's works, by Calvin's *Petit Traité de la Cène*— adopting his distinctive doctrine on the Eucharist—or by the council which opened at Trent in December, is not clear. It is certain, however, that 1545 was an important year in the history of Protestantism, and of its persecution in France.

Thus, by the end of the reign of Francis I, not only the Sorbonne, the *parlement*, the Church and the various inquisitors, but also the full power of the royal judiciary and administration were mobilized in the struggle against heresy. It was against these massive odds that Calvin had already begun, with careful deliberation, to mould and direct the reform movement in France. In 1538 he had founded his first church, at Strasbourg, for the French refugees; and, in 1545, the first Calvinist community in France was founded at Meaux, cradle of the French Reformation.[85]

It is important to remember that the French Protestant movement at this time was still extremely fluid. It had undergone the influence of Luther, Zwingli and Farel, and it was beginning to receive that of Calvin. Gradually he imposed control and direction on what were still separate and variegated pious groups. These arose in an ad hoc fashion, and the founders of the different churches were not ministers but "fidèles plein de zèle." "Church," therefore, would mean different things at different stages of development in different places. Calvinists came to draw a distinction between *églises plantées*, which were emergent communities, and *églises dressées*, which were fully constituted Calvinist churches with a pastor, or at least the share of one, since there were never as many pastors as churches. Sainte-Foy, Aubigny, Tours and Pau were among the first, between 1541 and 1546, to organize the administration of the Sacrament. But it was not until 1555 that

84. The first Sorbonne Index was completed on 13 August 1544; apparently no copy survived. It was reissued on 23 June 1545 and supplemented on 31 December 1546; Ibid., 21–27.

85. Mours, *Les Églises Réformées en France*, 10. It was decimated and subsequently re-founded.

Calvin's formal missionary effort began, when the first of his pastors, Jacques L'Anglois, went to Poitiers, "which long remained a mother-congregation of the French Reformed church."[86]

The example of Paris will serve to show the way in which, very much according to the Zwinglian pattern, these churches were able to arise and organize themselves anywhere. In this case, one Jean Le Maçon fled from persecution in Angers and went to Paris. There he and some others began to meet regularly in the house of a gentleman to pray and to read the scriptures. One day Le Maçon required the group to elect a minister in order to baptize his baby. After fasting and prayers they elected Le Maçon himself, who thus became their pastor. They then organized a consistory; this was how, in September 1555, the Paris church—one of the earliest—began. Meaux, Angers and Poitiers soon followed Paris; all (it is worth noting) were centers to which Francis had had occasion to pay special attention.[87] The next stage would normally be to appeal to Geneva for a trained pastor. Some "churches" dispatched and financed their own candidates for training; others simply paid for someone, but this trainee had to reach dauntingly high academic as well as personal and moral standards.

This spontaneous organization, and temporary self-sufficiency, explains how easily the churches could arise anywhere; also the discrepancy between the numbers of churches which might, at any moment, be said to exist, and the small number of pastors known to have been sent.[88] It also explains how easily such groups could become dominated by unsuitable persons or local pressure groups and become removed from truly pastoral or evangelical control. Calvin, who was much more conservative than Zwingli or Farel, constantly urged upon his followers the duties of patience, submission and obedience. While he did not approve of idols and images, he sternly reproved those who

86. Kingdon, *Geneva and the Coming of the Wars of Religion in France*, 2.

87. Viénot, i, 155; Mours, *Le Protestantisme en France*, 101–2.

88. Kingdon, 135–37, has been able to list eighty-eight pastors between 1555 and 1562. They often operated under several names and in various places.

willfully destroyed them. "Nous sommes bien esbahis," he once wrote to the church of Sauve in Languedoc, "qu'il y ait eu une telle témérité en celuy qui devoit modérer les aultres... *jamais Dieu n'a commandé d'abatre les idoles.*"[89] The churches might be strong, in the sense that they could arise and survive independently, but they were also alarmingly vulnerable, for example, to denunciation by anyone expelled for disciplinary reasons.

Saintes, whose church dates from 1556, affords a slightly different example from Paris. Philibert Hamelin, who in 1555 established a church at Arvert (Charente-maritime), stopped at the neighboring town of Saintes, where he delivered "de petites exhortations" to seven or eight persons. When he departed he urged them to continue to meet. The challenge was taken up by an artisan, probably Bernard Palissy, who, one Sunday, together with a comrade, gathered a meeting of nine or ten people and read from the Old and New Testaments. They agreed that six of them should take it in turn to exhort the meeting. Presumably they expounded the teaching of the Bible, to the best of their understanding, but they were apparently poor artisans of little education. This was the beginning of the church at Saintes, which soon acquired a pastor, Claude de la Boissière. He is described as a gentleman from Dauphiné, who was also poor, to the point of sometimes subsisting on applies and water. This small, clandestine community met "a plein minuit." Thus at Paris the pastor was elected; but at Saintes he came from elsewhere; the churches could be formed in either way.[90] Such communities represent the sort of original nuclei upon which Calvin began to work. They were frequently dispersed, and their ministers obliged to depart or move on. The consequent mobility is one reason why the movement tended to expand under the persecution which, in the reign of Henry II, was to reach its climax.

89. Bonnet, *Lettres de Calvin*, ii, 415-17, July 1561, Calvin to the church of Sauve; italics mine.
90. Mours, *Le Protestantisme en France*, 104.

2

The Climax of the Persecution,
1547–1559

HENRY II SHOWED LITTLE SIGN of sharing his father's genuine concern for the cultural values of the Renaissance, and he had, if anything, an even more pressing need than Francis I to acquire the wealth of the Church. With the growing independence of the Protestant German princes, shortly to be recognized in the religious peace of Augsburg, Henry was also less constrained by the susceptibilities of his German allies. This was a factor which had modified Francis's attitude and speech, even if it had not effectively influenced his religious policy. Henry may, temperamentally, have been more fanatical than Francis. However, the papal legate, Cardinal Trivultio, said that it was Henry's mistress, Diane de Poitiers, who incited him to greater severity.[1] Henry also inherited the heresy problem at a later and more disturbing stage, when its intractability had become apparent and its dimensions were greatly expanding. The crown had not at first been threatened by isolated patches of Lutheranism, although Francis had always taken seriously the offensive opinions of sectarians. Whether or not Henry ever grasped its content, the crown *was*, however, potentially threatened by Calvin's *Institution Chrétienne*—albeit proscribed—since it might prove instrumental in coordinating the French sectarians. But the transition from one phase of the Reformation to another was necessarily gradual, fluid and incomplete. It would take time to create more obedient Calvinist communities into which the Zwinglian sectarians might or

1. Lestocquoy, *Acta Nuntiaturae Gallicae*, xiv, 26, 44.

might not be quietly assimilated. To what extent either process occurred is a matter for conjecture, but not all the "churches," especially in the south, were as docile as Calvin desired.[2]

If Henry's reign was to bring the persecution of the Protestants to its savage climax, from which they gradually emerged as the Huguenots, this was at least partly because he was influenced, from his accession, by their bitterest enemy, Charles de Lorraine, brother of his boon companion, François de Guise.[3] For Lorraine who, as archbishop of Rheims, already claimed to represent the pope as *légat-né*, Henry promptly requested a cardinal's hat. The honor was duly conferred on 27 July 1547, the day after the coronation. Upon this occasion Lorraine exhorted Henry: "fais que la postérité dise de toi: si Henri II... n'avoit pas régné, l'Église romaine aurait péri de fond en comble."[4] Henry responded with a promise to exterminate—the language of war—"tous ceux que l'église lui désignera comme imbus d'erreurs."[5] Such words might have been a formal exchange: but the Protestants could afford no rash assumption, since the princes of the Schmalkaldic League had just been defeated by the emperor in Germany, while Calvin experienced resistance in Geneva.[6]

This, therefore, was a clear enough warning to the faithful of France, to whom on 24 July 1547 Calvin had addressed an open letter entreating them to steadfast courage and diligence in their religious practices.[7] There is no indication as to whom this was delivered, or by what means. But it shows that Calvin was actively fostering already existing contacts about a decade before we learn of the multiplication of formal Calvinist communities. If this was primarily because Calvin himself was not securely established in Geneva until 1555, it must also be partly explained by

2. Calvinists were, at least in theory, less dangerous than Zwinglians, since Zwingli had had no inhibitions about resistance.

3. Duc de Guise in 1550.

4. Viénot, *Histoire de la Réforme*, i, 212.

5. Weiss, *La Chambre ardente*, p. lxii.

6. The princes were defeated at the battle of Mühlberg, 24 April 1547.

7. Bonnet, *Lettres de Calvin*, i, 213–17, 24 July 1547, Calvin à nos très chers seigneurs et frères qui désirent l'avancement du royaulme de nostre Seigneur Jésus-Christ.

the severity of the persecution and the censorship in France, to which Henry II promptly attended.

The reign opened with an edict against blasphemy, 5 April 1547, and on 16 November 1547 Mathieu Ory was once again confirmed in his inquisitorial functions.[8] The following month, on 11 December, a royal edict confirmed the previous prohibitions against the production and distribution of religious works and the possession of those on the Index, of which Calvin's *Institution Chrétienne* was among the first.[9] Apart from emphasis, and a declaration of intent in the new reign, this ensured that censorship regulations were fully sanctioned and extended to the whole kingdom.

During the first three years of Henry's reign, the *parlement* of Paris alone issued over 500 *arrêts* against Protestants. This level of activity may have been partly due to the institution of the so-called *chambre ardente*, within the *parlement* of Paris, established to deal exclusively with heresy cases. This tribunal, which was more a matter of convenience than juridical innovation operated, according to the French Protestant historian Nathanael Weiss, from 2 May 1548—the date from which he found the registers—to January 1550. By 1547 the name *ardente* was already sometimes applied to the *chambres criminelles*, instituted by Francis I in 1515, to which heresy cases had been referred since the edict of 1 June 1540. The new *chambre ardente* was probably modeled on the example of Rouen where, in 1545, such a tribunal had been created, consisting of ten to twelve *conseillers* "des plus scavants et des plus zélés," appointed by the *présidents* to deal exclusively with heresy cases. This may have ensured that they were tried by extremists. Weiss, however, was unable to account for the origin of the famous, or infamous, *chambre ardente* in Paris, suggesting that it might have been instigated by the extremist *président* Pierre Lizet, before the new king departed in 1548 to inspect his eastern frontiers. No letters of creation, he said, had been found, but he thought it was probably constituted between 11 December 1547

8. Weiss, *La Chambre ardente*, p. lxiv.
9. Fontanon, *Les Édits et ordonnances*, iv, 373-74.

and 2 May 1548.[10] He appears, however, to have overlooked the statement at the end of the preamble to Henry's edict of 19 November 1549, which says: "... dès nostre nouvel avènement à la couronne... nous aurions pour plus grande et prompte expédition dedites matières et procez sur le fait desdites hérésies ... ordonné et establi une chambre particulière en nostre parlement à Paris, pour seulement vacquer audites expéditions, sans se divertir à autres actes."[11] This clearly dates the institution from Henry's accession. The preamble also relates this to the failure of all Francis's previous efforts to resolve the problem of heresy.

At the end of Francis's reign in 1547, procedures against the heretics were still regulated by the edict of 1 June 1540. Having aroused certain objections, it was supposed to have been clarified by the further edict of 23 July 1543. But this had never been published and the confusions and objections of 1540 still obtained. Henry II's edict of 19 November 1549 was therefore primarily intended to regulate these inherited problems.[12] The bishops, according to the verbose and complex preamble, had become lax in the execution of their duty to combat heresy, complaining that the edict of 1540 had encroached on their jurisdiction by requiring the *parlements, baillis, sénéchaux* and others of the judiciary to proceed against heretics. They claimed to have the exclusive cognizance of heresy within their dioceses. Henry's edict therefore reiterated the unpublished clarifications of 1543 that simple heresy was the exclusive province of the Church, adding (article 2) that as an exception in heresy cases, bishops might make arrests anywhere and not, as previously, only within their dioceses. Whenever heresy caused derivative and related offenses involving sedition—"scandalle publique" or "offense publique"—then ecclesiastical and lay authorities should cooperate: "... sera fait le proces à l'accusé... par les juges d'église et royaux ensemble." But, whereas the edict of 1540 had required the royal judges to refer all such cases to the *parlements* for judg-

10. Weiss, *La Chambre ardente*, pp. lxi, lxii, n. 1.
11. Haag, *La France protestante*, x, 16.
12. Fontanon, *Les Édits et ordonnances*, iv, 249–50.

ment, that of 1549 authorized them to prosecute and sentence as well; saving only a right of appeal to the *parlements*. The principal effect of this edict therefore—apart from attempting to placate and reassure the clergy—was to enhance the powers of the judiciary in heresy cases.[13] Letters patent of 22 June 1550— which give an astoundingly inaccurate account of the chronology and content of a number of previous edicts—simply brought the already confirmed powers of Mathieu Ory, *inquisiteur général*, into line with these modifications, permitting him to deal with heresy cases in cooperation with the Church, and without reference to the civil authorities.[14]

Up to this point the religious edicts had been largely concerned with prohibitions, the suppression of heresy, the punishment of related offences— generally described as sedition—and matters of jurisdiction and procedure. They had done little that was positive to arrest, and still less to exterminate heresy, which continued to flourish and increase. Besides the continued expansion of heresy, the crown was also faced with mounting problems arising from the negligence of the Church, conflicts of jurisdiction, conversions among members of the judiciary, an increase in public disorders and an overall degree of difficulty in implementing the law which was probably unknown within living memory.

Some of these difficulties were reflected in the composite edict of Châteaubriant of 27 June 1551, which has been described as "un vrai code de persécution."[15] This very long, comprehensive regulation, compiled during an intermission in the Franco-Hapsburg wars, marks a shift in emphasis away from a negative opposition towards a positive and pervasive persecution. Indeed, it might well be, if more were known about its execution, that we ought to date from this edict the beginnings of a revolutionary reaction in France; but at the moment this is conjecture. The Calvinist

13. By the edict of 1540 all cases were sent to the *parlements* for judgment; by that of 1543 all cases were to be reported to the *parlement*; by that of 1549 all the royal courts might sentence, and the *parlements* received appeals.

14. Fontanon, *Les Édits et ordonnances*, iv, 226–27.

15. Ibid., 252–57.

churches, however, must surely have arisen in the face of astounding odds, except where they were juridically protected by the conversion of those who should have suppressed them.

The preamble to the edict of Châteaubriant recapitulated the history of the edicts of religion from January 1534/35 to 1549, a summary which would be more useful if it were less inaccurate. Article 1 goes on to make a significant change in the juridicial procedure; in the case of laymen, the *parlement* and the presidial judges were now alone empowered to proceed against the disorders arising from heresy, and to pronounce judgment without appeal. Cases of simple heresy, however, were to be the sole province of the Church. This was the position according to the edict of July 1543, but not of November 1549 which (like that of 1540) equated heresy itself with treason. These new provisions in 1551 are particularly interesting in view of the statement in article 23 that the king had heard of judicial officials suspected of heresy and dereliction of duty. Furthermore, the *parlements* themselves—now potentially suspect—were required to hold *mercuriales* every three months to ascertain that none of their own members were tainted.[16] This was supported by the requirement of article 24 that there should be no appointments to judicial or municipal offices without a certificate of Catholicity. Although the presidial courts are referred to in earlier edicts, it appears that they had only just been fully instituted throughout the country by Henry II in January 1551; there were now thirty-two in the jurisdiction of the *parlement* of Paris. According to Nathanael Weiss, the *chambre ardente* had ceased to operate in January 1550. Could this, one is therefore bound to wonder, be an error for January 1550/51? However this may be, it does seem likely that the presidial courts—newly extended and nationwide, directly dependent upon the crown, whose members were certified Catholic—had been developed at least partially for the more reliable prosecution of heresy. Furthermore, this new endeavour to exclude Protestants from eligibility for certain offices introduced an element of

16. Article 25; the word refers to Wednesday, the day of the week on which these self-examinatory sessions were customarily held.

discrimination which attracted the most pertinacious resistance; eligibility became one of the Protestants' basic requirements, first accorded in 1570.

The juridical clauses were followed by no less than twenty articles (2–22) covering in exhaustive detail all matters of censorship; the possession, production, sale and dissemination of religious works; the rigid control of printing, and the inspection of bookshops. But even more vexatious and dangerous were the articles (27–33) relating to informing, which became mandatory. Informers were to receive one third of the confiscated property of the convicted, and it was an offense to ignore denunciations. Those who informed on illegal assemblies were, upon abjuration, pardoned similar offenses. Not only was it forbidden—as it had been since 1535—to shelter or assist heretics, but magistrates and *seigneurs haut justiciers* were actively to seek them out, and also to search houses for forbidden books. Thus persecution now violated the privacy of the home, and discreet and peaceful conduct was no longer any guarantee of safety. The edict also attempted to ensure that teachers in schools, academies, universities and even private tutors should all be Catholics. These were provocative clauses which became linked to the wider problem of eligibility for office. The control of literature, reading and teaching was even extended in theory (but without prospect of implementation) to a prohibition against the mere discussion of religion or religious matters by illiterate persons and foreigners. Furthermore, no one was to correspond with or send money to any exile in Geneva or other non-Catholic locality, and it was illegal simply to carry letters expressing heretical opinions. Presumably the number of exiles and contacts with them in Switzerland and Germany was already regarded as alarming. There followed property regulations intended to make flight more difficult, which doubtless exacerbated the smouldering resentment of those already in exile. Thus, the property of religious exiles was to be confiscated. The property of those who had sold it prior to departure was also to be seized, if it were established that the purchaser was guilty of collusion. These regulations would preclude any safe and prosperous exile, which might prove extremely dangerous to France.

As well as marking a shift from prohibitions to persecution, the edict of Châteaubriant was novel in that it prescribed certain positive religious observances from which abstention would be apparent, suspicious and dangerous. Thus, in the first place, it became obligatory to attend church, and as often as possible (and to refrain from parading about during the services). Not only were the bishops to be resident (and to require the same of their subordinates), but they were commanded to read in church every Sunday the articles of faith propounded by the Sorbonne in 1543, and to admonish their observance.[17] This is interesting in view of the fact that the subsequent decrees of the council of Trent, which closely followed the articles of the Sorbonne, were not to be received in France. Anyone licensed to preach had to conform to these articles, and no one might be so licensed who had ever been tainted with or suspected of heresy, unless his purgation were judicially certified. Finally, the *parlements*—which were possibly just beginning to exhibit signs of Protestant infiltration— were commanded to act with the utmost diligence, to report to the king, and to supervise inferior courts.

Thus with the opposition to heresy transformed into a positive persecution in the spheres of literature, education, the home, and property—which was certain to alienate members of the gentry—and with the exclusion of Protestants from many offices, there was little more that a government could do, short of violence. This was the direction in which France was moving. But for several more years the heresy problem developed while Henry II was preoccupied with foreign policy. This, in turn, had considerable repercussions on domestic and religious affairs, and the climax of the persecution in 1557. Indeed the events of 1552–57 provide an admirable illustration of the extent to which religious persecution in France was related to politics and, above all, to the unstable pressures of foreign affairs, of which it is therefore necessary to have some understanding.

The following years, 1552–54, witnessed a renewal of war with

17. These articles had already been ratified by the crown, 23 July 1543. *Catalogue des Actes*, iv, 473–74, no. 13224.

the emperor in the form of the Metz campaign, and a somewhat inglorious invasion of the Netherlands.[18] Meanwhile, the new papal nuncio, Santa-Croce, envoy of the pacifist pope Julius III, arrived in Paris on 21 August 1552. He was instructed to mediate peace between France and the Empire because of the mounting danger to Christendom (and the Papacy) from the heretics and the Turks, which resulted from the Franco-Hapsburg rivalry.[19] Naturally Santa-Croce was equally required to assist in what was, in a sense, the domestic aspect of the same struggle against heresy, and the dissemination of heretical literature, lest the movement should develop to the point where it could no longer be contained. This had happened in the Empire, in the case of Luther, and precisely because of the emperor's foreign wars. There was indeed a potential analogy. Whether or not it was on his own initiative, on 18 February 1553 Santa-Croce reported to Cardinal del Monte that the king had decided to create a special "heresy council," separate and apart, which was to attend to no other business ("appartato sopra le cose delle heresie, coiè che non attenda ad altro").[20] Perhaps the presidial courts, scattered in the provinces, did not fully replace the *chambre ardente* of the *parlement* of Paris which had been a central, if not a national organ. There is no indication that this heresy council ever materialized. Nevertheless, this may have marked the beginning of an attempt in the 1550s to reestablish the Inquisition on a formal, juridical basis, as in Spain. It has already been indicated that the Inquisition is too big a subject to incorporate here. Nevertheless, it is essential at this stage to make some allusions to it, in order to account for the emergence of the Huguenots in 1560, and to understand their juridical and political position, within the context of European affairs. The Huguenots were afraid of the imposition of an Inquisition—which necessarily involved the Papacy—and their struggle for survival was no purely French

18. This resulted in the conquest of Metz, Toul and Verdun, strategic positions in Lorraine.

19. Lestocquoy, *Correspondance de Santa-Croce*, 63-65, 18 May–19 June 1552, instructions for Santa-Croce.

20. Ibid., 143. He may have had the Spanish *Suprema* in mind.

concern. Indeed, the commingling of religious and political problems was already becoming complex.

Santa-Croce's peace policy, at least partly designed to switch attention to the problems of religion, found some support with the constable Montmorency, rival of the Guise brothers, whose immediate interests and future hopes lay in the prosecution of war. If Henry himself was keen to pursue his hereditary claims on Italy and Brabant, Santa-Croce tended to think—whether correctly or not—that it was nevertheless the emperor who was the main obstacle to peace.[21] Writing in October 1552, he thought that Henry might agree to treat on the basis of each retaining what they held. This is possible since, at that date, it would have legalized the French conquest of Metz which the emperor might otherwise retake.[22] But Henry was no match for his incompatible favorites, and Montmorency tended to be outmaneuvered by the Guises, though he probably prevailed in the affections of the king.

External circumstances, however, were drastically altered in 1553 by the news of the impending marriage of the emperor's son Philip to Mary Tudor. Philip might still, at this time, have inherited the entire Hapsburg empire, albeit after his cousin, Maximilian.[23] Thus the prospect of his union with Mary, solemnized in July 1554, created a violent reaction in France, and discussion of a major war with England by way of Scotland, whose dowager queen, Mary of Lorraine (regent from February 1554), was a sister of the Guises. This meant, in other words, an extension of the Franco-Hapsburg war across the Channel, not originally in the aggressive pursuit of a dynastic claim, but for more urgent considerations of defense. Dynasticism, however, was added thereto by the marriage in 1558 of the dauphin Francis to Mary queen of Scots. Mary's claim to the throne of England was supported by France after the accession of the Protestant Elizabeth in November 1558. This was a French dynastic response to the

21. Ibid., 35, 40.
22. Ibid., 93–95, 17 October 1552, Santa-Croce to Cardinal del Monte.
23. This was arranged by the Hapsburg family pact of March 1551.

marriage of Philip and Mary, albeit nearly four years later, as soon as the children were old enough. Because of this new aspect of the Franco-Hapsburg rivalry, in January 1554 the vidame de Chartres was appointed to command a considerable expedition to Scotland;[24] and in the summer of 1554 there was another campaign into the Netherlands. Santa-Croce, therefore, had no further hope of imposing peace and concentrating Catholic attention on the problem of heresy, which continued to increase in France in spite of the edict of Châteaubriant. This new and alarming European political pattern was to be even more drastically changed by further important events in 1555 and 1556.

In September 1555 the religious peace of Augsburg in the Empire vastly diminished the German princes' interest in French support against the emperor. At the same time, Philip relinquished his immediate claim to the Imperial crown; in October Charles V resigned to him the Italian possessions, Milan, Naples and Sicily, as well as the Netherlands, followed in January 1556 by the kingdom of Spain itself. These events altered the nature of the Franco-Hapsburg rivalry, which became predominantly Franco-Spanish. Similarly, the bellicose Neapolitan pope, Paul IV, nurtured a desire for war in order to evict the hated Spanish from Naples; his quarrel was really no longer principally with the emperor.[25] This led the pope, and his able and aspiring Carafa nephews, to seek an offensive-defensive alliance with France. They proceeded to negotiate with the French ambassador, Avanson, without awaiting the arrival from France of the requested envoy of rank.[26]

It was upon the business of this Franco-Papal treaty that the cardinal of Lorraine and his senior and rival the cardinal de Tournon—who had no sympathy with the Guise war policy—left for Rome in October 1555. There, on 15 December, they signed a slightly modified version of Avanson's alliance. The king

24. This consisted of 6,000 foot and 2,000 horse; Lestocquoy, *Correspondance de Santa-Croce*, 246, 13 January 1554, Santa-Croce to Cardinal del Monte.

25. This distinction does not seem to be very clearly made in contemporary correspondence.

26. The agreement with Avanson was signed on 14 October 1555.

of France took the pope and his house of Carafa under royal protection, and agreed to assist in liberating Naples from Spanish domination.[27] But, during the absence of the cardinals, the constable Montmorency (whose eldest son François was a prisoner of war and dearly ransomed) negotiated a truce at Vaucelles between France, the emperor and Philip. It was signed on 5 February 1556, just about the time when Lorraine was expected back from Italy.[28]

As a Neapolitan, Paul IV had much more to gain than Julius III from the Franco-Hapsburg rivalry and the renewal of war. But there was also a more venerable side to him, and he did share the concern of his predecessor, and of the cardinals Lorraine and Tournon, for the worsening state of religion in France. Indeed, his opposition to any form of Protestantism was known to be exceptionally violent. In 1520 he had sat on the commission appointed to deal with the affair of Martin Luther. More significantly, it was he who had reorganized the papal Inquisition for Paul III in 1542. Later, during his own pontificate, he issued the first papal Index in 1557, already preceded by that of the Sorbonne.

As pope and prince, Paul IV faced a serious situation in 1555, since this was not only a year of profound political change, but also critical in the history of Protestantism. In May, the month of Paul's election, John Knox returned to the now politically sensi-

27. This treaty and the subsequent Italian expedition might well have colored Spain's attitude toward France after the outbreak of the revolt of the Netherlands on France's frontier. Duruy, *Le Cardinal Carlo Carafa*, 88–89.

28. *CSPSp.*, *1554–58*, p. 253 and note *, 7 December 1555, Simon Renard to Philip from Cambrai. The Venetians refused to join the league, but the duke of Ferrara, a kinsman of the Guises, acceded; *CSPF.*, *1553–58*, p. 205, 18 January 1556, Peter Vannes to the council, from Venice; 207, 4 February 1556, Sir Edward Carne to Queen Mary, Rome; 207, 208, 5 February 1556, the truce of Vaucelles, negotiated by Gaspard de Coligny with the secretary Claude de Laubespine; 210, 10 February 1556, Dr. Wooton to Sir William Petre, from Blois; *CSPVen.*, *1555–56*, pp. 313–14, 12 January 1556, Soranzo to the doge; 335, 1 February 1556, Soranzo to the doge; 342–43, 9 February 1556, Soranzo to the doge.

tive kingdom of Scotland, where he proceeded to unite the Protestants. September witnessed the religious peace of Augsburg,
which gave recognition to Lutheranism in the Empire and,
shortly before Lorraine left for Rome, Calvin and his Company of
Pastors had become definitively established in Geneva. One consequence of this was the beginning of his formal missionary campaign in France and the organization of the first French Calvinist
churches. It was also from about this time that the nobility and
gentry were beginning to be converted in significant numbers.
This placed a new and alarming complexion on the French religious problem: from the point of view of the crown any defection
of the nobility, for whatever reason, was dangerous. In that year
no less than a record 119 nobles or gentry sought refuge in
Geneva. Their conversion and flight was presumably rendered all
the more dangerous by the punishing property clauses of the edict
of Châteaubriant. These refugees were shortly to provide some of
the political and military leaders of the Huguenot movement.
Furthermore, by allowing them asylum, Geneva almost automatically became involved in French politics. It was also in October
1555, as Lorraine made his way to Rome, that the Bourbon prince
de Condé and his suite visited Geneva, and were formally entertained, upon their return from war in Italy. This did not pass
unnoticed.[29]

While a study of these years strongly impresses one with the
obtuse preoccupation of princes and prelates with diplomacy and
war, this was not so complete as to exclude some secondary work
on the problems of religion. Thus Lorraine is said to have been
accompanied to Rome by "une troupe nombreuse d'évêques"
who, early in December, held conferences on the reform of
"abuses."[30] These, it transpires, were only problems arising out
of the concordat of Bologna. It seems likely, however, that religion, in a more general sense, accounts for the presence in Rome
of Tournon. His pacifist politics conflicted with the Guise war
policy, but he was much concerned with the state of the Church

---

29. Kingdon, *Geneva and the Coming of the Wars of Religion in France,*
59–60.
30. Romier, *Les Origines politiques,* ii, 243.

and the problem of heresy. In the two months between the conclusion of the treaty and the arrival, on 15 February, of the shattering news of the truce of Vaucelles,[31] Tournon, the pope and a
papal commission worked seriously on the problem of reform.[32]

This is as far as the evidence goes. It is not established that the
problem of heresy in France was discussed by either Lorraine—
who is not reported to have mentioned it upon his return—or by
Tournon. But as (by 1556) the problem of heresy was primarily a
French one, it is almost inconceivable that it did not arise. Furthermore, since he reestablished the Inquisition in Italy, this is
what one would expect Paul IV to have advised. Everyone knew
of the power of the Spanish Inquisition; in France it would ad-
mirably serve the ambitious purposes of Lorraine, and equally
accommodate what Tournon's biographer called his "désir sin-
cère de redresser une situation qui empire chaque jour."[33]

But, with the news of the truce of Vaucelles, politics once again
supervened, although the reaction of Gualtiero, nuncio in France,
was to press for more effective attention to the problem of religion. This may simply have been his perennial incantation.[34] The
reaction of the pope and his Carafa nephews was one of furious
political betrayal. This was why Cardinal Carlo Carafa went to
France in June 1556. His formal instructions related to converting
the truce into a firm peace and calling for a general council. His
real purpose, nevertheless, was to shatter the truce and reconsti-
tute the papal alliance. It is interesting that the correspondence of
this cardinal legate is practically silent on the problems of religion, which were not unobtrusive at the time. It was not (so far as
we know), until the end of his mission that he so much as mentioned heresy. Finally, however, on 11 August 1556, he claimed
laconically that Henry had agreed, almost completely, to what

31. Duruy, *Le Cardinal Carlo Carafa*, 109. Ten days to Rome was
about as fast as the journey could be made.

32. Lorraine had quickly gone away to seek the alliance of Ferrara and
Venice, and returned to court at Blois on 11 February 1556. Ancel,
Nonciatures de France, i, (2), 343, 14 February 1556, Gualtiero to Carafa.

33. François, *Le Cardinal François de Tournon*, 448.

34. Ancel, *Nonciatures de France*, i (2), 343, 7 February 1556, Gualtiero to Carafa.

the pope desired, "quanto ala cosa de i concordati et a le heresie."[35] He must, therefore, have received *some* instructions in this respect, though how formally is not clear.

It *can* only have been the Inquisition that Paul desired, Carafa proposed, and to which Henry had agreed, to judge from his letter of 13 February 1557 to Odet de Selve, his ambassador in Rome.[36] In this letter Henry said that while he had agreed to an Inquisition in France, "suivant la forme de droit, pour estre le vray moyen d'extirper la racine de telles erreurs [heresy]," the proposal had nevertheless raised certain difficulties. These arose from the opposition of the *parlement*. De Selve was therefore instructed to request the pope "très instamment" *that he should address his brief*—which suggests that Henry had reached a decision with Carafa—to a cardinal and other prominent churchmen, as he saw fit, "pour par eux et [leurdits] delegues estre procedé à l'introduction et observation de ladite inquisition, en la forme et manière accoustumée de droit, sous l'autorité du Saint Siège Apostolique, avec l'invocation du bras seculier et jurisdiction temporelle." The king undertook to support this with all his might. The request was granted on 4 March, and the pope agreed to address the brief to Lorraine.[37] Thus, on 26 April 1557, he appointed the three cardinals of Lorraine, Bourbon and Châtillon inquisitors general for the whole kingdom, with authority to delegate both the cognizance of heresy cases in the first instance, and for the hearing of appeals.[38] As Bourbon was a nonentity and Châtillon became a Protestant, Lorraine could be seen as the "grand inquisitor." Henry accepted and confirmed this papal

35. Ibid., 458-59, 11 August 1556, instructions from Carafa to Rucellai.

36. Ribier, *Lettres et Mémoires d'Estat*, ii, 677-78, 13 February 1556/57, Henry II to de Selve.

37. Ibid., 678-84, 28 March 1556/57, de Selve to Henry II.

38. Fontanon, *Les Édits et ordonnances*, iv, 227-28. As a nephew of the constable Montmorency, Châtillon might be regarded as a political enemy of the Guises. The Inquisition was to be imposed with the cooperation of the bishops in each diocese. Consequently letters patent of 1 May 1557 required archbishops, bishops and everyone having cure of souls to reside in their benefice upon pain of confiscation of revenue. Isnard, *Actes royaux*, i, 229, no. 1339.

brief by letters patent of 24 July 1557.[39] But he stipulated that the inquisitors should only delegate their powers to churchmen of proven quality, who were to act under oath to the council. The cardinals themselves were to establish appeals tribunals in the *parlement* towns. These were to consist of ten *notables personages*, of whom six (a majority) were to be *conseillers* of the *parlements*. At the same time, he sought to retain some control of the system by stipulating that the decisions of the appeals tribunals should be executed by royal officials.

The letters patent authorizing a form of inquisition in France were accompanied, on the same day, 24 July, by the edict of Compiègne.[40] This was the last and most savage of this first, repressive series. It therefore represents the juridical fulfillment of the king's undertaking to support the papal Inquisition with all the might of his secular arm. The preamble refers to six previous edicts which, "par malice des personnes et par negligence des officiers," had not been observed. Some had complained of the cost involved, some of the lack of obedience, and others of conflicts of jurisdiction; all of them inadmissible excuses. Consequently the numbers of heretics had greatly increased, and heresy had changed from being a matter of private opinion to one of open sedition. Thus—sweeping aside all previous distinctions—in article 1 the king menacingly declared: ". . . telles emotions sont autant a chastier et reprimer *par armes que par voye de justice*, et qu'à nous seul . . . appartient la correction et punition de telles seditions et troubles . . ."[41] This manifest declaration of war—to be pursued upon the termination of foreign war—is the origin of the Guise religious policy in the next reign, and it was largely they who incurred the odium.

Since the edict of Compiègne represented—juridically—the secular contribution to the newly decreed Inquisition, it was necessarily concerned with the mounting problem of law and order. Its principal item was therefore to impose the death penalty, without appeal, for all sacramentarians; all who preached

39. Fontanon, *Les Édits et ordonnances*, iv, 228–29.
40. Ibid., 258–59.
41. Italics mine.

(heresy) in public or in private; who offended against the Sacrament, images, the Virgin or the saints and who, in the furtherance thereof, raised seditions or popular assemblies; those who communicated with Geneva, and the bearers of condemned books, whether for sale or distribution.

This so-called edict of the Inquisition, together with the letters patent constituting the tribunals, were strongly resisted by the *parlement* of Paris. Affairs of state were certainly disrupted by the military crisis of 1557, when the king of Spain invaded France and captured Saint-Quentin on 10 August, thereby endangering Paris. This is at least partly why the king did not force the *parlement* to register the edicts until 15 January 1558. Nevertheless, there was such determined opposition that the tribunals were never set up, and in June 1558 the bull constituting the cardinal inquisitors is said to have been rescinded.[42] This was a setback, but not the end of the movement. According to Jules Delaborde, Lorraine and Arras (Granvelle) reacted to this by concluding a pact to exterminate Protestants and decided to strike first of all at François d'Andelot—a nephew of Montmorency. On the grounds that he had taken part in Protestant gatherings in the Pré-aux-Clercs in the faubourg Saint-Germain, d'Andelot was arrested on 19 May.[43] If this pact really did exist, then it was of fundamental importance, but there is no precise evidence for it.

The king, however, was certainly undeterred by this conflict over the edict of Compiègne and his confirmation of the papal brief. Shortly before the treaty of Cateau-Cambrésis (3 April 1559), which ended the Hapsburg wars, he had sworn a terrible oath: "Je jure qui si je peux régler mes affaires extérieurs, je ferai courir par les rues le sang et les têtes de cette infame canaille luthérienne." Immediately after the peace, Lorraine declared this royal intention to the truculent *parlement*. The king, he said, had

42. Pastor, *Histoire des papes*, xiv, 261. The registration of the edict and letters patent was noted by the nuncio, Lorenzo Lenzi, whose correspondence unhappily affords no further enlightenment. Lestocquoy, *Acta Nuntiaturae Gallicae*, xiv, 111, 26 January 1558, Lenzi to Carafa.

43. Lestocquoy, *Acta Nuntiaturae Gallicae*, xiv, 32; Delaborde, *Coligny*, i, 368.

wanted peace at all costs, in order to turn "plus à son aise" to the extermination of heresy.[44] This was substantiated by the letters patent of Écouen of 2 June 1559,[45] in which the king declared that he had been deflected by the needs of war (presumably since July 1557) from attending, as he would have wished, to the problems of religion. As a result, the problems had seriously worsened. Thus, the letters patent stated, the Protestants had "tout en un coup eslevéz... par turbes et nombres si effrénez, commettans tous les scandales qu'ils ont peu. ..." It was therefore more than necessary "de repoulser et reprimer ceste violence par une aultre plus aigre avec la force qu'il a pleu à Dieu nous mectre en la main," external peace having been concluded with England and Spain. This would appear to reaffirm the apparent declaration of religious war embodied in the edict of Compiègne.

Since, in June 1559, Henry was still detained by the marriage celebrations arising from the treaty of Cateau-Cambrésis, he intended to dispatch responsible persons to the provinces ("certains bons et notables personnaiges") to proceed with the extirpation of the heretics. All provincial officials were to assist them "avec main forte et armée," calling out, if need be, the *ban, arrière-ban* and municipal guards. Furthermore, the king would, if necessary, send "quelque bon nombre de gendarmerye." Clearly the king intended to brook no further opposition from the *parlement*. A week later, on 10 June, Henry himself appeared before the *parlement* to request from each of the *conseillers* his opinion on the punishment of heretics. Some of them risked advising the king that they should not be punished, until after the decisions of a general council. This was not unreasonable insofar as a council had been mentioned in the peace treaty and was generally expected. But it was not the advice that Henry wished to receive, and some seven offenders—including the celebrated Anne du Bourg—were forthwith arrested.[46] This resounding event, together with the king's violent declarations, precipitated an ex-

44. Pasquier, *Lettres historiques*, 33.
45. Viénot, i, 248; Romier, *Les Origines politiques*, ii, 362–64.
46. Pasquier, *Lettres historiques*, 33.

treme reaction and may reasonably be held to account for the flood of controversy and propaganda relating to self-defense and resistance. For even Calvinists—who were not, in their own estimation, sacramentarians—were theoretically permitted to resist in certain rather abstruse circumstances, although Calvin continued to enjoin the faithful to patient resignation, even in time of immediate peril.[47] Nevertheless, there could no longer be any doubt as to the king's intentions, and the idea of resistance was, from thenceforth, in the air. It was probably because he was planning to launch a major attack which, for the time being, would supersede judicial remedies, that Henry acquiesced in the frustration of the Inquisition. When his death averted that war, the Guises continued to support the policy of the Inquisition. It would have paralleled that of the Netherlands and Spain, but it was never possible to impose it.

On the morning of 30 June 1559, Henry ordered Montgomery—by whose lance he was to be fatally wounded that same afternoon—to command an expedition against the Protestants of Caux in Normandy.[48] It was natural, furthermore, since Philip II's representatives were in Paris for his marriage, by proxy, to Elisabeth de Valois, that they should have been discussing the intention, rather generally expressed in the treaty, to eliminate Protestantism. Philip II was willing to help the king within France—in spite of all Henry's past support of the Protestants against his father in Germany. The duke of Alva, however, Philip's personal representative, tended to oppose cooperation in an enterprise then favored by France and the pope to extinguish Geneva—source and cradle of Calvinism. Alva was afraid of provoking the Swiss cantons, which might then

47. See on Calvin's political philosophy, Mesnard, *L'Essor de la philosophie politique au XVIe siècle.* Kingdon, *Geneva and the Coming of the Wars of Religion in France,* 64; Geisendorf, *Théodore de Bèze,* 109–10. While in prison, Anne du Bourg wrote an attack on the tyranny of Henry II and was executed on 23 December 1559.

48. Lutteroth, *La Réformation en France,* 186–87. This was a first step towards the suppression of heresy by force, announced in the edict of Compiègne. Montgomery, well-known as a Huguenot lieutenant, did not become a Protestant until later; it is not known when. Marlet, *Le Comte de Montgomery,* 12, 19–20.

obstruct the "Spanish road" from north Italy to the Netherlands.[49] But, with or without Spanish help, there was still some such plan afoot. Calvin himself, in a letter of 29 June 1559 to the faithful of Paris, reminded them, for their consolation, that Geneva also was seriously threatened.[50]

This matter was the concern, among others, of the duke of Brunswick who, since the end of the Franco-Spanish wars, had feared the destruction of Protestantism at the hands of France and Spain. The treaty, which specified their amity, called for a general council, and embodied the marriage of Philip to Elisabeth de Valois, was sufficient to alert all Protestants without any more specific or subsequent declaration, such as the edict of Écouen. Thus, because of the "entreprises evidentes des princes d'Espagne et de France... pour detruire et renverser ... ceste cité," Brunswick went incognito to Geneva.[51] There he sent his secretary to inform the magistrates of the hostile intentions of France and Spain (the cooperation of Spain was doubtless assumed) against the city-state, through the agency of Savoy, their recent master. The duke of Savoy had newly married Marguerite, sister of the king of France, by the treaty of Cateau-Cambrésis. Brunswick is also said to have presented the council with some proposition for so diverting the Catholic monarchs and Savoy that they would be fully occupied in defending themselves and therefore unable to molest the Protestants. This, however, was to remain deeply secret; no one must know that such a proposition had ever been made.[52] Thus no one, it seems, has ever discovered what this diversionary project was. The council of Geneva apparently decided to wait upon events, being nervous about launching into such great matters before the powers had manifested their

49. Simancas, series B, Leg. n. 62–140, 26 June 1559, Alva to Philip II, quoted by Mignet, *Journal des Savants*, March 1857, pp. 169–71. Savoy had a claim to Geneva, his father Charles III having been dispossessed.

50. Bonnet, *Lettres de Calvin*, ii, 281–84, 29 June 1559, Calvin aux fidèles de Paris.

51. Archives d'Etat de Genève, Registres du Conseil, 55, f. 132v, 23 October 1559.

52. Gautier, *Histoire de Genève*, iv, 277–79, 293.

hostile intentions. The exact nature of these intentions is not clear and—conceivably on account of Spanish reluctance—neither then nor later did the enterprise of Geneva ever materialize. Nevertheless, the idea did not expire with Henry, when he died on 10 July.[53] It was resumed by the Guises and became woven into Catholic politics of the next thirty years or so. On 20 November 1560 Amblard Corna, an aged syndic of Geneva, was warned by Jean France from Paris of "l'entreprise de la maison de Guise... contre la ville de Geneve."[54] According to him, Lorraine had paid a substantial sum to six Englishmen, who were fabricating fireworks at the Arsenal in order to set fire to Geneva, which Savoy was to invest. The following January 1561, and probably referring to the same plans, the council of Berne also warned that of Geneva of "quelques menaces et malaisées entreprises contre vous," and urged them to great vigilance.[55] Furthermore, the Geneva enterprise was revived in the treaty of the Triumvirate, 1561,[56] and again by the Catholic League in 1585, although it did not actually feature in the Guise treaty of Joinville with Spain.[57]

Henry's accidental death in July 1559 modified the structure of European politics, and presumably also affected Brunswick's arcane design for diverting the fury of the Catholic monarchs. It could possibly have been one and the same as that embryonic project of certain German princes, together with François Hotman, professor of law at Strasbourg, and Jean Sturm, rector of the Academy, which, after the death of Henry II, was adapted into a plan to raise Antoine de Bourbon, king of Navarre, first

53. For example, Brunswick's own warning to the council of Geneva appears to have been in October 1559, three months after Henry's death.

54. Archives d'État de Genève, Portefeuilles historiques, 1689, 20 November 1560.

55. Ibid., 1667, 15 January 1560/61, council of Berne to Geneva.

56. Sutherland, *The Massacre of St. Bartholomew*, app. 348–49.

57. Martin, *Henry III and the Jesuit Politicians*, 156–57, 167; René de Luçinge, *Lettres sur les débuts de la Ligue*, 77, 80 and passim. See also Archives d'État de Genève, Registres du Conseil, 62, f. 34v, 2 April 1567. In 1567 the French Protestants garrisoned Geneva for its defense. Gautier, *Histoire de Genève*, iv, 559–600.

prince of the blood and allegedly a Protestant, to predominant power in France.[58] Similarly, by October 1559—when Brunswick warned the council of Geneva—it could have represented, in a more direct sense, the beginnings of the still mysterious conspiracy of Amboise which, it has been widely believed, originated in Geneva, city of refuge for a considerable group of French religious exiles. Whatever the truth behind these mysteries, Protestants were gravely disturbed by the fear of violence, proclaimed in the edicts of Compiègne and Écouen, and by the implications of the treaty of Cateau-Cambrésis between France and Spain. It is therefore not difficult to understand why the Huguenots should so swiftly have emerged as an identifiable Protestant opposition to the domination of Lorraine. As a cardinal, archbishop of Rheims, and *legat-né*, Lorraine still possessed inquisitorial powers, and his manifest intention was to proceed with Henry's policy of extermination in the reign of his young son Francis II.

58. See chap. 3.

3

Calvinism and the Conspiracy of Amboise, March 1560

THE CONSPIRACY OF AMBOISE arose directly out of the crisis which followed the sudden death of Henry II in July 1559. The disastrous thing about this new situation was that it superimposed a political upon an already advanced religious crisis. This had the effect of confusing the issues. The religious issue had been relatively clear. Controlled by the cardinal of Lorraine, or so it was believed, Henry II had regarded the Protestants not only as heretics, but also as seditious enemies of the kingdom. Accordingly he pursued them with a savage fury, seemingly foreign to his nature, and planned their systematic extermination once he was released from the preoccupation of foreign war. For this reason, the attempts of this distressed community to ensure its survival had slowly been sucking the Protestants towards the vortex of politics and diplomacy. So long, however, as Henry's stable rule continued—albeit increasingly resented in various quarters—the affiliations of the Protestant church with Bourbon and German princes, contracted in the search for protection, had little or no political significance. But when the accession of a youthful king precipitated a struggle for power between the persecuting house of Guise, who seized control of the court, and the supposedly pro-Protestant Bourbons, the fate of the Protestant church was automatically involved in the outcome of the political situation. By the same token, politics and religion suddenly became inextricably entangled, to the confusion of both and the sorrow of France, for religion was not a subject on which men were prepared to compromise. As the Protestant church was already the center of the religious crisis, both under Henry II and under the new régime, it was naturally also the center of attraction for those involved in the political crisis. As a result, the Protestants became a pawn in the international game of diplomacy, and were soon to be regarded as a faction in the State. Within a matter of weeks they were swept up in a mounting clamor of opposition, and their cause was rapidly embraced by many new and embarrassing recruits whose motives and interests had little in common with those of the evangelical movement.

The story of the conspiracy of Amboise reveals something of this process. But in order to understand the dual crisis from which it arose, it is necessary to examine both the previous history of the Protestant church of Paris and the political situation at the time of Henry's death.

The Protestant church of Paris, one of the earliest and most important of the French churches, was founded in 1555, under Jean le Maçon, seigneur de Launay, known as La Rivière. The following year he was joined, for a short while, by François de Morel, seigneur de Collonges, and soon after by Morel's brilliant young convert from the legal profession, Antoine de La Roche-Chandieu. Gaspard Carmel, who married a niece of Guillaume Farel, and Nicolas des Gallards, seigneur de Saules, both arrived in 1557. Jean Macar relieved des Gallards in 1558 and was himself replaced by Morel in October of that year. The crime of heresy carried the death penalty, and the extreme danger of their work was the reason for so many changes. The ministry was therefore performed quietly and secretly, against ever-mounting difficulties and dangers as the numbers of Protestants grew and the persecution increased. These young pastors were compelled to live a restless underground existence, similar to that of the Catholic priests in England. They had constantly to change their pseudonyms, alter their disguises and shift their lodgings. After only a month in Paris, Macar was obliged to move. Once they became "trop à découvert," as they put it, they went into hiding, withdrew to the country, or sometimes returned to Geneva. Their meetings were generally held at night in the heavily curtained rooms of private houses, and the proceedings were carefully organized. Normally the groups were small, which greatly increased the pastors' work, but by the summer of 1557 they were evidently becoming dangerously large. In spite of all their precautions they were sometimes discovered.[1] Thus on 4 September 1557, there occurred a calamity which had far-reaching effects. The Protestants assembled that night in a house in the rue Saint-Jacques and, from the opposite side of the road, were observed by the inmates of the Collège du Plessis, who collected stones and bricks and surrounded the house. Trouble ensued when the Protestants began to leave. They were unarmed, but some of the gentlemen, who naturally were wearing swords, managed to fight their way out. Of the rest, an estimated 132 were arrested by the *procureur du Châtelet*, who arrived to put an end to the affray. The prisoners were herded together in atrocious conditions. They were bullied and tortured, and some of them later burnt at the stake.[2]

The incident not only attracted unwelcome publicity, but was also one of the first of its kind to pose the problem of resistance. At least as early as April 1556 this problem had begun to worry Calvin, partly because he held resistance to be contrary to the word of God, and partly because he feared its consequences.[3] Hearing of the struggle in the rue Saint-Jacques from Nicolas des Gallards, who wrote without delay and sent the letter by Gaspar Carmel,[4] Calvin immediately wrote to the Paris church. He sympathized with their problems, but said that prayer should be their only redress, pleading with them to be patient and to attempt nothing contrary to the word of God; otherwise they could expect to incur "le salaire de nostre témérité." Deeply disturbed, he gave this advice, he said, because he well knew that "en telz effroiz on

1. Coquerel, *Précis de l'histoire de l'Église réformée de Paris*, p. xxv, 7 February 1558, Macar to Calvin. Most of the correspondence of Macar and Morel is printed in Latin in the *Calvini Opera*. Coquerel has translated large parts of it. The dates of the letters have been taken from the *Cal. Op.*, and not from Coquerel.

2. Coquerel, 19–20; Geisendorf, *Théodore de Bèze*, 88.

3. Bonnet, *Lettres de Calvin*, ii, 90–94, 19 April 1556, Calvin to the church of Angers.

4. Kingdon, *Geneva and the Coming of the Wars of Religion in France*, 62; Geisendorf, *Théodore de Bèze*, 89.

peut estre sollicité à beaucoup d'entreprises auquelles il est difficile de tenir bride." The letter ended with a solemn and now celebrated warning that it would be better for them all to perish, than that "l'Évangile de Dieu fust exposé à ce blame, qu'elle fist armer les gens à sedition et tumulte . . . car les excès et violences n'apporteront que stérilité."[5]

The prisoners taken in the rue Saint-Jacques continued to be an anxiety to the pastors. When Jean Macar arrived in January 1558 there were still twenty-one. We learn from his reports to Calvin how conditions worsened and tension increased during the year he spent in Paris. The frightened Protestants soon became unwilling to allow even small meetings in their houses. They were spied upon, not only in Paris but also in the surrounding villages, and special *commissaires* relentlessly tracked them down. But even more than the *commissaires*, they feared the fury of the people, whipped up by the Catholic priests who inaugurated from their pulpits a campaign of religious hatred. At the same time, the king breathed such fearful threats against them that as early as 12 April 1558, Macar informed Calvin that the wise and the clear-sighted saw in these early troubles the prelude to great calamities.[6]

During May there were a number of large but orderly gatherings in the Pré-aux-Clercs, in the faubourg Saint-Germain, for the purpose of singing psalms. At least one of these meetings was attended by the king of Navarre and François d'Andelot, brother of the admiral, Gaspard de Coligny, seigneur de Châtillon. The king became alarmed by the conversion of members of the nobility. He declared to the *parlement* that it was the Protestants who were his principal enemies and, on another occasion, said that they would tear the crown from his head. Catholic traducers gave out that the Protestants assembled in arms and would undermine the régime while the king was involved in foreign war. But Macar, who was there, insists that only a few gentlemen carried swords. This trouble resulted in greater activity on the part of the *commissaires* who made house-to-house searches—presumably in

5. Bonnet, *Lettres de Calvin*, ii, 139–45, 16 September 1557, Calvin to the church of Paris.
6. Coquerel, p. lxiv, 12 April 1558, Macar to Calvin.

the hope of catching the pastors—and in an increased number of arrests. It is all the more remarkable that Chandieu, who was captured in June, should have been released through the intervention of Navarre. Clearly he had escaped recognition.[7]

If the summer campaigns did something to deflect attention from the Protestants, they were seriously endangered in September by the treachery of a doctor who disclosed secret information about them. They narrowly escaped another disastrous incident, similar to that of the rue Saint-Jacques, by fleeing into the country through a hole in the city walls. When the campaigning season was over, the king openly proclaimed his religious war. Towards the end of 1558 the outlook was sombre indeed, and not for the Protestants alone. From the month of February onwards Macar, in his letters to Calvin, had been making accurate and disquieting observations about other aspects of French affairs. He emphasized the universal poverty and the king's financial expedients. Henry was alienating the royal domain and anticipating the revenues, yet he defaulted on his obligations. What was even worse, Macar likened those surrounding him to insatiable gulfs of avidity consuming his resources. Salaries and pensions went unpaid, and so did the troops, whose license was indescribable. "O confusion extrême," Macar groaned to Calvin in the month of March. Those who were not blind, he said, were aware of the wretched state of France, troubled by internal dissensions, with the enemy at the gates, and led by a man without judgment who disrupted everything. The reference was not to the king but to the cardinal of Lorraine, who Macar believed would end by overthrowing the whole kingdom.[8] This was an extraordinarily prophetic statement.

To Macar, this rot at the center was reflected in a breakdown of standards of conduct and a loss of propriety and respect for the law. He specifically mentioned the unpunished crimes and misdemeanors, the assassinations, and the general disorder and con-

7. Ibid., p. xxv, 7 February 1558; xxxiv, 27 March 1558; lxxv, 9 May 1558; xl, 22 May 1558; xliii, 25 May 1558, Macar to Calvin.
8. Ibid., p. lvii, 24 September 1558; xxxiv, 27 March 1558; xl, 22 May 1558; lxxiii, 21 March 1558, Macar to Calvin.

fusion, and repeatedly conveyed to Calvin the fear that France was threatened with calamity. While he could not guess what form the storm would take, he was sure the church would be at the heart of it.[9]

Calvin had always paid attention to reports from Paris and, besides preaching patience and obedience to the frightened and resentful Protestants, he had, for some time, been making strenuous efforts to bring pressure to bear on the king. For this purpose, towards the end of 1557, he had sought the cooperation of both the German Protestant princes and Antoine de Bourbon, king of Navarre, first prince of the blood. If Navarre could be persuaded to speak for the Protestants at court, the king might be forced to reconsider his policy of extermination. This was at once a powerful and a dangerous argument, but Calvin had not yet despaired of convincing the king that the Protestants were neither heretics nor rebels.

Immediately after the incident of the rue Saint-Jacques, Calvin sent a powerful embassy to Germany to plead for the princes' intercession on behalf of the prisoners.[10] This resulted in an embassy to France bearing a letter to the king, a copy of which, dated 1 December 1557, was sent back to Calvin. The letter appealed for mercy for the prisoners and assured the king that they were not "men loving sedition or other fanatic opinions."[11] Calvin himself tried to press home the same point. Writing to the king towards the end of the year, he enclosed a confession of faith designed to show that the Protestants were not heretics, and to persuade the king—as he had already tried with the *Institution Chrétienne* to persuade his father—that far from being rebels they believed that authority was ordained of God and that the civil laws must be obeyed.[12]

It was partly perhaps from disappointment at the results of the

9. Ibid., p. lxiv, 12 April 1558, Macar to Calvin. See also La Planche, 202. This belief that a moral degeneration was one of the principal causes of the civil wars was common in intellectual circles.

10. Geisendorf, *Théordore de Bèze*, 88–90.

11. *Cal. Op.*, xvi, 720–22; Kingdon, *Geneva and the Coming of the Wars of Religion in France*, 62.

12. Bonnet, *Lettres de Calvin*, ii, 151–58, late 1557, Calvin to Henry II.

German embassy that on 14 December 1557 Calvin addressed himself to Navarre, having received reports that he favored the Protestants. The letter was designed to flatter and encourage, and called upon Navarre to become "une lampe ardente," to champion their cause at court and obtain some mitigation of their sufferings. Calvin prompted Navarre with various lines of argument, and chose that moment to do so partly because of the forthcoming meeting of the estates general in Paris on 6 January 1558.[13] But it was not until March that Navarre reached Paris, ostensibly to congratulate the king on the successsful siege of Calais.

While Macar, in Paris, was waiting to see what effect this appeal might have, he received a letter from the Protestants of Poitou suggesting—as though it were a new idea—that a noble deputation should be sent to Navarre asking him to appeal for a German embassy to France, to press for an end to the persecution. In Macar's opinion they had already exhausted this means, which was burdensomely expensive. The negotiations which followed are complex and obscure. It appears, however, that Gaspard de Heu, seigneur du Buy, an agent of Navarre, passed through Paris at the beginning of March on his way to Germany on behalf of the Protestant cause. Three weeks later Macar wrote that du Buy had discussed a plan for a military alliance between Navarre and the count Palatine, so that if it came to an armed clash, all would have their forces ready in order to crush the enemies of the Gospel. This is the first we hear of the possibility of a resort to arms in France, and Macar would have nothing to do with it. Towards the end of March, du Buy went to Germany a second time and returned to Paris with a promise that the princes would write to the king. Soon after, he was arrested, which caused great alarm in the Paris church because of the papers he carried and the information he possessed. It was also unfortunate that he had implicated the church in his own offenses by linking its interests with the private intrigues of Navarre—or those which buzzed about his name—and with plans, however vague and in-

13. Ibid., 163–69, 14 December 1557, Calvin to the king of Navarre.

substantial, which envisaged civil war in France and the intervention of foreign powers. Since du Buy perished, his negotiations were probably all discovered and, if so, became grist to the mill of those who insisted that the Protestants were seditious. The importance of the matter was probably exaggerated, especially as Macar reported Navarre to have said that his interest in the German princes was to obtain their help in the recovery of the part of Navarre which was held by Spain.[14]

Calvin, meanwhile, pursued his own negotiations in Germany, partly in a further effort to obtain help for the prisoners.[15] As a result of one or other appeal, six German princes wrote to the king on 19 March 1558. They urged him to reform the Church and put an end to the persecution, adding something like a threat that an attempt to extirpate the Protestants by force would merely strengthen their efforts and would ruin his own subjects.[16] On 8 May, ambassadors arrived with a further letter, but their presence appeared only to irritate the king, who contemptuously increased the persecution while they were still at court. On 21 May—two days after the arrest of d'Andelot—Henry answered the letter, and bade the princes write to him no more: he meant to follow and impose the old religion, and declared that most of the

14. Coquerel, p. xxv, 7 February 1558; lxxvi, 4 March 1558; lxxiii, 21 March 1558; xxxiv, 27 March 1558; lxiv, 12 April 1558, Macar to Calvin. Gaspard de Heu, seigneur du Buy, was a former *échevin* and one of the leading Protestants of Metz. He became one of Navarre's principal intermediaries with the German princes. Arrested about April 1558, he was secretly executed at Vincennes in the first week of September 1558. He and La Renaudie were related through their wives, who were sisters. See the *Bull. Prot.*, xxv, 1876, pp. 164 seq.; also Haag, *La France protestante*, v, 515–16. Spanish Navarre was conquered by Ferdinand of Aragon in 1512. On Navarre's prolonged attempts to recover his lost inheritance, see my article "Antoine de Bourbon, King of Navarre and the French Crisis of Authority, 1559–1562."

15. Bonnet, *Lettres de Calvin*, ii, 182–89, 21 February 1558, Calvin to the duke of Württemberg; Geisendorf, *Théodore de Bèze*, 91; Ribier, *Lettres et Mémoires d'Estat*, ii, 677–78, 13 February 1556/57, Henry to de Selve.

16. *Cal. Op.*, xvi, 100.

Protestants were "perturbateurs du repos publicq et ennemys de la tranquillité et union des chrestiens." This, said Macar sarcastically, was the brilliant result of that embassy.[17]

In the first days of March 1558, when du Buy passed through Paris on his way to Germany, he informed Macar that Navarre had received Calvin's appeal with great pleasure. Navarre was expected at court at any moment and had said he was resolved to declare his religious opinions to the king. Hopefully, therefore, Macar wrote to him in the name of the whole church, and confided his letter to du Buy's kinsman, the baron de La Renaudie, who was evidently already in touch with the Paris church, and whose attendance Navarre had requested.[18] This, like other appeals to Navarre, was solely on account of his exalted rank, and marks the beginning of a prolonged endeavor on the part of the Calvinists to induce him to play the role in which they cast him. He appears to have been without strong religious convictions, and, though frequently accused of ambition, this is difficult to detect in his conduct. On the contrary, he would turn away from the struggle of life at court to the interests of his own little kingdom, openly admitting from time to time that this was what concerned him most. But even in Navarre he could not escape the implications of his rank, and he was submitted to great and varying political and diplomatic pressures from 1558 until his death at the siege of Rouen in 1562. He became the target of many derogatory judgments by the champions of those whose purposes he declined to serve. He frequently promised to remonstrate with the king, and may seriously have intended to do so, but whenever it came to the point, he remained silent.

In Paris, Navarre sent for Chandieu and James Hamilton, another prominent Protestant, and received them in bed at 8

17. Coquerel, p. lxxv, 9 May 1558; xliii, 25 May 1558; 1, 17 August 1558, Macar to Calvin. In August Macar himself took up the diplomatic struggle and went to the king's camp to see the ministers of the duke of Saxony who was said to be favourably disposed towards them. It is not clear, however, what he hoped to obtain. Ibid., p. liii, 26 August 1558, Macar to Calvin; *Cal. Op.*, xvii, 171, 21 May 1558, Henry II to the German princes.

18. Coquerel, p. lxviii, 6 March 1558, Macar to Calvin.

A.M. on 25 March. But their slight hopes in him had already been extinguished by his conduct at court, and they set no store on the promises he made them. While the Protestants urged him to speak for them at court, Lorraine, who was fully aware of the implications of such an alignment, did everything he could to prevent it. By methods of intimidation, which proved very successful, he made Navarre afraid of the possible results. Navarre refused to take the public and decisive step of absenting himself from mass, which would have entailed the king's public displeasure. But he did exert his influence with the *parlement* on behalf of the prisoners, rescued Chandieu from prison—while his own agent du Buy languished in the *château* of Vincennes—and mingled with the singers of psalms in the Pré-aux-Clercs. In May it was rumored that the king meant to detain him at court. In fact he remained there all the summer, and incurred the contempt of the Protestants for dancing so much of his time away. They soon reached the conclusion that he was incurably frivolous; but he was still too important to neglect. Thus in August, and in accordance with the wishes of Calvin, Chandieu entered Navarre's service as a member of his household, in the hope of being able to purge his entourage of some of the "vauriens" whose only care, Macar said, was to feather their own nests.[19]

While doing everything to win the support of Navarre, in whom they had so little confidence, in the middle of August Macar and Chandieu also waited upon his brother Louis de Bourbon, prince de Condé, who promised them "mountains and marvels" in the manner of princes, declarations which they received with prudent reserve. In the light of later events the meeting appears significant. It shows that by then, if not before, they had begun to look on Condé as a possible protector. His rank was second only to that of Navarre, while his character, in many ways, was very different. Soon after, he requested the services of a pastor, showing an interest in reform which presumably strengthened his association with the Paris church.[20]

19. Ibid., p. xxxiv, 27 March 1558; lxx, May 1558; xl, 22 May 1558; xliii, 25 May 1558; liii, 26 August 1558, Macar to Calvin.

20. Ibid., p. l, 17 August 1558; lx, 15 October 1558, Macar to Calvin.

A gap in the pastors' correspondence leaves us with little information between October 1558 and May 1559, months during
which the long war with Spain was brought to an end, and the
king prepared to turn upon his Protestant subjects. Notwithstanding the unabated arrests, imprisonments and searching
and sacking of houses, François de Morel, who succeeded Macar,
had the courage or temerity to hold the first national synod in
Paris in May. Thus he united the French churches into one organization at a critical moment in their history.[21]

It was possibly because of the presence in Paris of the Spanish
representatives for the wedding of Henry's daughter Elisabeth, to
Philip II, that the king chose the month of June 1559 to launch his
policy of extermination. Spies were placed in every *quartier* of
Paris; the Protestants were outlawed and, according to Morel,
judges were suborned. A goldsmith named Russanges was said to
have revealed the secrets of the Paris church, and the king possessed a long list of the names of Protestants from all walks of life.
These, Morel believed, he would track down systematically. It
was also in June that the king arrested several members of the
parlement who had dared to defend the Protestants, including
Anne du Bourg. The fate of du Bourg inflamed violent popular
passions on both sides and, in the months which followed the
death of the king, did more than anything else to exasperate the
Protestants beyond the point of endurance. Calvin was quick to
send his condolences on this new disaster, and to assure the
church that he had tried every human means in his power to help
them—he referred to his diplomatic efforts—but that the king
had proudly rejected every advance. He urged church members
to behave quietly and peacefully and to confound the agents of
Satan by the virtue of their lives. But even Morel seems to have
been growing restive. He complained that the fury of their
enemies was such that it violated "tout droit divin et humain," a
significant phrase, which indicates the lines along which he, or

21. Ibid., p. v, 17 May 1559, Calvin to Morel; Bonnet, "l'Église réformée de Paris sous Henri II. Ministère de François de Morel, 1558–
59," *Bull. Prot.*, xxvii, 1878, pp. 440–45, 8, 17 May, 11 June 1559, Morel
to Calvin.

others, were thinking. He considered withdrawing from Paris because his church was virtually disrupted.[22]

Such was the critical position of the Protestants of Paris at the beginning of July 1559. They had not, at this stage, made any demands or uttered any threats, but they were classed as traitors by the authorities, and treated like vermin by the Catholic majority of Paris. The king had sworn to destroy them and seemed likely to succeed. Yet so far Calvin's authority had prevailed upon his followers: they were a powerless minority and there was nothing they could do, or think of doing, against the Lord's anointed. But, when Henry died, the situation was radically altered, first by the hope and possibility of a drastic change of government and, when that hope faded, by the entirely new possibility, under a young king, of opposing the ministers who were held to abuse his authority. This is what the conspiracy of Amboise was concerned with, but not simply on account of the agony of the church. On the contrary, the new political crisis partially superseded the continuing religious crisis. The separate issues remained distinct in theory, while becoming entangled in action.

It is therefore not surprising that the king's fatal accident on 30 June should have been hailed by the Protestants as a judgment of God, or that they hoped, under a new regime, for an end to the appalling storm of persecution.[23] This hope was based on the belief that as the new king, Francis II, was too young to rule at the age of fifteen, the government belonged by right to Navarre, as first prince of the blood. It was therefore supposed that he would direct affairs and, presumably, summon the estates general. If Navarre had not inspired confidence in the past, no one could tell what he might achieve now. But, unhappily, he was in distant Guyenne and, while everyone was wondering what he would do, Lorraine and his brother the duc de Guise lost no time in securing their own position at court. They did so at the ex-

22. Bonnet, "l'Église réformée de Paris sous Henri II. Ministère de Francois de Morel, 1558–59," *Bull. Prot.*, xxvii, 1878, pp. 444 seq., 11 June, 3 July 1559, Morel to Calvin; Bonnet, *Lettres de Calvin, ii*, 281–84, 29 June 1559, Calvin to the church of Paris.

23. Coquerel, p. vii, July 1559, Morel to Calvin. Henry was wounded on 30 June but did not die until 10 July.

pense of the Bourbons, the queen mother, Catherine de Medici, and of the constable, Anne de Montmorency, who had been restored to power during the last year of Henry's reign.

While Navarre was absent, Catherine ill with grief, and Montmorency guarding the body of Henry II, the Guises quickly surrounded the young king and his mother—the very day that Henry died—and moved them from the Tournelles to the Louvre. This enabled the Guises to occupy the privileged lodgings formerly reserved for Montmorency and the king's mistress, Diane de Poitiers. Next they assumed possession of the *cachet* and within three days the English ambassador, Sir Nicholas Throckmorton, reported to Queen Elizabeth, "the house of Guise ruleth and doth all about the French king." The Tuscan ambassador made a similar report.[24] Within ten days the situation was already ominous. "Si ce règne continue," wrote Guillaume Ségond, a Provençal lawyer in Paris, "sommes pour avoir de grands assaults."[25] With a reckless disregard for vested interests and the personal animosities incurred, the Guises consolidated their advantage by assuming complete control of the army, the finances, the Church and all foreign negotiations. They attempted to place their own supporters as captains and *gouverneurs* of frontier towns and provinces, and removed all opponents from the court. In fact, according to the contemporary, La Planche, they stuffed every corner of the kingdom with their creatures.[26] While they were believed to have embezzled public money, officials and captains went unpaid, and the latter were ordered to depart on pain of death when they came to court to claim their due. Some of these—Castelnau and the young Maligny, to name only two—are known to have been drawn into the conspiracy of

24. Forbes, *A Full View of the Public Transactions*, i, 157, 13 July 1559, Throckmorton to Elizabeth; Desjardins, *Négs. Tosc.*, iii, 401, 14 July 1559.

25. 20 July 1559, Guillaume Ségond to the seigneur de Mauvans, quoted by Romier, *La Conjuration d'Amboise*, 18. The title of this book is misleading. It is a straightforward history of the reign of Francis II.

26. La Planche, 211. La Planche is known to have been anti-Guise, but there is no evidence that he was unreliable. Desjardins, *Négs. Tosc.*, iii, 402, 24 July 1559; B. N., Mss. Italien, 1720, f. 206, 16 July 1559.

Amboise. In less than two months, Lorraine was said by the Florentine ambassador to have become pope and king in France. According to the Protestant divine, Théodore de Bèze, he ruled absolutely, hated and feared by everyone, and he and his brother had so divided the kingdom between them that the king was left with an empty title.[27]

In the absence of Navarre, Condé struggled to defend the claims of the house of Bourbon against the Guise monopoly of power, and to delay important decisions until the arrival of his brother, to whom he sent an urgent dispatch.[28] To remove Condé from court, and involve him in expense, the Guises quickly sent him to the Netherlands to ratify the peace treaty.

On 31 July Navarre arrived at his ducal town of Vendôme and remained there for two weeks, awaiting the return of Condé before going to court. Extraordinary interest and significance has always attached to the conferences he held there with the many people who flocked to do him honor, to seek his help or to offer their support. Historians have never fully penetrated the mystery of these meetings, though it is clear that different forms of opposition were discussed. The Italian ambassador and the cardinal of Lorraine believed that the conspiracy of Amboise originated at this time. They were probably wrong, but there can be little doubt that *something of the kind* was considered. Already, in July, while Henry II lay dying, there had been rumors, proceeding

27. B. N., Mss. Italien, 1720, f. 206, 16 July 1559; Mignet, "Lettres de Jean Calvin," *Journal des Savants*, July 1857, p. 410; Desjardins, *Négs. Tosc.*, iii, 404, 27 August 1559; Naef, *La Conjuration d'Amboise et Genève*, 403, 12 September 1559, de Bèze to Bullinger. All accounts of the Guise dictatorship are very similar and no doubt basically true. In the absence, however, of any detailed research study, it is impossible to substantiate such charges as the embezzlement of public money, the corruption of justice, and filling the country with their creatures. H. O. Evennett has referred to the blackening of the cardinal's character by the Calvinist pamphleteers whose influence, he said, is still too evident. *The Cardinal of Lorraine and the Council of Trent*, 23, n. 2. Nevertheless, the charges made against the Guises were widely believed, and their government was violently resented.

28. Forbes, *A Full View of the Public Transactions*, i, 157–60, 13 July 1559, Throckmorton to Elizabeth; Romier, *La Conjuration d'Amboise*, 13.

from Condé's entourage, of a projected rising in favor of the Bourbons. Condé, who arrived on 11 or 12 August, his brother-in-law La Rochefoucauld, the prince de Porcien, and the vidame de Chartres are said to have been in favor of an immediate insurrection. Navarre's own position remains equivocal. No one appears to have known what he really wanted. Perhaps he did not know himself. He received Elizabeth's ambassador, Sir Henry Killigrew, "very gently," expressed a desire to enter into friendship with the queen and inquired whether she had any league with the German princes. His own relations with them are not clear. Some of them may have been urging him to take action, because it was widely believed that all Protestant powers were threatened by the treaty of Cateau-Cambrésis.[29] The Guises themselves were evidently afraid and amassed a supply of arms in Paris "to serve in case of innovation, if that any such matter should happen upon the arrival of the King of Navarre." They were also sending considerable sums of money into Germany, probably to provide for war in Scotland, possibly an assault on Geneva, or both; but forces raised for one purpose could easily be diverted to another.[30]

Not least of those who turned to Navarre and tried to galvanize him into action in the crisis of 1559 were the Protestants of Paris. Morel and the consistory wasted no time in sending La Roche-Chandieu to meet him. He had gone, Morel told Calvin, to remind Navarre of his rights and to inform him of their will and that of "toute la noblesse," lest he should neglect such an opportunity. It would be interesting to know what Morel meant by "toute la noblesse," for the phrase is clearly significant. Early in August Morel received Calvin's explicit instructions for dealing with the situation caused by Henry's death. Unfortunately these

29. This fear, which was widespread and continued to influence Protestant conduct for many years to come, was not without some foundation in fact. See the letter of 26 June 1559 from the duke of Alva to Philip II, quoted by Mignet, *Journal des Savants*, March 1857, pp. 171–72; also pp. 169–71.

30. Forbes, *A Full View of the Public Transactions*, i, 194, 8 August; 201, 15 August; 206, 25 August 1559, Throckmorton to Elizabeth; La Planche, 204, 213.

instructions are not available and our knowledge of what they contained is derived from Morel's reply. Calvin's purpose was that Navarre should be induced to hurry to court to assume the position due to his rank as first prince of the blood, and forthwith inaugurate a policy favorable to the Protestants. It was not that Calvin had any real confidence in Navarre, but that in the new circumstances occasioned by the king's death, he was too important to ignore. It is clear from the correspondence that Calvin had some elaborate plan for placing Navarre in power, and also that this was an adaptation of a previous plan, already contrived with certain German princes in cooperation with François Hotman, professor of law at Strasbourg, and their mutual friend Jean Sturm, rector of the Academy there.[31] But it is not clear what the plan was. The implication would appear to be that Calvin's instructions envisaged a veritable *coup d'état*, backed by foreign help, in order to put Navarre in his legitimate place at the head of the government. It is true that Calvin later referred to the permissibility of the use of force, at the same time deprecating bloodshed or the risk of bloodshed. It must be presumed, in the case of Navarre, that he was taking at least a calculated risk. The contradiction is not easily resolved. In a letter of 2 September to his friend Bullinger of the church of Zurich, Hotman referred to this matter quite plainly. Lamenting the way in which Navarre had miserably disappointed everybody's hopes, he said, "if you only knew . . . what conditions were offered him, what help was placed at his disposal." Although Calvin constantly preached patience and obedience, it is also clear from his own correspondence that he did envisage the use of force, if necessary, to install Navarre in power at the end of 1560. The explanation of the tenacity with which he pursued this purpose and declined to support any other, lies in his political philosophy. To Calvin, it was only through the

31. Coquerel, p. viii, August 1559, Morel to Calvin; Naef, *La Conjuration d'Amboise et Genève*, 298–99, 13 August 1559, Calvin to Jean Sturm. Navarre, as first prince of the blood, represented the "principal magistrate" in Calvin's political philosophy. For brief analyses of this part of the *Institution Chrétienne*, see Mignet, *Journal des Savants*, February 1857, pp. 93 seq., and Mesnard, *L'Essor de la philosophie politique au XVIe siècle*, 287 seq.

agency of Navarre and his legitimate claim to power that any alteration of the government in France could lawfully be undertaken.[32] In accordance with Calvin's instructions, and in order to arouse Navarre more thoroughly "et lui enlever toute crainte," Morel himself set out to meet him, arriving after the departure of Chandieu.

Morel worked on Navarre by every means he could and found him a little better disposed towards them than previously. The trouble was that he was being frightened by three of his own councilors who were acting as agents of the Guises—Monluc, the bishop of Mende, and d'Escars—who, Morel was convinced, were paid "pour l'enerver." This is confirmed by La Planche, who makes the same observation. Morel reminded Navarre that the government of France had been placed within his grasp by divine intervention, and that he might now assume power with the assent of all the orders—by which he meant the estates general. Everyone, he said, was sick of the rapacity and arrogance of the Guises. The situation could only worsen if they were allowed to fortify themselves in power, and the calamities of the church could surely not be forgotten. "Finally," wrote Morel significantly, in his report to Calvin, "in the event of someone barring his way, I explained to him how the adversaries could be reduced to silence, relying principally upon what I had seen in the instructions." As Morel was returning to Paris, his colleague La Rivière brought him another, similar set of instructions from Hotman, containing certain useful additions. Faced with what was apparently a definite proposition, Navarre began to hedge, saying that he would assert his rights in every way he could. If he succeeded, then he could easily help the afflicted. But if the injustice of his adversaries prevailed, he would return home again as quickly as possible. Stung by the ensuing torrent of Morel's reproaches, Navarre inquired of him how it was that Calvin disposed of such power ("un pareil pouvoir"), and on what princes he relied for

32. Dareste, "François Hotman, sa vie et sa correspondance," *Revue historique*, ii, 1876, p. 21, 2 September 1559, Hotman to Bullinger; Bonnet, *Lettres de Calvin*, ii, 345–49, December 1560, Calvin to the pastors of Paris; Naef, *La Conjuration d'Amboise et Genève*, 482.

help. Morel evidently did not know for certain and replied—perhaps a little pointedly—that Calvin never made frivolous promises. Assuming that it must be the German princes, Navarre declared that they were full of promises, but that when it came to the point, they seldom fulfilled them. Thus, Morel went on, "having neither accepted nor refused the proposition which I took him," Navarre enjoined him to secrecy, saying that they would continue the conversation in Paris. It was therefore not yet possible to say what could be hoped from him.[33]

Morel, however, knew Navarre, and there was little doubt in his mind as to what the outcome would be. In the same letter, therefore, he asked Calvin whether, in the case of Navarre's defection, there were not some other means of delivering the church from her present sufferings. He was aware, he said, that Calvin considered prayers and holy offices their principal means of succor. But he also pointed out that apart from the plan involving Navarre—which he clearly already considered abortive—Calvin had not proposed any "moyens moins sublimes." Morel himself went on to make a suggestion. When a minor ascended the throne, he said, according to the law of France the estates general ought to be summoned to appoint tutors and councilors for the duration of the minority. Thus, as it was licit to summon the estates, Morel queried whether Navarre alone had the right to do this? Could the demand not be made by anybody and, if refused, would it not be just for anybody to take up arms against the monopoly of tyrants and their small faction. The fact that Morel dared to raise the possibility of using force—in what he took to be permissible political circumstances—adds weight to the deduction that Calvin himself had sanctioned the use of force in support of Navarre. Unfortunately we do not know whether these were Morel's own ideas, or whether he was reporting discussions which were taking place around him. If the latter, then this report is probably among the first rumblings of Amboise, heard only five weeks after Henry's death.[34] Certainly these ideas were de-

33. Coquerel, p. x, 15 August 1559, Morel to Calvin.

34. Naef, *La Conjuration d'Amboise et Genève*, 402, 15 August 1559, Morel to Calvin.

veloped and expanded in greater detail in the pamphlet war which followed the conspiracy of Amboise, in which the rebels regarded themselves as a (self-constituted) estates general.

Navarre left Vendôme on 14 August and went to Paris, where he was subjected to a further campaign of intimidation by d'Escars and Mende. Among other affronts, he was excluded from the *conseil des affaires*. This was a matter on which he could have made a stand, and insisted on a definition of precedence in the State. When, on 22 August, the court prepared to leave Saint-Germain for Villers-Cotterêts, Navarre had acquiesced in the status quo, established in his absence, and even agreed that the Guise brothers should control the treasury and the army. Morel lamented this event which, he thought, threatened fearful trouble for the churches of France.[35]

Navarre had failed them utterly: he had even agreed to escort the king's sister Elisabeth to the Spanish frontier, to join her husband the king of Spain, and so escape from his embarrassments. Anticipating Chandieu's message by only a few hours, Morel inquired of Calvin on 23 August why they should continue to incur the danger of confiding themselves to Navarre. To Morel the danger seemed to be increasing, because of the ever greater stranglehold of the Guises on the government of France. Apart from anything else, he said that they were raising men, money and arms. "Où pense-tu," he abruptly demanded of Calvin, "que doive aboutir un pareil état des choses, quand toute resistance aura cessé?" One must not make predictions lightly, he went on, "nevertheless when I consider the ambition of these Guises, I cannot avoid the belief that the purpose of all these preparations is to seize control of the kingdom." As a counsel of despair, he proposed the mass emigration of the Protestants of Paris.[36]

35. François de Pérusse, comte d'Escars; Nicolas d'Angu, bishop of Mende. La Planche, 213; Romier, *La Conjuration d'Amboise*, 23; Forbes, *A Full View of the Public Transactions*, i, 212, 25 August 1559, Throckmorton to Elizabeth; Coquerel, p. xii, 23 August 1559, Morel to Calvin.

36. Romier, *La Conjuration d'Amboise*, 27 and n. 2; Coquerel, pp. xii, xiv, 23 August, 11 September 1559, Morel to Calvin. Negotiations for the evacuation of the Paris church to Strasbourg were still going on at the end of November. See Dareste, "François Hotman, sa vie et sa correspondance," *Revue historique*, ii, 1876, p. 22, 23 November 1559, Hotman to Bullinger.

Besides appealing to Navarre, Morel also sought help from the queen mother, Catherine de Medici. In the past she had shown some interest in reform and it was hoped that she might prove sympathetic. It was probably in July 1559 that Morel first wrote to her in the name of the consistory. Her reply was not discouraging, though it bore no fruit. Morel then wrote a second letter, probably in August. This one, he said was "assez vive," and the consistory obliged him to modify it. Morel is alleged to have given Catherine a solemn warning of impending "troubles et esmotions," if the case against Anne du Bourg was not quashed and the persecution abated, and it was probably in this letter that he did so. This was not intended as a threat on the part of the Paris church, but as a warning of the disaffection of others, "a hundred times more numerous," who had not yet placed themselves under ecclesiastical discipline, but who were conscious of the abuses of Rome, and who could not endure the persecution. This is a distinction of fundamental importance, and one which the government may not have appreciated, between members of the churches and other Protestants who might not even be known as such, and over whom the pastors had no control. Morel himself records that Catherine reacted angrily to his letter.[37] Morel's remarks about the estates general and his report of his correspondence with Catherine appear in the same letter to Calvin. Together they tend to confirm the suggestion that discussions, which were to lead up to the conspiracy of Amboise, were already taking place, and that Morel had heard of them, though he may not, of course, have known of their import. In spite of Catherine's irritation, he persevered in the attempt to arouse her sympathy and, through the good offices of Coligny, Condé and his mother-in-law, Madame de Roye, Catherine agreed to a secret meeting with Chandieu. Unfortunately it never took place.[38]

The severity of the persecution endured by the Paris Protestants in the previous summer of 1558 fully accounts for all Morel's efforts to obtain help, and for his warnings of impending trouble. He reported to Calvin that the cardinal's fury knew no limits.

37. Coquerel, 38; p. x, 15 August 1559, Morel to Calvin.
38. La Planche, 220; Forbes, *A Full View of the Public Transactions*, i, 226, 10 September 1559, Throckmorton to Elizabeth.

Scarcely a week passed without arrests, the sacking of houses, burnings at the stake, or someone being torn limb from limb. Even more serious, following the example of Paris, there was an upsurge of popular hatred against the Protestants all over France. La Planche said that Paris resembled a conquered city. Many Protestants had fled; their empty houses were sacked and their property stolen. Abandoned children roamed the streets and people were afraid to help them. Obscene libels appeared against the Protestants, who were blamed for all the anti-Guise publications. Early in September they suffered a further act of treachery whereby their houses and meeting places were revealed to the authorities. By an edict of 4 September 1559, houses used for illegal meetings were to be razed to the ground.[39] Morel's own name had been betrayed, and his features and clothing described. He hardly dared to venture outside. A mass of arrests resulted, and it was almost impossible to do anything to help the prisoners or to send them money. Some were confined without light or air, breathing in the stench of human excrement, and others were locked in torture cells, in which they could neither sit, lie nor stand. To Morel, their fate was worse than that of being burned at the stake, and there was not even a show of bringing them to justice. Sixty *commissaires* were appointed to make house-to-house searches in Paris, and Morel believed that the policy of extermination would soon succeed. He therefore tried to arrange for a mass emigration, either to England or to Strasbourg.[40]

The betrayal of the Protestant meeting places resulted in a raid on certain houses in the faubourg Saint-Germain, beginning with the house of one Visconte, where the authorities hoped to catch a group of Protestants eating meat on a Friday. Accordingly, the house was surrounded at dinner time, but the occupants offered a fierce resistance and most of them escaped. On the same occasion, Hercule Coiffart, the *bailli* of Saint-Aignan, was arrested in a neighboring house and found to be in possession of incriminating

39. Fontanon, *Les Édits et ordonnances*, iv, 259–60.

40. La Planche, 223–24; Coquerel, p. x, 15 August 1559, Morel to Calvin; p. xiv, 11 September 1559, Morel to Calvin; Bonnet, "L'Église réformée de Paris sous Henry II. Ministère de François de Morel, 1558–59," *Bull. Prot.*, xxvii, 1878, p. 245, 4 September 1559, Morel to Calvin.

papers containing remonstrances addressed to the king and the estates general, concerning both religion and political affairs. These documents were alleged to be "divinement biens faicts." This aroused speculation as to their provenance, since they could only have been drafted by educated persons of intellectual distinction, and could not be attributed to common rebels.[41] The discovery of these documents may very well be another pointer to the origins of the conspiracy. The date of this incident is not well attested, but is alleged to have been a Friday in August. It could therefore have been as early as the 4th. It is worth bearing in mind that there may have been some connection between the existence of such papers in the possession of a group of Protestants in Paris, and Morel's letter to Calvin of 15 August in which he made his remarks about the estates general and reported on his correspondence with Catherine. On the other hand, it might be more accurate to relate the concern, which he expressed in mid-August, to his journey to Vendôme—which probably occurred between about 4th and 10th—rather than to events in Paris.

Whatever the truth of this matter, it is evident that opposition was mounting and patience expiring. "Plusieurs," wrote La Planche, "se faschoyent de la patience chrestienne . . . n'obeissant rien moins en cela qu'à leurs ministres," a statement which, in fact, bears out Morel's warning. People began, said La Planche, to rise up against the Guises, as usurping tyrants. A demand arose for the Bourbon princes to assume control and summon the estates general, because of a widespread belief that the Guises meant to usurp the kingdom. This was not hysterical gossip, but the considered opinion of sober observers. We have already seen that Morel believed it. So did de Bèze. Everyone, said La Planche, was therefore forced to "penser à son particulier" and, unable to endure such oppression any longer, "commencèrent à se rallier ensemble pour regarder à quelque juste défense." Such things, he said, were generally "proposées et débatues ès compagnies."[42] More specific than this it is impossible to be. The Guises were evidently apprised of these things, to judge from their fur-

41. La Planche, 222–23.
42. Ibid., 229–34; Desjardins, *Négs. Tosc.*, iii, 402, 6 August 1559.

ther edict of 13 November 1559. Assemblies and conventicles, it declared, were being attended by "tant de diversitez d'hommes." Furthermore, it was alleged, they were being used to disseminate "infames et injurieux propos," and to incite people to "mutinerie et sedition." The edict therefore extended the death penalty to everyone holding or attending illicit meetings. Other letters patent of the same date made it obligatory to denounce such meetings, upon pain of punishment for heresy—death. Informers were to be protected and rewarded.[43] Evidently there was some odor in the wind.

These were the circumstances, political and religious, in which the conspiracy of Amboise had its roots, though its *precise* origins are veiled in obscurity and the evidence is entangled with that relating to other plots. There are strong grounds for believing that the plot passed through different stages before reaching the final form in which it took place, probably on account of a struggle for influence between the different elements involved. In the words of La Planche, these different elements comprised those who were moved by "un droict zèle" to serve God, their prince and their country; those who were moved by ambition and a desire for change; and those who were stung by a craving for revenge for injuries received at the hands of the Guises.[44]

The most readily available account of the origins of the conspiracy is that given by Lucien Romier, which needs to be considered carefully. He says that Condé turned to the idea of a conspiracy in August after he had finally despaired of his brother Navarre, and that secret discussions first occurred about 23 or 24 August 1559, when Chandieu and Navarre returned to Paris from Saint-Denis, and Navarre and Condé together sounded opinion in the city. The time would have been favorable for such meetings, since the court was conveniently occupied in moving from Saint-Germain to Villers-Cotterêts, and thence to Rheims for the coronation. Having inferred that the initiative came from Condé, Romier then shifts his ground and says that he may have been approached by someone ("quelqu'un de ses affidés put le

43. Fontanon, *Les Édits et ordonnances*, iv, 260. Both documents appear on the same page.
44. La Planche, 337.

suppléer"). He goes on to identify this person with Chandieu, whom he then closely associates with the early stages of the conspiracy. Condé, he says, appears to have begun by consulting the opinion of lawyers and theologians, and formulating a statement of the case against the Guises. Romier believes that after leaving Paris, Condé gathered his supporters at his house at La Ferté-sous-Jouarre before rejoining the court for the coronation. The plot was then finally concluded, he says, after the coronation on 18 September, while the court was once again conveniently absent, traveling in Lorraine. According to Romier, it was Chandieu, without any doubt, who coordinated the opinions of those whom Condé and Navarre had consulted in Paris.[45]

Romier goes on to link Chandieu with Condé's supposed itinerary when he left Paris, presumably about the end of August. It is true that Chandieu also left Paris and approached the court, probably during the first week in September. He stayed in a village near Rheims, in preparation for his secret meeting with Catherine which was to have taken place at this time. Throckmorton, in a letter of 10 September, indicated Chandieu's presence in the district—information, Romier says, that he could only have received from the prince's entourage. After the coronation, Chandieu is alleged to have departed suddenly, without waiting to see Catherine. Romier concludes from this that he made this journey in the prince's company and under his protection, "avec lequel il put poursuivre l'élaboration du complot."[46]

45. Chandieu is alleged to have written, and published in October, a pamphlet setting out the theme of the anti-Guise propaganda. Romier accepts this attribution and may be correct in doing so, but the connection between the pamphlet and Condé's inquiries in Paris has yet to be established. Romier, *La Conjuration d'Amboise*, 30 seq.; La Planche, 216; Condé, *Mémoires*, i, 357 seq.

46. Romier, *La Conjuration d'Amboise*, 31–34; Coquerel, p. xiv, 11 September 1559, Morel to Calvin; Forbes, *A Full View of the Public Transactions*, i, 226, 10 September 1559, Throckmorton to Elizabeth. Although Chandieu did not see Catherine at Villers-Cotterêts, it appears that certain other Protestants did. They took the opportunity of warning her that if the persecution did not cease, there would be "une merveilleuse confusion et desordre" in the kingdom. Catherine evidently received a favorable impression and later described the Protestants as "gens de parolle." La Planche, 298.

This account of Romier will not bear examination. In the first place, Condé's visit to La Ferté-sous-Jouarre, either before or after the coronation, is not well attested. He may not have gone there at all. Chandieu's journey, undertaken in the hope of seeing Catherine, is definitely established, but there is nothing to show that he had any communication with Condé at this time. Throckmorton's knowledge of his presence is not significant, and even if he had received the information from Condé, this would prove nothing since it was Condé's mother-in-law, Madame de Roye, who arranged the intended meeting with Catherine. Romier also interprets Throckmorton's letter of 10 September as indicating that Chandieu had already arrived. What it actually says is that Chandieu had already been ordered back to Paris, and without having seen the queen. There is therefore no reason to suppose that Chandieu lingered in the country for another eight or nine days, only to leave suddenly at the same time as Condé, immediately after the coronation. He had not, in any case, been at court, but in hiding some distance away. Even if Chandieu were involved in the conspiracy, it is difficult to believe that he would have jeopardized his mission to Catherine and risked his life by intriguing with Condé in a country village in the neighborhood of the court. There could be nothing more improbable, and the rest of Romier's story is equally unconvincing.

La Planche gives a different account. He clearly states that the initiative in the conspiracy came from an unspecified "compagnie." These people were agreed upon the necessity of seeking some legitimate form of defense "pour remettre sus l'ancien et légitime gouvernement du royaume," an objective which, at that stage, was political, limited and lawful. This group—not inconceivably those in possession of the documents "divinement bien faicts"—is said to have consulted the most learned jurists and theologians of France and Germany. As a result, it was claimed that they might legitimately oppose the government usurped by the Guises, and take up arms, in case of resistance, provided the princes of the blood, or one of them, would lead the enterprise. At this stage, La Planche went on, Condé was approached ("sollicité d'entendre à ces affaires"). The prince, he says, considered the matter carefully, and requested certain prudent and suitable persons to examine and inquire into the case against the Guises, in order to see what could and ought to be done, in all good conscience and for the benefit of the king and the commonwealth. It was the difficulty of implementing their objectives which turned the movement into a conspiracy. As the king was entirely controlled by the Guises, it was impossible to petition the council. It followed that the Guises must somehow be arrested and the estates general assembled. The problem was how and by whom this could be done ("à qui attacher la sonnette"). It was at this point that the services of the leader La Renaudie were enlisted and, according to La Planche, it was La Renaudie himself who proffered his services. Romier, without saying why, supposed that Chandieu presented La Renaudie to Condé. But we know that La Renaudie had been in touch with the Paris Protestants for at least eighteen months, and may well have been involved in the discussions from the start. He was a brother-in-law of du Buy and connected with Navarre, who summoned him in March 1558, and was possibly even one of his servants. It is therefore absurd to suggest that Condé only met La Renaudie through the agency of Chandieu in the summer of 1559, more especially since La Renaudie was persona non grata to Calvin.[47]

There is no reason to reject this version of La Planche: it is the most authoritative we have. It makes no mention of Chandieu, or of Morel, whom Romier also ignored. What then was the position of these pastors? Unfortunately it remains a matter for speculation. We know that they were both concerned, at some point, with discussions relating to a change of government. We also know that, faced with a choice between resistance and extermination, they desired some solution less sublime than that of prayer alone. We do not know who were the learned men who approved, or were alleged to have approved, the conspiracy, but it is quite possible that Morel and Chandieu may have assented to the original purpose—"remettre sus l'ancien et légitime gouvernement du royaume." Calvin himself approved of this. Bearing in mind, therefore, that the intention was not to organize a rebellion, but to devise a means of legitimate opposition, it is even conceivable that

47. La Planche, 237–38; Romier, *La Conjuration d'Amboise*, 35.

Chandieu may have been among those who approached Condé. It is true that he had been connected with Condé for some time and had a brother, Bertrand, in the prince's service. But further than this one cannot go. In the absence of proper evidence—and Romier produces none—it is impossible to agree that Chandieu, or any of the pastors, helped to organize the conspiracy in the form in which it took place. It is almost certainly the failure to make this distinction between the original purpose and what actually occurred which accounts both for the claim that the conspiracy was approved by those consulted, and for the fact that the pastors are said to have been implicated in the final scheme.

Chandieu's position is nevertheless bewildering since, late in September or early in October 1559, he went to Geneva to discuss the conspiracy with Calvin and the Company of Pastors. Romier, who assumes that the plot was finally arranged on 18 September, after the coronation, asserts that Chandieu went to Geneva in order to obtain Calvin's approval of the conspiracy, taking with him the indictment of the Guises which he is alleged to have drawn up for Condé. The hypothesis is ingenious but not supported either by probability or by the evidence produced. Chandieu's mission raises various problems but proves only one thing: that he knew something of what was going on and, by inference, the general nature of the conspiracy. It does not, as Romier appears to assume, prove his complicity.[48]

There are various possible reasons why Chandieu went to Geneva: to inform Calvin; because he had only just discovered what was happening; because he was alarmed by the turn of events; because he had been approached by some of the more cautious conspirators; or because he wished for a clear directive on the official attitude of the church. What little we know for certain about his mission comes from a letter of 16 April 1561 from Calvin to Coligny—although he concealed the identity of Chandieu—and from information recorded in Geneva in the course of a libel case in which Calvin, de Bèze and Chandieu were accused of complicity in the conspiracy. Jean Morély, Chandieu's accuser, alleged before the Seigneurie of Geneva that the original

48. Romier, *La Conjuration d'Amboise*, 57–58.

plans ("premiers propos") were "si equitables et tellement fondés en la Parolle de Dieu qu'il semblait la chose se debvoir entreprendre." Thus, Morély went on, Chandieu went to Geneva to discuss the matter with Calvin and the pastors, and subsequently informed the French churches that they had approved the enterprise. It must either be assumed that Morély's evidence was hopelessly garbled, or else that the report is incomplete, for the statement, as it stands, does not make sense. For his part, Chandieu denied having told the French churches that the ministers of Geneva approved the enterprise, "ainsi qu'elle a esté executée"; he knew that they did not. Here we have at least one clear statement amidst so much that is obscure, and there is no reason to doubt its veracity. In answer to another question, Chandieu said that he had spoken to Calvin of the tyranny of the Guises and of the need to establish a government of "the prince"—it is not clear which prince is intended—in view of the king's minority, and in accordance with the laws of France. These were, presumably, the "premiers propos," held to be in accordance with the word of God. According to Chandieu's evidence, Calvin replied that this was a purely civil matter, and that if Navarre and the estates general combined to restore order there was no objection to the Protestants lending their support ("il ne trouvait mauvais que les fideles... fussent du nombre").[49]

It is apparent, however, that Chandieu must—though not necessarily on the same occasion—have said more than the evidence states, and advanced some actual plan, since Calvin, in his evidence, claimed to have given Chandieu many reasons why the enterprise, "telle qu'elle estoit," was not based on the word of God. But if, Calvin went on, it were a question of supporting Navarre in an attempt to reestablish the proper order laid down by the laws of France, it would be permissible so long as it were done without the shedding of blood—a new development in Calvinist thought. Calvin here expressed himself ambiguously and without indicating the nature of the support he was prepared to

---

49. Bonnet, *Lettres de Calvin*, ii, 382–91, 16 April 1561, Calvin to Coligny. Naef discovered and printed this important material, *La Conjuration d'Amboise et Genève*, 452–53, 462, 469.

sanction. The letter to Coligny of 16 April 1561 is easier to follow. From this we may infer that there was a general discussion between Calvin and Chandieu on the legitimacy and the means of resistance. Realizing, Calvin said, that many people were deeply involved in plans for resistance, he gave a categorical answer that the idea—precisely which idea is not stated—must be abandoned. He tried to show that it was not founded in the word of God, and also that it was foolish, and could not hope to succeed. Chandieu, he said, disputed his answer, "voir avec quelque couleur," because there was no question of taking action either against the king or the royal authority, but only of calling for a government in conformity with the law. Meanwhile, if nothing were done, a horrible massacre was hourly expected, which would put an end to the reformed religion. Calvin says he replied—referring presumably to the project—that if a single drop of blood were shed, then it was preferable that all the Protestants should die a hundred deaths, than that the church should incur so frightful a responsibility. Nevertheless, Calvin again stated that if the princes of the blood, together with the *parlement*, demanded support for their rights in the common interest, it would be legitimate for all good subjects to go to their assistance. Here again, Calvin used an evasive expression—"de leur prêter main forte." In this version, the *parlement* is substituted for the estates general, and there is no reservation about the avoidance of bloodshed. The questioner then asked him, Calvin continued, whether the same plan were permissible if only one of the princes took part, an obvious reference to Condé. The answer again was an absolute negative, and Calvin believed that the project would therefore be abandoned. This could be taken to imply that plans for the conspiracy had not yet been completed, that Chandieu was not very well informed, or that Calvin had had an inflated conception of his own influence; certainly he regretted his loss of influence in the same letter to Coligny.[50]

As far as Chandieu is concerned, the evidence is still inconclu-

50. Naef, *La Conjuration d'Amboise et Genève*, 469; Bonnet, *Lettres de Calvin*, ii, 382–91, 16 April 1561, Calvin to Coligny.

sive. It implies a certain degree of sympathy with the conspirators because of his fears for the church, but this is in keeping with Calvin's own support of the "premier propos." We may deduce from Calvin's evidence that Chandieu must have mentioned Condé, and Romier assumes that Chandieu pleaded the cause of the conspirators, that is to say, supported the plans which were actually carried out. To this it may be objected that it is neither known what Chandieu said, nor whether he pleaded or merely reported; it is only known for certain that Condé was mentioned and that Calvin thought the proposition plausible, but inexpedient. The enigma remains, but the most likely explanation is that Chandieu described a plan proposing the substitution of Condé for Navarre, who was even then preparing for his journey to Spain. This would have been a strictly practical adaptation of Calvin's own plan. Many people, and perhaps Chandieu himself, must have thought the difference between the first and the second prince of the blood no more than a juridical quibble. Indeed, it is doubtful whether Calvin himself attached much importance to the distinction. It is clear that his absolute refusal to sanction whatever plan was suggested proceeded more from his fear of the consequences than from any theoretical consideration. Similarly, his violent disapproval of the enterprise which followed was based partly on contempt for La Renaudie and his methods, and partly on a well-founded conviction that anything so foolhardy was sure to be disastrous. It is impossible to explain this change in Calvin's attitude since the time of the conference at Vendôme, and Chandieu's mission to Geneva tends to suggest that it may have come as a surprise to him.[51]

While Chandieu was in Geneva, it seems likely that La Renaudie had begun to organize the conspiracy, and it is probably correct to assume, not that Chandieu failed to make a truthful report when he returned, but that he arrived too late to influence events. Condé, and military-minded gentlemen like La Renaudie, were clearly not going to wait upon Calvin's permission.

51. *Bull. Prot.*, i, 1853, pp. 250–52, 5 May 1560, Calvin to Pierre Martin, French translation.

Jean du Barry, seigneur de La Renaudie, sometimes known as La Forest, was a gentleman from Périgord. He was energetic, persuasive, embittered and unprincipled. He harbored a sense of injustice because of past troubles, and against the Guises in particular for the recent execution of his kinsman du Buy. He evidently had useful connections, and belonged to that section of society to which military adventures were a normal occupation. La Renaudie claimed to have received a mandate from Condé and proceeded, with more celerity than prudence, to organize what was, in effect if not in intention, a military coup. Thus the initiative passed into the hands of the country gentry or lesser nobility.[52]

In the late summer or early autumn, La Renaudie left Paris to make his preparations. He may have begun by visiting his native Périgord. Romier says that he was there in September, but his reference does not support the statement and the date of the visit remains uncertain. So does most of the itinerary, though we know that La Renaudie went to Geneva, probably in December. His arrival was a rude shock for Calvin, who thought his disapproval would kill the project. He was astounded, he said, in a letter to Coligny, when La Renaudie arrived in Geneva saying that he had been entrusted with the execution of the enterprise. Calvin knew La Renaudie, who had also been in exile, and had a very low opinion of him. He called him frivolous, vain and presumptuous, and condemned the enterprise as foolish and dangerous. The fact that Calvin was surprised by the arrival of La Renaudie suggests that the pastors in Paris did not know what was happening, otherwise Calvin would, presumably, have been kept informed. Had La Renaudie, for his part, known the results of Chandieu's mission to Geneva, he would surely have concealed his presence from Calvin, whose disapproval was, at the least, a grave disadvantage. Undismayed, La Renaudie set about raising men and money, using every means of persuasion to obtain support. He even continued to use Calvin's name, and extracted support by alleging his secret approval. Hearing of this, Calvin angrily tried to stop him. But, charged with the offense, La Re-

52. La Planche, 238, 318.

naudie replied with cool effrontery that he had lied if he had ever said that Calvin approved, for he knew that he did not.[53]

There is no doubt that La Renaudie lied, and used whatever lie suited his purpose best. Thus, he appealed to the exiled Protestant gentry by references to Coligny, from whom a call to arms would not lightly be ignored. Above all, he labored to propagate the opinion that the conspiracy was sponsored by Geneva and the churches. Nothing could have been more damaging or further from the truth. In this way, he deceitfully misled the well-intentioned and gained the support of numbers of people who were uncertain about the issues involved. Calvin himself was not well-informed. Nevertheless, he strove to restrain the Genevans, who were leaving the city secretly in small groups, and, above all, he tried to exert a direct influence on the French churches. To this effect, he twice wrote collectively to all the faithful of France. In these long and earnest exhortations, he called on the Protestants to suffer and, if necessary to die, to possess their souls in patience, and to seek protection in God because, he insisted, and in plain language, it was illicit to take refuge in the use of force. He knew, he said, that the temptation to self-defense was severe and difficult to overcome, but they must learn to prefer the honor of God and obedience to his word above the considerations of their lives on earth.[54]

It would appear that Calvin's influence prevailed, although some members of the church of Lyons contributed a small amount of material help, and there may, perhaps, have been

53. Boscheron Desportes, *Histoire du parlement de Bordeaux*, i, 130; Naef, *La Conjuration d'Amboise et Genève*, 543; Bonnet, *Lettres de Calvin*, ii, 382–91, 16 April 1561, Calvin to Coligny.

54. See, for example, the way in which the Protestants of Lyons appear to have been misled into believing that all the Protestant churches were taking part. Some question also arose about the possibility of turning Lyons into "une ville libre" on the Swiss model. Romier, *La Conjuration d'Amboise*, 69–70; Cimber et Danjou, série i, vol. iv, *Discours des premiers troubles advenus à Lyon*, 227; Bonnet, *Lettres de Calvin*, ii, 382–91, 16 April 1561, Calvin to Coligny; 297–306, November 1559 and 311–20, 1559, Calvin to the faithful of France; Paillard, "Additions critiques à l'histoire de la conjuration d'Amboise," *Revue historique*, xiv, 1880, pp. 311–12; Naef, *La Conjuration d'Amboise et Genève*, 542.

others. No evidence transpired that those who took part in the movement had been invited to do so by their pastors or consistories, with one exception—that of the pastor François Boisnormand, who was accused by some of the prisoners. Among those who were captured and interrogated at Amboise there was not one confessed member of the church of Paris. The bulk of La Renaudie's supporters were provincial nobles—some disgruntled like himself—and mercenaries, many of whom probably joined because, for once, they were actually paid. That La Renaudie had failed to obtain the support of the churches is suggested by the evidence of the second national synod which opened at Poitiers on 10 March 1560/61. Among other things, the assembly discussed whether it was permissable to preach without the consent of a magistrate. While no clear answer was given, it was decided that one must have regard to the times, and public tranquillity, and that seditions and tumults must be avoided. These were surely not church officials who had sent men and money to Amboise. The same piece of evidence supports the statement of Chandieu that he did not tell the churches the conspiracy was approved in Geneva.[55]

From Geneva, La Renaudie went on to Berne, and is sometimes said to have been to Strasbourg and to England. This is unlikely if only for reasons of time. He is generally believed to have toured the provinces of France, presumably to raise support and arrange for the meeting which he summoned at Nantes on 1 February 1560.[56]

---

55. La Planche, 275. On La Renaudie's supporters, see Romier, *La Conjuration d'Amboise*, ch. v; Bonnet, *Lettres de Calvin*, ii, 382–91, 16 April 1561, Calvin to Coligny; Mignet, *Journal des Savants*, July 1857, p. 416; Aymon, *Tous les synodes nationaux*, i, 22. It is not known how the conspiracy was financed.

56. For reasons of space it is impossible to discuss the part played by Protestant agents in Strasbourg in French affairs at this time. The evidence we have of the intense activity in this city is complex and obscure. While some of it may relate to the conspiracy of Amboise, it is not certain that it does. François Hotman was working enthusiastically at this time on a plan for the recovery of Metz from France—which he saw as a blow in favor of Protestantism. What other plots were brewing there is not clear either. Calvin later referred darkly to "d'autres praticques qui se

From the military point of view, the conspiracy was organized at Nantes, and the meeting is interesting for its curiously scrupulous deliberations, which appear to reflect the restraining influence of those who sought some effective means of opposition without becoming rebels. We do not know who attended the meeting, but "un bon nombre de noblesse et du tiers estat de toutes les provinces" are said to have been there. It was claimed that they represented a spontaneous and legitimate gathering of the estates. La Renaudie began by addressing the meeting at length, principally on the government of the Guises. He spoke of the decisions of the learned men who had been consulted— presumably alleging their approval—and asked whether the assembly would agree to support a prince or his lieutenant in an attempt to seize the tyrants, assemble the estates and provide the king with a suitable council. It was agreed that the project was just and necessary, provided there was to be no attack on the royal authority or the State. An oath was taken to this effect, and La Renaudie revealed his mandate from Condé. Condé was to declare himself and petition the king and the council, but only after the Guises had been safely arrested.[57]

The meeting then proceeded to consider how and when to carry out their intentions, how many men to use, which captains would command the forces and who should act as advisers to the leader or his lieutenant. The final details of this exploit were to be decided on the spot and nearer the time, by those responsible for its execution. It was formally stated that to do more than arrest

---

menoient de loing," which he claimed to have thwarted. Strasbourg was certainly a source of anti-Guise propaganda, and inquiries were made there as to whether the conspirators had any hope of receiving help from Queen Elizabeth. See Dareste, "François Hotman, sa vie et sa correspondance," *Revue historique*, ii, 1876, pp. 1 seq.; Romier, *La Conjuration d'Amboise*, ch. vi; Naef, *La Conjuration d'Amboise et Genève*, passim; Dureng, "La Complicité de l'Angleterre dans le complot d'Amboise," *Revue d'histoire moderne et contemporaine*, vi, 1904–5; *CSPF.*, *1559–60*, p. 412, 27 February 1960, Mundt to Cecil.

57. La Planche, 239. The form of the oath was as follows: "Protestation faicte par le chef et tous ceux du conseil de n'attenter aucune chose contre la majesté du roi princes su sang, n'y estat légitime du royaume."

the Guises would be unlawful. The assembly then appointed a council of "certain personnages de toutes les provinces." This council fixed the date of the enterprise for 10 March (it was subsequently delayed by about a week) and decided that five hundred gentlemen, drawn from all the provinces, should be assembled. This company was to assist the leader to capture the Guises, and a captain was appointed to command each local or provincial contingent. Finally, it was decided that men and money must be raised so that if the company of five hundred met with any resistance, they could defend themselves ("la force demoureroit au chef"), until they had been able to establish a legitimate government and bring the tyrants to justice. The meeting then dispersed, everyone to make appropriate preparations. La Renaudie went to Paris to see Condé, and to raise men, arms and horses.[58]

Shortly after the assembly at Nantes, the conspiracy was betrayed, information reaching the government from several different sources. As a result, the movement collapsed, and many of those involved were killed or arrested as they gathered in small bands in the neighborhood of Amboise. La Renaudie himself was killed on 18 March in the forest of Châteaurenault, and his secretary, La Bigne, was captured. Much of what is known about the nature of the movement is based on the documents taken from La Bigne. Among them was a statement of objectives opening with the oath of loyalty to the king. The purpose, the document declared, was to put an end to the government of the Guises and, by means of a legitimate assembly of the estates, to reestablish the ancient customs of France. The only reason why they appeared in arms for this purpose was because they feared that the

---

58. Ibid., 239–40, 255. The 500 gentlemen were followed by a thousand others, besides which there were various contingents on foot, many of them apparently unarmed. There is no mention of any forces coming from Burgundy, Brittany or, more curiously, Dauphiné. The original date for the execution of the plot is variously given as 6 and 10 March. The latter appears to be correct. Most of the lieutenants have been identified and, of those who survived, many were later active in the civil wars. See Romier, *La Conjuration d'Amboise*, 83–84; Mignet, *Journal des Savants*, July 1857, 418; Baum and Cunitz, *Histoire ecclésiastique des Églises réformées de France*, i, 290; La Planche, 239.

Guises would accuse them of sedition and employ the king's forces against them. A second document seized from La Bigne was a separate remonstrance, addressed to the king. It contained an article defending those Protestants who had voluntarily joined the movement, on the grounds that it was a political matter concerning the laws and the service of the king. Had it been otherwise, the document stated, they would never have become involved because of their principle of obedience, already openly declared in their confession of faith. For this reason, they condemned and disclaimed all "séditieux et perturbateurs de l'ordre de justice." They hoped to present the confession of faith to the estates general, in order to obtain some remission of the persecution which they suffered at the hands of the Guises. This apology, however, had no effect, and the Guises hastened to blame the Protestants and declare that they had taken up arms against the king. In reply, they published a further remonstrance. It was couched in similar terms, explained the loyal and political motives behinds the conspiracy, and again insisted that the Protestants involved had not taken up arms for the sake of religion. Such protests made no impression at the time, and are difficult to evaluate now, without knowing their precise origin.[59]

If the conspiracy of Amboise had succeeded, it would have been a bloodless, or almost bloodless coup d'état, accomplished by the lesser nobility, and Calvin and the churches would have rejoiced. Though the story is confused and the evidence is often vague, it seems reasonably clear that this bloodless coup is what what was really intended, at least by the more responsible of those involved. The movement began with an unspecified group of people, probably comprising at least a proportion of intellectuals. They were evidently Protestants in or around Paris, but we do not know whether any of them were members of the Paris church. Their original purpose was to consider by what legitimate means they could end the tyranny of the Guises and replace them by a government of the royal princes. This purpose, we may safely assume, corresponds to the "premiers propos," or

59. Romier, *La Conjuration d'Amboise*, 89-119; La Planche, 255; Condé, *Mémoires*, i, 405 seq.

the allegedly just and reasonable intentions, and was of immediate concern to all Protestants because their very existence was threatened by the régime. For this same reason the churches were accused of complicity in the act of insubordination which ultimately occurred. These original objectives were a legitimate concern of the pastors of Paris, who knew that Calvin himself had tried to replace the Guises by the king of Navarre. When this project was thwarted by Navarre himself, it was natural, in the midst of such fearful persecution, that they should have desired some alternative solution. We do not know whether they took any initiative in this matter, or merely reported the ideas of others, but Morel and Chandieu each put forward a suggestion. Morel proposed to elevate the importance of the estates general above that of the first prince of the blood, and call an assembly without his authority. If this were resisted, then he urged that it would surely be just to take up arms. The plan expounded—though not necessarily supported—by Chandieu was evidently that of substituting Condé for Navarre, an adaptation of Calvin's own original proposal.

These propositions were well within the spirit of Calvinism, though not, as it happened, the interpretation placed by Calvin on his own work. Neither of them was favorably received, and there is nothing to show that the pastors played any part in what followed. It is therefore impossible to agree with historians who fail to distinguish between the early and the later stages of the movement and, as a result, allege or infer that Chandieu was guilty of complicity in the actual conspiracy. It is true that he is alleged to have produced an anti-Guise pamphlet in October 1559, but the theme of this relates to the "premiers propos," and is not contrary to the spirit of Calvinism. There seems to be no reason for suspecting Chandieu at this stage, since he and his colleagues evidently managed to restrain the sorely tried Protestants of Paris, none of whom is known to have been present at Amboise.[60]

60. Théodore de Bèze has also been accused of complicity in the conspiracy. He was evidently guilty of certain minor indiscretions. He probably approved the "premiers propos" but almost certainly not the enterprise in the form in which it took place, since he tried to dissuade various people from becoming involved. See Naef, *La Conjuration d'Am-*

Calvin's own proposal having failed, he would accept no other: to him there was no legitimate alternative. But, unable to compromise, he was equally unable to convince all French Protestants of their duty to suffer and to die. From his point of view, this was not a negative attitude, but it was exasperatingly unrealistic to those who looked to him for guidance while feeling that there were limits to human endurance, and ought to be limits to the duty of obedience. Perhaps Calvin took refuge from this difficulty in his own inconsistencies. It appears, at least, from a letter to Sturm of 23 March 1560 that, having failed to prevent the enterprise, he hoped it would succeed. His political philosophy allowed for successful rebellions; their success made them legitimate. This may partly account for a certain evasiveness in Calvin's attitude, and for the somewhat unsatisfactory explanation of his conduct at this time in the long letter to Coligny of 16 April 1561. The non-participation imposed by Calvin on his followers was not a solution to the predicament of those who approved the aspirations, but condemned the methods, and perceived the disastrous folly of the conspirators. It was in vain that apologists tried to distinguish between Protestants acting in a political and in a religious capacity, or between the presentation of a petition in arms and participation in an insurrection. Such distinctions had little meaning in the realm of action, and no hope of acceptance by those in authority. By withholding support from this "cause civile," the churches lived up to Calvin's principle of obedience, and may have succeeded in delaying the deluge. But although their non-participation is historically impressive, it made no impression at the time. Indeed, it may not even have been generally known. The churches received no credit for this remarkable restraint, and were unable to dissociate themselves from the conduct of those who failed to accept their discipline or to emulate their example. It is difficult to avoid the conclusion that this was partly the fault of Calvin, who failed to clarify the position of the churches in the eyes of the world, and continued to provide a

---

boise et Genève, 414, 465 seq., 487–96; Geisendorf, *Théodore de Bèze*, 117 seq.; Kingdon, *Geneva and the Coming of the Wars of Religion in France*, 69 seq.; De Caprariis, *Propaganda et Pensiero Politico in Francia durante le Guerre di Religione*, i, 1559–1572, pp. 29–30.

retreat in Geneva for the disgraced and the exiled, thereby appearing to condone their offenses. It was no fault of Calvin that religion and politics had become disastrously entangled in France. But because he offered no material solution, he was forced to watch, with impotent distress, events which quickly proved the accuracy of his fears. Control of the Protestant movement passed from the disciplined evangelists into the hands of politicians and extremists, and the churches were forced into the struggle which ensued.[61]

61. De Bèze also indicated in 1561 that he had hoped the conspiracy would succeed. Geisendorf, *Théodore de Bèze*, 118, Naef, *La Conjuration d'Amboise et Genève*, 478–79, 486–87; Mignet, *Journal des Savants*, February 1857, pp. 95–96.

4

The Huguenot Struggle for Recognition, 1560–1562

BY 1560 THERE WERE MANY CONTEMPORARY NAMES for describing Protestants: *les Luthériens, les Calvinistes, les réformés, ceux de la religion prétendu réformée*—often known as *RPR*—*les sectataires, les consistoriaux*, and so forth. While these names meant several different things, they were indifferently applied. But the identity of the Huguenots seems to have been forged in the conspiracy of Amboise. This mysterious name appears to have denoted not simply those who shared a creed, but rather a nascent party, whose destiny therefore became a political matter. Since French refugees in Geneva returned to France to take part in the conspiracy of Amboise, it seems at least plausible that the epithet "Huguenot" was a corruption of the Swiss word *Eidguenot*. This had been the name of the Genevan faction which, from about 1520, had favored a Swiss alliance against the Savoyard prince-bishop. The name was therefore associated with the Genevan revolution which led to her independence. From about 1532, the cause of Genevan independence had become mingled with that of the Reformation, through the influence of her Zwinglian ally, Berne. Thus, before the *Eidguenots* themselves split into two hostile factions, about 1537, their name had come to represent independence from a Catholic overlord, and Protestantism.[1] But, however this may be, there certainly was, after the conspiracy of Amboise, a nascent Huguenot party. The nature of their original bond was less that they were all Protestants—which may or may not be strictly true—but rather

1. Monter, *Calvin's Geneva*, 35–44, 66.

that they were all opposed to the Guises who, primarily through the cardinal of Lorraine, dominated Church and State. The Huguenots' initial struggle for recognition was therefore necessarily accompanied by the development of leadership on the national level. This was bound to be politically and personally anti-Guise, and at least nominally Protestant. Such leadership was gradually assumed by the admiral Gaspard de Coligny, an unwavering Calvinist, and Louis prince de Condé—a somewhat ill-assorted partnership which was largely fortuitous.

At the time of Amboise, Coligny and Condé were both at court, but their closely related future was by no means yet apparent. Condé was opposed by the Guises on account of his challenging rank as a prince of the blood. Conversely, he was solicited by the Protestants in default of the first prince, his elder brother Navarre. Navarre's political and religious ambivalence greatly confused the problems and confounded the events of these critical years. Coligny was also an opponent of the Guises, both as a Protestant and as a nephew of their old rival, the constable Montmorency, who had withdrawn from court on the death of Henry II.[2] Here, therefore, at this relatively precise point in 1560, is the beginning of the long pro- and anti-Guise struggle which, at least until 1588, represents one way of studying the internal affairs of France on the national level. This might be compared with, and must be related to, the anti-Spanish struggle in the international sphere. Both these conflicts were confused by the intermingling of religious with political affiliations. Thus, from the start, the Huguenot struggle in France was linked, as the Protestant persecution had always been, to far-reaching issues.

Besides the emergence of the Huguenots, Amboise also marked the appearance of tension between the crown and the Guises, who had effectively alienated a significant proportion of the new king's subjects. The result was a drastic and permanent change in royal policy, from the extremism of Henry II to one of moderation. This was not a religious change. The crown was always Catholic and would greatly have preferred an unequivocally Catholic kingdom. Royal policy was tempered because law and

2. La Planche, 249.

order was the first essential of government; also because the Guises, with their papal and Spanish affiliations, presented a greater threat to the unstable throne of three weak kings than the supposedly seditious Calvinist minority.[3] This urgent preoccupation with law, order and authority was the principal concern of the crown between the conspiracy and the outbreak of civil war in June 1562. It was therefore clearly reflected in the eight religious edicts of the intervening period.

The Guises had reigned supreme since the death of Henry II, sustaining his policy of persecution. But once their régime was challenged at Amboise, Catherine de Medici, the queen mother, had some small opportunity to begin to exert her influence. This was invariably in favor of moderation. Indeed, Catherine had no alternative to moderation, if the crown were not to be dominated by an ambitious, ultra-montane war party, whose Spanish affiliations she greatly feared. It was one thing for Henry II to cooperate with the king of Spain in a struggle against heresy, but quite another for the Guises to do so in order to dominate the king of France. Certainly there is a significant difference between the Guisard edict of February 1560, when the conspiracy of Amboise was first betrayed, and the two which followed in March and May, when the Guise position was less secure. The edict of February 1560 is therefore the last of four persecutory edicts issued after the death of Henry II.[4] It referred back to the prohibition, in the edicts of September and November 1559, of illicit assemblies and conventicles. These, it claimed, had diminished in the big towns. But, by the connivance of royal judges and also of the nobility, such assemblies continued to be held in the smaller towns and villages and in seigneurial houses. This edict repeated the affirmation in that of November 1559—when there were already rumors of a conspiracy—that such religious meetings were being used for seditious purposes, and added: "aussi s'y font plusieurs conspirations contre la chose publique tendans à la sub-

3. The brothers Francis II, 1559–60; Charles IX, 1560–74; Henry III, 1574–89.
4. Fontanon, *Les Édits et ordonnances*, iv, 259–60, 4 September 1559, Villers-Cotterêts; idem, two *mandements* of November 1559, one dated 13 November and the other registered on the same day.

version de l'estat de nostredict Royaume" (preamble). There were no greater penalties to be imposed than those of Compiègne. But the text of the edict of February 1560 betrays the Guise fears of the nobility and gentry. By means of their seigneurial jurisdiction, they could not only protect the Protestants but also promote sedition and conspiracy. Such jurisdiction was difficult to control. The purpose of the edict was therefore to deprive of his jurisdiction or office anyone who should prosecute the Protestants but failed to do so. All such cases were to be reported to the *parlement* within one month.

The edict of February 1560 was closely followed by that of Amboise, 11 March, a day or two after the original date set for the execution of the conspiracy.[5] These were the first two edicts in which the text directly referred to current political affairs. This fact alone would suffice to establish that religion, and consequently the survival of the Huguenots, had become a political issue. The two edicts presented a remarkable contrast, and the influence of Catherine de Medici in the edict of Amboise is explicit. According to the preamble, the king—in whose name everything was transacted—is said to have conferred with his mother before bringing the matter to the council. The edict was also, according to La Planche, very much influenced by Coligny, who had forcefully proclaimed "le mescontentement de tous les subjects, pour le faict de la religion et les affaires politiques." He is said to have advised a relaxation of persecution, because the Protestants were too numerous to be exterminated. He also called for an "Edit en termes bien clairs et signifians,"[6] under which to live in peace, pending a council at which everyone should be heard.[7] This evidence of La Planche appears to be generally re-

---

5. Ibid., 261–62. Both edicts were issued at Amboise. The former is generally described as the *mandement* of February 1560, and the latter as the edict of Amboise.

6. Baum and Cunitz, *Histoire ecclésiastique*, i, 302.

7. La Planche, 247–48. La Planche says that the Guises had asked Catherine to send for Coligny and his brother, d'Andelot. They feared their involvement because of the large numbers of forces under their command. Presumably, if they *had* been involved, they would not have come.

flected in the edict. It was intended to extenuate a dangerous situation which persecution had done nothing to ameliorate. Though issued and registered at a time of crisis, the edict of Amboise was not a panic measure. It began by calmly examining the nature, variety and background of the problem. The pre-amble did indeed declare that the Protestants, of all sorts and condi-tions, had become so numerous that the rigors of the law, as embodied in the edicts of Châteaubriant and Compiègne, could only cause "une merveilleuse effusion de sang." The young king did not wish to sully the first year of his reign. Hoping therefore that clemency might prove more profitable, the edict offered a complete pardon for all past crimes of religion, provided the guilty lived henceforth as good Catholics. But it excluded pastors, and conspirators against the royal family, ministers, or the State—consequently anyone about to appear in arms before the gates of Amboise.

The edict of Amboise was followed, a few days later, by a specific pardon or amnesty for all who came in arms, provided they withdrew in twos or threes within forty-eight hours; oth-erwise they could expect no mercy.[8] Issued at the height of the crisis, this further document is interesting. Obviously a pardon represented the voice of moderation, and it incorporated permis-sion for one or two Huguenot deputies to present their re-monstrances and petitions. But the savage alternative to the con-ditions of the pardon was, however, equally clearly Guisard. Similarly, letters patent, issued on 22 March, excluded from the amnesty the leaders of the movement and those who had gone to Amboise in arms.[9] The explanation may be that the chancellor

---

8. Fontanon, *Les Édits et ordonnances*, iv, 262–63. The date of this pardon is variously given as 16, 17, 18 March. The king himself had announced it by 16 March. Hérelle, *La Réforme et la ligue en Champagne*, i, 30–32, 16 March 1560, Francis to the bailli of Vermandois.

9. La Planche, 262, 270. I have not found these letters patent, but Throckmorton reported on 12 April that "all the pardons proclaimed with trumpets at Amboise... were revoked at Tours in the same way." *CSPF.*, *1559-60*, p. 534, 12 April 1560, Throckmorton to Elizabeth; p. 505, 6 April 1560, Throckmorton to Elizabeth; the pardon would not be operative.

had only agreed to seal a commission naming the duc de Guise lieutenant general on condition of the pardon. It was therefore granted and promptly nullified.[10]

The duke's commission enabled the Guises to propagate without delay their own version of the affair. It was intended to establish that the conspirators were rebels against the crown, and to incriminate and tarnish the prince de Condé, whose superior rank was a threat to their preeminence. They began—unsuccessfully—by seeking to extort confessions from the principal captives to the effect that they had plotted to kill the king, and that Navarre and Condé were their leaders.[11] The real Huguenot purpose, to remove the Guises, summon the estates general—to which they intended to present a confession of faith—and provide the king with a different council, was explicit in the documents taken from La Bigne, secretary to La Renaudie.[12] The Huguenots are always said to have been under oath to respect the king, the princes, the State and the kingdom; and the principle of obedience was embodied in their confession of faith.[13] The Bigne documents explained that they came in arms for fear—even as petitioners—of being condemned as seditious, and victimized by royal forces.[14] Letters of 31 March sent to the *parlements*, the *baillis* and *sénéchaux* and their lieutenants described the tumult in such terms as "detestable rebellion" and "abominable treason," "qui tendoit a l'entiere subversion de nostre estat." A substantial share of the blame was placed on "aucuns prédicans de nouvelle Doctrine," the affair having been "délibérée soubz le masque de la Religion." The Calvinists as such, and by implication the churches, were therefore directly stigmatized.[15]

10. Condé, *Mémoires*, i, 342, n. 1, and 342–46, 17 March 1560, "pouvoir obtenu par le duc de Guise"; Michaud, série i, vol. vi, *Mémoires-journaux du duc de Guise*, 457–59.

11. La Planche, 263–65.

12. Ibid., 254–55. La Renaudie was killed on 18 March.

13. This was the confession of the national synod of Paris of May 1559, which was not published until after the first civil war. Condé, *Mémoires*, i, 411–33.

14. Baum and Cunitz, *Histoire ecclésiastique*, i, 289, and n. 2; La Planche, 254–55, 299.

15. Condé, *Mémoires*, i, 347–52, lettre du roi sur la conjuration d'Amboise, 31 March 1559/60. It cannot be fully analyzed here.

Although the letters patent of 31 March were subtle and complex, and by no means exclusively Guisard, they provoked a rapid and explosive Protestant reaction. This was because of the dual accusation of having taken up arms against the king, and in the cause of religion. Not only were both charges hotly and extensively refuted, but Lorraine, a "tyrant and usurper," was clearly designated as the Huguenot enemy.[16] The participation in the tumult of the persecuted Calvinist churches was categorically denied: "l'entreprise n'a esté faicte ny commencée à la persuasion des Ministres ny à leur adveu,"[17] although it was admitted that among those who took part in the tumult "il y en ait qui désirent vivre selon la réformation de l'Evangile"—something, perhaps, of an understatement.[18] They would never, the Protestants claimed, have taken up arms for that reason alone, had there not been "une cause civile et politique." While this was undoubtedly true, at the time, the Guises would respect no such distinction. Consequently, the post-Amboise conflict became inescapably politico-religious, and correspondingly complicated. From this conflict stemmed the Protestant struggle for recognition, and the now imperative need for lay leadership, twin pillars of protection and security.[19]

The oft-repeated and uncritically accepted allegation that Condé was the *chef muet* of the conspiracy appears to rest on the evidence of La Renaudie. He is reported to have said this at the preparatory meeting at Nantes, and to have shown his followers a commission from the prince.[20] This cannot, however, be regarded as good evidence, since Condé had a deplorably ill-advised habit of signing blanks. Furthermore, La Renaudie did not hesitate to proclaim the support of Calvin, who in fact despised him, and condemned his enterprise.[21] La Renaudie simply announced

16. Ibid., 353.

17. Ibid., 377.

18. Ibid., 410.

19. Ibid., 352–97, 405–10.

20. Baum and Cunitz, *Histoire ecclésiastique*, i, 286–87, 289–90; La Planche, 239.

21. The event, in fact, caused Calvin a "souffrance morale" which interfered with his work. *Bull. Prot.*, i, 1852, pp. 250–52, 5 May 1560, Calvin to Pierre Martyr.

what he wanted others to believe. After the *débâcle*, none of the leading captives incriminated Condé, in spite of savage efforts to induce them to do so. Furthermore, the letters patent of 31 March 1560, sent to the *parlements* and provincial officials, denied the assurance given that "aucuns princes" would embrace the enterprise as "chefs et conducteurs."[22] While this may have represented the failure of immediate efforts to inculpate Condé, any subsequent evidence against him would have been thoroughly publicized. But nothing positive was ever established against him. Since he had once been approached, the probability is that Condé was informed and aware of, rather than a party to, the conspiracy. But, whatever the truth, he could hardly escape incrimination, since he had, as a prince, a designated part in the Huguenots' plan to establish the Bourbons in place of the Guises. This was the implication of his rank, not the definition of his policy, and the matter must be treated as unresolved. To the Guises, however, Condé was either the Huguenots' obvious leader, or at least the obvious future leader, who must, at all costs, be quickly ruined.

Thus Condé's position at the end of March 1560 was inescapably hazardous. Throckmorton reported on 29 March that the prince was "greatly suspected and watched."[23] He is said to have been ordered not to leave court, and it is even claimed in the *Histoire ecclésiastique* that the Guises advised the king to kill him.[24] This becomes perfectly plausible in the light of all subsequent events until his murder in 1569. Some of his servants were molested, and his papers were searched. Condé himself was summoned by the king—presumably at the instigation of the Guises—who charged him with having been the leader of the conspiracy.[25] Condé responded by demanding a meeting of the

22. Condé, *Mémoires*, i, 349.
23. *CSPF.*, *1559–60*, p. 488, 29 March 1560 Throckmorton to Elizabeth; B. N., Mss. Italien, 1721, f. 38, 31 March 1560.
24. La Planche, 257, 267; Baum and Cunitz, *Histoire ecclésiastique*, i, 309.
25. Baum and Cunitz, *Histoire ecclésiastique*, i, 310. This must have been about the last week in March, before Lorraine left for Marmoutier near Tours on 4 April. *CSPF.*, *1559–60*, p. 505, 6 April, 1560, Throckmorton to Elizabeth.

princes, council and Chevaliers de L'Ordre du Roi. Furthermore, he challenged his accusers to stand forth and oppose him in single combat, an invitation which embarrassed Lorraine.[26] He hurriedly caused the king to ajourn the assembly, without debate. The reaction of the duc de Guise is not recorded. Presumably he though it ill-advised to fight a prince. Besides, there was always the possibility that the constable, or anyway his Châtillon nephews, might have championed Condé—a combination to be feared. Clearly the situation was fraught with dangers on both sides. Lorraine is reported to have urged in council that Condé should be arrested, but to have been opposed by Guise on grounds of expediency. Nevertheless, the cardinal "cerchoit [sic] sans cesse nouvelles occasions de luy faire proces."[27]

The Guises also became equally anxious to capture Navarre, since the Huguenots had apparently not yet completely despaired of arousing him to a proper sense of what they considered to be his duty.[28] Meanwhile the Guises ostensibly sought to conciliate Navarre, at the same time requesting him to arrest two pastors, David and Boisnormand—both known to be in his service—on grounds that some prisoners had incriminated them. The threat was thinly veiled.[29] Condé withdrew from court, probably to La Ferté-sous-Jouarre, contacted Navarre and joined him in Béarn.[30] Though specific evidence is lacking, he is said to have received many warnings of plots to kill him.[31] Whether or not this is true, in view of everything that happened later, the testimony of La Planche must be accepted as substantially correct.

If Condé ultimately became the Huguenots' princely leader, it was therefore largely for reasons beyond his control; but this was not to be for at least another year; arguably longer. In the mean-

26. Baum and Cunitz, *Histoire ecclésiastique*, i, 311.

27. Ibid., 309 seq.

28. Condé, *Mémoires*, i, 490–528, Remonstrance adressée au Roy de Navarre, undated.

29. Ibid., 398–402, 19 April 1560, Francis II to Navarre; La Planche, 247.

30. Aumale, *Histoire des princes de Condé*, i, 74. He had gone by 12 April, and very likely a week or so earlier. *CSPF.*, *1559–60*, p. 534, 12 April 1560, Throckmorton to Elizabeth.

31. La Planche, 276.

while, he was further pursued and outraged by the Guises, who left him no alternative, both in honor and in common sense, but to champion their enemies. This had little to do with religion.

It was therefore the definitively Calvinist admiral Coligny who first emerged as the Huguenots' effective leader. He strove to obtain their recognition, and to ensure their survival. As a nephew of the constable Montmorency, his position was already critical in 1560. When the conspiracy of Amboise was betrayed, it was the Guises who ordered him and his brothers (d'Andelot, colonel general of the infantry, and Cardinal Châtillon) to be summoned from home, apparently for fear of their military power.[32] Delaborde, Coligny's biographer, maintains that Coligny knew nothing about Amboise. He quotes Brantôme, who claimed to have heard this from La Bigne, La Renaudie's secretary. It sounds rather unlikely; but the explanation was that he would certainly have disapproved.[33] From the Guise point of view, summoning Coligny was probably a mistake: it provided him with an opportunity to proclaim the widespread discontent, and to demand a "bon edit" permitting freedom of conscience pending a general or national council.[34] Coligny's name was appended to the edict of Amboise, although it did not contain either the freedom of conscience or the council he is said to have demanded.[35] It is interesting to note that the harsh Guisard *mandement* of February 1560 (on the betrayal of the impending conspiracy) was not registered by the *parlement* until 7 March. This was only four days before the more temperate edict of Amboise, which—in that emergency—was not opposed by the Guises.[36] Their followers are said to have received appropriate explanations. This would be consistent with their allegedly having bartered an amnesty in return for the Guise lieutenancy, followed by measures excluding the principal beneficiaries.

32. Ibid., 247; Baum and Cunitz, *Histoire ecclésiastique*, i, 301; Delaborde, *Coligny*, i, 425, 430. He arrived on 24 February, Cardinal Châtillon on the twenty-fifth, and d'Andelot on 15 March.

33. Delaborde, *Coligny*, i, 430.

34. La Planche, 247–48.

35. Fontanon, *Les Édits et ordonnances*, iv, 262; Baum and Cunitz, *Histoire ecclésiastique*, i, 302.

36. Fontanon, *Les Édits et ordonnances*, iv, 261–62, [11] March 1560.

The tumult ensured that the Calvinist movement ceased to be clandestine, even though the churches had not been involved. Furthermore, if it is true that Coligny wished to include freedom of conscience in the edict of Amboise, then it marks the beginning of the overt struggle for recognition. Certainly the *mandement* of February, the edict of Amboise, the pardon, and the letters patent of 22 March 1560, exhibit a legislative confusion which strongly testifies to the existence of a struggle for power in the council. This struggle reached a grotesque climax in July 1561, but continued even beyond the edict of January 1562, by which Huguenot recognition was achieved.

In view of the treatment of Condé—a prince—it was not surprising that the Châtillons should also have withdrawn from Amboise. Nor is it surprising that Catherine de Medici should have sought the fullest possible information, and Coligny's advice. From his home at Châtillon, he replied that the Guises were the real cause of the trouble, because of their violent and illegitimate government. This, if juridically contestable, was widely believed, and the full case against them—only partly religious—was very extensive. Coligny therefore maintained that the troubles would never cease while the Guises remained at court, and he advised Catherine to "prendre elle même les affaires en main," to end the persecution and to enforce the amnesty which had everywhere been countermanded.[37]

It must have been about this time—shortly after the tumult—that the Protestants sent a number of gentlemen to petition the king at Chenonceaux, as conceded by the terms of the pardon.[38] Their uncivil reception at the hands of the Guises reinforced the

37. La Planche, 269–70.
38. This was probably late in April or the first week in May. Catherine was liable to visit Chenonceaux from Amboise. She was there on 20 April and 2 May. By 10 May Lorraine was at Chinon. This may well refer to the undated remonstrance printed in Condé, *Mémoires*, i, 405–10 which, to judge from its contents and his comments, may have been referred to by Throckmorton on 28 April as having been lately printed and spread abroad. But this is uncertain. *CSPF.*, *1559–60*, p. 597, 28 April 1560, Throckmorton to Elizabeth; ibid. *1560–61*, p. 8, 3 May 1560, Throckmorton to Elizabeth; p. 41, 10 May 1560, Lorraine to Throckmorton.

opinion, already expressed by Coligny, that troubles would never cease while the Guises remained at court. Thus, having been rejected a second time, "... chacun regarda de se sauver," and "aucuns aussi dressoyent autres entreprises dont la roine mere eut le vent."[39] Throckmorton reported on 19 May that 6,000 men had assembled near Romorantin "for the same cause that those this lent past came to this towne [Amboise]... and some alarme hath there been at Loches, where the king is presently."[40] This would account for an obscure edict, of Loches, recorded in the *Mémoires* of Condé, "portant abolition de tout ce qui s'est fait par le passé sur le fait de la religion."[41] This, if it was not modified by exclusion clauses, would have exceeded the edict and pardon of Amboise, by granting a total amnesty. But the full text is not printed. Throckmorton also learnt that before the end of June there would be 30,000 men in the field against the Guises.[42] The figure would seem to be suspiciously high. Later that summer Catherine was more fully informed of the Huguenot case by an immensely detailed remonstrance prompted, apparently, by her own enquiries. This was initiated by Chastelus, abbé de la Roche, *maître des requêtes*, drawn up under the pseudonym of Théophile.[43] It was said to have been presented to Catherine at the abbey of Beaulieu, "un jour de l'assomption," thus about the middle of August 1562.

The remonstrance of Théophile was a weighty indictment of the Guises, in particular, their disregard of the edict of Amboise—which had remained unprinted and therefore undistributed—and of the pardon; regulations which were "aucunement gardés." If government by the Guises continued, the remonstrance declared, and as Coligny had said, further trouble was inevitable. This, in itself, must ensure a Calvinist struggle for

39. La Planche, 270.

40. Forbes, *A Full View of the Public Transactions*, i, 468–69, 22 May 1560.

41. Condé, *Mémoires*, i, 539; Delaborde, *Coligny*, i, 449, also referred to the edict of Loches.

42. Forbes, *A Full View of the Public Transactions*, i, 465, 22 May 1560, Throckmorton to Elizabeth.

43. La Planche, 299–302.

recognition. Insofar as religion is concerned—which came second to the government—the remonstrance demanded a council "saint et libre," whether general or national, in which everything should be determined by "la parolle de Dieu." In the meanwhile, they requested freedom of conscience to live according to their confession of faith. The experience of forty years, it pointed out, had shown that the use of fire and sword was ineffective, and there were now too many Protestants—the numbers were certainly exaggerated—to be exterminated. The document inevitably enraged the Guises who, seeking to determine its provenance, unwisely maltreated and imprisoned its bearer, Camus. While the Protestants requested an edict to suspend the persecution pending a council, the Guises sought to impose the inquisition planned under Henry II. The *parlement* of Paris had resisted this for four months but now, it is claimed and was then widely believed, the Guises controlled the *parlement*. [44] The situation, however, was long past the control of any tribunal, even the Inquisition.

The edict of Romorantin, issued in these circumstances in May 1560, was neither tolerant nor inquisitorial. [45] With the Bourbons and Châtillons absent from court and the Guises still in power, no matter how shaken, it could hardly have been tolerant. According to La Planche, it was the temperate chancellor, L'Hospital, who prevented it from being inquisitorial. The edict of Romorantin is generally reputed to have been moderate, which is comparatively true, by the standards of Compiègne. This is because it revived the distinction between heresy and sedition, restoring the former to the sole jurisdiction of the prelates. They were to attend to its extirpation by their own good example—prayer, preaching, persuasion, and the decrees of canon law. The edict, however, comes out very strongly against what are designated as "assemblees illicites, et forces publiques," any participation in which constituted *lèse-majesté*. Such offenses were placed under the sovereign jurisdiction of the royal *cours présidiaux*; preachers, authors of placards, cartels and libels, and printers, salesmen or distributors of the same were held to be similarly guilty of treason. On the

44. Ibid., 299–305.
45. Fontanon, *Les Édits et ordonnances*, iv, 229–30.

face of it, the principal significance of this edict would appear to be the exclusion of the *parlements*, both from the jurisdiction over crimes of heresy, as well as illicit assemblies and public disorders in this connection—certainly the last thing the Guises desired. The restoration of heresy to the jurisdiction of the Chruch, and the explicit and complete exclusion of all civil courts in such cases (article 1) would have the effect, without making the statement, of revoking the death penalty for heresy. It would also leave unmolested Protestants who behaved discreetly. But, even when they did not, they would be subject to far less hostile—and in some cases, positively sympathetic—tribunals than the notoriously Catholic and allegedly Guisard *parlements*. Thus, if the Protestants gained no positive concession, Romorantin was far from being the "édit de l'inquisition" which the Guises reputedly still desired. As one might expect, it was resisted by the disfavored *parlements* and not registered in Paris until 16 July. If not for what it achieved, which was probably very little, it is important for what it illustrates. It was an astute effort, on the part of a powerless government, to avert an extremely dangerous situation and to thwart the hostile purpose of the Guises. But it did not positively concede anything they opposed. On the other hand, it was a grievous revelation of the deadlock character of the conflict, and of the political and administrative nature of the problem of religion, which the tumult of Amboise had only served to exacerbate. Had the edict of Romorantin been observed, it could, in theory, have done much to placate the Protestants and diminish their suffering. It is therefore interesting evidence of an aspiration which was more clearly manifested in the notably clement *lettres de cachet* of 28 January 1561.[46] These letters effectively marked the beginning of Catherine's regency. After Romorantin, there was no further edict, whether Guisard or moderate, in the whole intervening period from May 1560 to January 1561. This would seem to be further evidence of the paralyzing intensity of the struggle for power.

Early in 1560 the country was in a state of turmoil or, as some

46. Michaud, série i, vol. vi, *Mémoires du prince de Condé*, 570–71.

believed, imminent insurrection. Advised by Coligny, Catherine and L'Hospital decided to call an assembly of notables—a proper constitutional procedure. Clearly *something* had to be done, and this measure was not opposed by the Guises.[47] Possibly they hoped to dominate such an assembly, and it might have been a means of recalling the Bourbons to court. However this may be, the assembly opened at Fontainebleau on 21 August 1560, when the remonstrance of Théophile was freshly in mind.[48]

Coligny had offered pro-Protestant advice ever since he was summoned to court in February 1560. But it was not until the assembly at Fontainebleau that he could be said to have emerged as the Huguenots' leader, and in a specifically Calvinist sense. Consequently, the assembly was also a milestone in their struggle for recognition. Condé's position in the summer of 1560 was much less clearly defined, and the two future leaders had not yet, so far as we know, had any occasion to cooperate. If Condé were leading anything at all, which is doubtful, then it was some continuation of Amboise, against the government of the Guises. Any such enterprise would inevitably have carried religious implications, but could hardly have been described as a religious movement. The Bourbons, however, did not attend the assembly. Some people believed that had they come quickly, and in force, they could have ousted the Guises and implemented the program of Amboise. This was because the old constable Montmorency (who was engaged in an acrimonious quarrel with the Guises over the estate of Dammartin) came with his sons and his Châtillon nephews, well accompanied by over 1,600 persons.[49] The combination of Navarre, Condé, Montmorency and his sons, together with Coligny and his brothers, could not have been resisted by the Guises. When hostilities began, two years later, Navarre and

47. B. N., Mss. Italien, 1721, ff. 150–51v, 8 August 1560.

48. The assembly consisted of the council, provincial *gouverneurs*, various seigneurs and captains and the Chevaliers de l'Ordre du Roi, whose membership the Guises augmented by seventeen for the occasion—"un premier desordre . . . à cest ordre," wrote the punning Estienne Pasquier; *Lettres historiques*, 46.

49. B. N., Mss. Italien, 1721, f. 155, 16 August 1560.

Montmorency both sided with the Guises. The Montmorency sons were inactive, and only Coligny and his brothers joined Condé on the Huguenot side. This was a decisive difference.

This dramatic appearance in strength of the Montmorency clan at Fontainebleau was undoubtedly prompted by motives of self-defense, and tends to show that religion, as such, was not yet a predominant issue dividing the nobility. In general the proceedings of Fontainebleau also bear this out. Nevertheless, it was with religion that Coligny concerned himself.

On his departure from Amboise, Coligny had gone to Normandy at the request of Catherine. She wished him to pacify the province and to obtain information.[50] There he is said to have celebrated the cult in a house in Dieppe. When he emerged, for the assembly at Fontainebleau, he brought two substantially similar petitions, one addressed to the king and the other to Catherine. They were read aloud by the secretary of state, de Laubespine.[51] The burden of the petition addressed to the king was that his loyal and obedient subjects, spread in large numbers throughout the kingdom, requested a church, or other suitable premises, in every town, in which to celebrate the cult by day. This would be a sure way of terminating the present troubles, and obviating those which appeared to be imminent. Furthermore, these subjects offered to pay additional taxes, in order to prove that they were wrongfully accused of tax evasion. The text of these petitions, as printed in the *Mémoires* of Condé, does not precisely tally with the summary of their alleged contents in the "Récit de ce qui s'est passé à l'assemblée de Fontainebleau."[52] According to this source, the petition to the king expressly condemned the events of Amboise. These are said to have been perpetrated in the name of religion—but without consent of the Calvinist churches—by seditious persons from whom they wished to be dissociated. Also, according to this source, the peti-

50. Very likely this journey to Normandy also had something to do with the affairs of Scotland. Delaborde, *Coligny*, i, 446, 459.

51. Condé, *Mémoires*, ii, *supplement*, 645–48, gives the text of both petitions.

52. "... et mesmes si mestier estoit, ne refuserions de payer de plus grands Tributs," Lalourcé et Duval, *Recueil des pièces originales*, i, 66–118.

tion addressed to Catherine contained an additional clause inviting royal officials to inspect their lives, morals, meetings and procedure. This is a proposal which was later contained in the Protestant petition of 11 June 1561,[53] and subsequently included in the edict of January 1562. The version of these petitions printed in the *Mémoires* of Condé appears and claims to be the formal text, "collation faite avec l'original." Nevertheless, the purely evangelical point of view of the Calvinist communities, expressed in the *Récit* account, clearly illustrates the initial dichotomy in the Huguenot movement.[54] While its various strands were to become inextricably plaited together, they did not thereby cease to have a separate existence. This dichotomy continued, in subtle ways, to complicate the problems and bedevil the leadership of the Huguenot movement.

Having emerged at Fontainebleau as the Calvinist leader, Coligny served the interests of the Calvinist churches, without interruption, for the rest of his life. It was not for nothing that he became the Protestant hero and martyr although, as a *grand seigneur*, he also had personal, class and political interests to defend. He was necessarily concerned with every aspect of the Huguenot cause. The same could never be said of Condé, although he was loyal enough in his way, and was ultimately murdered by the same enemies. But, as a prince of the blood, he was subject to inescapable personal and political conflicts and, to him, the churches were a secondary concern. The wonder is that two such different leaders should have cooperated so well, for both these kinds of leadership were simultaneously necessary once the movement had led to hostilities. Indeed, one might even postulate a triple leadership, pastoral, seigneurial, and princely, though they were not always clearly defined.

By April 1560, after the events of Amboise, it was already too late for the Bourbons to compound the dual political and religious

53. Condé, *Mémoires*, ii, 372. The two texts have not, however, simply been confused. The version given by Baum and Cunitz, *Histoire ecclésiastique*, i, 316–17, mentions higher taxes and the supervision of royal commissioners.

54. This dichotomy is a complex problem which might well form the subject of a separate study.

role. The Huguenots' struggle for recognition and survival, and
the effort to secure their juridical position, is primarily concerned
with the more purely Calvinist strand; hence the importance of
the first petition for *temples,* and of Coligny's performance at the
assembly of Fontainebleau. Coligny's turn to speak came on the
third day, 24 August. Apart from supporting the contents of the
petitions, he objected to the special, additional guard with which
the Guises had surrounded the king. His inaccessibility was a
major cause for complaint in the extensive literature of opposition. Coligny is reported to have said that it was dangerous for a
king to appear to be afraid of his people; they, in turn, would fear
and suspect the king. Coligny further called for an estates general,
and a suspension of persecution pending a council, whether general or national. There was no longer anything new in all this—it
was only to be expected—but all sources agree that criticism of
the royal guard infuriated the duc de Guise. He hotly denied that
it was misguided and unnecessary, "et y a grande apparence que
dès lors se forma en son cueur la haine contre l'ammiral qu'il a
tousjours gardée depuis."[55] Guise also objected that the two petitions were unsigned. When the admiral offered to obtain 10,000
signatures, Guise angrily returned that he could oppose a million,
"dont il seroit le capitaine." "Cecy," wrote Pasquier, "nous est un
certain prognostic que l'un et l'autre ... seront quelque jour conducteurs de deux contraires partis, qui ne sont encores formez."[56]
Thus the Guises had not only clashed with Condé at Amboise,
but now also with Coligny. This time it was definitely over religion, for Coligny did not, in any direct sense, threaten the Guises
politically.

The outcome of the assembly of Fontainebleau was a decision
to summon the estates general for 10 December 1560, and an
assembly of the clergy on 20 January 1561, to prepare for a council. It appears also to have been rather vaguely agreed that, where
no sedition occurred, persecution should meanwhile be suspended. Lorraine is reported to have said at Fontainebleau that,
for the moment, those who went unarmed to preaching, sang

55. La Planche, 362.
56. Pasquier, *Lettres historiques,* 46.

psalms and absented themselves from mass, should not be perse- ← Ⱃ
cuted. L'Hospital, however, issued a warning in his report to the
parlement of Paris: "N'a este donnée liberté d'introduire nouvelle
secte, ne impunité d'icelle pour l'avoir renvoyé à la congnoissance
aux juges de l'eglise"—a reference to the edict of Romorantin.
L'Hospital also recommended that the prelates should use their
ecclesiastical authority with moderation, preferring "douces et
aimables exhortations" to severity.[57]

This was the beginning of the road to recognition; it was also
juridical chaos. The edicts of persecution had been undermined,
but not revoked. No religious concessions had been made, yet the
Protestants, if peaceful, were to go unmolested. Just what would
or would not be tolerated must therefore depend on immediate
local conditions. Clearly nothing more could be expected to happen before the meeting of the estates general and the assembly of
the clergy at which, it had been announced, anybody was to be
permitted to express an opinion and depart in safety.[58] In the ←
meanwhile, it was forlornly hoped that everyone would behave
reasonably and with moderation. This was not at all what the
Guises had in mind. They were more than ever determined to
exterminate the Protestants and pursue the Bourbon princes. At
the end of October Navarre and Condé were lured to Orléans
on the pretext of the estates general. Condé was arrested and
irregularly condemned.[59]

The sudden death of Francis II on 5 December, after a short
illness, changed everything, literally over night. The next day
Catherine became regent for Charles IX, in conjunction with
Navarre. Condé was reprieved, and the Guises, though still in the
council, no longer exercised the power of the crown. Thus, with
an estates general also about to open, and an assembly of the

57. La Planche, 363–64; Baum and Cunitz, *Histoire ecclésiastique*, i,
324; Delaborde, *Coligny*, i, 473; Condé, *Mémoires*, i, 574–78, discours de
L'Hospital au parlement de Paris, 7 September 1560; 578–80, 10 September 1560, letters summoning the clergy to Paris for 20 January 1561.

58. Condé, *Mémoires*, i, 578–80, 10 September 1560, letters summoning the clergy; Paris, *Négociations*, 486–90, edict of 31 August 1560.

59. Just what the Guises had in mind belongs to the full story of the
origins of the civil war, and cannot be entered into here.

clergy scheduled for the following month, the political demands of the Huguenots had virtually been met.[60]

Both Coligny and Condé returned to the council in March 1561 which must, presumably, mark the beginning of their cooperation in leadership. They were both influential at court during 1561, although we do not hear very much about either of them until the beginning of 1562.[61] The prospects of the Huguenots were, at least theoretically, enormously improved in the new reign. Thus the year 1561 naturally witnessed a powerful resumption of the struggle for recognition.

This struggle had already recommenced with the estates general, which opened on 13 December 1560, although members had been unrealistically forbidden to discuss religion.[62] This could have been averted by countermanding the estates because the king had died. But it was hoped that they would ratify the regency and vote substantial sums of money. L'Hospital therefore tried to divert them from religion, on the grounds that the pope had already announced the resumption of the council of Trent for the following Easter.[63] Accounts of the estates general are confused, incomplete and lacking in dates. It appears, however, that the Protestants declared themselves to have been wronged by accusations of having tried to establish their religion by force of arms. They denied the impossibility—expressed in his opening harangue by l'Hospital—of good relations between persons of different religions. They appeared inclined to turn to Navarre— to whom their *cahiers* were presented—presumably as being more Calvinist than Catherine, albeit doubtfully so. The *noblesse*, however, recognized Catherine, from whom they hoped for support, and presented a written petition requesting *temples* for themselves—a scandalous attitude which is hard to explain.[64]

---

60. The assembly of the clergy was postponed to 25 February, but did not take place.

61. Sutherland, *The Massacre of St. Bartholomew*, 14, n. 4.

62. Baum and Cunitz, *Histoire ecclésiastique*, i, 430–31.

63. The papal bull announcing the council was published on 20 November 1560. Baum and Cunitz, *Histoire ecclésiastique*, i, 429–30. Easter 1561 was on 6 April.

64. Ibid., 487–90.

In view of these events, the timing of the *lettres de cachet* of 28 January 1561, otherwise known as letters for the release of prisoners, was clearly not an accident, but was calculated to conciliate the *noblesse*. [65] The letters also resumed the spirit of the edict and pardon of Amboise, and the edict of Loches, which had certainly never been implemented. While Romorantin might be placed in the same category, the *lettres de cachet* is the first regulation to emphasize, in the first instance, the problem of law and order: "Regardant," it begins, "... principallement aux choses plus nécessaire pour... maintenir la tranquillité publique..." The principal provision was the release of all prisoners held for religious offenses and the cessation of all prosecutions, even in the case of those who had assembled in arms or contributed money. The sole exception was the leaders of sedition—a further emphasis on the problem of public order. *Léttres de cachet* were uniquely issued upon the sovereign authority of the king, the *cachet* being his personal seal. Since the accession of Charles IX, this was held by Catherine, in place of Lorraine. The letters of 28 January stated, however, that they were to have the same validity as letters patent; these, for good reasons, had been deferred. Clearly the *parlements* would not have registered, without obstruction or delay, letters patent amounting to an amnesty. They had already been offended by the edict of Romorantin, which the *lettres de cachet* now confirmed. This was, therefore, another step, at least in theory and in law, towards the cessation of persecution.

The edicts of Amboise and Romorantin and the January *lettres de cachet* had all arisen from political crises. The next edict, of 19 April 1561, also followed a serious crisis: a quarrel between Navarre and Guise over power and authority had almost overthrown the government and brought the nobles to the brink of civil war. [66] Since Navarre had been there all the time, the quarrel may very well have arisen from the return of Condé and Coligny to the council. This inspired the Protestants with hope—and ←

65. Michaud, série i, vol. vi, *Mémoires du prince de Condé*, 570–71.
66. La Ferrière, *Catherine de Médicis, Lettres*, i, 586, 3 March 1561, Catherine to Limoges.

some audacity—and was extremely inauspicious for the Catholic cause.[67] This crisis was barely over when a session of the estates of Paris and the Ile-de-France met on 20 March to elect deputies for a further assembly of the estates general, scheduled to open at Pontoise on 1 May.[68] Contrary to their instructions, the Paris estates not only discussed, but also challenged, the regency. But Catherine and Navarre emerged confirmed in their regency partnership; each needed the other. In order to avoid any further embarrassment, and similar happenings in other local estates, the Paris assembly was dissolved and the estates general postponed to 1 August, at Melun.[69] Letters patent, issued on 25 March, announced the formalized regency partnership of Catherine and Navarre, and summoned all the local estates to meet on 25 May, and the provincial estates on 10 June, to consider the voting of money. They were forbidden to discuss either the government, which was settled, or religion, which was not. To determine the problems of religion, it had been decided to "faire venir... des plus grands, dignes et vertueux personnaiges... gens de saincte vie, doctrine et savoir, pour prendre d'eux advis sur ce qui se devra faire... attendant le fruict d'un bon Concile." In other words, there was to be some sort of national council, pending the outcome of a general council.[70] Meanwhile, everyone was to live "catholiquement sans aucun scandale."

The Guise reaction to the crisis of March 1561, to changes in the composition of the council, the regency partnership of Catherine and Navarre and their relatively liberal religious policy, was to form a close, Catholic cabal, known as the Triumvirate.[71] It consisted of Guise himself, Marshal Saint-André and the constable Montmorency, who together virtually controlled the army. Montmorency, though formerly an enemy of the Guises, was unshakeably Catholic. The Triumvirate was the nu-

---

67. Sutherland, *The Massacre of St. Bartholomew*, 14–15, 14, n. 4.
68. A further meeting of the estates general was called because no money was voted at Orléans.
69. De Ruble, *Antoine de Bourbon*, iii, 62–64.
70. Condé, *Mémoires*, ii, 281–84, 25 March 1561, lettre de convocation des états généraux.
71. Michaud, série i, vol. vi, *Mémoires-journaux du duc de Guise*, 464–65.

cleus of a Catholic league, which they looked to Philip II to direct. Thus the Triumvirate was dedicated to the preservation of Catholicism, primarily through the power of Spain. Their first and immediate purpose was to win Navarre from the new religion, lest he convert the king, and to persuade Navarre to turn, with them, against that pernicious sect. If they were successful in this, "seront lors faciles et abregez les moyens de la guerre future." But, if Navarre refused, Spain was to make preparations during the winter, and fall upon his kingdom of Navarre in the south of France. Should he and his followers put up any resistance, Guise would declare himself "chef de la confession catholique." Armed with a commission to extirpate all Protestants in France, Guise would then undertake the destruction of the whole house of Bourbon. It is not clear who was to issue the commission—presumably the pope. The idea was to be revived in 1563, shortly before the murder of Guise. While this war of extermination was taking place in France, the emperor was to prevent the Protestant princes from sending help. The Protestant cantons in Switzerland were to be extinguished with the help of the Papacy, and Geneva, source of the infection, by the duke of Savoy. These things having been accomplished, the Catholics would then attack the Protestant princes of Germany, and other neighboring countries, which meant England. It is therefore clear that, from about April 1561, the Triumvirate *intended to exterminate Protestantism by means of war, not only in France but also elsewhere in Europe.* From the very beginning, the struggle for power and the struggle for religion were one and the same endeavor. This was a long-term program, not a specific project and, in view of what happened in the next thirty years, there is no reason to doubt its general veracity.

Navarre was to be seduced by the prospect of his heart's real desire, namely compensation for Spanish Navarre, conquered by Ferdinand of Aragon in 1512. It appears, however, that the intentions of the Triumvirate were not kept secret for very long.[72] Catherine, therefore, realizing what was at stake, skillfully enter-

72. B. N., Mss. Fr., 6618, f. 8, 29 August 1561, de Laubespine to Limoges.

tained Navarre with similar hopes. Consequently there followed a prolonged struggle for his allegiance, which the *Triumvirs* finally won; but not until February 1562.[73]

The important religious festival of Easter, which fell on 6 April, was the occasion of numerous clashes and disturbances, both in Paris and in the provinces. This unfortunately tended to strengthen the Catholic contention that the Protestants were seditious. Not long before, Jean de Morvillier, bishop of Orléans, had described the troubles and seditions as being beyond human counsel and remedy.[74] Referring to demands for pastors, Calvin wrote to Bullinger on 24 May, "on assiège ma porte comme celle d'un roi."[75] This was the time of maximum Calvinist expansion, and the movement had run out of pastoral control. "Cest manière de faire ne me plaist aucunement," de Bèze wrote to Jeanne d'Albret, "ce brisement de sépultres est entièrement inexcusable."[76] In these extremely critical circumstances, the edict of 19 April was intended to be conciliatory.[77] Not surprisingly, it emphasized the problem of public order and the prevention of mutual provocations, insults and outrages, which were expressly prohibited. While there could, at that moment, be no question of positive concessions, the edict passed as being pro-Protestant in the eyes of angry Catholics. This was because it prohibited the molestation of people in their own houses, which, its opponents asserted, obliquely authorized preaching in private. Furthermore, it reiterated the provisions of the *lettres de cachet* for the release of prisoners, and permitted the return of religious exiles and the recovery of their property, provided they abjured. This provision for the recovery of property rescinded one of the more vexatious clauses of the edict of Châteaubriant. The April edict was sent

73. Sutherland, "Antoine de Bourbon, King of Navarre and the French Crisis of Authority, 1559–1562," in *French Government and Society 1500–1850*, Ed. J. F. Bosher.

74. B. N., Mss. Cinq Cents Colbert, 394, f. 37, 7 March 1561, Morvillier to Rennes.

75. *Bull. Prot.*, xiv, 1865, p. 319, 24 May 1561, Calvin to Bullinger.

76. Rochambeau, *Lettres d'Antoine de Bourbon et de Jehanne d'Albret*, 233, 13 May 1561, de Bèze to Jeanne d'Albret.

77. Condé, *Mémoires*, ii, 334–35.

directly to royal officials, dispensing with registration by the
parlement of Paris. The Guises were then obstructing Condé's
application to the *parlement* for a declaration of innocence in respect of the charges brought against him at Orléans.[78]

Tension of every kind was considerable and serious disorders,
especially in Paris, continued into the summer. It was clear that
proper discussion of the specifically religious issues could not
much longer be safely postponed. According to Chantonnay, the
Spanish ambassador, the edict of April threw all Catholics into
desperation.[79] Thus, immediately after the coronation on 15
May, Lorraine called for an assembly of princes, seigneurs, and
the council in the *parlement* of Paris, "pour y faire solennellement
une bonne loy inviolable."[80] This would put an end to the cir-
cumvention of the *parlement*, a procedure which favored the Protestants. Furthermore, the proposed new edict must surely avert a
religious *colloque*—namely a disputation between Catholics and
Protestants. This probability accounts for the important Protestant petition of 11 June 1561. It was presented by the seigneur
d'Esternay, a Protestant of Picardy and a follower of Condé, on
behalf of the "deputez des Eglises esparses parmi le Royaume de
France."[81] The second Calvinist national synod, which had met
at Poitiers on 10 March, decided that each province should elect a
Protestant representative to reside at court in order to supervise
the affairs of their churches. They constituted a redoubtable pressure group, and Esternay was one of them.

The order and content of the petition of 11 June appears to
reflect the Protestant anxiety that, if Lorraine were to force the

---

78. Baum and Cunitz, *Histoire ecclésiastique*, i, 507; Delaborde, *Coligny*, i, 506–7; Condé, *Mémoires*, ii, 373–94. Coligny appears to have been
at home at this time. B. N., Mss. Fr., 3192, f. 27, 9 April 1561, Coligny
to Catherine.

79. Condé, *Mémoires*, ii, 7, 22 April 1561, Chantonnay to Catherine.

80. Baum and Cunitz, *Histoire ecclésiastique*, i, 509, 516.

81. Condé, *Mémoires*, ii, 370–72; de Ruble, *Antoine de Bourbon*, iii,
101. Aymon, *Tous les synodes nationaux*, i, 114–16. Esternay was one of the
leading Protestants whom Lorraine tried to murder in August 1568,
along with Condé and Coligny. Sutherland, *The Massacre of St. Bartholomew*, 76.

religious issue in an assembly of notables, the Protestants would be deprived of an opportunity to expound and defend their confession of faith in a national *colloque*. They were inevitably hoping for such an opportunity, because it had been conceded, in principle, by the letters patent of 10 September 1560, after the assembly of Fontainebleau. The letters had summoned an assembly of the clergy for 20 January 1561.[82] That had been postponed to 25 February, but still no assembly took place. The most recent summons, of 25 March, had not repeated the general permission for anyone to attend. The June petition denied that the Protestants were either seditious or heretical, and requested the king to consider their cause and to have it examined: "prendre cognoissance de nostre cause, et commander que nostre Doctrine et nostre vie soyent examinées selon la parole de Dieu . . . ." This, it said, they had in no wise contravened. They therefore presented their confession of faith and requested permission to expound and defend it; also to recall various exiles, with a guarantee of safe conduct. Clearly there could be no such disputation if Lorraine were to succeed in obtaining what he considered "une bonne loy inviolable."[83] It is to be presumed, from the rest of the petition, that the relatively liberal provisions of recent edicts had not been implemented. Thus it requested, in the meanwhile, an end to persecution in public and in private, protection against violent outrages, and the release of religious prisoners. Finally, it requested permission to hold services in public—which would demonstrate Protestant innocence—and repeated the demand of August 1560 for *temples* or other premises, since they were too numerous to meet in private houses. This is followed by the proposal that, to eliminate any question of sedition, and to establish their declared loyalty and obedience, their meetings should be supervised by royal officials. The very next day, 12 June, the prelates were summoned to meet on 20 July.[84] This was not an

82. Condé, *Mémoires*, i, 579.

83. Baum and Cunitz, *Histoire ecclésiastique*, i, 509.

84. Le Plat, *Monumentorum ad Historiam Concilii Tridentini*, iv, 704–5, 12 June 1561.

announcement of the desired *colloque*, but it was at least an essential preliminary.

Lorraine's proposal for an assembly of the council in *parlement* was, nevertheless, adopted, and the Protestant petition was submitted to it. Extensive deliberations, described by Pasquier as "les pourparlers de Paris," lasted from mid-June for about a month.[85] Evidence relating to these discussions, and the events which led to the *colloque* of Poissy in September, is confused and incomplete. It is clear, however, as one might expect, that the debate was heated, and the assembly of some 120 to 140 persons was fairly equally divided. According to Pasquier, Catherine imposed a secret, written vote on the motion, "qu'il falloit ou suivre l'Eglise Romaine . . . ou vuider le Royaume avec permission de vendre ses biens." This was carried by a majority of only three.[86] So small a majority in so great a matter inevitably created an uproar. Once again, there was an angry exchange between Coligny and the duc de Guise, who menacingly declared that he would not hesitate to employ his sword in the execution of the proposed edict.[87]

The edict, published at the end of July, was unsatisfactory to everyone.[88] It was regarded by the Protestants as a disappointing setback because it prohibited all their meetings, in public or in private (article 4). Those held in private had been at least tacitly permitted by the edict of 19 April. The moderates, however, obtained confirmation of the edict of Romorantin, which excluded the jurisdiction of the *parlements* in heresy cases. Banishment was to be the maximum punishment for simple heresy, pending the outcome of a general or national council. This edict therefore expressly excluded the death penalty, which was now reserved for the possession of firearms. The carrying of swords, knives and daggers was also severely restricted. On the

---

85. Various dates are given, the longest being 18 June to 19 July 1561.
86. Pasquier, *Lettres historiques*, 64; de Ruble, *Antoine de Bourbon*, iii, 101.
87. Pasquier, *Lettres historiques*, 65.
88. Fontanon, *Les Édits et ordonnances*, iv, 264–65.

pro-Protestant side, article 7 contained a complete pardon and rehabilitation, without exception, for all religious offenses— including sedition—committed since the death of Henry II. This was followed by the remarkable stipulation that magistrates were not to pursue people indiscreetly or "abuser de l'execution du contenue en ces presentes," a transparent invitation to ignore the clause prohibiting private meetings. This curious, contradictory, self-defeating, provisional edict further reflected the dangerous state of administrative and legislative paralysis, already noted in May 1560. Pasquier described the edict as neutral, although his analysis suggests that he saw it as marginally pro-Protestant.[89] This opinion was emphatically not shared by the pastor La Rivière, who declared the edict to have been made to satisfy "le roy Philippe et le pape et pour tyrer quelque argent des ecclesiastiques."[90] The pastor Merlin, however, reassured Protestants that Condé intended them to go on meeting, but quietly, and in small numbers.[91] It was given out that the edict would never be executed. This was later confirmed by L'Hospital, in his speech to the assembly of Saint-Germain in January 1562. The edict, he said, had been tacitly abrogated and never implemented.[92] It is small wonder, therefore, if provincial officials like Montpézat, *sénéchal* of Poitou, complained of the ambiguity of the edicts, so that "chascun les interprete pour favoriser son opinion."[93]

The scrambled edict of July can hardly have been a disappointment, since nothing constructive was to be expected. The hopes of the Protestants were now fixed on receiving a proper

89. Pasquier, *Lettres historiques*, 64–65.

90. Bibliothèque de Genève, Mss. Français, 402. f. 59, 10 August 1561, La Rivière to de Bèze; Baum and Cunitz, *Histoire ecclésiastique*, i, 520, n. 1.

91. Delaborde, *Les Protestants à la Cour de Saint-Germain*, 78–80, 14 July 1561.

92. De Ruble, *Antoine de Bourbon*, iii, 103–4; l'Hospital, *Oeuvres*, i, 449–50. This appears to be a corrupt text. It is described as being a speech to a commission of the estates at Pontoise, 26 August 1561. It is clear, however, that it was addressed to the assembly at Saint-Germain in January 1562.

93. B. N., Mss. N. A. F., 5850, f. 11, 9 July 1561, Montpézat to Catherine.

hearing at the forthcoming national council. Indeed, the "députés en cour" had already elected their Protestant representatives by 11 July. But it was not until 25 July that they were actually invited by letters patent: "tous nosdits subjects de quelque estat, qualité et condition qu'ils soyent, qui auront... à remonstrer quelques choses, qu'ils puissent seurement... et sans aucune craincte, venir... en ladite Assemblée... de Poissy."[94]

In August, while the clergy were in session at Poissy, the Protestants began to arrive. They were represented by twelve leading pastors, including de Bèze; Pierre Martyr arrived later. There were also about twenty lay deputies. The clergy, however, appeared disinclined to meet them. In their initial session, on 1 August, they had already decided not to discuss doctrine, which should be left to Trent. They would confine themselves to the reform of abuses. On 14 August Cardinal de Tournon proposed that they should send to the king "pour mettre ordre aux huguenots et dévoyés," which hardly suggested a conciliatory attitude towards those who had assembled under safe conduct, to seek a solution to the problem of religion. Clearly this was embarrassing for Catherine. She summoned everyone to Saint-Germain on 24 August partly, no doubt, to witness a formal reconciliation between Guise and Condé. This charade served the necessary purpose of enabling them both to appear at court.[95]

These adverse circumstances explain why the Protestants should have presented another petition, on 17 August, asking to be heard. If they were to be heard at all—which was still doubtful—they feared that it would not be according to any just rules of procedure.[96] This is what the petition was about, and their fears were all too fully justified. While Catherine forced the prelates to consider the petition, Lorraine and others complained to the king, on 29 August, of Huguenot outrages, at the same time offering him a "certain" sum of money.[97] On 5 September

94. *Bull. Prot.*, xiv, 1865, pp. 363–64, 11 July 1561, Marlorat to Calvin; Condé, *Mémoires*, i, 41–42.
95. De Ruble, *Le Colloque de Poissy*, 21.
96. Baum and Cunitz, *Histoire ecclésiastique*, i, 543–44.
97. De Ruble, *Le Colloque de Poissy*, 24–25.

there was an attempt to set fire to the convent in which the prelates were meeting and, on 8 September, a dozen theologians from the Sorbonne came to prevent the *colloque* from taking place.[98] Consequently the Protestants petitioned again, that same day. The *Sorbonnistes* were rejected by the crown, but the Protestants' petition had neither been conceded nor fully answered when the *colloque* opened next day, 9 September. It is clear that the crown had been obliged to insist on its opening, and neither the circumstances nor the atmosphere were favorable to the Protestants. It was not at all the free, open and holy council that had for so long been envisaged. Furthermore, on 19 September, the cardinal legate of Ferrara arrived, for the express purpose of traversing the proceedings.[99] In this he was supported by Diego Lainez, general of the Jesuits.

The full story of the *colloque* of Poissy is a specialist study apart,[100] but there is one aspect of it which must be emphasized here. Just as Catherine had, with some difficulty, prevented it from being completely sabotaged at the outset, so she also struggled to sustain it. When the controversy focused on the problem of the Eucharist, she adopted a proposal to appoint a small committee to tackle the problem in private. This committee was composed of five moderate Catholics, described by de Bèze as "gens doctes et traictables,"[101] and five pastors. They were required to devise "quelque raisonnable confession touchant ce point de la Cène."[102]

The committee began work on 29 September. It studied a number of different formulae, but without reaching full agreement. One of these formulae was presented to the prelates on 1

98. Baum and Cunitz, *Histoire ecclésiastique*, i, 555; de Ruble, *Le Colloque de Poissy*, 26.

99. De Ruble, *Le Colloque de Poissy*, 32–34.

100. See on this: Nugent, *The Colloque of Poissy*; Sutherland, "The Cardinal of Lorraine and the *colloque* of Poissy, 1561: A Reassessment," *Journal of Ecclesiastical History*, July 1977.

101. Bibliothèque de Genève, Mss. Latin, 117, f. 1, 3 September 1561, de Bèze to the elector Palatine.

102. Nugent, *The Colloque of Poissy*, 161, seq.; de Ruble, *Le Colloque de Poissy*, 40–45.

October. They immediately condemned it. The next day, they disclaimed the Catholics on the committee and threatened to expel them from the assembly. When, on Catherine's insistence, a further formula was submitted to the prelates on 4 October, they appointed a commission to examine it. Having thus appeared to take the proposal seriously, they denounced it as captious and heretical. At the same time, they produced an alternative, Catholic formula. Its wording was such that no Protestant could possibly accept it. On 9 October the cardinal of Lorraine clearly aligned himself with this majority opinion. Lorraine had genuinely wanted the *colloque* to succeed, by means of agreement on a moderate, Lutheran formula. But, when this endeavor had failed, he reverted to character.

This was the end of the *colloque* of Poissy. Probably everyone of goodwill had looked to a council—whether national or general—as the one true means of reaching a religious solution. But who had ventured to look beyond? *Given the desire, it was* possible to produce a formula compounding different points of view, provided that a Real Presence was neither denied nor too explicitly defined. But, apart from the intransigence of many members of the *colloque*, the problem of what to do with a compromise formula would still have remained.[103] It is hardly plausible that France, in 1561, could have adopted and enforced a Gallican confession. Besides, any agreement reached at Poissy would surely have been rejected at Trent. It was unrealistic, however defensible, to proclaim the criterion of heresy as conformity to, or deviation from, the demonstrable word of God, as contained in the Old and New Testaments. In this respect the Calvinists were justifiably confident in the learning and ability of their leaders. But the difficulty, which had somehow become obscured, was that of withdrawal from, or submission to, the Church of Rome. So that while, on one level, compromise and conciliation were not impossible, there did also exist a clash of absolutes. If it is difficult

103. Various formulae discussed are printed in Nugent, *The Colloque of Poissy*, 233–40. Two of the more Calvinist proposals are printed in the *CSPF.*, *1561–62*, p. 342, 30 September 1561, translated from the original Latin.

to determine the point of no return in the affairs of France, it was certainly not later than October 1561.

The provisional edict of July 1561, pending the outcome of the council, was therefore followed, on 20 October, by a far more savagely Catholic regulation.[104] This, presumably, represented the triumph of the prelates, since it did not reflect the attitude of the regency. Certainly it played strongly into the hands of the clergy, from whom the government badly needed money; and they could hardly have been in a stronger position. Thus capital punishment was reintroduced. This was not specifically for heresy, but for what one is tempted to suspect they deplored even more, namely, the seizure of, or interference with, churches and Church property; also for mutual abuses and offensive entry into each other's houses. It repeated the prohibition against the possession of firearms, which were all to be surrendered to royal officials. The Gallican Church was a major vested interest, and this edict reveals what the prelates were most concerned about.

After the failure of Poissy, therefore, the Huguenot struggle for recognition and survival was never more desperate, acute and starkly dangerous. But the immediate departure from court of the Guises,[105] however ominous in itself, temporarily strengthened the Protestants and moderates. Catherine was advised to call yet another assembly. This one was to draft a further provisional edict—apparently during the royal minority, and presumably pending the outcome of the council of Trent. It was also to reply to the pressing demand for *temples* renewed by the estates general of Pontoise.[106] It was beginning to be widely felt that the pressure to permit preaching in *temples* could not much longer be resisted. It was already happening illegally and was going to happen anyway. Meanwhile the Protestants presented yet another petition, requesting their *temples* and the revocation of the edict of July.[107] Little time was wasted after the closure of the *colloque* of Poissy.

104. Fontanon, *Les Édits et ordonnances*, iv, 265–67.

105. Valois, "Project d'enlèvement d'un enfant de France," *Bibliothèque de l'École des Chartes*, lxxv, 1914, p. 44, 21 October 1561, de Laubespine to Limoges.

106. Baum and Cunitz, *Histoire ecclésiastique*, i, 742.

107. Condé, *Mémoires*, ii, 575–78, undated, but about November or December 1561.

By 12 November an assembly had already been summoned, to consist of the council plus two representatives from each of the eight *parlements*.[108] This was doubtless on the advice of Coligny, among others, since it is exactly the type of assembly for which he had called during the *pourparlers de Paris* in July. According to Chantonnay, he had been supported by Navarre, Condé and one of the Montmorency sons.[109]

The assembly of Saint-Germain opened early in January 1562.[110] It was addressed by the chancellor, L'Hospital, who was courageously outspoken in emphasizing the real issues. He said that persecution and doctrinal conciliation had both failed, and that those who still advised the former, advised war. The immediate problem therefore was civil and administrative: it was not to decide which of the two confessions was the better, but whether or not to authorize preaching. Extreme Catholics once again did their utmost to traverse proceedings. But, as l'Hospital later told the truculent *parlement* of Paris, the State could only be restored to one religion by the extermination or banishment of all the Protestants, and neither expedient was feasible. This accounts for the edict of 17 January 1562, "brief, de tolerer ce scandale pour eviter un plus grand."[111]

The principal outcome of the assembly of Saint-Germain, as contained in the edict of January 1562, was to authorize preaching. But it rejected the central Protestant demand for *temples* by a majority of twenty-four. Catherine de Medici, who had spoken last, and at length, must have supported this majority, to judge from the approval of Chantonnay, the Spanish ambassador, and the cardinal legate Ferrara, who said that she wished to satisfy "sinon en tout du moins en partie ces esprits fascheux." As Ferrara reported, her hope and intention was to "pacifier les

---

108. Šusta, *Die Römische Curie*, i, 304, 12 November 1561, Ferrara to Borromeo.

109. *Archivo documental Español, Francia*, ii, 279–84, 7 July 1561, Chantonnay to Philip II.

110. Pasquier said 3 January; *Lettres historiques*, 81. Santa-Croce said 7 January; Sainte-Croix, *Lettres*, 20, 15 January 1561. The latter date hardly seems possible.

111. Pasquier, *Lettres historiques*, 81–85; Fontanon, *Les Édits et ordonnances*, iv, 267–69.

troubles... par toutes les voyes les plus faciles et les plus douces."[112] The right to preach was, after all, the principal concession which permission to build churches would have embraced. Salvation could only lie in the promulgation, acceptance and enforcement of a reasonable compromise which, it was already clear, was not going to be a doctrinal one. This was why the Protestants welcomed the edict, not without reservations, but as a hopeful beginning.[113]

Apart from its vital concession, the edict was otherwise predominantly Catholic in tone. Even the pope thought it, on balance, rather more favorable to the Catholics than to the Protestants.[114] Article 1 began by reiterating from the edict of October 1561 that all Church property, revenue, and so forth, was to be restored; no other churches were to be seized or built, anywhere; there was to be no interference with the working of the Catholic Church and no iconoclasm, all upon *pain of death*. It was still expressly forbidden to meet publicly or privately by day or by night within the towns, but meetings for religious purposes were permitted outside towns. In some cases this was to be with the supervision of royal officials, such as the Protestants themselves had proposed in their petition of 11 June 1561. Prohibitions were repeated against mutual abuse, incitements and provocations; also against the possession of firearms and—a new development—the enrollment of men and the raising of money. These were sinister indications of the fear of impending war. The death penalty was reimposed for a second offense in the distribution or printing of placards and libels. It is interesting to note that article 14 expressly stated that the purpose of this edict was "la conservation du repos general et universel de nostre Royaume, et pour obvier a tous troubles et seditions." As with the ultimate edict of Nantes, no one claimed that this was good, or even satisfactory; but it was necessary in the interests of peace.

112. D'Este, *Négociations*, 14–16, 17 January 1562, Ferrara to Borromeo; Condé, *Mémoires*, ii, 20, 22 January 1562, Chantonnay to Tisnacq. Chantonnay was more explicit than Ferrara.
113. Bibliothèque de Genève, Mss. Fr., 402, f. 3, 22 January 1561/62, anonymous letter written from Saint-Germain to the pastors of Geneva.
114. Šusta, *Die Römische Curie*, ii, 413–18, 15 March 1562, the pope and Borromeo to Ferrara; also 416, n. 3.

Permission to assemble for religious purposes outside the towns meant, at least in theory, that everyone was accommodated. It is simply for this reason that, all else forgotten, the edict of January was subsequently regarded as the best. With the exception of the abortive peace of Monsieur, 1576, all later edicts were restrictive, specifying particular *lieux du culte*, to the exclusion of all other places. This raised the most acrimonious quarrels and insupera- bly difficult administrative problems, always leaving a proportion of Protestants deprived.

With permission to hold assemblies for all peaceful purposes, the edict of January ends the initial Huguenot struggle for recognition. Unlike previous legislation, it was a practicable, unambiguous, strictly reasonable compromise. But it did not bring peace. There is a sense in which it was already too late, although, on the national level, there were to be no hostilities for a further six months.

The edict was immediately denounced and resisted by the Catholics, in particular the *parlement*, which withheld registration until 6 March. Meanwhile, on receipt of *lettres de jussion*[115] the *parlement* obtained a declaration of 14 February which, though partly interpretative, also proclaimed the edict to be "par manière de provision et sans que par nostre dite ordonnance nous ayons entendu approuver deux religions en nostre Royaume."[116]

This fierce struggle over the registration of the edict, at a time of intense political crisis, was hardly reassuring for the Protestants. As a result of the unremitting efforts of the emissaries of Spain and the pope, Coligny and his brother d'Andelot (colonel general of the infantry) were forced to quit the council by about 17 February. Cardinal Châtillon, their other brother, left a few days later.[117] Coligny was never again to be suffered to return to

---

115. *Lettres de jussion:* orders to the *parlement* demanding immediate and unqualified registration of royal legislation.

116. Fontanon, *Les Édits et ordonnances*, iv, 269–70, declaration of 14 February on the edict of January 1562.

117. Sainte-Croix, *Lettres*, 39, 22 February 1562; *Archivo documental Español, Francia*, iii, 312–19, 3 February 1562, Chantonnay to Philip II; 328–35, 11 February 1562, Chantonnay to Philip II; 345–47, 14 February 1562, Chantonnay to Philip II; 382–92, 28 February 1562, Chantonnay to Philip II.

the council without violent opposition from the Guises. Thereafter, Navarre capitulated to the *Triumvirs*. As lieutenant general and commander-in-chief, the importance of this change can hardly be exaggerated, and was not overlooked by the Guises.[118] The civil war, which the Triumvirate projected, had not begun with a campaign against Navarre, because he was too easily outwitted. The obvious target therefore became the edict of January, and it is remarkable that it was ever registered at all, even with the reservation, "sans approbation de la nouvelle religion, le tout par manière de provision."

Since all expedients had already been tried, long since, the notion that successive edicts were provisional, pending some true solution, had worn undeceptively thin. No one expected the resumed council of Trent to solve the Protestant problem, whatever else it might achieve. Far from being in any way constructive, the pope, his emissaries and allies remained consistently provocative. The predictable reservation of the *parlement* did not, however, alter the substance of the edict of January, and its registration, on 6 March, enabled the Protestants to claim that they had taken up arms in defense of the law. So far as Condé was concerned, he also had his life to consider. This was significantly different from taking up arms in defense of religion, which the Calvinist confession forbade, and from which, in any general sense, they had so far refrained. In one respect at least, the crisis in France was quite simple: either the edict of January, or something very like it, must be accepted, otherwise considerable numbers of people were prepared to fight for it. Thus, the Calvinists had received grudging, contested and ineffective recognition. The ensuing struggle for survival passed into the military sphere, and the proposals of the Triumvirate were said to have been taken by Lorraine to the council of Trent.[119]

118. Delaborde, *Coligny*, ii, 22–23; Sainte-Croix, *Lettres*, 47, 13 March 1562.

119. Preamble to the "treaty of the Triumvirate," Michaud, série i, vol. vi, *Mémoires-journaux du duc de Guise*, 464–65.

5

The Struggle for Security, 1563–1570

THE CIVIL WAR—and those which followed it—achieved very little in a military sense.[1] Although the Catholics—who disposed of the royal forces—were the more successful in the field, neither side could definitively conquer the other. Nor could their quarrels ultimately be settled in the field. It was to be predominantly political and financial, rather than military, circumstances which fashioned the treaties and edicts of peace by which—at least juridically—the Huguenots were slowly reintegrated into society.

In an immediate sense, the first civil war had arisen from the refusal of the Triumvirate and the Catholics to accept the edict of January 1562, granting the Huguenots recognition and limited, supervised toleration. This edict, at least with the addition of a clause conceding the possession of *temples*, could have pacified the purely religous problem in 1562. The edict had, paradoxically, been considered necessary in the interests of peace. It therefore appears that, given the disastrous weakness of the crown, and the Catholic success in dividing the co-regents, Catherine de Medici and the king of Navarre, war had become unavoidable. So there began a pattern of action and reaction, which was to be constantly repeated in ever more dangerous circumstances until, eventually, Henry IV was strong enough to impose his authority and suffi- cient acceptance of the edict of Nantes. This, also, was declared by the king to be necessary in the interests of peace. Each succes-

---

1. The military history of the Huguenot struggle is a study apart which cannot be entered into here.

sive peace treaty from 1563 to 1598 was to incorporate an edict of religion—the so-called edicts of pacification—which, in the ensuing period of "peace" the Catholics successfully subverted.[2]

In the first civil war, the Catholics reduced the Protestant city of Bourges, in September 1562, followed in October by Rouen, where Navarre was fatally wounded. Then, in December, the duc de Guise won the first pitched battle of the wars, at Dreux. But he lost his confederates, the marshal St. André, who was killed, and the constable Montmorency, who was captured; so, on the Protestant side, was the prince de Condé. This, therefore, disrupted the Triumvirate and rendered the duc de Guise more important than ever, as the only remaining hope—in the military sphere—for the execution of its policy.

For a month or more before the battle of Dreux, Catherine de Medici had been moving heaven and earth to achieve a peace settlement; peace at home and abroad was her most constant policy.[3] This was strongly opposed by the Catholics, who were exploiting the forces of the crown. But it was favored by Condé, probably because he claimed to have "certain proof" that the duke intended his destruction, and that of his party. There is evidence that Condé was aware of the terms of Triumvirate policy. A copy of the so-called "treaty of the Triumvirate" appears among his papers, and he is said to have published it in April 1562.[4]

Guise was blamed for the breakdown of the peace negotiations, although he was not entirely unyielding so long as his army was in need of rest.[5] Guise had no personal interest in making peace,

2. This study is concerned with what happened on the national level. The fate of the edicts in the provinces is a matter for numerous local studies.

3. B. N., Mss. Fr., 3180, f. 114, 12 December 1562, Fresne to Nemours; *CSPF., 1562*, pp. 515–16, 5 December 1562, Throckmorton to Elizabeth; 517–18, 6 December 1562, Throckmorton to Elizabeth; 529–34, 9 December 1562, the prince of Condé's negotiations.

4. *CSPF., 1562*, pp. 533–34, 7–9 December 1562, articles of the prince de Condé; Condé, *Mémoires*, iii, 209–13.

5. Forbes, *A Full View of the Public Transactions*, ii, 263–65, 5 January 1563, d'Andelot to Elizabeth; La Noue, *Mémoires*, 607.

and Spain and the Catholics were relying on him for the continuation of the war.[6] At the end of January 1563, Saint-Sulpice, the French ambassador in Spain, sent his secretary, La Mothe-Fénelon, to inform Catherine of Philip's efforts to obstruct the conclusion of peace.[7] This should probably be related to the activity of Lorraine during the council of Trent. After the victory of Dreux, Lorraine is said to have urged the formation of an international league of Catholic princes for the maintenance of religion, especially in France. This was to be sustained by the king of Spain, and placed under the protection of the pope. The pope was to appoint a leader for France whom all Catholics would be required to obey until the heretics had been completely exterminated. This proposal is said to have been warmly received—presumably by Pius IV—and it was agreed that Guise should be' that leader.[8]

Although Lorraine had more urgent and more personal reasons than anyone else for wanting such a Catholic league, the idea was neither new nor exclusively French. It must, in any case, have been at least as old as the Triumvirate. The wealthy Cosimo dei Medici, duke of Tuscany, had allegedly made a similar proposal to Pius IV. Pius is said to have adopted the idea with ardor and to have formed such a project in May 1562, although he met with little response in Madrid or Venice. Indeed, in the autumn of 1561, Pius had already declared his intention to depose both the king of France and the queen of England, in favor of Philip II, if

6. Cabié, *Ambassade en Espagne*, 123, 27 March 1562/63, Saint-Sulpice to Catherine (secret).

7. Ibid., 112–13, 31 January 1563, Saint-Sulpice to Catherine; 114, 5 January 1563, Saint-Sulpice to the court (secret).

8. Maimbourg, *Histoire de la Ligue*, 12–14. Lorraine is said to have used Sebastiano Gualtiero, bishop of Viterbo, as his intermediary with the pope. Gualtiero had been the nuncio in France from May 1560–October 1561. Frémy, *Essai sur les diplomates du temps de la Ligue*, 27; Lestocquoy, *Correspondance des nonces en France. Lenzi et Gualtiero, légation du cardinal Trivultio*, 15–16. The whole question of the origin, at this time, of a Catholic league, fostered by Lorraine, is one that I hope to investigate further.

they refused to obey him and conform.[9] Besides France and England, Geneva and Protestant Germany were also to follow, although, in the event, the Netherlands were to attract more urgent attention. In January 1563, before the civil war was over, a number of Spaniards were reported by the council of Berne to have arrived at Genoa for the "practique" of the pope, Spain, Savoy, and others against France. Spain was also making preparations in Germany.[10] Thus Sir Thomas Smith reported Lorraine to have been "marvellous busy about the Emperor, Swiss catholics and German Papist Princes."[11] This was all in accord with Triumvirate policy, for which Guise was the designated leader. It amply accounts for his adamant refusal to lay down arms after his arrival in Paris in March 1562, and supports the opinion that the Catholics fully intended to make war, contrary to the policy of the crown.

Had the civil war continued in 1563, Guise might well have executed Triumvirate policy in France, their first objective. But, were Catherine to succeed in making peace—for her determination was notoriously formidable—Chantonnay and the Catholics evolved a means by which to frustrate it. Sir Thomas Smith, the English ambassador, reported on 17 February that there was a council at Paris "kept" by the cardinal of Guise (the duke's brother), the nuncio Santa-Croce, the cardinal legate of Ferrara, and Chantonnay, the Spanish ambassador. They are said to have resolved that if peace were concluded they, the Parisians and the Catholics would reject it, unless the pope allowed it. As there could no longer be any peace which did not sanction some degree of toleration, the pope would obviously not allow it. In this case, they planned to "declare the Duke of Guise to be the protector of the Roman and Catholic Church. So by that means he will remain

9. Pastor, *Histoire des papes*, xvi, 106–7; Šusta, *Die Römische Curie*, i, 280, 18 October–December 1561, instructions to Brocado, going to Spain.

10. Archives de Genève, P. H., 1716 (no pagination), 22 January 1562/63, conseil de Berne to that of Geneva.

11. *CSPF.*, *1563*, p. 138, 17 February 1563, Smith to the privy council.

Lieutenant, and continue in arms, and be aided with money by the Pope and such as profess the Popish religion."[12]

Whether in war or in peace, therefore, the duc de Guise was the pivot of national and international Catholic policy. But, on 18 February 1563, he was fatally wounded on the outskirts of Orléans by Poltrot de Méré, a native of Aubeterre in Angoulême. He died six days later, completing the destruction of the Triumvirate, whose policy was to be largely shouldered by Lorraine. Poltrot was a relative of La Renaudie, leader of the conspiracy of Amboise, and had his private, festering reasons for desiring the death of Guise. But he was only one among many who wanted "to stay" the duke, because he would certainly not have agreed to any treaty of peace after the fall of Orléans, which was imminently expected.[13] Poltrot, in his deposition of 21–22 February, claimed to have heard of some wider plot, and that there were to be other similar deeds.[14] The Venetian ambassador reported him to have said that this was the first of a whole series of immense murder plots, which included all the Catholic nobility.[15] Two months later, the diary of the council of Trent records the report of a conspiracy to murder Catholic leaders. Lorraine had heard that he was first on the list.[16] This was possibly no more than a distant echo of Poltrot's deposition, which is certainly not reliable. But, considering the theatrical nature of the Triumvirate, the fact that Guise had already been assassinated, and the subsequent history of the civil wars, there is nothing inherently improbable in such a report. Besides, reports of this kind did not depend for their effect upon their veracity. The scanty evidence would certainly not support the interpretation that Poltrot murdered Guise on account of a nascent Catholic league; he is unlikely to have been well informed. One cannot, however, assume that, but for Poltrot, the duke would have survived, and it is

---

12. Ibid., 142, 17 February 1563, Smith to the privy council.
13. B. N., Mss. Italien, 1722, ff. 681–82, 17 February 1563.
14. De Ruble, *L'Assassinat de François duc de Guise*, 56 seq.
15. B. N., Mss. Italien, 1722, f. 689, 27 February 1563.
16. *Concilium Tridentinum* II. *Diarium pars secunda*, 676, April 1563.

14. De Ruble, *L'Assassinat de François duc de Guise*, 56 seq.

reasonable to suppose that, on both sides, the leaders went in fear and danger of sudden death.

The importance of the murder of the duc de Guise can hardly be exaggerated.[17] It was a calamitous precedent which triggered an extensive chain reaction. Apart from averting the fall of Orléans, the Huguenot military headquarters, it had other weighty consequences. In the first place, it shattered the Catholics' plans, national and international, which turned upon the duc de Guise. By the same token, his death finally enabled Catherine de Medici, with the help of the princesse de Condé, to bring together the two noble captives, Montmorency and Condé, and clinch the peace for which she had long been striving.[18]

The edict of Amboise, which Catherine achieved on 19 March 1563, was partially modeled on that of January 1562.[19] But it was more complex and contained various important differences. Not surprisingly, it reflected the problems arising from the war itself, to which the preamble is devoted. The principal differences lie in the toleration clauses, which indicate the relative importance of the Protestant nobility, and the strength of the Catholics. The nobles obtained special privileges to exercise the cult at home—clauses which Coligny indignantly opposed. He had no part in the negotiations and condemned the settlement as a recipe for ever greater troubles.[20] But for everyone else, the cult was allowed only in the suburbs of one town per *bailliage* or *sénéchaussé* and not, as previously, anywhere outside the towns. The cult, however, might also be exercised in one or two places in towns where it was held up to 7 March 1563. It is possible that this article 5 may have considerably increased the total number of places, and is likely to have included the most Protestant. However, it was later interpreted to mean towns which had then been held by force, which was not the same thing. This edict of Am-

17. I hope to analyze elsewhere the evidence relating to this still mysterious event.

18. B. N., Mss. Fr., 6607, ff. 48, 49, 51, 54, 55 [1563], the princesse de Condé to Catherine.

19. Fontanon, *Les Édits et ordonnances*, iv, 267-69.

20. *Revue des documents historiques*, iii, 1875, pp. 175-76, 16 March 1562/63, Coligny to the count Rhinegrave, from Caen.

boise is the first to mention the problems of lay property and offices, all of which had to be restored, notwithstanding seizures, decrees or judgments issued since the death of Henry II; probably a legal impossibility. These clauses were supported by a total amnesty for every wrong or injury arising from the war, and a prohibition, upon pain of death, against the further pursuit of any such wrong. In theory, this should have included the murder in February 1563 of the duc de Guise. In practice it did not. The edict also prohibited all associations, the raising of men and money, and all assemblies not explicitly allowed. This last stipulation was to reappear in the final edict of Nantes, and was intended to prevent the Huguenots from holding political, as distinct from religious, meetings.

Thus the cult clauses were weighted in favor of the nobility, whereas the real problem was located in the towns. There was still no clause permitting *temples* but, on the other hand, they were not expressly prohibited. The sensible supervisory clauses of the edict of January were dropped, and there was no reference to any previous edict. The choice of the *lieux du culte*, as they were called, in the *bailliages* and *sénéchaussées* was bound to be fiercely contentious, and was easily subject to villainous manipulation. This was an unnecessary administrative problem to inflict on the weakened royal government, which had no hope of prevailing against any substantial local opposition. This difficult and dangerous work soon had to be entrusted to special commissioners—precursors of the *intendants*—who received a detailed commission, quite as long as the edict itself, on 18 June 1563.[21] The only right of appeal against them was to the council. A full account of their difficult work would be most illuminating. We know, however, that it was largely unsuccessful, and a further declaration of 14 December 1563 referred to their problems of interpretation and the many unforeseen circumstances.[22] France contained a great variety of regional differences, but the edict was couched in the most general terms, probably drafted in a hurry, and with primarily political problems in mind. A further declara-

21. Fontanon, *Les Édits et ordonnances*, iv, 274–76.
22. Ibid., 276–79.

tion, of Roussillon, 4 August 1564,[23] actually imposed the death penalty both for acts of iconoclasm on the one hand and, on the other, for interference with the legal celebration of the cult. It repeated that this might only be held as specified in the edict. Ministers who ignored the restriction were to be banished for their first offense and beaten for their second—a ludicrous example of the careless drafting which contributed to the juridical chaos of the time.

It is interesting to note, by way of comparison, that although the crown had been too weak to protect the Huguenots, there was nothing unenforceable about the toleration clause of the edict of January 1562. It was purely permissive and required neither interpretation nor administrative machinery. But the predictable failure to administer the complex edict of Amboise was one contributory cause of the second civil war (September 1567–March 1568).

If the peace of Amboise had been facilitated by the death of the duc de Guise, paradoxically, the same event was also to destroy it. Bereft of the duke, who was to have continued in arms as knight errant to the Papacy, the Catholics were obliged to revise their tactics. They had to devise some new means by which to sabotage the peace and pursue the destruction of Triumvirate enemies. This was the purpose of the Guise-Châtillon vendetta. The vendetta derived from the murder, for which the duke's family promptly elected to blame the admiral, Coligny. This enabled them to make a virtue of necessity, adapting Catholic policy to the altered circumstances, though nothing could repair the loss of their great military leader.

In effect, the vendetta was an extension to Coligny of the Triumvirate policy against the Bourbons. Navarre was dead, and Coligny was now a much more dangerous adversary than the prince de Condé. Besides, like his late brother, Navarre, Condé might still be exploited as a princely figurehead; but for this he would have to be publicly blameless. Thus, although there was at least a prima facie case against the prince—who had himself been unforgiveably imperiled by the Guises in 1560—the Catholics

23. Ibid., 279–81.

made repeated efforts to seduce him to their allegiance. Had they succeeded, this would have isolated Coligny, who could then more easily have been framed as a rebel. It was therefore convenient and politic to proclaim the culpability of Coligny, and to launch against him a murderous vendetta.

Apart from the long-term future of Triumvirate policy, it was, in any case, essential to ruin Coligny in order to disrupt the peace. Otherwise, together with the king and Catherine, he might have done much to implement it. There was also a danger that Coligny might reunite with his Montmorency relatives to forge a center and royalist party. The old constable, until the war, had long been an enemy of the Guises. Thus the Catholics had to have something more than his now legalized Calvinism to level against Coligny. They needed some fresh pretext, however specious, for remaining in arms, for threatening his life, and for continuing to exclude him from court and council, which it was still indispensable for Lorraine and the Catholics to dominate. Consequently they seized upon the evidence of Poltrot. In his deposition, extorted under torture and subsequently retracted, Poltrot had claimed to be in the service of Coligny.[24] On 12 March 1563 Coligny categorically denied any complicity in the murder, though he incautiously admitted to having rejoiced. Coligny demanded a full confrontation with Poltrot and also his safekeeping for this purpose.[25] But, to the contrary, he was swiftly executed on 18 March, the day before the peace of Amboise would have amnestied his crime. More important, however, Poltrot's death ensured that the allegations against Coligny could never be resolved. Consequently it afforded the Guises the spurious but invaluable grievance of a denial of justice. These tactics were adroit and effective. This implacable vendetta was to determine Coligny's subsequent role in the Huguenot struggle, because it could be sustained so long as he succeeded in remaining alive.

If Coligny's life had been in danger since his emergence as a

24. De Ruble, *L'Assassinat de François duc de Guise*, 56 seq.
25. Du Bouchet, *Preuves*, 521–22. The date is wrongly given as 22 March 1562/63. Coligny's letter was also signed by La Rochefoucauld and Théodore de Bèze.

Protestant leader and the formation of Triumvirate policy in 1561, it was far more directly and continually threatened after the inception of the vendetta—successive edicts of pacification in 1563, 1568 and 1570 notwithstanding. Indeed, he was never to be safe again, and his personal danger was notorious. Already on 12 March 1563, the English ambassador Sir Thomas Smith recorded his anxiety for Coligny "so long as Aumale [the late duke's brother] and the Guisians be so greate about the queen mother, making such a brute to ron upon the admirall."[26] Furthermore, they threatened him in arms when he sought, for the first time, to return to the court in May 1563,[27] and repeatedly demanded justice against him in the *parlement,* which Coligny had already impugned. On 16 May 1563 the king evoked the matter to himself and forbade either party to offend the other.[28]

Coligny remained at home at Châtillon during the summer of 1563, while Condé assisted Catherine to recapture Le Havre from England, his wartime ally. Thereafter, seeing the queen in extremity as the result of a heavy fall from her horse, the Guises went in force to Meulan planning, if she died, to seize the young king. Contemptuously ignoring his previous evocation, although Charles was now declared of age, they again demanded justice in the *parlement.*[29] The king repeated his evocation, referring the matter to the council. Only then, according to his own evidence, did Coligny permit his followers to assemble. This was evidently necessary since, in October, he complained to the king of a warning that Aumale had dispatched two gentlemen to kill him.[30] The following month the Guises sent a substantial force to prevent Coligny from returning to court near Fontainebleau. On this oc-

26. Forbes, *A Full View of the Public Transactions in the Reign of Queen Elizabeth,* ii, 358, 12 March 1563, Smith to Elizabeth.

27. *CSPF., 1563,* p. 344, 17 May 1563, Middlemore to Cecil; B. N., Mss. Italien, 1724, ff. 56–58, 15 May 1563; Delaborde, *Coligny,* ii, 263–65.

28. B. N., Mss. Fr., 3193, ff. 51–52, 16 May 1563, *arrêt* du conseil, printed in Du Bouchet, *Preuves,* 537–38.

29. B. N., Mss. Italien, 1724, ff. 143v, 30 September 1563; f. 145, 30 September 1563; *Bref discours,* 13–14.

30. B. N., Mss. Fr., 20461, f. 69, 8 October 1563, Coligny to Charles IX; Delaborde, *Coligny,* ii, 295–301.

casion he called their bluff and, well accompanied, went to Paris about 20 November and resumed his place in the council. But, according to Sir Nicholas Throckmorton, he was in great danger, and narrowly missed assassination in the Louvre.[31] The Guises withdrew, but impugned the jurisdiction of the council in criminal cases, whereupon Coligny counterpetitioned for the evocation to stand. Faced with this deadlock, on 5 January 1564 the king suspended the matter for three years, or during pleasure, and licensed both parties to depart.[32] The situation was therefore hardly reassuring, more especially since the resourceful Lorraine was about to return from the council of Trent, with the status of legate *a latere*. Coligny withdrew some ten days before Lorraine arrived on 29 January 1564.[33]

The possible implications of Coligny's brief return to court had vexed and alarmed all Catholic extremists, who were determined to ensure his future exclusion.[34] Thus the struggle in France, which focused on the Guise-Châtillon vendetta, became greatly intensified. Lorraine immediately strove to reassert his control of the council, an endeavor in which he was both skillful and favored by circumstances. The intensified struggle also became increasingly internationalized: the Catholics were sustained by the Papacy and Spain, while the Huguenots looked first to the Netherlands and, albeit in rather different ways, beyond them to England and Germany.

Whether or not there were formal hostilities, from this time on there was to be no real peace and still less, for the Huguenots, security. On the contrary, there were plentiful rumors of Spanish and Catholic "practices," that the court was bent on subjecting

31. *CSPF.*, *1563*, p. 600, 26 November 1563, Throckmorton to Elizabeth.

32. *Archivo documental Español, Francia*, vi, 27–29, 5 January 1564, extraict des registres du conseil privé; 32, 8 and 10 January 1564, Chantonnay says the decision was taken on 4 January; B. N., Mss. Italien, 1724, f. 189, 29 December 1563, ff. 192–93, 12 January 1564.

33. *Archivo documental Español, Francia*, vi, 73, 23 January 1564, Chantonnay to Philip II. Coligny had gone to Châtillon four days before.

34. One might call this two months, the longest Coligny was ever to spend at court after his expulsion in February 1562.

the Huguenots to the papists, and that Philip II and the house of Guise would serve this turn. Before she embarked on the great itinerary of the court round France, during 1564–66, Catherine was warned that Chantonnay, the Spanish ambassador, and his brother Granvelle, Philip's minister in the Netherlands, would seek to rekindle the civil wars. Certainly the vendetta in no wise abated while she was away, and hostilities were only narrowly averted. "De jour à aultre," the Catholic Simon Renard wrote on 6 October 1564 to the duchess of Parma in the Netherlands, "s'accroist l'inimitié et partialité, par les practiques que meynent ceulx de la maison de Guyse pour venger la mort du feu sgr. de Guyse, pour réinpétrer le crédit qu'ilz ont eu par le passé... [et] procurer leur ruyne par vengeance publique et criminelle."[35] This was a succinct statement of Guise policy from an impeccably Catholic source. The following January, 1565, Lorraine openly clashed with François duc de Montmorency, *gouverneur* of Paris. Montmorency challenged Lorraine's claim to be allowed to enter the city in arms, and resisted his progress. The situation became so dangerous that Coligny actually hastened to his cousin's support, and France was very close to the renewed civil war that all extreme Catholics desired.[36] This went not only for the French, but also for the Spanish, of which Catherine received ample evidence at Bayonne, where the courts of France and Spain held a spectacular meeting in June 1565.

Even before the meeting, the duke of Alva who, to Catherine's regret, represented Philip II, had rudely informed the French ambassador, Saint-Sulpice, of the folly of imagining that France could "parvenir" without Spanish help, and remedy the "maux et périls qui nous environnaient de tous côtés."[37] At the meeting itself, Alva found Catherine steadfastly unreceptive to the argument that she should employ force to destroy heresy; significant evidence, since Catherine was then acting independently of the council. Alva therefore turned to the Catholic leaders who sur-

---

35. *Bulletin de la Société de l'histoire du protestantisme français*, xxxvi, 1887, p. 640.

36. Cabié, *Ambassade en Espagne*, 344–45, 4 February 1565, St. Etienne to Saint-Sulpice.

37. Ibid., 7–11.

rounded Catherine and, ignoring the queen, prepared to act in concert with them. According to Alva himself, the idea was formulated of concentrating upon the removal or, in other words, the "elimination" of five or six of the Huguenot leaders.[38] This proved to be a turning point in the story of the primarily personal and domestic vendetta. Thereafter it gradually merged into a wider, international, Catholic policy to eliminate the principal Huguenot leaders, of whom Condé, as a Bourbon, had already been explicitly endangered by the Triumvirate. This "elimination" idea was not actually new, but it now assumed a new impetus. In July, a month later, Lorraine revealed to Granvelle the existence of an association of the Guises, the duc de Montpensier and others to support Catholicism, seeking Philip's participation.[39] Since all the French Catholic extremists followed Lorraine, it is difficult to believe that there was no connection between his intrigues and those of Alva.

In view of all that had happened since the peace of Amboise in March 1563, including, during the summer of 1564, a strenuous effort to detach Condé from the Protestants,[40] it is not surprising that the Huguenots should have sought to strengthen their links with the Netherlands. This was done on the personal level between members of the nobility, some of whom were kinsmen, and also between the Calvinist churches, which, it must be remembered, were well-organized communities, capable of contingency planning. Only a matter of days after the conclusion of the conference at Bayonne, Granvelle wrote to warn Philip of the progress of Calvinism in the Netherlands, and also of the close and regular correspondence between Montigny, brother of count Horne, and his Châtillon cousins in France.[41]

The judicial settlement of the vendetta was therefore critically urgent for the peace and security of the kingdom since, on the one

38. Weiss, Granvelle, *Papiers d'État*, ix, 298, 21 June 1565, Alva to Philip II.

39. Ibid., 399–403, 15 July 1565, Granvelle to Philip.

40. Ibid., viii, 126–27, 6 July 1564, occurrents in France; Sutherland, *The Massacre of St. Bartholomew*, 50.

41. Weiss, Granvelle, *Papiers d'Etat*, ix, 404, 18 July 1566, Granvelle to Philip II.

hand, Coligny was now regarded as a dangerous enemy of Spain and, on the other, the mounting power of Lorraine endangered the crown of France. The returning court reached Moulins in January 1566, where the king was particularly vulnerable because he was seriously ill. The events of Moulins clearly indicate Lorraine's grip on the destiny of France, as well as the importance to him of the vendetta. On 29 January, Charles IX sought to terminate the vendetta by a simple *arrêt* in council, declaring Coligny's innocence of the murder of Guise.[42] But Lorraine had already contumaciously declared that he would honor no adverse verdict; also that his brother, Aumale, would seek the admiral's life. This statement came very close to a declaration of war against the Huguenots, in total disregard for the authority of the crown.[43] Nor were these idle threats. In March, during a resounding row in the council with the chancellor, L'Hospital, over the interpretation of the edict of Amboise, Lorraine openly and explicitly admitted that he sought to ruin the Protestants.[44] In May and June there followed reports of a "secret practice" to kill the admiral, as well as his brother d'Andelot (who had narrowly escaped an ambush in January) and La Rochefoucauld, by a "great concourse of people." Condé also complained of persons lying in wait for his life.[45] Not only, therefore, was the vendettta rather invigorated than terminated, but Lorraine and the French Catholics had adopted the "elimination" policy outlined by Alva in a letter to Philip II at the time of the Bayonne conference. Such a policy could be continuously pursued, even if the crown were to succeed in averting war.

It is therefore not surprising that disturbances in the Nether-

---

42. Archives de Chantilly, papiers de Condé, série K, iv, f. 134, no date, contemporary copy of the *arrêt;* B. N., Mss. Fr., 3193, f. 31, 30 January 1566, Coligny to the duchess of Ferrara.

43. B. N., Mss. Fr., 3193, ff. 52v–57v, ce qui se passa à Moulins.

44. Ibid., 3951, ff. 100v–107v, 15–16 March 1565.

45. *CSPF., 1566–68,* p. 9, 23 January 1566, Smith to Leicester; 70, 21 May 1566, Hoby to Cecil; 82–83, 24 May–8 June 1566, Hoby to Leicester and Cecil; B. N., Mss. Italien, 1726, ff. 19v–21v, 23 May 1566; Desjardins, *Négs. Tosc.,* iii, 525, 2 June 1566.

lands later in 1566, followed by the appointment of Alva as military governor, should have had grave and alarming repercussions in France.[46] With his approach along the eastern frontier of France, in the summer of 1567, general consternation rose to crisis point, and the king summoned 6,000 Swiss troops. When Alva began to persecute the nobility in the Netherlands, Lorraine augmented his policy of intimidation in France. In a seemingly parallel assault on the nobility, he appointed certain "centeniers" in Paris and other large towns, to swoop upon seigneurial houses, on the pretext that they had been admitting more people to the cult than the edict allowed.[47] Out of the fears aroused in the Netherlands and France by the conference at Bayonne, the conviction grew that Alva and Lorraine were working together. Large numbers of gentlemen fled across the frontier to join the prince de Condé. This tended to confuse the issues, which were in fact widely different, and to augment the interest of Spain in the affairs of France.

Catholics in France were said to be bragging that, with the arrival of Spanish forces in the Netherlands, the king would revoke the edict. It was naturally suspected that this was why he required 6,000 Swiss. The Huguenots and the Netherlanders were, it appeared, to be simultaneously suppressed. Condé protested to Catherine, who declared that the king would never break the edict so long as she could help it.[48] But the stark fact was that she could *not* help it. According to Sir Henry Norris, Lorraine had "greatly entered into the favour of the King who will neither ride, go, or [sic] eat without his good cousin.... "[49] At the end of August 1567, a proclamation was published ordering all law officers to attest their Catholic faith, and to confess at least once a year.[50] Meanwhile, the Protestants were necessarily

46. Navarrete, *Colección de documentos inéditos para la historia de España*, iv, 388–96, 31 January 1566/67, instructions for Alva.

47. *CSPF., 1566–68*, pp. 327–28, 23 August 1567, Norris to Elizabeth; 328, 23 August 1567, Norris to Cecil.

48. Ibid., 330, 29 August 1567, Norris to Elizabeth.

49. Ibid., 327, 23 August 1567, Norris to Elizabeth.

50. Ibid., 331, 30 August 1567, Adolph Blyleven to Gresham.

preparing to defend themselves: "certain cornets of reiters" were said to be hovering in Lorraine, ready to come to the aid of the Protestants "who prepare themselves and gather money secretly."[51]

In mid-September Norris reported the "appearance of civil tumults." This, he said, was because the king, by consent of his council, was about to revoke the edict of Amboise and publish the decrees of the council of Trent.[52] Clearly Lorraine had completely established his ascendancy in the council. Furthermore, certain specific articles were prepared for the overthrow of religion. These articles prohibited any further Protestant assemblies or preaching, under pain of death at the stake. Similarly all pastors were to leave the country or face the same penalty. Everyone was to live by the Catholic faith and according to the decrees of Trent. All governors of provinces were to assist, "with force of justice," in the execution of these decrees, upon pain of deprivation. Other articles provided for the reform of abuses. When these articles were concluded in the presence of the king, "much was said by the Cardinal of Lorraine in favour of the Catholic religion." Furthermore, his nephew, Henri duc de Guise, now aged seventeen, "did then protest to live and die in the same, to the effusion of his blood in defence thereof."[53] It was expected that the articles would shortly be published, together with the decrees of Trent which the king had, allegedly, already signed.[54]

About 11 September, Michel de Castelnau, seigneur de Mauvissière, was sent to Condé "to understand why he assembled with such force about him." Condé replied that he wished "to maintain the liberty of the Gospel, which the King was determined to suppress," and he feared the foreign forces which the king had raised.[55] Both these fears arose from Lorraine's control

---

51. Ibid., 330–31, 29 August 1567, Norris to Elizabeth; 338, [13 September] 1567, Norris [to Leicester].

52. Ibid., 338 [13 September], 1567, Norris [to Leicester].

53. Idem.

54. Ibid., 340, 15 September 1567, Norris to Cecil; 341, 16 September 1567, advertisements out of France.

55. Ibid., 338 [13 September], 1567, Norris [to Leicester].

of the king and council, and the knowledge of Catherine's helplessness, despite her assurances; early in September the court was at Lorraine's own house, La Marche.[56]

At the same time as he was trying to revoke the edict and enforce the decrees of Trent, Lorraine actively sustained the vendetta. Already the admiral "by secret means deciphered some practice that wholly tended to his confusion." Consequently he withdrew to his house and did not return to court with his two brothers at the end of July.[57] Now, in mid-September, the vendetta was publicly assumed by the young duc de Guise, who "began to renew the quarrel of his father's death, saying he could not be content unless better justice were done." When asked by the queen mother "whether he would not stand to the arrest [sic (*arrêt*)] of the Privy Council given for the Admiral's innocency" at Moulins, he haughtily refused, answering that "if there had been 500 arrests he would never let that pass so unrevenged." This added a dangerous new dimension to the quarrel. Coligny, "being advertised," replied that he "was constrained for his safety to have a better guard about him than hitherto, and that he doubted not by the help of his friends to make the Duke recoil."[58]

In these circumstances, the Huguenots had either to face annihilation, personal and religious, or else to fight. With the Guises in control of the king and the council, and Alva in command in the Netherlands, Triumvirate policy was once again a deadly threat. Nor was there anything parochial in the scope of Lorraine's aspirations. In the midst of this crisis, he was evidently scheming to "fetch away" the infant prince James of Scotland, so that he should not be educated as a Protestant.[59] But, of more immediate significance, Lorraine turned to Alva for help the moment civil war began, and proposed to him that if Charles and his brothers were to die, Philip would be able to claim the throne of France in the right of his wife, the Salic Law being a mere

56. Ibid., 335, 6 September 1567, Charles IX to Elizabeth.
57. Ibid., 305, 31 July 1567, Norris to Leicester.
58. Ibid., 341, 16 September 1567, advertisements out of France.
59. Ibid., 342, 18 September 1567, Norris to Cecil.

pleasantry.[60] Even Alva was dumbfounded by this. It was therefore in vain that, after Bayonne, Catherine had forbidden the cardinal to have any communication whatsoever with Philip's servants.[61]

Hostilities began on 26 September 1567 with what is known as the "incident de Meaux." This was a Protestant *prise d'armes*, of which the principal purpose was to capture Lorraine and break the Guise stranglehold on the court. It was only by controlling the king and the council—his objective since his return from Trent—that Lorraine might revoke the edict and proclaim the decrees of Trent. But, unfortunately, the Guises escaped—"by the grace of God and their good Turkish horses."[62] Once again, in the following February, 1568, Lorraine escaped "very hard" at Rheims from an assault on his coach.[63]

Condé is reported to have submitted certain demands to the king within a day or two of the "incident." According to the Tuscan ambassador, Petrucci, he demanded security of religion and the expulsion of foreigners, especially Italians. Foreigners would have embraced the Guises, disobligingly described as Lorrainers. By Italians, Condé may have meant many men, but the principals are likely to have been Albert de Gondi, comte de Retz—a murderous enemy—and his cousin Jérôme de Gondi, Italian bankers and relatives of Roberto Ridolfi; Louis de Gonzague, duc de Nevers; and Jacques de Savoie, duc de Nemours, who notoriously loved and later married the duchesse de Guise, widow of the murdered duke. Thirdly, Condé demanded reform of the council—from which, of course, the Huguenot leaders were excluded—and the reduction of taxes.[64] The chancellor, a moderate, was swiftly sent to negotiate with Condé. By 1 Oc-

60. Gachard, *Correspondance de Philippe II*, i, 593–94, 1 November 1567, Alva to Philip II. Charles and his brothers were far from robust and all tended to be acutely ill at the same time.

61. Weiss, Granvelle, *Papiers d'État*, ix, 400, 15 July 1565, Granvelle to Philip II.

62. Desjardins, *Négs. Tosc.*, iii, 528–31, 29 September 1567; 535, 8 October 1567.

63. *CSPF.*, *1566–68*, p. 413, 9 February 1568, Norris to Cecil.

64. Desjardins, *Négs. Tosc.*, iii, 530–31, 29 September 1567.

tober his terms had risen to the free exercise of religion everywhere; the expulsion of foreigners; the abolition of all taxes imposed since the reign of Louis XII; a public account of the finances of the last seven years; four *places de sûreté*; and the restitution of offices to everyone dismissed on grounds of religion.[65] This is the first we hear of demands for complete toleration, *places de surêté* and the retention of offices, clauses which were subsequently to recur again and again.

These were demands which could not possibly be granted in the circumstances of 1567. Besides, the failure of the "incident" had burdened the Huguenots with the responsibility for having laid an ambush for the king, although he escaped, escorted by his controversial 6,000 Swiss. This was already bad enough; but it led to a siege of Catholic Paris, when the king was in residence, an offense which the populace was not to forgive. These regrettable events probably terminated Condé's chances of ever resuming his rightful place at court. The Huguenots were therefore guilty of tactical errors which placed them grievously in the wrong. This error also strengthened Lorraine's determination to "eliminate" their leaders, and supplied him with more tenable pretexts.

Not only the Huguenots, but France herself was in serious danger, should Catherine and the helpless king prove unable to resist the strong Catholic pressure against heretics, or to achieve a settlement before foreign Catholic forces poured into France. The pope took it upon himself to require the king to dispense with the services of the chancellor, and of Marshal Montmorency who should be disarmed. In return for papal "help," Charles was expected to rely wholly upon the duke of Savoy and other Catholic captains: Montpensier, Nemours, Monluc and Aumale. As the pope himself informed Savoy that he had sent money to the cardinal of Lorraine, there was no kind of assurance that this "help," if rejected by the king, would not be turned against him.[66] But this would take a little time. In the meanwhile,

---

65. *CSPF.*, *1566–68*, pp. 348–49, 30 September 1567, Norris to Elizabeth.

66. B. N., Mss. Italien, 1726, ff. 149–50v, 7 October 1567; f. 158, 24 October 1567; Archives de Genève, P. H., 1839, 15 November 1567, Condé and others to the council of Geneva, no pagination; *CSPF.*,

Catherine was, once again, striving for peace, with the help of her moderate supporters in the council.[67] Negotiations, however, were almost inevitably unsuccessful, since the queen and the moderates had been unable to ensure even the retention of the edict, let alone its implementation.[68]

Negotiations were then resumed at the end of November, and pressed by Condé in December.[69] By January 1568, the duc d'Anjou, now lieutenant general of the kingdom,[70] was in favor of peace and a return to the edict of Amboise. This did not so much reflect his real opinion as the inability of the Catholics to mobilize and exploit their forces. The army was paralyzed by camp quarrels, while the Protestants were expecting the arrival of German mercenaries.[71] As Condé laid siege to Chartres, the "little" peace of Longjumeau was concluded on 23 March.[72] Both sides were suffering severe financial difficulties but the Huguenots enjoyed at least a temporary military advantage. This was to help the royal commissioners in concluding peace, but did not enable them to make any significant concessions. The Protestants were, however, more successful in obtaining some guarantees for better observance of the edict. But it was from the king, not from their enemies, that these guarantees were sought.

Articles of 4 March 1568, presented by Châtillon, La Rochefoucauld and Bouchavannes to the royal commissioners, expressed some of their past difficulties and present fears. These all related to contentions which had arisen over the implementa-

---

1566–68, p. 350 [September 1567]; Hirschauer, *La Politique de St. Pie V*, 98–101, 101–3, two letters of 16 October 1567, the pope to della Torre; De Potter, *Lettres de St. Pie V*, 7–8, 18 October 1567, the pope to the doge of Venice; 9–10, 18 October 1567, the pope to the duke of Savoy; 11–12, 16 November 1567, the pope to the duke of Savoy; Lettenhove, *Relations*, v, 29, 19 October 1567, Clough to Gresham.

67. Sutherland, *The French Secretaries of State*, 148.

68. B. N., Mss. Italien, 1726, ff. 151v–54v, 15 October 1567.

69. Delaborde, *Coligny*, ii, 503.

70. B. N., Mss. Fr., 3951, ff. 118–23, 12 November 1567, letters patent.

71. Ibid., 15544, f. 75, 19 January 1568; B. N., Mss. Italien, 1726, ff. 187-v, 3 January 1568; Desjardins, *Négs. Tosc.*, iii, 563, 2 January 1568.

72. Fontanon, *Les Édits et ordonnances*, iv, 289–91.

tion of the last edict, and to problems of security. In the first place, they had been afflicted with inconvenient cult towns, and had experienced great difficulty and expense in getting them changed. They therefore wanted the king himself to name the towns—one in each *bailliage* or *sénéchaussée*—in which the cult was to be permitted. For the better observance of the edict, they wanted the princes, the council, *gouverneurs* and all royal officials to be required to swear to observe it, thereby explicitly binding hostile Catholics. Once published, the edict was not to be distorted by declarations and interpretations because—though they did not say so—the edict of Amboise had been vitiated in this way. Furthermore, they asked to be allowed recourse to the king himself, whenever they suffered injustice or oppression. They required the king to guarantee their right to hold assemblies of ministers, and to educate their children in the Protestant towns. In order to circumvent the malice of disobedient officials, they requested a *chambre* in each *parlement*, composed of those "qui se trouvent les plus paisibles et moings passionez," to supervise the execution of the edict and to hear Protestant cases. In order to secure a safe return to their homes and property, they wanted the edict to be published without delay, and the *gouverneurs* to protect them from molestation.[73]

That all these points were conceded, is an interesting commentary on the true religious policy of the crown. This may also be the reason why the Huguenots agreed, at Longjumeau, to a renewal of the edict of Amboise, "selon sa première forme et teneur, levant et ostant toutes restrictions, modifications, declarations et interpretations, qui ont esté faites depuis...."[74] It was much less the edict itself than its non-observance to which they objected. The crown, however, was powerless to fulfill its guarantees and it will be seen that, in 1570, some of these same, vital points were to be written into the edict itself. The peace of Longjumeau does not mark any new stage in the Huguenots' progress; clearly nothing had been settled. The only real dif-

73. B. N., Mss. Fr., 3410, ff. 63–64. I am indebted to Dr. Joan M. Davies for having kindly transcribed this document for me.
74. Fontanon, *Les Édits et ordonnances*, iv, 289–91, 23 March 1568.

ference made by the second war and peace was that—temporarily—Lorraine had failed in his efforts to revoke the edict and publish the decrees of Trent as a preliminary to the extermination of the Huguenots. He had also seen that their leaders were not so easily to be caught, like rats in a trap.

Naturally, as in 1563, the ambassadors of Rome and Spain had employed themselves "all they possibly may to impeach this accord," and had constantly urged that it was impossible to have two religions in one realm. Philip, for his part, had offered a large sum of money to keep the war going.[75] In the opinion of Norris, the Catholics had been afraid of Condé's expected reinforcements, and also of the queen of England whom they understood to be "in readiness with her navy." Apart from the perennial problem of finance, it seems rather more likely that Lorraine wanted to be free to send his brother, Aumale, with an expedition to Scotland for the delivery of Mary and the restoration of religion.[76] However this may be, the affairs of Scotland, England and the Netherlands were about to impinge very closely on those of France, and strongly influence the Huguenot struggle.

Lorraine had evidently been obliged or induced to agree to peace, but this did not mean that he meant to observe it. As in 1563, the Catholics set about devising the means by which to destroy it. After the peace had been concluded, Lorraine held a meeting of those extremist members of the council, "sworn enemies to the religion," who had supported his revocation policy. Together they conspired to surprise and seize the Protestant cities of Orléans, Soissons, La Rochelle and Auxerre. The seigneur de Sansac, the vicomte de Martigues, the seigneur de Chavigny and Marshal Brissac were appointed to undertake these exploits. It was also determined to reinforce the garrison of Paris and to take other, similar precautions in the provinces. It was probably as a result of this nocturnal council that a secret *mandement* was shown to the principals of garrison towns, instructing them to persecute, vex, tax and generally harass and ill-treat the Protestants, in order to drive them out of their homes. Lorraine

75. *CSPF.*, *1566–68*, pp. 401–2, 23 January 1568, Norris to Elizabeth.
76. Ibid., 433–34, 28 March 1568, Norris to Cecil.

also intended, as in 1563, that while the Protestants dispersed, the Catholics would remain in arms. He would either place or secure supporters in all the main towns, and make sure of controlling the key points of communications.[77] Thus, having "by covert means" retained the greater part of their forces, while the Huguenots were disarmed and deprived of their strongholds, "it would be more easy to work their wills of the principals of the religion."[78]

This conspiracy was, however, promptly leaked to Cardinal Châtillon, and Norris reported it on 30 March. La Rochefoucauld galloped away to the camp to "stay the heralds from publishing the peace," but he was too late. The duc de Montmorency, one of the royal commissioners, protested in the council that he had been greatly abused. But the king swore that he had no knowledge of the matter—which was probably true. Charles was neither sufficiently in control of events, nor intellectually capable of such duplicity; it can only be another illustration of the deep cleavage within the government. Charles declared it to be a practice of the cardinal (of Lorraine) but that nevertheless he, the king, would proceed with the peace; whereupon he wrote to the prince de Condé to that effect. Norris goes on to indicate that much better terms were under discussion between the king and the prince.[79] But, if Lorraine could not, in time of war, fully control the Catholic high command, the king could not, in time of peace, ensure such terms as Lorraine rejected. The Huguenots necessarily feared for their persons, and the "little peace" was no peace at all but, as Norris was to say, more dangerous than the war. About five months later, Norris declared that more Protestants had perished in the "peace" than had lost their lives in the war. Daily murders were committed without any punishment to the offenders, and people were dragged from their houses and drowned. "The which thing," Norris said, "was meant when the

77. PRO/SP/70/105, a memorandum in the possession of La Forest Bochetel, brother-in-law of the secretary Claude de Laubespine, a moderate and a loyalist. *CSPF.*, *1566–68*, p. 436, 30 March 1568, Norris to Cecil.

78. *CSPF.*, *1566–68*, p. 436, 30 March 1568, Norris to Cecil.

79. Idem. The exact timing of these events is not clear. They occurred between 23 and 29 March. The peace was published on 27 March.

peace was yet in treaty, as appears by the letters intercepted from the Cardinal of Lorraine to the Duchess of Guise."[80]

Lorraine's determination to destroy the peace of Longjumeau was shortly assisted by the serious illness of Catherine de Medici. According to a memorandum of La Forest Bochetel, Lorraine planned to seize the young king (as, in similar circumstances, he had planned in 1563), secure the city of Paris and "executer par tout le Royaume le desseign quils avoient auparavant [projecté]." Whether or not this again included inviting Philip II to occupy the throne of France, it is to be presumed that Lorraine meant to revoke the edict of Longjumeau, publish the decrees of Trent, expel the pastors and exterminate Calvinism. This "desseign" was to follow Alva's proposal and begin with the elimination of the Huguenot leaders. This was determined in a council meeting at which one man was appointed to each Huguenot leader and dispatched to seek out and assassinate him. Both these schemes came to nothing, however, because Catherine had recovered by mid-May, and the Huguenots were warned and proved impossible to surprise.[81]

The failure to dispose of the Protestant leaders in May 1568 proved to be disastrous for Lorraine because dramatic events, occurring simultaneously in Scotland, England and in the Netherlands, distracted his attention from domestic affairs. These events also brought about an immediate expansion of his objectives, which were nevertheless hampered by the continued existence of his Protestant enemies at home. In April 1568 William of Orange published his *Justification*. This was followed, at the end of May, by a dramatic victory of William's brother, Louis of Nassau, at Heiligerlee; events which quickly drove Alva to the violence he had always advocated. In the same month of May, Queen Mary fled from her adversaries in Scotland and took refuge with her embarrassed cousin in England. Mary had a notorious claim to the throne of England and, in spite of her dubious marriage to the earl of Bothwell, was regarded as eligible.

80. Ibid., 515–16, 7 August 1568, Norris to Elizabeth.
81. PRO/SP/70/105; *CSPF.*, *1566–68*, pp. 458–59, 17 May 1568, Norris to Cecil.

This gravid development was therefore fraught with dangers and possibilities, which closely concerned her uncle, Lorraine. Indeed, Mary's sudden availability inspired what was surely Lorraine's most ambitious endeavor, undertaken with complete disregard for the policy of the French crown.

As he was out of favor with the French king, Lorraine was quick to see that the duc d'Anjou might serve his turn, in many ways even better than the king himself. He proposed to resuscitate the idea of an international Catholic league, and, in order to combine this with his elimination policy in France, Lorraine required a princely figurehead. Consequently he sought to exploit the authority and aspirations of the duc d'Anjou who, as heir apparent and lieutenant general, possessed vice-regal powers. Anjou had been appointed lieutenant general following the death of the old duc de Montmorency in 1567, in order to supersede the claims of the prince de Condé to promotion as constable. After the "incident de Meaux," if not before, Condé was persona non grata. While, in theory, Anjou's appointment kept command of the armies in royal hands, it also rendered him a potential rival of his brother the king; especially with Lorraine at his back. Lorraine, seeking to build up the power he could wield through Anjou, induced the Parisians to demand him as their *gouverneur* in place of Marshal Montmorency. Control of Paris had long been one of Lorraine's objectives.[82] At the same time, Lorraine offered Anjou 200,000 francs per annum from the Church, "to sustain the Romish religion, whereto the Pope the King of Spain and other Papistical Princes have promised all help in everything that he attempts to the ruin of them of the religion."[83]

If Charles persisted in making peace with his heretics, his lieutenant might yet be employed against them. But Lorraine began by dangling before the youthful prince a much more romantic enticement. He proposed to bring Mary back to France, where she would be induced to yield to Anjou all her estate in

---

82. *CSPF.*, *1566-68*, pp. 476-77, 7 June 1568, Norris to Elizabeth. Montmorency was removed, but it was Alençon, Anjou's brother, who took his place, presumably as a compromise decision. Ibid., 494, 5 July 1568, Norris to Cecil.

83. Ibid., 476-77, 7 June 1568, Norris to Elizabeth.

Scotland and in England—which could only have been through the crown matrimonial. Mary had been Anjou's sister-in-law, but the pope is said to have consented.[84] The moderates, however, who had supported the peace, were aware of Lorraine's tactics. Already on 2 May, when Catherine was ill, a council was held in her room, at which the three marshals Montmorency, Damville and Vieilleville opposed the lieutenancy of Anjou. As commander-in-chief of the royal forces at the age of sixteen, he would be a considerable liability to the marshals. But they were even more concerned to remove "the platform of the Cardinal of Lorraine's devices," for Anjou's appointment had been strongly urged by the pope.[85] At the end of June, Montmorency and Lorraine are said to have been "admitted chief of the Privy Council."[86] Since their purposes were quite opposed, and the pope regarded Montmorency and the chancellor as his principal enemies in the council, this was symptomatic of the continuation of a serious struggle for power.[87] It was to produce great confusion, not to say contradiction in "royal" policy, and caused the young Anjou to be pulled this way and that. It was in order to undermine Lorraine's "devices to hold his credit with Monsr. D'Anjou" that Catherine and Montmorency initiated negotiations for his marriage to Queen Elizabeth. Even though she "never meant the same should take place," this was still a useful ploy to counteract the even less plausible marvels promised by Lorraine. Thus they hoped to "work him out of favour."[88]

As the continued existence of the Huguenot leaders in France was likely to hinder Lorraine's enterprise of England, he made a further attempt, about this time, to detach the prince de Conde from the Huguenots. Not only would this have strengthened the Catholic faction with the authority of an older prince than Anjou,

84. Idem., 481, 17 June 1568, Norris to Cecil; 489-90, 28 June 1568, Norris to Cecil.

85. Ibid., 453-55, 12 May 1568, Norris to Elizabeth.

86. Ibid., 490, 28 June 1568, Norris to Cecil.

87. Hirschauer, *La Politique de St. Pie V*, 101-3, 16 October 1567, the pope to della Torre.

88. *CSPF.*, *1566-68*, p. 487, 23 June 1568, Norris to Cecil.

but Lorraine also needed a general. Thus it was probably then that he offered Condé the command of the enterprise, although the timing of this is uncertain. Condé, in any case, indignantly rejected his overtures.[89] In the meanwhile, the activities of Alva in the Netherlands were also calculated to alert and enrage the Huguenots, who were obviously expected to react adversely to the execution, on 5 June, of Egmont, Coligny's cousin, and Horne, among numerous other noblemen. Consequently, on the very same day, La Valette, Chavigny and Tavannes were detailed to murder Condé, Coligny, and d'Andelot, respectively. But they found their counsel revealed and their victims so well protected that nothing was attempted.[90]

This reverse did not, however, deter Lorraine from his enterprise of England. Early in July Norris was gravely warned that France, Spain and the pope were conspiring to destroy the queen of England, "whereby the Queene of Scotts might succeed hir Majesty."[91] This was shortly confirmed by Châtillon, who also gave news of Lorraine's connection with "divers particular persons in England, who mind to make some insurrection." This correspondence was conducted through the Spanish ambassador in England, through Alva in the Netherlands, and also by way of Rome.[92] Both Coligny and d'Andelot—in the light of their own experience—believed Queen Elizabeth to be in imminent danger

89. Ibid., 474, 4 June 1568, Norris to Elizabeth; Haynes, *State Papers*, 473–75, 6 October 1568, instructions for M. de Cavaignes. Condé here refers to having been offered the command in August, three or four days before his departure from Noyers. The instructions are briefly calendared in English in *HMC Hatfield*, i, 364–65, instructions for M. de Cavaignes going to England, 6 October 1568. This was not the date of the document but the date on which the instructions were delivered at Windsor.

90. *CSPF.*, *1566–68*, p. 477, 7 June 1568, Norris to Elizabeth; 489, 28 June 1568, Norris to Cecil.

91. Ibid., 489–90, 28 June 1568, Norris to Cecil; Haynes, *State Papers*, 466, 7 July 1568, Norris to Cecil.

92. *CSPF.*, *1566–68*, p. 500, 14 July 1568, Norris to Elizabeth; 502, 14 July 1568, Norris to Cecil. This was the continental background to the rising of the northern earls, followed by the Ridolfi plot.

from Italians sent by Lorraine to practice against her.[93] Norris could not identify them, but he confirmed that Lorraine was "a most cruel enemy to the queen and her country." Martigues, he warned Cecil, was ready with his forces shortly to go to England to rescue Mary. The Spanish ambassador, then on his way to England, had had a long conference with Lorraine before going on to Alva in the Netherlands.[94]

It was the Huguenot reaction to affairs in the Netherlands, and the consequent renewal of civil war in France, which averted this enterprise of England in the summer of 1568. Alva's assault on the nobility, early in June, led to large numbers of refugees crossing into France. They elicited immediate support from the Huguenots who began to assemble forces in Picardy. Late in July a preliminary expedition under the captains Mouvans and Cocqueville was intercepted by Marshal Cossé at St. Valéry, with heavy casualties. Cocqueville and three others were executed.[95] Nevertheless, many other leading Huguenot captains were biding their time, until the awaited invasion of the Netherlands by William of Orange.[96] Late in August, just as he was ready to move, a formal alliance was drawn up between William of Orange and Condé and Coligny, whereby they guaranteed each other full mutual support. If either party were to be at peace, then it would go to the assistance of the other.[97] When William crossed the Rhine from Cologne, he was expecting some 7,000 to 8,000

93. Ibid., 505, 23 July 1568, Norris to Cecil.

94. Martigues was *gouverneur* of Brittany. Ibid., 508, 29 July 1568 Norris to Cecil.

95. Ibid., 505, 23 July 1568, Norris to Cecil; 509, 29 July 1568, Norris to Cecil; 512, 2 August 1568, Norris to Cecil.

96. On 7 September 1568 Mouy (who was murdered during the third civil war) pleaded for the help of 3,000 Englishmen because he was trapped between Dieppe and St. Valéry. Ibid., 544, 9 September 1568, Norris to Cecil.

97. Van Prinsterer, *Archives ou correspondance*, série i, vol. iii, 282–86, August 1568. While there is no evidence that this treaty was ever signed, the fact that it was drafted is, in itself, significant; both sides acted as though it existed. I am grateful to Dr. J. J. Woltjer for his help and advice on this point.

French to invade the Netherlands.[98] Henceforth, the affairs of the Netherlands and those of the Huguenots were to be inseparably linked. Coligny's unfruitful conception of reuniting France in her former anti-Hapsburg policy and making war on Spain in the Netherlands dated from this time. It should be noted, however, that this was the antithesis of the sort of factional, religious war which actually occurred, and which he vainly sought to avert.

This was the first of several occasions upon which it was essential, at all costs, to prevent a major invasion of the Netherlands. Consequently, it was events in the Netherlands which explain the timing of Lorraine's next coup against the Huguenot leaders, fixed for 25 August 1568 for he had not, in the meanwhile, been so dazzled by his enterprise of England as to neglect the affairs of France. He rather appears to have promoted a nation-wide organization, both by means of careful appointments and by Catholic associations.[99] These were ready to fall upon the Huguenots, each in their own area, lured by the hope of confiscated property. Previously it had been "the meaner sort of men" who had principally suffered. Now Lorraine, like Alva, meant to attack the nobility, "so that they will shortly be forced either to yield up their lives or fly to arms."[100] In either case, they would be unable to campaign in the Netherlands. In the event, it was actually William of Orange and Louis of Nassau who came to the assistance of their allies in France.[101]

98. Ibid., 260, July 1568, William to his brother Nassau; this suggests that the treaty was valid. William invaded early in September.

99. Condé told the king of a "confrerie du St. Esprit" which was said to be arming the gentry in Burgundy. Archives de Chantilly, 1213, ff. 15–18, 12 July 1568, Condé to Charles IX.

100. *CSPF., 1566–68*, p. 516, 7 August 1568, Norris to Cecil. Condé later declared that they had taken up arms for the preservation of the nobility as well as for religion, after having tried all legitimate and peaceful means to prevent extermination of the religion and those who professed it. Haynes, *State Papers*, 473–75, instructions for M. de Cavaignes going to England.

101. Orange entered France on 17 November 1568. La Ferrière, "La Troisième guerre civile et la paix de St. Germain," *Revue des questions historiques*, xli, 1887, p. 85; B. N., Mss. Fr., 5783, Jules Gassot, Discours sommaire, ff. 8 seq.

Late in August forces were converging on Burgundy, where Condé and Coligny were living. Furthermore, the comte de Retz, with Rochefort and des Croissettes, were there, it is said, with a dozen Italians, "qui se vantent de faire merveilles."[102] When he was ready, Lorraine assured Catherine and the sick king that, with the proffered help of Spain and the pope, they "might exterminate the religion whensoever they would."[103] He appears to have envisaged that once the leaders were dead, his extensive preparations would enable him to exterminate or overwhelm the Protestants everywhere, thereby opening the way for his enterprise of England.[104] This was seasoned Triumvirate policy. Once again, however, the Huguenot leaders received timely warnings.[105]

On 23 August, just as William was expected to enter the Netherlands, Condé and Coligny fled with their families from Noyers (Yonne). Condé intended to go to the house of his brother-in-law, La Rochefoucauld but had, instead, to go to La Rochelle. This was the only remaining Protestant stronghold, which Lorraine was planning to besiege from the sea.[106] In his opinion, the Protestants would be lost if La Rochelle were to fall.[107] At the same time, the vidame de Chartres, Montgomery and La Noue evaded Martigues in Brittany; La Rochefoucauld escaped from the sieur de Ruffec, and Jeanne d'Albret, mother of Henry of Navarre, eluded Monluc in Gascony.[108] They all took

102. PRO/SP/70/105.
103. Idem; *CSPF.*, *1566–68*, p. 538, 2 September 1568, Norris to Elizabeth.
104. PRO/SP/70/105. This gives the details of Lorraine's preparations.
105. Condé had been steadily complaining of machinations against him, and of the ill-treatment of Protestants generally. See for example, Archives de Chantilly, 1213, ff. 15–18, 12 July 1568, Condé to Charles IX; ff. 19–23, 27 July 1568, Condé to Charles IX; Archives de Chantilly, papiers de Condé, série i, vol. ii, f. 231v, 30 July 1568, Condé to Charles IX.
106. *CSPF.*, *1566–68*, p. 516, 7 August 1568, Norris to Elizabeth.
107. Ibid., 538, 2 September 1568, Norris to Elizabeth.
108. Marlet; *Montgommery*, 68–69; Bastard d'Estang, *Jean de Ferrières*, 99–100; Amirault, *François de la Noue*, 19–22; Roelker, *Queen of Navarre*, 299–301.

refuge in La Rochelle, except for Châtillon, who escaped to England.[109] There, in a long discourse to William Cecil, he detailed the Protestants' *gravamina* since the peace of Longjumeau. It is the best account we have.[110]

The flight of the Huguenot leaders was not a rising, and Condé was extremely careful not to repeat past mistakes. The day before his departure, he sent his secretary to the king to explain what he was doing.[111] He departed unarmed with, he said, more cradles than lances and more coaches and carts than warhorses.[112] But he appears, however, to have been succored by forces on the way, which was probably very necessary, but not prearranged.[113] At successive stages on the journey, he continued to issue statements—to Marshal Vieilleville, and to Monluc in Guyenne, to make it clear that he did not intend war. But, when his letter to the king was received on 26 August, a *mandement* was issued to assemble an army, in order to obtain by means of war against him what the conspiracy had failed to achieve. The *mandement*, Condé said, was the first he heard, by way of a reply and, on 30 August, his envoy was arrested.[114]

Lorraine moved swiftly in order to counter the Huguenots' complaints and declarations. On 25 August he issued two proclamations—in the name of the king, who was gravely ill and quite inactive. These were calculated to make the Huguenots appear to be the aggressors. One proclamation declared that mas-

---

109. B. N., Mss. Cinq Cents Colbert, 24, f. 182, 5 September 1568, Châtillon to Charles IX; printed by Marlet, *Correspondance d'Odet de Coligny, cardinal de Châtillon*, 89–90, 5 September 1568, Châtillon to Charles IX, from Sénarpont, near Amiens.

110. Châtillon's Discourse [September] 1568; printed by Atkinson, *The Cardinal of Châtillon in England*, 93–106.

111. B. N., Mss. Cinq Cents Colbert, 24, f. 178, 22 August 1568, Condé to Charles IX; printed by Aumale, *Histoire des princes de Condé*, ii, 357–58.

112. Cecil Papers, 4, f. 33v [September 1568], Declaration of the prince de Condé. The document bears the date 23 August. This refers to the date of their departure and not to the document.

113. *CSPF., 1566–68*, p. 534, 29 August 1568, Norris to Elizabeth.

114. Cecil Papers, 4, ff. 32v–33 [September 1568], Declaration of the prince de Condé.

ters of requests had been sent to various places to investigate Protestant complaints. These had all proved to be either groundless or greatly exaggerated. The second proclamation announced that the Huguenot leaders had taken up arms, but ordered that Protestants who respected the edicts were not to be molested.[115] What, therefore, had they to complain about?

Since war in France was inevitably going to involve the Netherlands and England, which was potentially highly dangerous, Catherine immediately sent word to Condé to "stay at some place where she may come and confer with him."[116] If any further proof is needed that her policy was not that of Lorraine, this letter was intercepted by the Catholics. On 1 September, a proclamation in the name of the king commanded leaders of the gendarmerie to assemble at Orléans under Anjou because, it stated, the chiefs of the new religion had taken up arms. In fact it had already been resolved that, if they escaped from the traps which were laid for them, Montpensier in Anjou, Martigues in Brittany, du Lude in Poitou and Monluc in Guyenne would assemble troops with which to close in upon La Rochelle.[117] Lorraine, at least according to Norris, had planned to make his enemy appear in the wrong, and it was easy to sneer at their disclaimers once they were gathered at La Rochelle.[118]

By the beginning of September, or before, it was determined to march against Condé, and war was assumed to have begun.[119] Possibly assisted by Châtillon, Queen Elizabeth declared, with uncharacteristic promptitude, that she would intervene. Norris delivered this message to the king, queen and council on 8 September, and subsequently submitted it in writing. Her decision, the message said, rested upon "the duty due to her subjects, the friendship she has for the King, and the preservation of her own

115. *CSPF., 1566–68*, p. 531, 25 August 1568.
116. Ibid., 534–35, 29 August 1568, Norris to Elizabeth. Norris reported the "great bruit" of English preparations for war.
117. Ibid., 537, 1 September 1568, proclamation; PRO/SP/70/105.
118. *CSPF., 1566–68*, pp. 537–39, 2 September 1568, Norris to Elizabeth.
119. Ibid., 539, 2 September 1568, Norris to Cecil.

estate."[120] Then, and later, Elizabeth made it quite clear that she distinguished between the king (or more likely Catherine) and Lorraine, to whom the import of her message was perfectly plain. He affected to rejoice that the intervention of Elizabeth in France would inflame Philip and the emperor against her, and so facilitate the enterprise of England.[121] At this same time, Condé issued a declaration from La Rochelle in which he stated that he took up arms, not against the king, "but only to protect those of the religion from the tyranny and oppression of their enemies." He protested before God that he had no alternative, after having done everything possible for the peace of the kingdom.[122]

If Lorraine had once again missed his mark, he had nevertheless obtained the war which he otherwise needed. It was not, however, entirely convenient, both because it deferred his English plans and also because he did not control the army. This was the greatest weakness that Lorraine was never able to surmount. Three marshals, Montmorency, his brother Damville and Vieilleville all refused to serve, thereby emphasizing the deep division in the council. But Catherine's protests went unheeded, that she would have no wars, and that the king (who in mid-September was still unable to leave his bed) would reconcile his nobility with clemency.[123] Nevertheless, Lorraine still had to face stout opposition in council from the chancellor L'Hospital

120. Ibid., 544, 9 September 1568, Norris to Cecil; 545 [10 September 1568], message delivered by Norris to the king.

121. Sir Nicholas Throckmorton feared an all-out ideological war at this time. He was alarmed by what would become of England when "the like professors with us shall be utterly destroyed in Flanders and France." He referred, of course, to religion. *HMC Hatfield*, i, 363–64, 18 September 1568, Throckmorton to Cecil. Norris also reported that if Alva was successful in the Netherlands, he would, forthwith, invade England. *CSPF., 1566–68*, p. 542, 6 September 1568, Norris to Cecil; 548, 15 September 1568, Norris to Elizabeth. Much money was allegedly being spent on purchasing the nobility of Scotland. Ibid., 532, 27 August 1568, Norris to Elizabeth.

122. *CSPF., 1566–68*, p. 544, 9 September 1568, Declaration of the prince de Condé.

123. Ibid., 541–42, 6 September 1568, Norris to Cecil.

until, eventually, he was forced to retire. Only then did Lorraine finally obtain the edict for which he had striven exactly a year before followed, on 25 September, by the suppression, among others, of all the judicial and financial offices held by the Protestants.[124] The edict of Saint-Maur, registered on 23 September, was, in a sense, Lorraine's manifesto and triumph. The preamble represented an extreme Catholic statement of all the troubles in France since the death of Henry II. In this respect it was a justification of his policy, or, at least, useful propaganda. The edict itself revoked that of Longjumeau, prohibited any religion but that of Rome, and ordered all pastors to leave the country within two weeks—a policy which had been propounded at Bayonne. The Huguenots were therefore almost back where they had started, and a major conflict was bound to ensue.

The renewal of war did not, however, cause Lorraine to abandon his attempts to catch the Huguenot leaders, who were still the principal obstacles in his path. Thus, on 30 September, as the war was just beginning, Norris informed Cecil that fifty Italians had each received 1,000 crowns apiece "to empoison wine, wells and other victuals to the destruction of the Prince of Condé and the Admiral."[125] If this sounds somewhat colorful, it should be remembered that these elusive men had already survived for far too long. Their removal was not only urgent, but vital to Lorraine, and all who subscribed to his international Catholicism. Furthermore, it would be most advantageous if their destruction could now be represented as acts of war. Consequently strenuous efforts were made to eliminate them. Condé was the first to fall, murdered as a prisoner after the battle of Jarnac on 13 March 1569. D'Andelot also died, at Saintes, on 7 May 1569; whether of poison, a camp fever, or both, has never been ascertained. De

124. Ibid., 537, 30 September 1568, Norris to Elizabeth; Fontanon, *Les Édits et ordonnances*, iv, 292–94; *CSPF., 1566–68*, p. 583, 16 December 1568, letters patent concerning the execution of the edict of 25 September 1568. Another edict of 14 December 1568 deprived Protestants of all State offices. Ibid., 583.

125. *CSPF., 1566–68*, p. 558, 30 September 1568, Norris to Cecil. There are numerous documentary references to the use of Italians as hired assassins.

Spes, the Spanish ambassador in England, informed Alva that d'Andelot had been poisoned by a Florentine, and that the same had been tried on Coligny and La Rochefoucauld, who were unaffected. Coligny and La Rochefoucauld were, in fact, seriously ill at that time, but they recovered. Norris reported a similar rumor, but he did not mention La Rochefoucauld.[126] However this may be, Alava, the Spanish ambassador in France, and the pope, Pius V, both claimed to have put pressure on Catherine to follow up the victory of Jarnac by the death of the Huguenot leaders; Alava specified Coligny, d'Andelot and La Rochefoucauld.[127] There were other, very similar incidents in the summer of 1569 and, on 13 September, the *parlement* issued an *arrêt de mort* depriving Coligny of honors, offices, and property, and placing the substantial price of 50,000 *écus* on his head.[128] This was warmly applauded by the pope.[129] Early in October, after the murder of Coligny's first lieutenant, M. de Mouy, there were reports by Alava and Norris that six soldiers had plotted to murder the admiral and the chief of those about him. Charles de Louviers, seigneur de Maurevert claimed to have been one of these. It was he who shot Mouy, circumstances having prevented him from assaulting the admiral.[130] Maurevert was to make a further attempt, which also failed, on 22 August 1572, two days before the massacre of St. Bartholomew. After the battle of Jarnac and the murder of Condé in March 1569, efforts were made to obtain possession of the young generation of princes, Henri prince de Condé, and his cousin Henry of Navarre. When these

126. Lettenhove, *Relations*, v, 396, 1 June 1569, de Spes to Alva; *CSPF.*, *1569–71*, p. 79, 27 May 1569, Norris to Cecil.

127. Vaissière, *De Quelques assassins*, 97–99, Alava's report of 7 April 1569 of an interview with the queen; De Potter, *Lettres de St. Pie V*, 36–38, 28 March 1569, the pope to Charles IX; 62, 26 April 1569, the pope to Anjou.

128. B. N., Mss. Fr., 5549, ff. 57 bis., 13 September 1569, *arrêt* of the *parlement*.

129. De Potter, *Lettres de St. Pie V*, 74–76, 12 October 1569, the pope to Charles IX.

130. Vaissière, *De Quelques assassins*, 102–3, 9 October 1569, Alava to Alva; *CSPF.*, *1569–71*, p. 130, 10 October 1569, Norris to Leicester and Cecil.

efforts failed, they too, according to Norris, were included in yet another attempt to dispatch Coligny in January 1570.[131] Clearly Coligny and the other Huguenot leaders were not intended to survive the third civil war, which their elimination in August 1568 should—at least in theory—have averted.

According to the usual pattern, there were intermittent peace negotiations during the war. In the summer of 1569 peace was desired both by the Catholic commanders—because their forces were decimated by famine and sickness—and by Coligny, who was now seconded by Louis of Nassau. But Coligny required guarantees for complete freedom of religion.[132] Such a peace was inevitably opposed and obstructed by Spain and the pope and, in order to prevent it, Alva himself was prepared to invade France. In other words, the continuation of war in France was a Spanish priority.[133]

Negotiations were resumed in November 1569, with the onset of an early winter. By December articles of peace had been drafted under several heads, including religion, property, justice and guarantees—matters which were to dominate all future negotiations until the end of the wars. The queen of Navarre was determined that there should be no peace which did not guarantee religion, and thought that the treaty ought to include the Protestant princes of Germany. "As the danger is common, so should be the defence."[134] This is another illustration of the extent to which

131. *CSPF.*, *1569–71*, p. 174, 27 January 1570, Norris to Elizabeth.

132. Ibid., 94, 9 July 1569, Norris to Cecil; Delaborde, *Coligny*, iii, 560–65, Coligny's petition, July 1569.

133. *CSPSp.*, *1568–79*, pp. 159–60, 1 June 1569, Alva to Phillip II. Alva's concern with France was, at that moment, largely negative. He did not want a war with England while Elizabeth still held Spanish property impounded after the affair of the Spanish treasure ships in December 1568. He was also afraid that if peace returned to France, Anjou would be married to Mary queen of Scots, which would involve the French enterprise of England. But, if Alva were to invade France, Spain might obtain a free hand in England and might herself dispose of Mary. One might add that Spain was still involved with the revolt of the Moriscos, and war in France was greatly to her advantage.

134. *CSPF.*, *1569–71*, pp. 144–45, 24 November 1569, the queen of Navarre to the princes of Navarre and Condé. Now that Navarre, first

the Huguenot cause had become international. However different their domestic circumstances, Protestants of different kinds in France, England, the Netherlands and Germany were all menaced by militant Catholicism, mainly directed from Rome. This factor also accounts for the Huguenots' hesitation late in 1569. It was not a moment to relax, just when the rising of the northern earls was stirring in England, because Lorraine was anxious to intervene and, among other things, to carry off the young king James VI of Scotland.[135] The Scottish regent, Murray, was murdered on 23 January 1570, which was not considered to be a coincidence. After the collapse of the northern rising there were, if anything, even more compelling reasons why the French Catholics should not be released from domestic trouble to embark on the enterprise of England. By the beginning of February, there were substantial preparations for this enterprise, and Elizabeth's excommunication, on 25 February, was calculated to facilitate her replacement by Mary.[136] The pope also provided considerable financial help. This was a great and prolonged emergency, which evolved into the Ridolfi plot in 1571.

It was therefore obvious that the Huguenots were going to demand, and to hold out for, everything they wanted. They had, after all, taken up arms in defense of their lives, religion and property, and they would not be lulled or tricked into any further agreement which did not at least purport to guarantee their security. Considering the history of the vendetta, and the more general policy of "elimination," it is hardly surprising that security should have become a Huguenot obsession. The Catholics had a way of remaining in arms, and the Huguenots were never again to submit to the sole defense of the law. They repeated, ad nauseam, that they did not oppose the crown; but it had remained power-

---

prince of the blood, was nearly sixteen, Jeanne d'Albret briefly assumed greater importance in Protestant affairs, but she was always regarded as a difficult character. Ibid., 145, 24 November 1569, advertisements from France; 159, December 1569, articles for the pacification of France.

135. Ibid., 149, 10 December 1569, Norris to Cecil.

136. Ibid., 174–75, 27 January 1570, Norris to Elizabeth; 181–82, 5 February 1570, Norris to Elizabeth; 193, 25 February 1570, Norris to Cecil.

less to fulfill its obligations. Now the Catholics had found that winning battles did not dispose of the war. Nor, on the other hand, could Lorraine ever, possibly, accept the Huguenots' demands. The two sides had, therefore, reached a state of deadlock, quite apart from the wider considerations which, in fact, were constantly impinging on Huguenot fortunes. The issue of war or peace in France concerned all Europe, directly or indirectly, and so did the contents of the next edict of pacification.

Queen Elizabeth offered the king mediation, and to the Huguenots money—some measure of her deep concern—and Châtillon maintained that England and the German princes should all be required to guarantee the new peace.[137] Thus encouraged, the Huguenots stood out for freedom of religion, and much journeying and hard bargaining ensued. Given a little patience, circumstances were gradually beginning to favor them. In the first place, by February 1570, almost all the council wanted peace as the only practicable policy.[138] These were the circumstances, foreign and domestic, in which Lorraine began to lose his vital grip on the council, the foundation of his power. If he could no longer sustain the war, then he was bound to be overtaken by others who could, and would, conclude a reasonable peace. Thus the moderates became correspondingly more effective, just as they had in 1568, before the peace of Longjumeau.[139] In April 1570 the Protestant commissioner, Téligny, was forbidden to negotiate either with Lorraine or in his presence or that of his followers.[140] This suggests that the disgrace of their mortal enemies, Lorraine and the Guises, was, in effect, a Protestant prerequisite for peace, just as it had been in October 1562;[141] certainly peace could be achieved in no other way. Temporary concessions in France, for the sake of the enterprise of England,

137. Ibid., 191, 23 February 1570, instructions for Norris; 200–1, 9 March 1570, Châtillon to Cecil.

138. B. N., Mss. Italien, 1727, ff. 118v–19, 6 February 1570.

139. Ibid., f. 144v, 6 April 1570.

140. Desjardins, *Négs. Tosc.*, iii, 624, 26 April 1570; B. N., Mss. Italien, 1727, f. 148v, 7 April 1570.

141. *CSPRome, 1558–71*, p. 108, 18 October 1562, Santa-Croce to Borromeo.

would have been Lorraine's only conceivable face-saving expedient.[142] But his extreme Catholic policy had never been adopted by the crown, and would no longer command support in the council. Lorraine therefore had no way to turn and, by early May, he appears to have regarded peace as inescapable.[143] Peace did not, however, follow immediately, because the Protestants were in a position to raise their demands. Thus, while articles were under discussion late in June, Coligny made a swift advance towards Paris, and forced a truce. That assisted the conclusion of peace; besides, necessary arrangements for the king's marriage to Elizabeth of Austria could not be completed so long as the war continued.

The fall of Lorraine, in July or August, was probably sealed by the disgrace of his nephew, Henri duc de Guise, for having audaciously aspired to the hand of Marguerite, the king's sister.[144] Whether this was a desperate maneuver on the part of Lorraine—since Marguerite was destined to marry his enemy, Navarre—or simply a disastrous coincidence, is uncertain. But, by 11 August, at the latest, Lorraine had been excluded from the council.[145] The peace of Saint-Germain, which was then concluded, shattered Lorraine's designs and high ambitions. As the Huguenots' most dangerous and indefatigable enemy, he was disarmed.[146] But the papal policy of international Catholicism, of which he had been the greatest protagonist, naturally survived his fall from power; nor was he a negligible force at one remove. The extremists, however, had lost the initiative and, temporarily, their policy became rather more arcane, and difficult to trace.

The edict of Saint-Germain, signed on 8 August 1570, is the

---

142. *CSPF.*, *1569–71*, p. 274, 20 June 1570, Norris to Elizabeth.

143. Ibid., 255, 4 May 1570, Lorraine to ——— [?] This document appears to be misplaced.

144. Ibid., 291, 9 July 1570, Norris to Elizabeth and Norris to Cecil.

145. Desjardins, *Négs. Tosc.*, iii, 639, 10 August 1570; 640, 20 August 1570; *CSPF.*, *1569–71*, p. 314, 11 August 1570, Norris to Elizabeth; 343, 23 September 1570, Norris to Cecil.

146. Lorraine returned to power with his protégé Anjou, when he became Henry III in the summer of 1574; he died the following December.

first of the edicts of pacification which could be described as clearly pro-Protestant.[147] It reflected the Huguenots' achievements in the bitter and bloody third civil war, and their unshakable determination never again to accept insufficient terms and safeguards. Indeed, it would hardly be an exaggeration to describe it as a Calvinist charter, standing—juridically—midway between the edict of January 1562 and the ultimate edict of Nantes, 1598. It was conspicuously better drafted than its predecessors, all of which were explicitly superseded. This edict replaced a great deal of confusion by juridical precision.

The purpose of the edict was to restore peace and amity. It provided for the restoration of Church property and the mass, on the one hand, and for freedom of conscience on the other. The religious privileges of the aristocracy, embodied in the edicts of Amboise and Longjumeau, were retained. For everyone else the cult was permitted in two towns per *gouvernement*, and in all places in which it was held on 1 August 1570—an unknown number. Avoiding the cardinal error of previous edicts, the particular cult towns were specified and must, therefore, have been convenient for the Protestants. This was very much less than the complete toleration they had originally claimed. But it was not so much the degree of toleration which counted, as the extent to which the edict was respected. This was the first edict to include certain guarantees, which the Huguenots had stipulated since the earliest negotiations. Thus they obtained four *places de sûreté*, for two years: the strategic towns of La Rochelle, Cognac, La Charité (bridging the Loire) and Montauban, indicating the Huguenot concentration in the south and west. These *places* were primarily required to provide bases, and to ensure the personal safety of the hunted leaders. They made their headquarters at the Atlantic port of La Rochelle, thereby securing communications with England and the Netherlands. The experience of 1568 underlined the importance of such a refuge. This was a substantial safeguard. It gave teeth to the edict, and undermined the specification that only the king might retain arms (article 10). A further guarantee

147. Fontanon, *Les Édits et ordonnances*, iv, 300–4, registered on 11 August 1570.

clause was that royal officials were required to swear to observe
the edict; and the *parlements* were ordered to register it forthwith;
both demands which had been advanced in 1568. Besides a degree
of toleration and physical protection, the edict of Saint-Germain
was the first which sought to allow all that was necessary for the
rehabilitation and reintegration of Protestants into society, from
which they had been increasingly ostracized. The edict therefore
comprised a number of important civil rights which were essential to peaceful coexistence. These rights included equality of
taxation and of eligibility for all offices, schools, academies, hospitals, and the like, and something approaching equality before the
law. Law cases between persons of differing religions were to be
heard by the *baillis* or *sénéchaux* and, in the *parlements*, Protestant
litigants might impugn up to four judges in any one case. All
sequestered property was to be restored, as well as all offices, of
which the Protestants had been deprived at the outbreak of war.
If, therefore, after three civil wars, the restoration of the
Huguenots into society was still not to be achieved for a further
twenty-eight years, this was not because the juridical framework
had never been provided.

6

The Huguenots and the
Netherlands, 1570–1572

THE FALL OF LORRAINE, which had accompanied the liberal edict of
Saint-Germain, exposed the discrepancy between the will of the
crown and that of the extreme Catholics. While the discrepancy
dated from about 1560, it had never before been so nakedly apparent. Now the only possible policy for the crown was that of
reconciliation with the Huguenots, whose place in society it had
newly recognized and guaranteed. This relationship entailed a
corresponding shift in royal policy towards England. England
was similarly endangered by Spain, the Guises and their followers, and Elizabeth had carefully maintained the vital distinction
between supporting the Huguenots and opposing the crown. The
principal instruments of the crown's dual policy were to be the
Bourbon marriage, namely of the king's sister, Marguerite, to
Henry of Navarre, and that of Anjou, his brother and heir apparent, to Queen Elizabeth. Thus the young Navarre, now titular
head of the Huguenot party, was to be integrated into the court,
for which the Catholic justification was his future conversion. This
was not at all what his inflexibly Calvinist mother, Jeanne d'Albret
envisaged. Thus the project was fraught with difficulties and
long delays. Implicit in the implementation of the new edict, the
Bourbon marriage, and the whole policy of reconciliation was the
return to court of Coligny and the Huguenot leaders. This return
could not, however, be facilitated simply by a shift in royal policy, because of the inability of the crown to escape from extreme
Catholic pressures, which had not been terminated by the disgrace
of the Guises. On the contrary, the frustrated Catholics rallied to

their compliant figurehead, Anjou, and opposed both royal and Huguenot policies with resourceful tenacity. They were still supported by Spain and the pope, with Alva nearby in Brussels, and it was to be they who triumphed, once again, through the ultimate murder of Coligny in August 1572 and the massacre of St. Bartholomew which followed. Thus, although the Bourbon marriage was eventually achieved, the two years from August 1570 to August 1572 witnessed the complete collapse of the policy of reconciliation. The crown was then seen to have failed, both in war and in peace, and there was no third course to be followed. Consequently an almost unbridgeable chasm opened between the crown and the Huguenots.

Late in 1570, however, this ruinous failure was by no means inevitable. These two years might, just conceivably, have seen the development of greater stability and peace in France, had it not been for one thing: the fatal Huguenot involvement with the Netherlands. There had been shared undertakings in both the second and third civil wars, and, owing to the hostility of Spain—and Alva in particular—their fortunes were now confounded. Indeed, on the national level, Huguenot affairs became partially subsumed by those of the Netherlands, the hub and focus of European conflict. This, in turn, was the cause of a disastrous dependence—both of the Huguenots and of the crown—on Queen Elizabeth, who, primarily concerned with the defense of England, skillfully deluded them both. Nothing was more calculated to inflame the hostility of Spain, the papacy and French Catholic extremists than involvement in the Netherlands. Like the abortive coup of August 1568, the murder of Coligny in August 1572 was timed to avert a major Huguenot invasion, diverting hostilities from Hainault to the fourth civil war in France.[1]

In 1570 the Netherlands were calm, so there were no immediate demands upon the Huguenot leaders. From the relative safety of La Rochelle, Coligny was concerned with the implementation of the new edict. Elizabeth sent over the puritan Sir Francis

1. The similarities between the situations in August 1568 and in August 1572 should not be overlooked.

Walsingham to support the peace, but chiefly for the Huguenots' encouragement. He returned to France in January 1571, as resident ambassador, and was to be their firm friend and champion.[2] Neither Walsingham nor Norris were at all hopeful that the new peace could last, because the nobility were in no way reconciled.[3] Furthermore, the Catholics immediately began their usual opposition. In August 1570, the pope had already commanded Lorraine to disrupt the peace negotiations which, unknown to him, had in fact been concluded.[4] The cardinal de Bourbon was also required to "troubler et renverser les projects et l'acte d'une paix."[5] Although there had been major changes at court, Lorraine and his supporters were still able to operate, through the entourage of Anjou. They were strongly backed by the pope and the nuncio, Frangipani, who declared his intention to sustain continual Catholic pressure on Charles and Catherine, "oportune e importune."[6] He was joined by an extraordinary nuncio, Bramante, to whom the king defended himself as best he could.[7] But his necessary prevarications, in the face of so much Catholic clamor, fostered villainous rumors from Catholic sources as to his true motives and intentions with respect to the Huguenots.[8] Thus the delicate bud of Huguenot confidence was quickly blighted. In January 1571, Coligny arrested two men, said to have been hired by Lorraine to assassinate him.[9]

2. Digges, *The Compleat Ambassador*, 1–5, 11 August 1570, instructions for Walsingham; 5–6, 15 August 1570, Elizabeth to Walsingham.

3. *CSPF.*, *1569–71*, p. 326, 31 August 1570, Norris to Cecil.

4. De Potter, *Lettres de St. Pie V*, 116, 14 August 1570, Pius V to Lorraine.

5. Ibid., 117–20, 14 August 1570, Pius V to the cardinal de Bourbon; 121–24, 23 September 1570, Pius V to the cardinal de Bourbon.

6. Hirschauer, *La Politique de St. Pie V*, 116, 2 September 1570, Frangipani to Rusticucci; De Potter, *Lettres de St. Pie V*, 125–29, 23 September 1570, Pius V to Lorraine.

7. Hirschauer, *La Politique de St. Pie V*, 139–52, Bramante's parting audience, undated, late 1570 or early 1571.

8. For example, Charles secretly declared in the *parlement* that he never meant to support two religions. La Mothe, *Correspondance diplomatique*, iii, 361, 9 November 1570, La Mothe to Charles, secret.

9. Desjardins, *Négs. Tosc.*, iii, 646–47, 27 January 1571.

These were depressingly familiar situations; and they could not remain static. During these two years the court was most frequently dispersed. While it was some advantage that no one really dominated the council, this vacancy exposed the fatal inadequacy of the king, who was swayed by every breeze and seemingly grasped only immediate issues. Making a feeble bid for independent action, he was unable to agree with his mother, whom he needed, and quarreled violently with Anjou, his brother and heir who, exploited by the cardinal and his faction, could be dangerous. As the Catholics adhered to Anjou, even to the point of treason, Charles was correspondingly thrown back upon the Huguenots. It was, however, *he* who was induced—if unreliably—to support *them*, rather than vice versa, if only because he had no steady purpose of his own. This resulted in royal involvement in a sectional cause, which Charles, for a variety of reasons, was unable to sustain.

It was particularly unfortunate, in the face of such grave difficulties, that once the war was over, the Huguenots became deeply divided. Their lack of coherent leadership greatly contributed to their undoing. Because of their rank, the young princes, Navarre and Condé, were the titular leaders, but they were both under the influence of Navarre's mother, Jeanne d'Albret. Everyone else detested her, and found her impossible to work with; nor, religion apart, did her interests really coincide with those of the other Huguenot leaders. Thus there was no Huguenot agreement about the two royal marriages, or about a proposed Netherlands enterprise—separate matters which became inextricably entangled.

The Bourbon marriage, on which both Charles and Catherine were firmly set, seems to have aroused no Protestant enthusiasm. Jeanne d'Albret was far from sure that it represented her son's best interests, while Coligny and his older generation of supporters were definitely opposed to it. To his younger lieutenants, such as Téligny, Louis of Nassau and the Flemish exiles it was irrelevant, except as a concession with which to bargain for royal support of their Netherlands plans. Coligny, to his dying day, labored for the success of the edict of Saint-Germain, but he could not share Catherine's conception of the means of reconciliation. They would have been ingenious, were it not that she had no others. The Anjou and Bourbon marriages might, together, have brought the crown considerable safeguards, gaining English support—or at least in the eyes of Spain—defusing the Anjou faction, which also threatened Elizabeth, and drawing the princes and Huguenots back to court. For, if they did not return, then the Catholics surely would.

To Coligny also, as a Huguenot leader, it was essential to find some way of securing English support. This is why he favored a marriage between Navarre and Queen Elizabeth. As this would have precluded both the marriages sought by the crown, it was a major policy disagreement. The Navarre proposal had already been put to Queen Elizabeth by Châtillon, through the agency of Sir Nicholas Throckmorton, before the conclusion of the treaty of Saint-Germain.[10] To Coligny, it had the attraction of securing the English alliance for the Huguenot party. In this way the Huguenots would retain their prince—whom they needed as a Protestant counterweight to the Catholics' figurehead, Anjou—and also be free from any dangerous dependence on the crown. Unfortunately, the match offered no corresponding advantages to Queen Elizabeth, who rather wanted to caution Spain by parading her intimacy with the French king. So it was objected that Navarre was too young and too small, and the matter lapsed. French exiles in England then began to work instead for the Anjou match, a policy which was shortly to be adopted by the crown.[11] Late in 1570, Elizabeth's deteriorating relations with Spain inclined her towards France. Thus, ably conducted by Châtillon, the matter "reached daylight" by the end of that

---

10. La Mothe, *Correspondance diplomatique*, iii, 300, 5 September 1570, La Mothe to Charles IX; 357-59, 9 November 1570, La Mothe to Catherine, secret; 359, 9 November 1570, La Mothe to Catherine; Ibid., iv, 224-25, 7 September 1571 (*sic*), La Mothe to Charles IX. The French exiles had been alarmed by Elizabeth's resumption of marriage negotiations with the archduke Charles of Austria. *CSPVen.*, *1558-80*, p. 458, 27 September 1570, Soranzo to the Signory.

11. La Mothe, *Correspondance diplomatique*, iii, 289-301, 5 September 1570, La Mothe to Charles IX; 358, 9 November 1570, private letter to Catherine; Ibid., iv, 224-26, 7 September 1570, La Mothe to Charles IX.

year.[12] In theory, at least, the Anjou match should have brought the Huguenots the alliance of England as well as more harmonious relations with the crown, and it was probably supported by all but a minority—possibly the elder generation—who, like Coligny, opposed it. As originally broached in England, however, towards the end of the third civil war, it had been a joint Franco-Flemish initiative, with the purpose of engineering Anglo-French support for the rebellion in the Netherlands. But all these calculations were hypothetical. That Anjou, Lorraine's Catholic protégé, could hardly be brought to support such a policy, was an obstacle they chose to ignore; that Queen Elizabeth—already gravely troubled at home—could never be brought to support such a policy, was a difficulty they failed to perceive.

While these marriage negotiations proceeded in 1571, the corollary of a Netherlands enterprise was strongly canvassed in France. William of Orange had left France after the siege of Poitiers in 1569 to prepare a second invasion of the Netherlands. But his brother, Louis of Nassau, and many exiles remained behind in France. Once the civil war was over, Nassau and some of the younger, more dynamic Huguenots, led by Téligny, turned their attention to organizing a Netherlands enterprise to coincide with William's invasion. During the peace negotiations, in the summer of 1570, the idea had been floated of making peace in France in order to carry the war into the Netherlands, which could have been generally advantageous to both sides. A degree of condescension by Queen Elizabeth towards the French and Flemish exiles in England fostered the vain conceit of doing this with English support.[13] Coligny himself, in his petition of July 1569, had suggested such a transference of the war.[14] But then, as later, it may not have been generally understood that he was thinking in terms of the "Italian" wars, which had preceded the treaty of Cateau-Cambrésis. While this solution was now hopelessly anachronistic, it was undeniably patriotic, and remained his ideal

---

12. Ibid., iii, 417-20, 29 December 1570, La Mothe to Catherine; 438-42, 18 January 1571, La Mothe to Catherine.

13. Ibid., 256-57, 25 July 1570, La Mothe to Charles IX.

14. Delaborde, *Coligny*, iii, 560-65.

to the end. Coligny emphatically did not wish to campaign in the Netherlands unless the king of France declared war on Spain. It is important to understand that this attitude was not shared by his confederates, who maneuvered him into precisely that predicament. From one source or another, the idea of transference survived, together with much confusion of thought as to what it entailed. There is a possibility that the Huguenots, who had contracted the peace of Saint-Germain very much on their own terms, may have extracted from Charles IX some imprudent undertaking concerning the Netherlands; but this is uncertain.[15] However it may be, a group of Huguenot and Flemish exiles were soon to prevail upon him. He was young, and resented the unjustified military reputation which Anjou had acquired in the third civil war. Nassau tempted Charles, persuading him that he would obtain substantial advantages in the Netherlands without incurring the risk of war with Spain. This was just the sort of unrealistic involvement with the king that Coligny feared.

The persuasion of the king took place while the Anjou marriage negotiations were making progress. For Charles, interference in the Netherlands would guarantee a maximum of Catholic hostility, French, Spanish and papal. If, however, he could be sure of English cooperation, it might—just—be a viable proposition and a possible means of emancipation; otherwise it was chancy in the extreme. It was, however, only for a matter of weeks that the two initiatives advanced simultaneously. As soon as the marriage negotiations showed, as Châtillon said, "quelque fondement,"[16] the Catholics successfully poisoned Anjou against it, disparaging Elizabeth as a barren heretic, among other "dishonourable arguments."[17] Their counter-attractions were a proposal to make him commander of the Holy League against the Turk[18] or, alternatively, to lure him with money into a Guise project for a descent

15. According to de Spes, who may have been unduly suspicious, they, or some of them, had granted to the king one fifth of their property. *CSPSp.*, 1568–79, p. 280, 25 September 1570, de Spes to Philip II.

16. La Mothe, *Correspondance diplomatique*, iii, 455, 31 January 1571, La Mothe to Catherine.

17. Digges, *Compleat Ambassador*, 37, 8 February 1571, Walsingham to Cecil; 43, 18 February 1571, Walsingham to Cecil.

18. Ibid., 26, 28 January 1571, Walsingham to Cecil.

upon Ireland. This would be to divert English attention from the Netherlands.[19] Already, by the beginning of February 1571, Anjou had announced that he would not marry Elizabeth. The vital English negotiation could not, however, be allowed to lapse and, if necessary, Catherine would substitute Alençon for his brother.[20]

By about the end of April 1571 Charles had been persuaded to sanction a developing Netherlands enterprise, for which his reward, at that stage, was to be Hainault and Artois.[21] But all this had been devised in the absence of Coligny. He was informed, but had neither approved nor consented to the plan for which, nevertheless, Charles was going to need him. Catherine was another who disapproved of the enterprise, because of the probability of war with Spain. But Nassau was in the service of Jeanne d'Albret and, together, they could obstruct the Bourbon marriage. That was both Charles's and Catherine's priority policy and, swiftly concluded, it might well have facilitated the English marriage.

The French court dispersed towards the end of April 1571, while Charles awaited the outcome of the negotiation in England. He hunted his way towards Normandy and Brittany, apparently hoping to meet Coligny, Nassau and other Flemish leaders. He evidently held some important secret meeting on 12 July at the château of Lumigny, which belonged to La Noue, one of Téligny's colleagues. While the evidence is poor and garbled, it would appear that Protestant agreement to procure the Bourbon marriage was there extracted, in return for royal support of a Netherlands enterprise.[22] Whether or not Nassau had been at Lumigny, he definitely attended a slightly less obscure meeting at Fon-

---

19. Ibid., 34–36, 8 February 1571, Walsingham to Cecil; 38, 8 February 1571, Walsingham to Mildmay; La Mothe, *Correspondance diplomatique*, vii, 185, 19 February 1571, Charles IX to La Mothe.

20. La Mothe, *Correspondance diplomatique*, vii, 178–80, 2 February 1571, Catherine to La Mothe.

21. Desjardins, *Négs. Tosc.*, iii, 657–61, 23 March 1571; La Huguerye, *Mémoires*, i, 24–25.

22. La Huguerye, *Mémoires*, i, 25; Lettenhove, *Documents inédits du XVIe siècle*, 133–34, rapport sur la conférence secrète de Lumigny, 19 July 1571.

tainebleau from 28 to 30 July 1571. This meeting is an important landmark in a confusing story, because it was then that a *specific* enterprise was determined, and is said to have been approved by the king. This was a plan to partition the Netherlands between France, England and the Empire. France was to receive Flanders and Artois; Brabant, Guelderland and Luxembourg were to go to the Empire, under the authority of William of Orange, while England's share was to be Zealand and places on the west coast. Nassau had argued that the enterprise was honorable and legitimate, easy to execute and a wonderful opportunity for Charles. Charles, indeed, may have thought that the recovery of Flanders and Artois could yield him a measure of much-needed prestige, and might commend itself to traditionalists. No doubt Nassau also supposed that the prospect of important acquisitions would prove irresistible to Queen Elizabeth, and lure her into agreement. If so, it shows just how little he and his colleagues understood what they were doing.

It was intended to execute this ambitious plan—after the Bourbon marriage—in the following spring of 1572; the date was never more precise. It gradually becomes clear that everyone had agreed that the Bourbon marriage was to precede the enterprise. This, and the vital proviso that the project was conditional on the support of England, were two principal reasons why the enterprise miscarried.[23] Elizabeth exploited this God-sent advantage with a faultless sense of timing, while the Bourbon marriage was easily delayed. Instead of leading to glory and aggrandizement, the enterprise ended in danger, defeat and the massacre of the Huguenots. The policy of transference was a boomerang.

Just when everything depended on the cooperation of England, the English negotiation collapsed. As England was convulsed by the dangers of the Ridolfi plot, Elizabeth had come to accept the necessity of the Anjou marriage and had so far yielded in matters of religion that she was prepared to omit it from the treaty.[24]

23. Digges, *Compleat Ambassador*, 123-28, 12 August 1571, Walsingham to Burghley.
24. If the French thought Anjou's honour preserved, in that his religion was not denied to him, so was hers in that she had not assented to it. Ibid., 111, 9 July 1571, Elizabeth to Walsingham; 116, 7 July 1571,

Frantic efforts, however, on the part of "hinderers" on both sides of the Channel destroyed what slight confidence had ever existed between Elizabeth and the French.[25] The Ridolfi plot was not yet over, and Catholics still believed that Anjou might yet be married to Queen Mary II of England. Meanwhile, he was bribed with a large annual pension from the clergy; it was even proposed that he might replace Don John of Austria as general of the Holy League, and La Mothe reported him to have received a secret commission from the pope to exterminate the Protestants in France.[26] As Anjou stood out for the impossible, namely public assurance as to his religion, Paul de Foix, a good friend to England, was sent to salvage what he could of the negotiation.[27] If the marriage negotiation was all too easily frustrated, "amity," at least, could be secured without the consent of Anjou or the Catholics. A straight alliance was what everyone concerned now began to hope for.

Both the Bourbon marriage and the enterprise of the Netherlands, and probably also an alliance with England, required the return of Coligny to court. Early in July 1571 Charles had determined to send for him, and later in the month Catherine actually did so. Coligny acknowledged her letter on 3 August but wrote only about matters arising from the edict.[28] There seems to have been some confusion among Protestants as to *why* Coligny was absent. Walsingham reported their wanting Elizabeth to intercede for him, as he should not be suffered to live "in such a corner as Rochel." Walsingham was aware of the need for Coligny's cooperation in matters of great trust, because of the insufficiency

Leicester to Walsingham. It appears that Elizabeth did not mean to give way to any Catholic demands.

25. La Mothe, *Correspondance diplomatique*, iv, 165, 9 July 1571, La Mothe to Charles IX.

26. Ibid., 208–9, 6 August 1571, La Mothe to Catherine. This was quite possible, especially as potential commander of the Holy League. Charrière, *Négociations de la France dans le Levant*, iii, 165–68, 8 August 1571 François de Noailles to Fizes; Digges, *Compleat Ambassador*, 119–20, 31 July 1571, Walsingham to Leicester.

27. Digges, *Compleat Ambassador*, 118–19, 31 July 1571, Walsingham to Burghley; 119–20, 31 July 1571, Walsingham to Leicester.

28. B. N., Mss. Fr., 15553, f. 153, 3 August 1571, Coligny to Catherine.

of others, and the king's own addiction to pleasure.[29] In other words, the inexperienced king was out of his depth. The boot, however, was on the other foot: both the Huguenot party and Coligny had been committed in his absence to much that he could not approve of. Neither the admiral himself, nor those most concerned for his safety, wanted his return to court; nor did they think it necessary. After the conference at Fontainebleau, Charles went to Blois—half way to meet Coligny. There he awaited the results of de Foix's embassy, and applied to the pope for a dispensation for the Bourbon marriage.[30] In preparation for the expected return of Coligny and the princes, he labored—but in vain—to resolve the vendetta. This still endangered Coligny and thwarted the royal policy of reconciliation.[31]

Meanwhile, Bricquemault, Coligny's elderly representative at court, who had been present at Fontainebleau, had grave misgivings about the wisdom of the Netherlands enterprise. Not only was it betrayed to Alva, but he naturally had no confidence in the king. Charles, for his part, had begun to issue the steady stream of disavowals and assurances to Spain which he sustained until the débâcle a year later.[32] Bricquemault's servant, La Huguerye, records a three-day meeting attended by all the "négociateurs" at which his experienced master tried to reduce the Netherlands partition plan to something more realistic. It would appear, from what happened later, that his modifications were accepted. La Huguerye and Bricquemault were agreed that the Huguenots would have been wiser to act alone, without the king, and they condemned Nassau for the dangerous position in which he had placed Coligny.[33] La Huguerye also records, rather vaguely, discussions which followed at La Rochelle, either late in August or early in September 1571. Nassau is said to have been charged

29. Digges, *Compleat Ambassador*, 121–22, 12 August 1571, Walsingham to Burghley.

30. B. N., Mss. Fr., 3951, ff. 134–35v, 19 January 1572, Charles to Ferrals, ambassador in Rome.

31. La Huguerye, *Mémoires*, i, 32–33; Digges, *Compleat Ambassador*, 121–22, 12 August 1571, Walsingham to Burghley.

32. La Huguerye, *Mémoires*, i, 26–31, 50, 90.

33. Ibid., 33–34, 49–57.

with the difficulty and danger of the Protestants' position, considering Charles's disavowals to Spain. He was also blamed for making an agreement with the king which entailed the return of Coligny to court. Furthermore, Nassau made Charles an undertaking to procure the Bourbon marriage, whereas Coligny and his supporters still favoured the marriage of Navarre to Elizabeth.[34]

This project was raised again in the summer of 1571 when it was believed that the Anjou negotiation had failed. It seemed to Coligny that Nassau had deliberately committed the party to the French crown, when it was really England that they needed. Nassau, however, had been warned by Walsingham that they should so "direct their doings that they may stand in no need of England."[35] Nassau, in fact, needed both England and France. The trouble was that his interests were never to be fully aligned with those of Coligny and the Huguenots. The whole burden of Coligny's argument was that the Netherlands enterprise should be founded upon England and English support—for three principal reasons. He did not want to lose Navarre, their princely figurehead who, the Catholics argued, would be converted as a result of his marriage to Marguerite. Secondly, Coligny had no confidence that Charles would really undertake a war against Spain—the only circumstances in which Coligny would willingly support a French enterprise of the Netherlands. Nassau, however, persisted in maintaining that his enterprise need not lead to war between France and Spain; consequently, the king's real attitude was irrelevant. The third reason why the Coligny group maintained that the enterprise of the Netherlands should be founded only on English support, excluding the king of France, was because they were anxious to save Coligny from having to return to court. Jeanne d'Albret was not, however, disposed to consider the English marriage for her son. She rightly believed it to be in any case unattainable. Coligny therefore found himself irretrievably committed to the policy of Nassau, and his own

34. La Mothe, *Correspondance diplomatique*, vii, 242–43, 25 August 1571, Charles IX to La Mothe.
35. *CSPF.*, *1569–71*, p. 506, 12 August 1571, Walsingham to Burghley.

extremists. It was decided that he no longer had any option but to return to court.[36] Had he done otherwise, he would, presumably, have forfeited his already tenuous hold over the Huguenot party.

Coligny's return to court should have proclaimed the success of the policy of reconciliation. It was, however, ill-timed, short-lived, and abortive. It was not, in the first place, auspicious that Coligny had felt it necessary to insist on capitulations amounting to no less than eleven articles before he would consent to leave La Rochelle. Article 5 required the king, Catherine, Anjou, Alençon and all the nobles and marshals to provide Téligny with a written assurance as to Coligny's safety.[37] He also extracted an affirmation of royal support for the edict of Saint-Germain. Coligny arrived on 12 September, escorted by Marshal Cossé, and well surrounded. There was, however, little that he could do. The resolution of the Netherlands enterprise awaited Elizabeth's reply,[38] while agreement on the Bourbon marriage, to which Coligny was opposed, was known by 26 September to have been concluded.[39] There remained the matter of the dispensation.

If Coligny's return was gratifying to the king, it is hard to perceive that there were other advantages. It was difficult to explain away to Philip II, who was told that, on Coligny's insistance, Charles had consented for the sake of peace.[40] Philip, who had some cause to be alarmed, had already expressed the opinion that the only good reason for recalling Coligny was to ensure his arrest and execution. Aumale was at court and, whether or not he had signed the required assurance, the Guises had not yet agreed

36. La Huguerye, *Mémoires*, i, 49, 57, 59-60, 77-79, 88-89, 91; *CSPF.*, *1569-71*, p. 506, 12 August 1571, Walsingham to Burghley; Roelker, *Queen of Navarre*, 351.

37. Desjardins, *Négs. Tosc.*, iii, 694-701, 10 August 1571.

38. Digges, *Compleat Ambassador*, 135-36, 15 September 1571, Walsingham to Burghley (pages missing in British Library copy).

39. Douais, *Lettres de Charles IX à M. de Fourquevaulx*. 360-61, 28 September 1571, Charles IX to Fourquevaulx; Gachard, *Notices et extraits*, ii, 348, 28 September 1571; *CSPF.*, *1569-71*, p. 538, 26 September 1571, Walsingham to Burghley. Walsingham said that the marriage was thoroughly concluded.

40. Douais, *Lettres de Charles IX à M. de Fourquevaulx*, 362-63, 26 September 1571, *mémoire*.

to terminate the vendetta. Lorraine had an agent at court, Marmoustiers, and was said to be gathering the Guises at Joinville to determine family policy in the light of this development.[41]

De Foix returned from England about 20 September 1571, expecting a distinguished envoy to follow him shortly.[42] This may have been why there was "great consultation" on the Netherlands enterprise[43] and, by 8 October, the king had resolved upon it. Catherine, however, succeeded in having the decision rescinded, since they still did not know what Elizabeth would do. Her support seemed all the more unlikely in that Anjou flatly declined the match.[44] There is no mention, in all this, of the influence of Coligny, except that the nuncio, Frangipani, said it should not be exaggerated. It is doubtful if the nuncio and the Catholics distinguished between shades of opinion in the Huguenot party, or between the French and the Flemish. Frangipani added that Coligny did not obtain everything he asked for, and that he would soon leave for Châtillon.[45] This may partly have referred to money. But it seems most likely that, since the Netherlands enterprise was to take place, Coligny had been trying hard to persuade the king to declare war on Spain. This, at least, was believed by Zúñiga, the Spanish ambassador in Rome.[46] Such a declaration would have committed the king and pledged national resources. It would also have protected Coligny against the grave dangers of repudiation by the king and the revenge of Alva. Besides, however poor an ally Elizabeth might be, Coligny could not afford to see England overthrown. The duke of Norfolk had been arrested on 7 September and Philip was resolved to spare nothing in fur-

41. Desjardins, *Négs. Tosc.*, iii, 701, 22 August 1571; 706, 19–20 September 1571.

42. Digges, *Compleat Ambassador*, 136, 23 September 1571, Walsingham to Burghley (pages missing from the British Library copy).

43. *CSPF., 1569-71*, p. 538, 26 September 1571, Walsingham to Burghley.

44. Ibid., 545, 8 October 1571, Walsingham to Burghley.

45. Hirschauer, *La Politique de St. Pie V*, 172–73, 14–15 October 1571, Frangipani to Rusticucci.

46. Serrano, *Correspondencia diplomatica*, iv, 485–86, 16 October 1571, Zúñiga to Philip II; La Mothe, *Correspondance diplomatique*, iv, 319, 22 December 1571, La Mothe to Charles IX.

thering what had been begun. This included the death of Elizabeth, the release of Mary and the re-Catholicizing of England.[47] On 7 October Spain carried off the spectacular victory of Lepanto.[48] There were many reasons, therefore, for wanting Charles IX to declare war on Spain. Such a war could have averted the militarily crazy enterprise of the Netherlands, and it may have been thought that a French declaration would have disposed Elizabeth to support them. This would not, in fact, have been the case, since she naturally preferred to see others fight her battles for her. Charles, however, was not a free agent, and the entire council was opposed to war—though by no means all for the same reason. Coligny's entreaties, which were reported to Philip II by mid-October, can only have confirmed his opinion that the admiral should be arrested and executed. The pope was explicitly of the same opinion.[49]

Charles left Blois on 18 October 1571 and Coligny went home to Châtillon. Charles was daily hoping for plain news from England, and intended to reconvene the court in about three weeks' time, when the two princes, Navarre and Condé, were expected. On the advice of the nuncio, according to his own account, Charles had already summoned Guise, Aumale and Mayenne—but not Lorraine—in order to force a reconciliation with Coligny.[50] Charles's policies were not, however, as close to maturity as he may have thought. In the first place, Elizabeth had decided not to send over a distinguished envoy until she had received a report following the return of de Foix. The Ridolfi plot and the battle of Lepanto had persuaded Elizabeth of the necessity of a French alliance, but de Foix found Anjou "so coldly affected" that he had no hope of the matter, while Charles was not disposed to

47. Gachard, *Correspondance de Philippe II*, ii, 195–97, 30 August 1571, Philip II to Alva.

48. The majority of the ships were actually Venetian, but the commander was Don John of Austria.

49. Desjardins, *Négs. Tosc.*, iii, 732, 28 November 1571, anonymous letter to François de Médicis.

50. Hirschauer, *La Politique de St. Pie V*, 172, 14–15 October 1571, Frangipani to Rusticucci.

declare war against Spain.[51] Elizabeth seems to have been inclined, in these circumstances, to draw closer to Coligny. She
"somewhat opened her mind" to the Huguenot lieutenant,
Montgomery, who saw her early in December.[52] He was, however, a relative of Sir Arthur Champernown (Artus Chamber-
nant) and it is not clear that he went to England on behalf of
Coligny. Knowing his need and desire for an English alliance,
Elizabeth wished to seek Coligny's advice, and wanted him to be
at court, to assist her envoy, Sir Thomas Smith, who was ready
to depart.[53] But for some reason he did not arrive until the beginning of January 1572. By this time, the situation in France had
changed, and Coligny was unable to return to court.

In mid-November the Spanish ambassador, Alava—who had
been recalled at the end of August—suddenly fled to the Netherlands.[54] This was the first overt sign of an obscure conspiracy
which Sir Henry Killigrew called "some practice of the Catholics
who favour Spain."[55] It was also in favor of Anjou; designed to
frustrate the three royal policies, and to prevent the return to
court of Coligny. About the same time Guise, as *gouverneur* of
Champagne, entered Troyes with a large following. It was reported that the Guises were collecting money and that Guisard
followers were assembling in Paris, where serious disorders occurred.[56] The Protestants, hearing these things, gathered round

51. *CSPF.*, *1569–71*, pp. 538–39, 26 September 1571, Walsingham to
Burghley.
52. La Mothe, *Correspondance diplomatique*, iv, 296, 30 November
1571, La Mothe to Charles IX; Digges, *Compleat Ambassador*, 153, 6
December 1571, Leicester to Walsingham.
53. Digges, *Compleat Ambassador*, 153, 6 December 1571, Leicester to
Walsingham; La Mothe, *Correspondance diplomatique*, iv, 291, 26
November 1571, La Mothe to Charles IX.
54. La Mothe, *Correspondance diplomatique*, vii, 279, 30 November
1571, Charles IX to La Mothe; *CSPF.*, *1569–71*, p. 561, 19 November
1571, Walsingham to Burghley.
55. *CSPF.*, *1569–71*, p. 569, 3 December 1571, Killigrew, advertisements from France.
56. Ibid., 582–83, 30 December 1571, advertisements from Walsingham;
Desjardins, *Négs. Tosc.*, iii, 738, 4 December 1571; 742–43, 24
December 1571.

Coligny at Châtillon. Coligny sent to inquire whether he was to take the Catholics for friends or foes. Charles shortly learned that the house of Guise threatened to be revenged upon Coligny.[57] They were reported to be advancing on Châtillon, and suddenly France was again on the brink of civil war. Killigrew reported that Coligny had secret intelligence as to what he might expect if he went to court, which both sides were supposed to do.[58] It was alleged that Saint-Gouard was planning to destroy Coligny upon arrival. Saint-Gouard was a relative of de Retz and his cousin, Jérôme de Gondi. Both were relatives of Ridolfi. Gondi had recently been to Spain and Saint-Gouard was about to go as ambassador.[59] Those who thought that his perdition was the only reason for recalling Coligny had evidently been at work. In these circumstances, Charles actually offered him the protection of armed forces, and countermanded his summons.[60] The Guises were also ordered to stay away.[61]

There could no longer be any doubt that the edict of Saint-Germain had made no difference. So long as the vendetta continued, the Guises would not suffer Coligny to take his place in the council; and they flaunted their ability to exclude him. He was now the key figure in all three royal policies which the Catholics were bent on destroying. He was urgently needed at court to assist Sir Thomas Smith to construct an English alliance—marriage or no marriage—and he was also the only Frenchman, of any standing, who wanted the king to declare war on Spain. But Charles could neither safely favor and employ him,

57. *CSPF.*, *1569–71*, p. 576, 17 December 1571, Killigrew to Burghley.
58. Ibid., 581, 29 December 1571, Killigrew to Burghley.
59. Champion, *Charles IX, la France et le contrôle de l'Espagne*, i, 420 seq.
60. B. N., Mss. Fr., 3193, f. 25, 13 December 1571, Coligny to Charles IX.
61. Desjardins, *Négs. Tosc.*, iii, 744–45, 28–29 December 1571. The conspiracy, which is still mysterious, was a far-reaching affair. It could have been intended to place Anjou on the throne. It was probably connected with the plotting of Ridolfi, who came to France in mid-September to meet his Gondi kinsmen on his way from Spain to the Netherlands. Coligny was then at court and de Spes was deported from England shortly after. *CSPF.*, *1569–71*, p. 573, 14 December 1571, speech declared to the Spanish ambassador.

nor yet safely abandon him. The Guises and the Catholics collectively were still too powerful. They were once again trying to manipulate policy and control the court. In December 1571 and the following January, the king made another attempt to terminate the vendetta which now lay between him and prosperity. Coligny requested the king to examine Guise on the subject, and both parties were required to state their pretentions. The Guises, however, again rejected the royal settlement of Moulins and demanded redress from the king. This was refused.[62]

Considering the advantageous position of the Catholics, it was not surprising that Anjou announced demands which amounted to a final refusal to marry Queen Elizabeth, just as the negotiations were beginning with Smith. This created an angry and tearful commotion and Smith, who had recently been involved in investigating the Ridolfi plot, immediately proceeded to draft treaty articles, which were sent to England without delay. A treaty of alliance was now inevitable, although the French wanted an offensive agreement and the English only a defensive one. Unlike Smith, who urged Burghley to prevent the queen from procrastinating, Elizabeth was still in no hurry.[63] It was at least the opinion of Jeanne d'Albret that—even now—Elizabeth would not agree to an alliance with France until the Bourbon marriage was concluded. The timing of events, and the active help of Walsingham, bear this out.[64]

Everything now depended on the Bourbon marriage which the Catholics were still striving to prevent. In mid-January a nuncio, Salviati, arrived, followed on 7 February by a legate, Cardinal Alessandrino, just as Jeanne d'Albret was expected with Nassau.

62. Douais, *Lettres de Charles IX à M. de Fourquevaulx*, 372–74, 26 December 1571, Charles IX to Fourquevaulx; Desjardins, *Négs. Tosc.*, iii, 744–45, 28–29, December 1571; *CSPF.*, *1569–71*, p. 584, no date, occurrences in France; Ibid., *1572–74*, pp. 35–36 [3 February] 1572, news from France.

63. *CSPF.*, *1572–74*, pp. 8–11, 8 January 1572, Smith and Killigrew to Elizabeth; 11, 7 January 1572, Anjou's demands; 11–13, 9 January 1572, Smith to Burghley; 14, 10 January 1572, Smith to Burghley; 19–20, 17 January 1572, Smith to Burghley.

64. Digges, *Compleat Ambassador*, 175–76, March 1572, Walsingham to Burghley; Roelker, *Queen of Navarre*, 374.

She might easily have turned back, and Alessandrino's masterly timing created a maximum of embarrassment.[65] The legate's mission was to destroy all three royal policies, and he offered the king 4,000 Spanish troops if he would break off the Bourbon marriage and make war on the Huguenots.[66] If Charles refused to do this, or to join the pope's Holy League, he could expect to be punished. Alessandrino could obstruct the essential Bourbon marriage by blocking the dispensation, and this was his angry parting shot. But, as he rightly admitted, Catherine was determined to proceed, nonetheless.[67] There were, however, many other difficulties, besides those raised by the papal envoys, and the negotiations were not concluded until 4 April, after the appointment of commissioners, including Nassau and La Noue, who were impatient for a settlement.[68] This was quickly followed by the English alliance—the treaty of Blois—hastened, no doubt, by developments in the Netherlands.[69]

While commissioners thrashed out the details of the Bourbon contract, Nassau had proceeded with plans for the Netherlands enterprise, and Charles again addressed himself to the problem of the vendetta, since Coligny's return to court was increasingly urgent. While Charles was not immediately successful, early in May Guise suddenly capitulated. This is difficult to explain, unless it was that the Guises thereby obtained a dual advantage. The duke himself was enabled to return to court, while the rest of his family rejected the settlement because Lorraine was still unwelcome. They may also have realized that Coligny would be easier to catch if they let him go to court.[70]

65. Hirschauer, *La Politique de St. Pie V*, 181–82, 9 February 1572, Alessandrino to Rusticucci.

66. Desjardins, *Négs. Tosc.*, iii, 748, 14 February 1572.

67. Ibid., 750, 23 February 1572; Serrano, *Correspondencia Diplomatica*, iv, 673, 22 February 1572, Alessandrino to Castagna, nuncio in Spain.

68. Digges, *Compleat Ambassador*, 184, 29 March 1572, Walsingham to Burghley; Roelker, *Queen of Navarre*, 382.

69. *CSPF.*, *1572–74*, p. 87, 19 April 1572. Scotland had proved to be a problem in the case of the English negotiation.

70. Ibid., 64–65, 29 March 1572, Walsingham to Burghley; Desjardins, *Négs. Tosc.*, iii, 771, 28 April 1572; 772, 12 May 1572; B. N., Mss. Fr., 3188, f. 27, 5 May 1572, Nançay to Bouchage.

The Bourbon marriage—which was arranged but not yet celebrated—the English alliance, and the resolution of the vendetta were the three principal requisites for the Netherlands enterprise, and they all came too late. On 28 March, while all three negotiations were still in progress, William's sea beggars had intercepted the returning Netherlands fleet and, on 1 April, descended on Brill, before Alva's citadel at Flushing was complete, or the town safely garrisoned.[71] Consequently, although he was not yet ready, William of Orange issued a declaration from Dillenburg on 14 April, which amounted to a declaration of war.[72] The precipitation of war in the Netherlands, before anything in France was ready for the enterprise, produced a series of crises through the summer, which ended in the massacre of St. Bartholomew. The problem for the Huguenots and the Flemish was that they needed to depart forthwith. The problem for Charles and Catherine was not only their determination to complete the Bourbon marriage at all costs—and they were great—but also that the treaty of Blois had not secured the help of England in an offensive war. The burning question, therefore, which came to dominate all others, was that of war with Spain. To Coligny, the king was irretrievably committed, and war was in any case inevitable. Apart, however, from the tergiversations of Elizabeth, there were other compelling reasons why Charles was unable or unwilling to declare himself publicly in favor of war. Not only was the powerful Catholic faction against the war, but also Catherine, the marshals and the entire council, with the sole exception of Coligny.[73] Charles was therefore committed to a policy that he refused to avow and was unable to execute. This was exactly what Coligny had always feared.

After the seizure of Brill, Alva immediately sent an envoy to Charles to discover his intentions. Not without some delay, and after having promised help to Nassau, Charles returned the envoy

71. La Mothe, *Correspondance diplomatique*, iv, 427–28, 14 April 1572, La Mothe to Charles IX.
72. *CSPF.*, *1572–74*, p. 81, 14 April 1572, proclamation of the prince of Orange.
73. If anyone else did support Coligny in the council, this has not been recorded.

with every possible assurance of friendship.[74] This was the first of many such assurances and disavowals which Charles sustained from May until August, while he awaited the answer from England. Given both these conditions—the Bourbon marriage and the support of England—it seems likely that he would have declared war. The Huguenots were suspended in this hope, although there remained the problem of the adverse council, and also the known power of the Catholics to act. But, as week after week went by, without the two conditions being fulfilled, Charles's disavowals became increasingly transparent, and his danger correspondingly greater. Charles's sole advantage, throughout these waiting months, was the preoccupation of the pope with his Holy League, and of Philip II with the Turks, together with the sheer unpreparedness of Alva. Nevertheless the suspense produced explosive tensions in France between the Huguenots and the Catholics, both of them straining hard in opposing senses.

The immediate problem after the capture of Brill was, as Walsingham put it, how to "proceade." It was essential both to prevent Alva from taking Flushing, and also to create a diversion in the south. It is apparent that Nassau had agreed to await the Bourbon marriage, but events had overtaken him: Navarre was ill and not expected before June at the earliest.[75] Because Alva was not yet ready, Nassau saw in this situation a supreme opportunity, if only it could be swiftly grasped. Téligny did his best to galvanize the king, while Nassau may possibly have gone to consult Coligny. But Charles only temporized, writing cryptically to Nassau that he would do something to help as soon as circumstances permitted.[76] It was therefore without royal consent, but surely with Coligny's approval, that Nassau departed suddenly, in the middle of May, taking with him a number of his Huguenot

74. Lettenhove, *Relations*, vi, 415, n. 1, 22 April 1572, letter of Walsingham to Burghley; Gachard, *Correspondance de Philippe II*, ii, 250, 22 May 1572, Alva to Philip II.

75. Navarre suffered a relapse and was even longer delayed. Desjardins, *Négs. Tosc.*, iii, 781, 28 May 1572.

76. Lettenhove, *Documents inédits du XVIe siècle*, 169–70, 27 April 1572, Charles IX to Nassau.

confederates.[77] His enterprise was, as he confied to Walsingham before leaving, "to give Alva an alarm," and he meant it literally. After capturing Valenciennes and Mons on 23 and 24 May 1572,[78] he sent La Noue, Genlis and Bouchavannes in an audacious bid to capture Alva himself in Brussels. It was indeed Alva that everyone feared, and Nassau hoped thereby to do what he had vowed: to execute the enterprise of the Netherlands quickly, without incurring war with Spain. It might, nonetheless, have been supposed that war would shortly have resulted.[79] Unfortunately, this exploit was a spectacular failure, which therefore carried provocation to extremes. Far from having saved the situation, Nassau had created a much worse one. By the end of May, there were many Frenchmen in the Netherlands and war with Spain was generally expected, whatever Charles might be saying. It was indeed very close.[80]

It was not because of this crisis, but in order to ratify the English treaty, that the court reassembled in Paris at the beginning of June 1572. With the vendetta at least formally settled, Coligny, flanked by 300 horsemen, arrived on 6 June.[81] In facing the extreme danger of Paris, Coligny had two purposes. One was to persuade the king, in view of what had happened, to give him permission to follow Nassau to the Netherlands. He believed that if he did not go, Alva would have extinguished all resistance within a couple of months. It was then to be feared that he would turn on France. It was also feared that Charles might save his own skin by permitting Alva to turn on the Huguenots.[82] Whether or

77. Digges, *Compleat Ambassador*, 202, 21 May 1572, Walsingham to Burghley.

78. Gachard, *Correspondance de Philippe II*, ii, 258–59, 24 May 1572, Alva to Philip II; 259–60, 29 May 1572, Alva to Don Diego de Zúñiga, ambassador in Paris.

79. Valenciennes was promptly retaken. Ibid., 259, 29 May 1572, Alva to Don Diego de Zúñiga; 260, 1 June 1572, Alva to Philip II; Digges, *Compleat Ambassador*, 204, 29 May 1572, Walsingham to Leicester; 204–5, 29 May 1572, Walsingham to Burghley.

80. Gachard, *Correspondance de Philippe II*, ii, 259, 29 May 1572, Alva to Zúñiga.

81. Theiner, *Annales Ecclesiastici*, i, 338, 9 June 1572, Frangipani, bishop of Gajazzo, to Cardinal di Como.

82. Desjardins, *Négs. Tosc.*, iii, 784, 10 June 1572; 785, 24 June 1572.

not he were really so base, he would have been powerless to intervene. Coligny's second reason for braving the city of Paris was to see the English ambassadors, who arrived on 8 June.[83]

Finding among the embassy two puritans, Sir Henry Middlemore, a kinsman of Sir Nicholas Throckmorton, and Sir Arthur Champernown, a kinsman of Montgomery, Coligny invited them to supper. This meeting shows that Coligny had not changed his opinions. He tried hard to persuade them of the immediate opportunity in the Netherlands to bridle Philip II, which called for a "resolute determinyd order" between England and France. Coligny, in fact, was seeking a further, offensive treaty, which he hoped de Foix would be pursuing in England. Besides ratifying the treaty of Blois, de Foix was earnestly seeking the Alençon marriage, and Elizabeth's immediate help in the Netherlands. But the English ambassadors were wisely reticent. Coligny's mind was on the original partition plan, which allowed England substantial gains. Otherwise he might have heeded Middlemore's only significant remark, that England "colde least lyke that Frawnce shuld commaunde Flawnders." The matter proceeded in England to a draft treaty, but Elizabeth was indeed afraid of French success in the Netherlands and, carefully hedging her bets, drew stealthily closer to Spain.[84] As it was, neither Charles nor Coligny appears to have understood that Elizabeth would continue to keep them waiting until it was too late.

Before the English departed, on 22 June, the council began a prolonged debate on the problem of war with Spain.[85] They were still engaged in this exercise when Genlis returned from Mons on 23 June. Alva's son, Don Fadrique de Toledo, was closing in on Nassau, and Alva was expected to be ready to leave Brussels in mid-August.[86] All the depositions in the council strongly op-

83. Hirschauer, *La Politique de St. Pie V*, 184, 9 June 1572, Frangipani to Gregory XIII.

84. Ellis, *Original Letters*, 2nd series, iii, 3–11, 17 June 1572, Middlemore to Burghley; 12–22, 18 June 1572, Smith to Burghley.

85. *CSPF.*, *1572–74*, p. 135, 22 June 1572, Walsingham to Burghley.

86. Lettenhove, *Relations*, vi, 436, July 1572, John Lee to Burghley; Piot, Granvelle, *Correspondance*, iv, 270, 22 June 1572, Morillon to Granvelle; Gachard, *Correspondance de Guillaume le Taciturne*, iii, p. xix; Alva left Brussels on 26 August 1572.

posed war. Coligny continued to press the king for an open declaration, but in vain. It was then that he determined, if necessary, to go alone, in the very circumstances he had always striven to avoid.[87] But he had not yet finally given up hope of England and of Charles and, meanwhile, he was required to wait for the Bourbon marriage, for which Navarre did not arrive until 8 July; nor was there yet any dispensation.[88]

For Charles, the first essential was to restrain Coligny because, if he were to lead an army across the frontier—with or without permission—he could not plausibly be disavowed. Charles therefore agreed to covert assistance, presumably on condition that Coligny himself awaited the marriage. Thus, about the middle of July, Genlis slipped back to the Netherlands with orders to seize Cateau-Cambrésis—according to Walsingham, with 4,000 foot and 600 horse. At the same time, Charles issued a covering proclamation recalling his subjects from Mons, and forbidding others to depart upon pain of death.[89] This was as much as he would do, since the English negotiation had broken down. He sent another envoy to implore Elizabeth to declare war on Spain. In this he was supported by Coligny, who told Elizabeth that he could not act himself until after the Bourbon marriage. Nevertheless they earnestly hoped that she would continue to assail the Netherlands coast.[90] Charles gave out that the Bourbon marriage would take place in about two weeks, and the inference was that he would then join Elizabeth in open war.[91] Apart from his two preoccupations, the Bourbon marriage and English support, Charles dared not take overt action so long as Don John of Austria was detained at Messina with all the forces intended to support the Holy League against the Turks, because he could easily have

87. Desjardins, *Négs. Tosc.*, iii, 785, 24 June 1572.

88. Ibid., 792, 7 July 1572; Navarre was coming the next day.

89. Digges, *Compleat Ambassador*, 221–22, 13 July 1572, Walsingham to Burghley; *CSPF.*, *1572–74*, pp. 145–46, 12 July 1572, Walsingham to Burghley.

90. *CSPSp.*, *1568–79*, p. 402, 7 August 1572, intelligence from England to Alva.

91. La Mothe, *Correspondance diplomatique*, vii, 302–3, 14 July 1572, Charles IX to La Mothe.

fallen upon the undefended southern provinces of France. This restraint was carefully calculated by Philip II.[92]

Coligny's agreement to wait might well have paid off, were it not for the headstrong folly of Genlis. With his return, the situation in the Netherlands could probably have been stabilized for a few weeks, had he not disobeyed his precise instructions and gone straight to Mons. There, on 17 July, his force was overwhelmed with heavy losses, and he and many others were captured. This Protestant disaster was received by the Catholic populace of Paris with tumultuous rejoicing.[93] Once again Alva sent to Charles, to know whether or not he acknowledged Genlis. Charles not only disavowed him, but so far groveled as to offer Alva his congratulations. Charles's continued assurances of peace carried no weight, however, since captured documents were hopelessly incriminating, allegedly indicating plans for a general rising in the Netherlands, and disclosing efforts to persuade Charles himself to invade. Furthermore, Genlis, who was tortured, claimed to have been acting under royal commission, and almost certainly exaggerated the force which Coligny was about to deploy.[94]

Charles's one and only remaining hope was to restrain Coligny, while galvanizing England into action. If Coligny once crossed the frontier, the situation would, ironically, be beyond control both for France and for Spain. Charles immediately sent over to

92. *CSPF., 1572-74*, pp. 145-46, 12 July 1572, Walsingham to Burghley. Don John was authorized to leave by 16 July. Hurtubise, *Correspondance du nonce Salviati*, i, 168, 28 July 1572, Galli to Salviati. Serrano, *Lepanto*, ii, 358-61, 1 August 1572, Don Juan de Zúñiga, ambassador in Rome, to Philip II.

93. Piot, Granvelle, *Correspondance*, iv, 319, 20 and 22 July 1572, Morillon to Granvelle; idem, n. 1; Lettenhove, *Relations* vi, 459-60, 18 July 1572, avis; Gachard, *Correspondance de Philippe II*, ii, 269-70, 19 July 1572, Albornoz to Cayas; *CSPF., 1572-74*, p. 153, 18 July 1572, news from Antwerp.

94. *Bulletin de la Commission royale d'Histoire*, série ii, vol. iv, 1852, pp. 342-43, 12 August 1572, Charles to Mondoucet; Gachard, *Correspondance de Philippe II*, ii, 262, 14 June 1572, Albornoz to Cayas; 269-70, 19 July 1572, Albornoz to Cayas; Piot, Granvelle, *Correspondance*, iv, 328-29, 27 July 1572, Morillon to Granvelle; 341, 4 August 1572, Morillon to Granvelle; Lettenhove, *Les Huguenots*, ii, 490 seq.

England La Mole, a servant of Alençon, explaining the danger of declaring himself openly. La Mole carried similar letters from Coligny, with an account of the forces he had in readiness.[95]

It was after the defeat of Genlis that tensions on both sides began to reach breaking point. If Coligny did not leave in time, and with adequate forces, Orange would be overthrown. In that case, not only would Charles have been unable to protect the Huguenots, but all France, as well as England, would have been in grave danger. The forces of Catholicism might then have won the desperate struggle of the sixteenth century, in which power and ideology were inseparably joined. To Spain and the Catholics, on the other hand, it seemed that Don John had unwisely left Messina before Alva was ready.[96] Substantial French forces, possibly supported by England in the west, might enter the Netherlands at any moment, relieve Mons, and march on Alva in Brussels. This was manifestly what the French had in mind. The one diplomatic means of preventing this was to obstruct the Bourbon marriage. Lorraine was in Rome at the time, and doubtless doing his best. He was also in touch with Alva, and had warned him to be vigilant and to guard against trouble from France.[97] Philip's ambassador in Rome, Don Juan de Zúñiga, was also doing his best, trying to ensure that a dispensation would only be granted on terms that Navarre could be expected to reject.[98] Philip was already anxious before the overthrow of Genlis, which proved to be rather an embarrassing victory. He was glad to hear that the pope was sending a special nuncio, Salviati, to put pressure on France to preserve the peace with Spain and to join the Holy League. He required his ambassador to impress upon the pope that he had far more dangerous enemies, nearer home, than the Turks. Consequently, if he did not find some way of altering French policy, he warned the pope

---

95. Lettenhove, *Relations*, vi, 480–83, 7 August 1572, Antonio Fogaça to Alva.

96. Alva was seriously hampered by lack of money. Gachard, *Correspondance de Philippe II*, ii, 266–67, 2 July 1572, Alva to Philippe II.

97. Ibid., 267–68, 18 July 1572, Alva to Philipe II.

98. Serrano, *Lepanto*, ii, 367–69, 19 August 1572, Zúñiga to Philip II.

that he would be unable to attend to the Holy League and the affairs of the Levant.[99]

When Charles unwisely congratulated Alva on the defeat of Genlis, and protested that he wanted peace, Philip and Alva both called his bluff.[100] Early in August Philip told Rossano, the nuncio in Spain, that the Huguenot defeat had been considerable, because their most valorous leaders had died. Thus, if Charles wished to purge the kingdom of his enemies, now was the time to do it. If he were to combine forces with Spain, the rest could be destroyed, more particularly since the admiral was in Paris, where the people were Catholic and loyal. *There, in Paris, it would be easy to dispose of him, once and for all.*[101] Philip, clearly, was not concerned about the danger involved. He would then employ all his strength and resources to liberate the kingdom and restore it to its pristine splendor and safety, from which his own would be derived. Such Spanish help was precisely the calamity that Catherine had constantly feared since the death of Henry II in 1559. Philip was planning to put this proposition to Charles. Meanwhile Alva had swiftly written to much the same effect. Having, as he said, already killed so many of Charles's enemies, he offered to deliver him from the rest.[102] It seems unlikely that Charles ever received Philip's macabre invitation, but Rossano's report provides an unambiguous statement of the Catholic policy of elimination. This, therefore, was the danger, not only to Coligny and the Huguenots, but also to France herself.

Coligny was extremely anxious about the prisoners of Mons. Having been disavowed, they were subject, not to the laws of war, but to the notorious cruelty of Alva. He was naturally thirst-

---

99. Ibid., 348–49, 14 July 1572, Philip II to Don Juan de Zúñiga; Hurtubise, *Correspondance du nonce Salviati*, i, 155–60, 16 July 1572, Salviati to Boncampagni.

100. Gachard, *Correspondance de Philippe II*, ii, 267, 14 July 1572, Philip to Alva; 269–70, 19 July 1572, Albornoz to Cayas; 270, 21 July 1572, Philip II to Alva; 271, 2 August 1572, Philip II to Alva.

101. " . . . dove potria se volesse facilmente levarselo dinnanzi per sempre," Theiner, *Annales Ecclesiastici*, i, 327–28, 5 August 1572, Rossano to Cardinal di Como.

102. Idem.

ing to revenge the insolent raid on Brussels, in which Genlis had taken a leading part. Coligny wanted to ransom the prisoners, and the French agent, Mondoucet, interceded for their better treatment; but Alva laughed derisively.[103] Philip was no longer the only one to utter threats, and passions in France were rising. Coligny is said to have sent for Jérôme de Gondi and ordered him to find the Spanish ambassador. The message was that if he did not obtain the release of the prisoners, he would be murdered in Paris, and no other Spaniard would be safe in France.[104] Gondi was a cousin of the comte de Retz and, notoriously, Zúñiga's paid informant of council business. If this report is correct, it could be of fundamental significance.

The situation was now explosive. At the end of July Charles, who detected a hardening of the papal attitude to the dispensation, addressed to Lorraine a final ultimatum. He said that he was obliged to take essential measures for the protection of his State and that, with or without a dispensation, he would proceed with the marriage.[105] He was evidently heeding Coligny's warnings. Early in August, alarming rumors that Elizabeth meant to recall all her subjects from the Netherlands were the cause of two stormy council meetings in Paris, at which it was decided to have nothing to do with war. This was because the pro-Spanish members of the council had put Catherine in "such a fear that the enterprise cannot but miscarry without the assistance of England." Coligny did not, however, "give over," but urged the king to recognize his peril.[106] The Huguenot reaction was violent. They threatened to take matters into their own hands, and it was unlikely that Coligny would be able to control them much longer. Furthermore, they threatened to savage the comte de Retz, who, it was claimed, had promised more than one ambassador—presumably Zúñiga and Salviati—to obtain that council resolution against war.[107]

103. Gachard, *Notices et extraits*, ii, 520, 17 August 1572, Mondoucet to Charles IX.
104. Desjardins, *Négs. Tosc.*, iii, 800, 23 July 1572.
105. B. N., Mss. Fr., 3951, f. 142, 31 July 1572.
106. Digges, *Compleat Ambassador*, 233, 10 August 1572, Walsingham to Burghley; Desjardins, *Négs. Tosc.*, iii, 801, 6 August 1572.
107. Desjardins, *Négs. Tosc.*, iii, 801, 6 August 1572.

According to one account of the massacre of St. Bartholomew, the banker de Retz had received 25–30,000 *écus* to prevent the Netherlands enterprise.[108]

Coligny was quick to reassure William of Orange that he would be coming, in any case, with 12,000 foot and 3,000 horse.[109] According to Walsingham, however, in spite of the council decision, Coligny did obtain "somewhat" from the king. As Alva shortly complained of the presence of troops on the frontier, it is to be supposed that Charles had again agreed to a measure of covert support, in return for a pledge that Coligny himself would wait.[110] Charles instructed his agent, Mondoucet, to inquire of Alva whether the forces he was raising were directed against France. While he believed they were not, he had nevertheless been obliged to take some precautions.[111] Charles had, at last, acquired some sense of urgency: without awaiting his reply from Rome (which could hardly have come in less than three weeks), he proceeded, on 18 August, to celebrate the Bourbon marriage.

The dispensation and the marriage were therefore no longer a means of deferring war, and decisions in council were no guarantee. Philip had seen only one alternative. Between 16 and 19 August, Coligny received from Jean de Mergey, servant to La Rochefoucauld, the last of many warnings that his life was in danger.[112] He wrote to his wife, on the day of the marriage, confiding his aversion from staying in Paris. His mind, however, was on problems arising from violations of the edict. That he had not obtained permssion to leave before 25 August was all that he

108. *Le Tocsain contre les autheurs du massacre de France*, 24. While this source cannot be regarded as reliable, the allegation is entirely plausible.

109. Van Prinsterer, *Archives ou correspondance*, série i, vol. iii, 490–91, 11 August 1572, Orange to his brother count Jean.

110. Digges, *Compleat Ambassador*, 234, 10 August 1572, Walsingham to Leicester; Gachard, *Notices et extraits*, i, 409, 11 August 1572, Alva to Charles IX; B. N., Mss. Fr., 3193, ff. 68–69.

111. Gachard, *Correspondance de Philippe II*, ii, 273–74, 31 August 1572, Alva to Philip II. Mondoucet saw Alva on 16 August.

112. Jean de Mergey, *Mémoires*, 574–75. The text says five or six days before the execution. It is not entirely clear whether this referred to the assault against Coligny on 22 August, or the massacre on 24 August.

said about the Netherlands.[113] Since Alva was having great difficulty in assembling his army, Coligny's departure on 25 August might—just—have been in time. This, at least, was to be the anguished lament of William of Orange, who believed that they had been on the point of overwhelming Alva.[114] Others must also have shared that opinion since, by 25 August, Coligny had perished in the massacre of St. Bartholomew.

The massacre of St. Bartholomew comprised three distinct events. The first was an abortive attack on Coligny in the rue de Béthizy on Friday morning 22 August. The second was the murder of Coligny, together with his principal followers, during the night of Saturday 23-24 August. This was followed or accompanied by the massacre, in the popular sense. Writing to Mondoucet in the Netherlands on 26 August, Charles gave him an account of the initial assault on the admiral. This, he had rightly feared, would be followed by even worse trouble. The Protestants had declined to await justice at his hands, and undertook their own revenge against everyone they held in suspicion. In order to forestall this "si pernitieuse entreprise," he had been obliged to permit and enable the Guises to fall upon the admiral, who had been killed together with all his adherents. This, however, had been accompanied by a popular commotion, as a result of which many of the Protestants in Paris had been murdered. Furthermore, there was a danger of similar events happening in all the towns of France.[115]

Charles was left in a most desperately dangerous position, and Mondoucet urgently needed to know as much of the truth as possible. The king's account appears to be generally correct, but

113. Dufey, *La Saint-Barthélemy*, in *Paris révolutionnaire*, iii, 356-57, 18 August 1572, Coligny to his wife.

114. Van Prinsterer, *Archives ou correspondance*, série i, vol. iii, 505, 21 September 1572, William to his brother count Jean (pages misplaced in British Library copy).

115. *Bulletin de la Commission royale d'Histoire*, série ii, vol. iv, 1852, pp. 344-45, 26 August 1572, Charles to Mondoucet. Salviati said that the whole city rose in arms. Hurtubise, *Correspondance du nonce Salviati*, i, 204, 24, 27 August 1572, Salviati to Galli.

incomplete. When Charles wrote that "he" had been obliged to authorize the Guises to assassinate Coligny, he was referring to a decision of the *conseil privé*.[116] This decision derived from the extremity of the danger to the court and to the capital, which forced others to concur in the Catholic policy of elimination, which was then executed. But it is true that a Guisard party burst into Coligny's lodgings and slaughtered him.[117] Charles omitted to add that he had issued an edict, at about 3 A.M., seeking to arrest the massacre and pillage, for this was not a point to be impressed upon Alva.[118] Nor did Charles, in any way, account for the original assault. He may even have thought this unnecessary, since Coligny had been a Catholic target for over a decade, and he was probably ignorant of the circumstantial details.

For some weeks past, Coligny alone had pressed the king to make war on Spain. Why, therefore, if he were going to be murdered, was this left so late? As the corollary amply demonstrated, his murder in those particular circumstances was an absolutely desperate enterprise, only to be adopted as a very last resort. When the council had decided against war, Coligny was still held in check by the impending Bourbon marriage. Once it had taken place, however, nothing but his removal could prevent him from invading the Netherlands in support of Orange. Coligny was not only accompanied in Paris by most of the leading Huguenots, but they also held some 4,000 horse and 12,000 foot in readiness nearby. Fuming with anger and grief, and threatening fire and fury after the first assault, Téligny, his son-in-law, was fully capable of ravaging the court and capital. A veritable act of war had therefore to be undertaken, for Coligny himself no longer walked abroad, and his lieutenants were too dangerous to ignore.

In the absence of Lorraine, de Retz, Gondi and Anjou, as well as the other Guises, formed the nucleus of the group of court

116. Isambert, *Recueil général des anciennes lois françaises*, xiv, 256, 22–23 August 1572.

117. Salviati named Guise, Aumale and Angoulême. Hurtubise, *Correspondance du nonce Salviati*, i, 202, 24 and 27 August 1572, Salviati to Galli.

118. Theiner, *Annales Ecclesiastici*, i, 329, 24 August 1572, Salviati to Cardinal di Como.

extremists. Anjou had long been at the center of Catholic plots and plottings, albeit no initiator. He was on dangerously bad terms with his brother the king, and had violently opposed his policies since the peace of Saint-Germain. If it is true that de Retz had received 25–30,000 *écus* to prevent the Netherlands enterprise, then carrying the council against war had proved insufficient. While this evidence is unconfirmed, de Retz's Spanish affiliations were no secret. Nor were the wishes of Philip II, while the pope had compelling reasons to find some way, as Philip had said, of altering French policy; otherwise he would be bereft of Spanish help in the Levant. Not long before, the Tuscan, Petrucci—a Catholic, and sympathetic—had described de Retz as "obbligato al Re di Spagnia, ed intrigato con i Guisi."[119] De Retz's wife, Claude-Catherine de Clermont was a cousin of Saint-Gouard, the French ambassador in Spain. De Retz was one of those who had failed to trap Condé and Coligny in 1568, while the hired assassin was Maurevert, a Guise protégé, who failed to shoot Coligny in 1569. The house in which he lurked had been allotted by the court to Madame de Nemours, formerly wife of François duc de Guise, who used it for members of her family.[120] Guise participation—the culmination of the vendetta—would seem the obvious means of executing what was most likely a group decision, followed by verbal instructions; this, however, is conjecture.

The murder of Coligny—but not the massacre—had been the only remaining way of averting his invasion of the Netherlands and a war with Spain. While neither Charles nor Philip wanted war, neither, paradoxically, could have avoided it. But the massacre did not, automatically, prevent a punitive invasion by the infuriated Alva, at a moment when Charles was supported by neither the Catholics nor the Protestants. It was therefore because of this great fear of invasion that the king staked a claim to the credit—in Catholic eyes—for what had happened. On 26 August,

119. Desjardins, *Négs. Tosc.*, iii, 787, 26 June 1572; Pommerol, *Albert de Gondi*, passim.

120. Hurtubise, *Correspondance du nonce Salviati*, i, 197, 22 August 1572, Salviati to Galli.

at the same time as writing to Mondoucet, Charles made a statement in the *parlement* to the effect that everything had been done on his instructions.[121]

Thus, although Charles was probably innocent of Huguenot blood, in any direct sense, the crown was disastrously implicated in the massacre, for which it incurred the responsibility. The Bourbon marriage was of no avail—even before the celebrations were over—and the whole policy of reconciliation was irredeemably shattered. Charles proclaimed his adherence to the edict, but his credit was exhausted. Coligny had died—and in vain—for the sake of the Netherlands, and his principal achievement for the Huguenots, the peace of Saint-Germain, was swept away by the fourth civil war.

121. Desjardins, *Négs. Tosc.*, iii, 811, 27 August 1572, Petrucci to Concini; Institut de France, Fonds Godefroy, 290, f. 25, letters patent, undated draft by Villeroy; Isambert, *Recueil général des anciennes lois francaises*, xiv, 257–59, 28 August 1572.

7

The Struggle for Reintegration, 1572–1576: The Peace of Monsieur

THE DEATH OF COLIGNY and the massacre of St. Bartholomew were a watershed in the Huguenot struggle for recognition, and proved to be almost as catastrophic for the crown as for the Huguenots themselves. Since the peace of Saint-Germain the Huguenots had, to some extent, sheltered the king from the Catholic extremists. Now he was in their power and the Huguenots would never trust him again; Charles had no way to turn. In August 1572 neither the king, the Catholics nor the Huguenots were prepared for renewed civil war. Consequently there followed a period of considerable anarchy. This was heightened by the declining health of Charles IX and his death, less than two years later, in May 1574. If the Huguenots had nothing more to hope for from Charles IX, they had everything to fear from the accession of Anjou as Henry III and, with him, the return to power of his mentor, Lorraine. No one knew precisely how the massacre had come about. Nevertheless, Anjou's involvement was generally believed, while Lorraine had labored for a decade or more to achieve something very like it. There was little prospect that the moderation of Catherine de Medici would prevail in the coming reign, nor could the Huguenots even be certain that she would still protect them, to the extent of promoting a reasonable edict. It is against this background of turbulence and fear that one must seek to understand the Huguenot efforts to protect themselves by means of a comprehensive organization which manifestly challenged the authority of the crown.

The fourth civil war was unlike the first three, which had been anticipated and, to some extent, prepared. Although the Protestants also rose in arms in other parts of the country, especially Languedoc and the south, on the national level warfare was confined to the siege of La Rochelle by a dangerously mingled "royal" and Catholic force—even though the king had declared his adherence to the edict of Saint-Germain. There appears to have been a considerable element on the "royal" side which was violently opposed to the Guises and all their extremist adherents, now stained by their role in the massacre. The young duc d'Alençon—still untried and untainted—emerged about this time as the chief of these adversaries. This was very dangerous, just when the Huguenots were leaderless and the king was completely discredited. Alençon was on notoriously bad terms with the king, as well as with Anjou—who ranked as a Guisard—and he was bound to attract a hopeful following, if only because of his station. What, exactly, was going on, remains extremely obscure, but Catherine—who probably knew—was urgently concerned to remove Anjou, lieutenant general and commander-in-chief, from the hostility of his "allies." It appears to have been largely for this reason that she labored to have him honorably exiled to the throne of distant Poland. It was also by this improbable eventuality that she and her faithful moderates forced the conclusion of the peace of La Rochelle in July 1573.[1]

This curious half peace was, according to its wording, principally concluded with the Protestant strongholds of La Rochelle, Montauban and Nîmes, but was also intended to apply to the whole country. The explanation probably lies in the prolonged difficulty in reaching any agreement at all. This partial and abortive compromise was therefore primarily a crude device for extricating Anjou, together with much of the court, from the camp at La Rochelle. The peace achieved little else. It is clear, as one might expect, that the Protestants were seeking to reaffirm their edict of Saint-Germain which, in fact, had never been rescinded. Thus the first three articles of the peace of La Rochelle—declaring

1. This is also known as the edict of Boulogne, namely the *château* of Madrid in the Bois de Boulogne, Paris. Haag, *La France protestante*, x, 110-14.

an amnesty, prohibiting all forms of recrimination and restoring Catholicism and all Catholic property—directly corresponded to articles 1, 2, and 3 of Saint-Germain, while those relating to justice were similar. The military clauses also followed the previous edict, where still appropriate, introducing only the new principle of four hostages in respect of each of three privileged towns, La Rochelle, Montauban and Nîmes. The principal and astounding difference between the two edicts lay in the toleration clauses. According to articles 4 and 5, the inhabitants of the three towns were permitted to hold the cult within their own houses and property, but not in public. Elsewhere Protestants were accorded nothing but freedom of conscience, except that *seigneurs haut justiciers* might celebrate christenings and marriages privately at home, with a small attendance of up to ten non-members of the family. They were not authorized to celebrate the Sacrament. For everyone else the *baillis* and *sénéchaux* were to provide for burials; that was the bleak total. Thus the cult was allowed only in private houses in three cities, in spite of a general recognition of the existence of the Protestants, who might, with certain reservations (article 9), depart without prejudice to their property rights.

Such an edict, without any general toleration clauses, could not and did not bring peace. Instead it promoted confusion and endemic civil war, from which, on the national level, the crown and the Catholic leaders had withdrawn. Thus, from 1573 to 1576 there existed neither peace nor war, but a fluctuating state of increasingly dangerous chaos which favored all ambitious malcontents and fishers in troubled waters. The problem of the partial peace was most acute in the Midi, where the Protestants had taken up arms after the massacre, and two of the three specified cities, Montauban and Nîmes, had not been represented at the negotiations of La Rochelle. It was therefore on the pretext of discussing the new edict that they obtained permission from the duc d'Anjou to assemble at Montauban to discuss the treaty.[2] This is how the Protestant petition of 25 August 1573 originated.[3]

2. Anquez, *Histoire des assemblées*, 3.

3. Haag, *La France protestante*, x, 114–21, requête de l'assemblée de Montauban.

This surprisingly moderate petition embodied, according to the preamble, all the "particularités necessaire à l'entretenement d'une vraye et entière paix." It was therefore fundamental in its influence on all subsequent edicts,[4] which may, like the previous ones, be classified in groups. Just as the edicts of January 1562, Amboise, and Longjumeau were all annihilated by Lorraine's triumph, the edict of Saint-Maur in 1568, so the related edicts of Poitiers, 17 September 1577, Nérac, 28 February 1579, and Fleix, 26 November 1580 were, in turn, completely demolished by the Guisard treaty of Nemours in July 1585. Thus the whole tortuous, cyclical process had to begin for a third time, and in ever greater anarchy, bitterness and travail.

The Protestant petition of 25 August 1573 was drafted in the name of the "*vicomtes, barons et gentilhommes*" and their adherents, and the deputies of the churches of twenty-two specified areas of southern France. Its purpose was stated to be a durable peace and "vraye réintégrance d'amitié entre tous . . . subjects des religions." The first essential, it declared, was therefore to restore some measure of confidence between themselves and the crown. This was an interesting and judicious comment, since a breakdown of confidence was a fundamental cause of the duration and complexity of hostilities in France. According to the petition, the restoration of confidence required, in the first place, a series of clauses relating to the massacre of St. Bartholomew, an event which had shattered all illusions and dashed all hopes. The petitioners reminded the king of his letters of 24 August 1572. These were, presumably, the letters of that date addressed to provincial *gouverneurs* in which Charles had declared his wishes and his intention to sustain the edict of Saint-Germain, despite the events in Paris. Thus the Protestants requested the establishment, wherever necessary, of special, impartial tribunals to try those allegedly responsible for the provincial massacres. In this way the king would begin to "arracher la juste et grande deffiance qu'ils

---

4. This, it must be understood, is a juridical statement, since it was actually immediate current affairs which determined the timing and content of each edict. Certain basic Huguenot requirements, however, obtained all along.

[the massacres] ont conceue." Furthermore, they required a public exoneration for all those involved in the alleged conspiracy
against the king following the assault on Coligny, which the death
of the admiral and other Huguenot leaders was held to have
preempted.[5] This request was to ensure that no one should subsequently be molested on this pretext of having conspired against
the king, or for having taken up arms in self-defense in or after
August 1572. Exoneration was equally required for all action
relating to the conduct of those hostilities. Posthumous exoneration was also demanded for the victims of the massacre, of whom
Coligny, La Rochefoucauld, Arnold de Cavaignes and François
de Beauvais, seigneur de Bricquemault, were named, since this
permitted the restitution of property and rights of inheritance.

After the problems arising from the events of St. Bartholomew,
the principal requirement of the petition inevitably related to
religious liberties. Given the opportunity to state their own
terms, the Protestants demanded complete freedom of the cult
everywhere for everyone, in public and in private, and exemption
from contributions[6] and observances contrary to their religion.
Curiously enough they added to this, not a demand for churches
(*temples*), which they probably held in any case, but guaranteed
burial rights ("la liberté d'honneste sépulture") which were often
riotously opposed. Further categories of requests related to civil
rights and liberties, equality without respect to religion in admission to schools and colleges, with staff of both confessions;
equality of tax liability, eligibility for posts and offices, compensation for loss of property, protection for property acquired, and
judicial impartiality. All these matters had been covered in the
edict of Saint-Germain, but the petition goes beyond the edict in
its juridical requirements. We find here the origin of the *chambres
mi-parties*, first granted in the peace of Monsieur, 1576, and well
known as the final judicial guarantee embodied in the edict of
Nantes. The petition requested that cases between litigants of

---

5. This is interesting evidence that the "conspiracy" theory of the
immediate origins of the massacre was generally disseminated. Sutherland, *The Massacre of St. Bartholomew*, ch. xviii.
6. Exemption from contributions was never granted, even in 1598.

both religions should be heard by equal numbers of Catholic and Protestant judges. For this purpose they wanted a *chambre mi-partie* to be established in some peaceful town within the jurisdiction of each *parlement*—but not, be it noted, *within* the *parlements* themselves. The petition also requested that cases between litigants of the same religion should be heard by judges of that persuasion. Concessions of this kind, however, had been and would be useless if their implementation were not assured. Thus implementation, together with personal security—from which the idea of the *places de sûreté* had arisen—were recognized as being the key problems. "Reste le point principal . . . les moiens d'une vraye et juste seurté pour la tenue durée et entretien . . . des promesses et ordonnances de V. M. sur tout ce que dessus pour une ferme et durable paix." The petition then revived a subversive idea, formerly raised during the negotiations of Saint-Germain, which no government could possibly have admitted. This was the guarantee of such an internal settlement by foreign Protestant powers: Germans, Swiss and English. In this connection there were also requests relating to the location and command of garrisons, a matter which became a constant cause of dispute. Rather surprisingly, *places de sûreté* were not mentioned as such, but the petition appears to assume their existence by specifying that the Protestants should guard their own *places* themselves, nothing having been demolished or, in other words, fortifications intact and arms retained. Finally, the petition elaborated on the principle of oaths of loyalty, and good faith in respect of the regulations. Such oaths were to be renewed annually for five years before a special assembly for whose composition various proposals were made. The oaths were to embody a promise both to observe the agreement, and to offer life and service in its defense.

These, therefore, were the essential concessions and safeguards, drafted by the Protestants in August 1573, for their reintegration into society and the maintenance of a durable peace. They might have been described as a charter for the "*zelés de religion*," and they were never lost sight of, although from about 1575 the movement was to be increasingly dominated by political leaders whose principal aims were not those of securing religious liberties and civil rights. The outward moderation of this petition must therefore not be taken too literally. If it did not go so far beyond the terms of Saint-Germain as to be labeled revolutionary, there was, nevertheless, a nascent revolutionary organization behind it, whose purpose was far removed from a "vraye réintégrance d'amitié," and which was shortly to be exploited by the nobility in arms. It is therefore only in the light of the events of 1573–76 that the fundamentally important peace of Monsieur can be explained and understood.

While the fourth war was still going on, four Protestant assemblies had already been held, at Nîmes, Millau, Réalmont and Anduse. They produced *règlements* which laid the foundations of the notorious Protestant "state within the State." Their purpose appears to have been no less than the transfer of sovereignty from the crown to elected assemblies and carefully controlled councils. The Protestant estates of Bas-Languedoc had assembled at Nîmes and drew up articles for submission to the king. It was their meeting at Montauban, together with deputies from Guyenne, which produced the deceptively reasonable petition of 25 August 1573. This was signed by the vicomte Paulin, the Protestants' own substitute *gouverneur* of Haut-Languedoc. Three deputies, Yolet, Philippi and Chavagnac, together with several delegates to this assembly, were to present the petition at court.[7] By the end of 1573, nothing had been achieved, the king was seriously ill, and the disorders in Languedoc were increasing. In December the Venetian ambassador reported "mille innovationi et si teme di peggio."[8] The Tuscan, Alamanni, seemed to be of much the same opinion that "ogni cose è in maggior confusione che mai, e senza presta rimedi si cammina alla destruzione del regno."[9] The likelihood of renewed war was much greater than any hope for peace. France therefore entered upon a prolonged period of dire peril and multiple conflict, which led to the royal capitulation of May 1576.

Without awaiting the answer to their petition, the Huguenots held a further assembly at Millau, in December 1573, on the

7. Anquez, *Histoire des assemblées*, 6.
8. B. N., Mss. Italien, 1728, ff. 149–50, 2 December 1573.
9. Desjardins, *Négs. Tosc.*, iii, 894, 16 December 1573.

pretext that as negotiations might be protracted, and expectations slow to materialize, it was "très-necessaire à tous ceux de la Religion de se tenir sur leurs gardes et conduire prudemment pour s'opposer aux pratiques, machinations, entreprinses secrettes et surprinses que les ennemis brassent . . . à la totale ruine desdits de la Religion."[10] Thus, for their mutual protection, so they claimed, they formed themselves into a "union civile de l'Eglise réformée" under the assembly of Millau. Consequently they drew up a new *règlement*, dated 16 December 1573, which increased and extended their organization and stiffened the terms on which they would negotiate with the royal commissioners.[11] This organization was revolutionary both in its form and in its purpose, and appears to have promoted a dangerous dichotomy between the leadership and the rank and file.[12] It not only extended the area under Protestant control, but also provided for an army, military discipline, finance, justice and municipal administration.[13] Thus, while the petition of 25 August 1573 showed the religious and civil aspects of the Huguenots' activity, this *règlement* of December 1573 showed the political. The king was required to abrogate his sovereignty by endorsing these dispensations. Thus, in spite of the fact that the truce with the Huguenots of Languedoc, originally concluded in August 1573, had been extended until 20 February 1574, they were more prepared to resist than to conclude the durable peace demanded in the petition.[14] So they sent these totally unreasonable demands to the royal *gouverneur*, Damville. The king prepared to send troops to Languedoc and Provence, while ineffective efforts to negotiate also continued.[15]

10. Haag, *La France protestante*, x, 122.

11. Ibid., 121–26; Anquez, *Histoire des assemblées*, 7–12.

12. This statement would admittedly be difficult to illustrate, but such a division does seem to have emerged and was later referred to by Henry of Navarre. See p. 291.

13. Anquez, *Histoire des assemblées*, 10.

14. Mesnard, *Histoire civile, ecclésiastique et littéraire de la ville de Nismes*, v, *preuves*, 109–15, 25 August, 11 October and 29 November 1573, articles of truces. I am indebted to Dr. Joan M. Davies for this reference.

15. B. N., Mss. Italien, 1728, f. 176, 7 January 1574; f. 182, 22 January 1574; f. 192, 31 January 1574; f. 209, 18 February 1574; f. 215, 24 February 1574; f. 221, 28 February 1574.

The Huguenot intransigence in December 1573 is probably explained by the fact that some sort of conspiracy or rebellion was planned for the beginning of March 1574.[16] Madame Duplessis-Mornay recorded that Alençon "projetoit diverses pratiques contre le Roy son frère"—who was dangerously ill. In the event of failure, Alençon planned to escape to England, presumably to solicit haven and help from the queen. He was also himself solicited by the Flemish and by the Huguenots' organization which, at the time, was in need of a prince.[17] From then until his death in 1584, Alençon greatly complicated the Huguenot problem, since he shared their aversions without espousing their cause. The disturbances of March 1574 must surely be regarded as a succession crisis in which Alençon, Queen Elizabeth, the Netherlands and the Huguenots all had their reasons for fearing the seemingly imminent accession of Henry III. At the same time, there was some fresh quarrel between the Guises and François duc de Montmorency, who had played a consistently moderate role at court since the peace of Saint-Germain. The Guises sought to engineer Montmorency's departure, just as they had, until the massacre, sought to exclude Coligny from court.[18] This prolonged struggle against the power of the Guisard extremists—formerly embodied in Coligny—continued without interruption to be the real pivot of French domestic affairs. It was, however, much less obvious than before the massacre, because their principal adversaries, including Alençon and the Montmorency family, as well as the Huguenots, shared little—if anything—else in common. To these must be added Henry III himself, once the interests of the crown were his. The partial, shifting and improbable affiliations which so confuse the following years can only be understood in terms of common hostility to the Guises and their adherents.

For Charles IX the wheel had come full circle. The Guise-Châtillon vendetta was over, because Coligny and his brothers were dead. But once again the duc de Guise—this time the young

16. Both 10 and 14 March are mentioned but it seems, in any case, that the timing miscarried.

17. La Ferrière, "Les Dernières conspirations du règne de Charles IX," *Revue des questions historiques*, xlviii, 1890, pp. 429–31.

18. Desjardins, *Négs. Tosc.*, iii, 903–5, 1 March 1574; 905, 5 March 1574.

duke, Henri—was too powerful at court for there to be any peace with the Huguenots while his family and faction prevailed. Montmorency, though not a Protestant, was Coligny's cousin, and had always been pro-English. According to La Noue, a Protestant lieutenant in arms in the west, a rising had been planned for 14 March, when Alençon and Navarre were to have gone hunting and then escaped to Mantes. Navarre had been detained since the time of the massacre, when he was forced against his will to become a Catholic. This, and the failure of his marriage to Marguerite de Valois, accounts for his need and desire to "escape." By descent and inclination his role still lay with the Huguenots, whose titular leader he had been before his marriage and Coligny's death in the massacre. The escape plan, however, miscarried because its execution was advanced by ten days. The flight of the princes was consequently prevented, and they confessed to Catherine.[19]

What really happened is still far from clear, except that various dangerous processes were evolving simultaneously. Contemporaries themselves were bewildered. According to the Tuscan, Alamanni, a Huguenot rising, which threatened the king at Saint-Germain, was said by some to have been a plot by Alençon and Montmorency to kill the Guises. This, in either case, was reminiscent of the "incident de Meaux." The "incident" had occurred on Michaelmas day 1567, and contemporary use in 1574 of the term *Michelade* may be significant.[20] Others maintained that Alençon had meant to flee and absent himself from court until the Guises, who competed with him for power, had been dismissed.

The Venetian ambassador, Cavalli, expressed at this time the general fear and uncertainty in France: something, somewhere, was expected to happen—"qualche maggior fiamma"—possibly in the form of massive help to the Huguenots from Germany or

---

19. La Ferrière, "Les Dernières conspirations du règne de Charles IX," *Revue des questions historiques*, xlviii, 1890, pp. 449–51, 454; Desjardins, *Négs. Tosc.*, iii, 908–10, 11 March 1574. Alamanni said that the plot had been disclosed by the queen of Navarre, who had always favored the Guises. This is plausible, since she was alleged to have been in love with the duke.

20. I am indebted to Dr. Joan M. Davies for this information.

England. The comte de Retz, a Catholic extremist, had been summoned to return from Poland via Germany to find out what was happening there. Spain, the ambassador said, was preparing a huge armada, and his Tuscan colleague, Alamanni, reported that Giuliano del Bene had been sent by Savoy, probably upon Spanish instigation, to obstruct any peace with the Huguenots.[21] Catherine was preparing to send Saint-Sulpice and the secretary of state, Villeroy, to Languedoc. At the same time, the king was also planning to send out various small forces. But it is difficult to see what enemies they could identify, or what objectives they could aim at. Cavalli further reported Montmorency to have told a friend that the king would do nothing but send people hither and thither "per conto della pace," and the Huguenots could never have confidence in the king until the government was changed.[22] This was a renewal of the problem of the control of the council.

On 8 March 1574 the dying king was moved to the greater security of Vincennes and the imprisoned princes were more closely watched. But there was, reportedly, no lack of people blowing in Alençon's ears to persuade him to leave court and lead the rebel malcontents. It was doubtless for this reason that he was said to be "caressed" at court, where, on 25 January, he had been promised the rank of lieutenant general, though in fact he did not receive it. Spain—and therefore the Guises—the report goes on, were afraid that he and his followers might take action in the Netherlands, especially since Henri prince de Condé had gone to Picardy.[23]

It was therefore not surprising that, at the beginning of April 1574, another conspiracy should have erupted at court, whence the princes are said to have been about to flee. But, once again, the plot was allegedly betrayed, this time by Madame de Sauve, wife of the secretary Fizes, with whom both Navarre and Alençon are said to have been in love—an inauspicious basis for a joint

21. Desjardins, *Négs. Tosc.*, iii, 919, 22 April 1574.
22. B. N., Mss. Italien, 1728, ff. 251–52, 26 March 1574; ff. 255–61, 28 March 1574.
23. Desjardins, *Négs. Tosc.*, iii, 908–9, 11 March 1574.

enterprise.[24] What anyone had really been trying to do is not well authenticated; probably too many disparate things for any clear success. This time—one might venture to suggest because Charles was dead—the marshals Montmorency and his kinsman Cossé were also implicated, and they and the princes were all imprisoned. The involvement of the marshals, and the other Montmorency brothers, Méru and Thoré, who escaped to Germany with Condé, meant that Montmorency's brother Damville, the *gouverneur* of Languedoc, was potentially dangerous.[25] It was impossible to arrest him, nor was he precisely dismissed, but his authority was disavowed.[26] This degradation drove him into alliance with the Huguenots, who now had more to gain from war than from peace. Never before had this been the case, and it necessarily added to the danger of the crown, inaugurating a period in which either faction might take the offensive.[27] Such was the desperate situation when Charles IX died on 30 May 1574. Catherine once again became regent, since Henry III was absent in Poland. Henry made no attempt to hurry home and, to the Huguenots, the recurrence of a regency was a God-sent pretext for increasing their demands.

Having agreed to a six months' truce to run from June 1574, an assembly was reconvened at Millau on 16 July. There the previous *règlement* on the structure of the Protestant "state" was confirmed, and the absent Condé was elected "chef gouverneur général et protecteur." He was, nevertheless, to be very strictly controlled by the organization, which began to reveal its true com-

24. La Ferrière, "Les Dernières conspirations du règne de Charles IX," *Revue des questions historiques*, xlviii, 1890, p. 457; B. N., Mss. Italien, 1728, f. 272, 10 April 1574; f. 274, 14 April 1574; f. 278, 19 April 1574. According to the Venetian, the alarm was raised on 10 April and the plot was to have been executed on the eleventh. La Ferrière says that Alençon was to have fled on 8 April.

25. Sutherland, *The French Secretaries of State*, 180–81.

26. According to Dr. Joan M. Davies, no one really knew how to dismiss a *gouverneur* who refused to relinquish office and could not be caught. The position was therefore confused.

27. Desjardins, *Négs. Tosc.*, iii, 910, 16 March 1574; 911, 24 March 1574; 912, 30 March 1574; 913–14, 14 April 1574; 918, 22 April 1574; 925, 5 May 1574.

plexion.[28] The Huguenots demanded that Condé should govern in the name of the king, and they called for the release of Navarre and the marshals. They were not, apparently, concerned about Alençon. The king, upon his return to France, was required to summon the estates general, and to receive the Protestant petition of 25 August 1573, which they presumably intended the estates to sanction. Finally the Huguenots adopted the repudiated Damville as their own *gouverneur* and commander in the absence of Condé.[29] This, in turn, ensured Damville the power base he needed to hold out in Languedoc against the prince dauphin, who, in May 1574, had been appointed to supersede him. Thus the peace and edict which had been the original purpose of the Protestant petition of August 1573 was even more remote. In September 1574, when the king finally reached Lyons, deputies went to demand freedom of the cult and the cession of *places de sûreté*. Damville, however, would conclude no agreement so long as his brother Montmorency was held a prisoner.

Henry III appeared to be oblivious of the gravity of the crisis awaiting him, while the Huguenots exploited his procrastination to become ever more invincibly organized. They met again at Nîmes in December 1574, when the truce was about to expire, and confirmed both their union and the appointment of Damville, which was formalized in January 1575.[30] Thus fortified, they again presented the king, at Avignon, with their outrageous "peace" proposals; meanwhile Condé prepared to invade France from Germany. Still left to their own devices, while the king was occupied with his marriage and coronation,[31] the following February 1575 the Huguenots drafted a further comprehensive *règlement* which completed the organization of their notorious "state within the State." The *règlement* of Nîmes consisted of eighty-four articles creating a complete political, administrative, finan-

28. Anquez, *Histoire des assemblées*, 13.

29. B. N., Mss. Italien, 1728, ff. 401–5, 17 September 1574.

30. B. N., Mss. N. A. F., 7178, ff. 134–35, 12 January 1575, articles of Damville's union with the association of Nîmes. I am indebted to Dr. Joan M. Davies for this reference.

31. B. N., Mss. Italien, 1728, ff. 538–58, 12 February 1575.

cial, judicial and military organization for the Protestants. The "basic communities," namely the churches, were grouped into provinces, each directed by a governor. He was assisted by a permanent council which was itself appointed and supervised by a provincial assembly. At the summit of this organization was a general assembly, originally composed of three deputies from each province, all under an elected protector—Condé—who served as their supreme commander. At first the *règlement* embraced only the southern parts of France, roughly from La Rochelle to Auvergne; but gradually other provinces joined until all the Protestants were formally united. Such, then, was the organization which the contemporary historian, J.-A. de Thou described as "une nouvelle espèce de république... séparée du reste de l'etat." This organization long outlasted the Huguenot liaison with Damville and his followers, the *catholiques unis*—an awkward expedient which collapsed in March 1577.[32]

Short of a long and catastrophic war, which the king was in no position to wage and had no stomach to undertake, the Huguenots were now, in February 1575, in a position to insist on more or less their own terms. Thus, when it suited them, and not before, on 11 April 1575 twelve commissioners from the prince de Condé presented another petition. Although the regency was over, they still demanded a meeting of the estates general, permission to celebrate the cult everywhere, *places de sûreté*, judicial guarantees, and the punishment of the authors of the massacre. These provisions were drawn from among the ninety-one articles agreed to at Nîmes, in which may be found all the Protestant demands.[33]

Negotiations on this basis in the early summer of 1575 were predictably unsuccessful. The king was ill, and had never dominated or controlled the affairs of his kingdom since his dilatory

32. Anquez, *Histoire des assemblées*, 13–21, 10 February 1575; de Thou, *Histoire universelle, livre* lx.

33. B. N., Mss. Italien, 1728, f. 564, 17 February 1575; ibid., 1729, ff. 1–2, 1 March 1575; f. 4, 12 March 1575; f. 9, 12 March 1575; f. 23, 27 March 1575; ff. 28–29, 31 March 1575; ff. 31–32, 7 April 1575; ff. 41–42, 12 April 1575; Desjardins, *Négs. Tosc.*, iv, 36–37, April–May 1575.

return from Poland. He wanted, as he was always to want peace. This eluded him, as it was always to elude him, because he never acknowledged his danger until it was too late to avert it. He had neither the energy, the right sort of ability, the power, nor the means to obtain and enforce peace.[34] Condé's commissioners departed in May having rejected, according to the king, his reasonable terms. He commanded them to return before the end of July, but only a few of them came, declaring that they could do nothing without the others. In fact they were determined to break the negotiations and "porter les choses aux dernières extremités." About this time Alençon entered into what he called a "league" with the elector Palatine and Condé.[35] Helped, once again, by some of those who had tried to rescue him in 1574, Alençon finally escaped from court on 15 September 1575.[36] He and the Huguenots were, for the moment, useful to each other, and he played along with them for a while, to their mutual advantage. It would appear that Alençon and the Huguenots were simultaneously in arms against the same enemies, but only partially in pursuit of the same objectives, since Alençon was not so myopic as to lose sight of the throne. According to Henry, the Huguenots were attempting to take most of the *bonnes villes*, seeking to attract the Catholic gentry, and soliciting foreign aid. Their intention was, indeed, to make war, when Condé and his forces arrived from Germany. The king therefore called out the royal forces to be commanded by Montpensier, Guise and himself.[37]

34. Desjardins, *Négs. Tosc.*, iv, 38, June–July 1575.

35. *CSPF.*, *1575–77*, p. 190, 27 November 1575, Instructions for Monsieur de la Porte; 304, 2 April 1576, Instructions for Randolph. It is likely that Alençon acceded to the agreement between Condé and Casimir, the elector's son, of 27 September 1575; ibid., 295–96.

36. Ibid., 140–42, Dale [to Smith and Walsingham, 21 September 1576].

37. Gomberville, *Mémoires de Nevers*, i, 93–94, 10 [17?] September 1575, Henry to the *gouverneurs*, *baillis* and *sénéchaux*; 435–36, advertissement sur la négociation de mai 1575; Desjardins, *Négs. Tosc.*, iv, 43, August–September 1575; B. N., Mss. Italien, 1729, f. 107, 1 June 1575; ff. 136–41, 5 July 1575; ff. 150–53, 18 July 1575; f. 171, 15 August 1575; ff. 215–23, 11 September 1575.

After his flight from court, Alençon made his way to Dreux and, on 17 September 1575, issued a "declaration" which amounted to an extensive condemnation of the Guises.[38] It had already been maintained, early in 1574, that the Guises were determined that no peace acceptable to the Huguenots should be concluded or implemented.[39] Alençon proclaimed that he had escaped "pour prendre la cause publique en main," and to oppose not the king, but the pernicious counsel and designs of those who disturbed the kingdom. He called rather vaguely for reforms, a council, and a meeting of the estates general from which all foreigners should be excluded. This was the usual way of referring to the Guises—possibly also to the Guisard dukes of Nevers and Nemours, who were both Italians. Alençon described his enterprise as holy and praiseworthy, and called upon princes, *seigneurs*, gentlemen and bourgeois to support him with men and money. He did not, however, announce what it was they were to fight for.

Alençon's "cause publique" included huge personal demands. These he presented to his mother, Catherine de Medici, who caught up with him between Blois and Chambord about the end of September.[40] By this time the German forces were already in Lorraine, which may be one reason why the marshals Cossé and Montmorency were released in October on Alençon's request. The approach of the Germans made Alençon disinclined to negotiate with his mother. Thus for some weeks they played cat-and-mouse in the region of the Loire, and Alençon became increasingly intransigent. While the king prepared for war, Catherine opted for a truce. This she obtained with difficulty, and it was really only a capitulation in order to avert the foreign invasion. To this end the king agreed to pay 500,000 *livres* for

38. B. N., Mss. Fr., 3342, ff. 4–5, 17 September 1575, Alençon's declaration.

39. Desjardins, *Négs. Tosc.*, iii, 900, 16 February 1574; 903, 1 March 1574.

40. Ibid., iv, 43, August-September 1575; B. N., Mss. Italien, 1729, ff. 136–41, 5 July 1575; ff. 150–53, 18 July 1575; f. 171, 15 August 1575; ff. 215–23, 11 September 1575; ff. 272–76, 3 October 1575.

Alençon's *reistres*, if they refrained from crossing the Rhine. Henry also agreed to pay forAlençon's garrisons, and to disband his own forces. Alençon was allowed to hold Angoulême, Niort and Bourges; also Saumur and La Charité, which both commanded the Loire. Condé was granted Mézières in the Ardennes. The cult was permitted in all these *places de sûreté*. It was therefore already obvious that the ensuing peace conference would have to accept the principal Protestant conditions, as specified in the petition of 25 August 1573.[41]

The six months' truce of Champigny from November 1575 to May 1576 purchased the Huguenots time in which to prepare for war while seeking, for preference, an acceptable edict. The truce also represented a royal effort to detach the Huguenots and Damville from Alençon and Montmorency; this, in turn, would isolate Condé.[42] In this respect, it was a failure; and the truce itself was troubled in December by Condé's approach in arms. Late in January 1576 his forces were in Burgundy.[43] These already perilous circumstances were rendered even more critical when, at the beginning of February, just as Condé's forces were about to cross the Loire, Navarre escaped from court. He went to Poitou on his way to Béarn and shortly took the field as leader of the Huguenots.[44] This could have permitted them to mount a military pincer movement upon the Catholics, who controlled the king. The truce, however, did not expire until May. Thus, characteristically ignoring its virtual breakdown, Catherine worked feverishly to obtain a settlement. For this purpose she

41. Desjardins, *Négs. Tosc.*, iv, 47, November 1575; 52, 15 November 1575; 53, 21 November 1575; B. N., Mss. Italien, 1729, f. 272, 3 October 1575; f. 308, 11 October 1575; f. 346, 3 November 1575; f. 357, 7 November 1575; f. 362, 14 November 1575; f. 367, 22 November 1575; f. 376, 30 November 1575; Gomberville, *Mémoires de Nevers*, i, 99–104, trève générale [21] November 1575, Champigny.

42. B. N., Mss. Italien, 1729, f. 376, 30 November 1575; f. 455, 25 January 1576.

43. Ibid., f. 384, 6 December 1575; f. 390, 16 December 1575; f. 458, 25 January 1576.

44. Desjardins, *Négs. Tosc.*, iv, 56, February–March 1576; B. N., Mss. Italien, 1729, f. 483, 12 February 1576; f. 571, 3 April 1576.

restrained the royal forces from attacking Condé, as he approached from the east, although it was reported that Spain was seeking to bribe Damville to obstruct the conclusion of peace.[45]

Peace—at virtually any price—was clearly essential: the crown was faced with a truly formidable combination which it was ill-prepared to combat. While so incongruous a coalition could never have stabilized, there was a real danger, in the summer of 1576, that it might have toppled the monarchy before its members disputed the spoils. Henry made no attempt either to dissociate himself from the Guisards, or to divide the assorted enemies who opposed him in that image. Catherine did what she could, at least to avert ruinous hostilities. These were the circumstances which account for the peace of Monsieur and the edict of Beaulieu (Indre-et-Loire), 6 May 1576.[46] This most liberal of all the edicts was really a royal capitulation, and proved to be a catastrophic precedent for the reign of Henry III.

The peace of Monsieur began by expressing the king's desire to reconcile his subjects in "une parfaite union et concorde." Consisting of sixty-three articles, it was long and comprehensive, because, superseding all others, it had itself to contain everything, and to incorporate the demands of the basic petition of 25 August 1573. Juridically it stood halfway between the edict of Saint-Germain, 1570, and that of Nantes in 1598, which bore a marked resemblance to them both. All three, therefore, had many clauses in common. Articles 1 to 3 again repeated those of Saint-Germain and La Rochelle, declaring amnesty, the prohibition of recrimination, and the restoration of the Catholic religion and Church property. This was extended in other articles, such as the observance of Catholic festivals, the degrees of consanguinity and the payment of ecclesiastical dues. But, as well as providing for the protection of the Catholic church, it necessarily made

45. B. N., Mss. Italien, 1729, ff. 503–8, 27 February 1576; ff. 571–74, 3 April 1576. Clearly, if Spain could have bought Damville, this would have been a major coup for the Catholic faction, which was, at that moment, in great danger.

46. Haag, *La France protestante*, x, 127–41.

the important concessions demanded by the Protestants. Thus it was the only edict in the entire series to permit the exercise of the cult "libre public et général... par toutes les villes et lieux... sans restriction de temps et de personnes." Furthermore, it also permitted, at last, the possession and construction of *temples*. [47] These were the edict's distinctive features. Finally, in the presence of royal officials—as in the edict of January 1562—the Protestants were also allowed to hold provincial consistories and general synods. The same article 4, however, also reverted to the hope that a free and holy general council would restore everyone to "une mesme foy religion et creance." This was presumably to safeguard the king. Like the edict of Saint-Germain, that of Monsieur sought to obviate and settle all sources of quarrels and divisions by providing for the restoration of all real and moveable property, income, titles, inheritances, offices, privileges, franchises and jurisdictions. The corollary to this was equality of taxation and the specification of civil rights, already introduced into the edict of Saint-Germain. The vital principle of eligibility for offices, specified in several scattered articles, was extended to a positive undertaking that Protestants would actually receive appointments. This concession was tenaciously cherished over the years, and, after manifold vicissitudes, all these basic demands were ultimately incorporated into the edict of Nantes.

The equally vital juridical protection, first provided by Saint-Germain, was both revived and extended in articles 18 to 21. Thus it was the peace of Monsieur (and not the edict of Nantes, as is commonly supposed), which instituted the famous *chambres mi-parties* in the *parlements*. [48] This provided that cases between persons of opposing religions were to be tried before equal numbers of Protestants and Catholics. These *chambres*, to act as sover-

---

47. Article 8; this was omitted, it was implausibly alleged by inadvertence, from article 11 of the edict of Poitiers, but restored by article 2 of Nérac in 1579.

48. Articles 18 to 21. In the edict of Saint-Germain the *chambres* were established not within the *parlements* themselves, but within their jurisdictions.

eign courts, were composed of two *présidents* and sixteen *conseillers* in Paris, and two *présidents* and ten *conseillers* elsewhere. Protestant offices were to be created to provide the requisite personnel.

The circumstances in which the edict was concluded account for the specific nature of its various, scattered articles of pardon, rehabilitation and exoneration relating to the nobles who had opposed the crown and indulged in such activities as were necessary for war. Alençon, Navarre, Condé and Damville were all personally named, as well—significantly enough—as the prince of Orange and Jean Casimir, son of the elector Palatine. Thus it appears that the impending war would, yet again, have embraced the struggle in the Netherlands. Damville was thereby reinstated in Languedoc, which in practice he had never relinquished.

Articles intended to assuage the memory of St. Bartholomew and rehabilitate its victims were derived from the petitions of 25 August 1573 and 11 April 1575. Article 58, binding the king to summon the estates general within six months, asserted—as a face saver—that Henry's own, prior intention to call them had been thwarted by the disturbances. In fact it reflected imperative Protestant demands; also those of Alençon.

The petition of August 1573 had placed especial emphasis on the problem and importance of guarantees and implementation. Thus the 1570 innovation of *places de sûreté* was another principle incorporated into the peace of Monsieur, and ultimately carried to triumphant and alarming extremes in 1598. The original four towns held by the Protestants now became eight, situated in Languedoc, Guyenne, Dauphiné and Provence. As a corollary to this, it was not surprising that the edict of Beaulieu should have extended the enforcement clauses of Saint-Germain in respect of all those required to swear to observe the agreement. Its implementation was now placed in the especial care of the marshals and *gouverneurs*—in both cases military officials. They were to publish and enforce the edict immediately, without awaiting its registration by the *parlements*, which clearly were expected to refuse. Once again, as in Saint-Germain, anyone who opposed the edict in arms was liable to the death penalty; non-violent resistance was to be otherwise punished.

The peace of Monsieur temporarily averted the erupting civil war in the spring of 1576 and achieved, juridically, more or less what the Huguenots really wanted. But, in the process, they had become a dangerous, revolutionary power in the State. The Catholics, who were no whit more altruistic, never regarded the peace as more than an interim, extorted under duress from the helpless Henry III. While the Protestants could never trust him, his worst trouble was to come from the Catholics.

8

The Struggle against the Catholic Leagues, 1576–1589

THE PERSONALITY AND REIGN OF HENRY III are highly enigmatic, and the years between the peace of Monsieur in 1576 and the formal constitution of the Catholic League in 1584 are possibly among the least familiar of the ancien régime. But their problems and tensions cannot be circumvented if one is to pursue the Huguenots' struggle for recognition. In this struggle to obtain their minimum requirements, clearly defined since 1573, the Huguenots continued to be violently opposed by all Catholic agents and extremists. As these included the king of Spain, the conflict in France must always be seen in relation to war in the Netherlands, because of their influence on the problems of war and peace in France. This is merely to emphasize the obvious continuity of French domestic and foreign history. Similarly, the story of these years was yet another variation on the old theme: the creation, destruction and reconstruction of a modus vivendi between the crown and the factions, as they evolved in the society and State of France.

Where the massive efforts of Catherine de Medici had repeatedly failed, the timid and bewildering prevarications of the equally pacifist Henry III were scarcely even heeded, and could seldom be heard above the menacing voice of international Catholicism. As a prince, Henry had lent himself to extreme Catholic policies, whether voluntarily or otherwise; now, as king, he was confronted by the clandestine "practicing" of Spain, the subversive disregard of his Catholic subjects, and the chronic distrust of his openly hostile Protestants. For them, Coligny's death was unavailing: it had merely destroyed the acceptable edict of Saint-Germain, while the crucial problem of French intervention in the Netherlands had simply been deferred by the massacre. By 1576 the Netherlands problem had become, if anything, even more acutely dangerous, focused on the king's brother and heir presumptive, the weak, ambitious Alençon, now known as the duc d'Anjou,[1] who resumed this part of Coligny's burden, but without the simplicity of his motives. Anjou was lured and flattered by Flemish proposals and, spasmodically as in 1576, he threatened to carry the Huguenots with him. If he had nothing to offer the Huguenots, as such, he stood, nevertheless, for opposition to the Guisard extremists and, in effect if not in theory, to the king. This unstable liaison was desperately serious, since it magnified Catholic resistance to the implementation of any peace.[2] In practical terms, this frustratingly elusive conflict between the Protestants and Damville's *catholiques unis* on the one hand, and the Catholic extremists on the other, nourished personal villainy and brigandage, communal strife and general anarchy. Less destructive, if no less subversive energies on both sides were channeled into seditious organizations, with their concomitant, plain civil war. The conflicting forces at work within these years were probably beyond the control of any insolvent sixteenth-century monarch; certainly beyond that of a sick and sensitive mystic, as Henry III appears to have been.

In the months which followed the peace of Monsieur, Anjou was enticed by the Netherlands. Catherine, for her part, sought to obtain closer relations with Navarre, much as she had formerly sought to conciliate first his father, Antoine de Bourbon, and later Coligny. Besides, she wanted to keep him detached from Anjou. Henry III, like Charles IX, seriously tried to impose the required oaths of fidelity, and to enforce the new edict of pacification. But, if former peace treaties had provoked extreme Catholic opposition, there was never any prospect that the more or less dictated terms of Monsieur would be accepted, or that the Protestants would ever enjoy its advantages. It therefore remained to be seen,

---

1. Alençon took his brother's former title of duc d'Anjou from the time of the peace of Monsieur.

2. B. N., Mss. Italien, 1729, f. 862, 22 October 1576.

during the following months, in what way it would be frustrated and destroyed.[3] From the summer of 1576, after the peace of Monsieur, the Catholics no longer merely isolated the king by opposing the edict and the Huguenots, but gradually began to oppose and threaten the crown itself. This development was, in turn, to modify Henry's policy and attitude to the Huguenots, and inevitably affected the nature of their struggle for recognition.

One should probably beware of overformalizing the Catholic initiatives which immediately followed the peace of Monsieur. They were overtaken by events and never crystallized. There was, on the one hand, a straightforward defensive movement of Catholic solidarity against the excessive leniency of the edict. But there were also more menacing and subversive ideas afloat in a sinister atmosphere. To what extent they were shaped into definite intentions is uncertain; nor does the personal role of the duc de Guise emerge with any clarity.

Henri duc de Guise had been nurtured by his uncle Lorraine, and brought up in mortal hatred of the Bourbons, Châtillons and Montmorencys. For Lorraine, the death of Coligny and the massacre of St. Bartholomew had been a beginning rather than an end. Events in France and the Netherlands since 1568 had frustrated his hopes of an international Catholic league, and his enterprise of England. After the peace of La Rochelle in 1573, there were rumors of renewed Guise machinations; rumors which help to account for the conduct of all anti-Guisards and the confused events of 1573–76. According to Louis de Maimbourg, Lorraine's death, in December 1574, had again disrupted "the plan," which Guise was thenceforth determined to promote as soon as he could.[4] While this opinion was probably deduction, in the light of hindsight, it was probably also true. The idea of a "plan" must not be taken too precisely. It represented the long-term and evolv-

3. Desjardins, *Négs. Tosc.*, iv, 77–78, 5 August 1576; 81 [August–September] 1576; 82, 28 September 1576; 85, 5 November 1576; 94, 16 December 1576; B. N., Mss. Italien, 1729, f. 724, 15 May 1576; f. 860, 8 October 1576; f. 862, 22 October 1576; f. 871, 6 November 1576; f. 873, 6 November 1576.

4. Maimbourg, *Histoire de la Ligue*, 14.

ing Catholic program of the Triumvirate, which, of course, included the enterprise of England.

In January 1576 Dr. Dale, the English ambassador, had reported a secret league between Guise, Nemours, Nevers and the chancellor, René de Birague, against "all that would have any peace, and if it should be made, to begin a sharp war again."[5] It has been seen that the Catholics were temporarily in considerable danger, and this reaction is what one would have expected. Lorraine's conception of a Catholic league had inevitably included Spanish support. This was indeed its weakness, since neither really wanted the other to achieve their common objective of replacing Queen Elizabeth by Mary queen of Scots. Nevertheless, Henri duc de Guise soon began to look towards Madrid, and later became a Spanish pensioner.[6] It was rumored at the time, and has since been widely recorded, that Guise met Don John of Austria when he passed through France on his way to the Netherlands—at high speed and incognito—on 30-31 October 1576. According to Pierre de l'Estoile, they were to meet in Luxembourg, where Don John arrived on 3 November. P. O. Törne maintains, however, that historians have been misled by Brantôme, and that the story of this meeting was invented in the seventeenth century.[7] Nevertheless, the rumors of such a meeting, reported by l'Estoile, prove the existence of the idea and the plausibility of such an event. Nothing is likely to have been determined at any such hurried and clandestine meeting, if only because Don John had departed without his instructions.

The alleged outcome, however, contained more than a grain of

---

5. *CSPF.*, *1575-77*, p. 233, 24 January 1576, Dale [to Smith and Walsingham].

6. Törne, "Philippe II et Henri de Guise, 1578," *Revue historique*, clxvii, 1931, p. 334.

7. *CSPF.*, *1575-77*, pp. 407-8, 29 October 1576, allegedly from M. de Villiers to Walsingham. This must be an editorial error since the letter appears to be from Philip II, writing from Pardo, who refers to his brother, Don John. Many of the documents in this volume are assembled in the wrong order. See also: ibid., 418, 10 November 1576, occurrents; Törne, *Don Juan d'Autriche et les projets de conquête de l'Angleterre*, 1568-78, ii, 36-44; L'Estoile, *Journal de Henri III*, vol. i, 143.

truth, and whether or not they actually met, they certainly shared a measure of common interest. Don John was to conquer England and Scotland—always an intended extension of the suppression of the Netherlands—and marry Mary Stuart, Guise's cousin. Don John's instructions, dated October 1576, included the statement that having restored the king's authority and the observance of the (Catholic) religion in the Netherlands, Philip might then "give the law to his heretic neighbours, who at present have their foot upon his neck and keep up these intestine wars [in the Netherlands] in order to destroy his greatness."[8] The reference was both to England and to France, where the Guises had been, and were again to be his agents. There is no doubt that the marriage of Don John to Mary Stuart was mentioned at this time, and apparently intended as his reward for the conquest of England.[9] In the hostilities which followed the abrogation of the peace of Monsieur in 1577, Don John is said to have "preferred his Spaniards to the king," then temporarily leader of the Catholic cause.[10] After the subsequent edict of Poitiers, in the autumn of 1577, Guise assisted Don John by raising 4,000 men in France.[11] In April 1578 Guise entered into negotiations with the Spanish ambassador, Vargas, for an invasion of England which he was to command. During the following years Guise was involved with the Jesuits in designs on Scotland and England and the deposition of Elizabeth in favor of Mary.[12]

8. *CSPF.*, *1575-77*, p. 409-10, October 1576, instructions for Don John of Austria. Anjou was actively "practising" in the Netherlands at this time and Don John reported the presence of 6,000 cavalry near Luxembourg in November 1576. The figure sounds dubiously high. Ibid., 423, 19 November 1576, Wilson to the privy council; 448, 17 December 1576, Laurence Jonson to Daniel Rogers; 458, 26 November 1576, Don John to Jeronimo Rodas.

9. Ibid., 565-68, 28 April 1577, Paulet to Walsingham. Paulet's informant was the secretary of the duc de Guise. Ibid., 576-77, 9 May 1577, Paulet to Walsingham. It is the report, not the evidence, which is retrospective.

10. Ibid., 536-38, 4 March 1577, Paulet to Burghley.

11. Törne, "Philippe II et Henri de Guise, 1578," *Revue historique*, clxvii, 1931, p. 324.

12. See for example, Martin, *Henry III and the Jesuit Politicians*, chaps. iv, viii and footnotes.

Don John's reciprocal support of the Catholic cause in France allegedly included Guise designs on the throne.[13] Whether the duc de Guise really harbored designs on the throne as early as 1576 is very hard to estimate. In the first place, it was not a matter for free discussion. It might have been an inchoate aspiration, or an idea which simply existed, latent in his mind. It might also have existed, and perhaps more forcefully, in the minds of older and more experienced Catholic extremists for whose purposes the young duke was indispensable. We can follow neither the processes of his mind, nor even the stages by which he assumed control and direction of the Catholic movement in France. Guise was still only twenty-five, just nine months older than Henry III, who had, from 1567, been closely connected with the career of Lorraine. It is likely that the two Henrys had some recently shared experience in the emotive business of the massacre. Lorraine, however, must have realized that Henry—as king—would never be capable of resisting the Huguenots, and he may have prepared the duc de Guise to exploit the king, just as he had himself exploited Anjou as heir apparent. It is not certain whether Henry ever trusted Guise, at the beginning of his reign. He seems not to have brought his mind to bear on the problems of his kingdom. He may simply have taken Guisard support for granted—at least while Lorraine was still alive—without realizing that his accession to the throne would sever him from the loyalties of the past. The severance, however, would not have been immediately obvious, since it was not until after the capitulation of 1576 that Henry could possibly have been accused of anything prejudicial to the extreme Catholic cause. But, while Henry desperately needed peace, the Guises and the Catholics stood most to gain from war. The peace of Monsieur had the catastrophic effect of alienating the king from much of Catholic France, and provided the Guisards with a supreme opportunity to reactivate the "plan." Thus began the fatal enmity between Henry III and the duc de Guise. While these one-time comrades ought to have been allies, Guise had inherited the mantle of Lorraine and—so it would appear—was not content to serve the king of France.

The correct interpretation of the crisis of 1576–77 may well be

13. Forneron, *Les ducs de Guise*, ii, 250.

in terms of Henry's anxiety to avert the fearful consequences of a rift between himself and Guise. Catherine de Medici had faced the same dangerous problem in 1560–62. But she was greatly assisted, though only in this respect, by the murder of François duc de Guise in 1563. As a result, the family and faction had lacked a military leader until Henri grew to manhood. This, in turn, had enabled her to ward off the danger from Spain, of which she was always aware. Lorraine, as a prelate, had been obliged to work through the council, which necessarily obviated, on his side, any overt break with the crown. From past experience, Henry III knew as much as anyone of the dangers of a Catholic league focused through the Guises on the kingdom of France. In 1576 these dangers were potentially greater than ever before, since the young duke was then available to assume a military command. He was therefore virtually certain to be importuned by all Catholic activists, of whatever disposition, and likely to be credited with their most subversive sentiments. He may possibly have inherited a network of provincial clientage, contrived by Lorraine, although this is a matter for research.

There is not, however, any direct evidence for the activity of Guise himself in creating the first, rather nebulous—French—Catholic league of 1576, though it is usually assumed to have been his work.[14] In reality there was not one clearly formulated league, but rather an unspecified number of provincial associations, springing from the first of them in Picardy. Any mention of *the* League, however, almost certainly referred to that of Picardy. In June 1576, a few weeks after the peace of Monsieur, Jean d'Humières, whose city of Péronne had been ceded to Condé as a Protestant stronghold within his *gouvernement* of Picardy, addressed to all Catholic princes, noblemen and prelates a manifesto entitled "traité de la Confédération entre les catholiques... dite la Sainte-Ligue."[15] Whether before or after this event is not clear but, on 8 June 1576, Henry III wrote to d'Humières deploring

14. There had been other, earlier Catholic leagues, from about 1560, but not, so far as is known, on the scale of 1576.

15. Haag, *La France protestante*, x, 141–42, June 1576, traité de la Confédération conclue à Péronne, dite la Sainte-Ligue.

the fact that the inhabitants of Péronne refused to accept the terms of the month-old treaty and admit the cult. Furthermore, the people were seeking support among the nobility of Picardy. Péronne could not be made an exception. Six days later Henry wrote to Bellièvre that Péronne had refused to admit Condé's garrison and was receiving money from other towns, "et qu'ils constituent avec elles des ligues." These towns were Amiens, Abbéville, Saint-Quentin, Beauvais and Corbie. Thus the original Catholic league was a league of cities in Picardy, protesting against the introduction of the Protestant cult under the terms of the peace of Monsieur. The Venetian ambassador reported that there were Spanish agents encouraging this resistance because they did not want a garrison of the Protestant prince de Condé in Péronne, on the frontier of the Netherlands.[16] Thus Henry III knew from the outset what was going on.

The manifesto of Péronne contained the seeds of a revolutionary movement whose articles amounted to a declaration of war on all opponents. Though it would appear to be ranged against their powerful "state" organization, the Protestants were nowhere specified. While the articles formally subscribed to the protection of the king, this was on condition that he obeyed the league. Thus he was to be presented with certain articles by the estates general (to be summoned by the terms of the peace of Monsieur), recalling him to the religious duties of his coronation oath. The signatories also declared their intention to execute faithfully the decisions of the estates, the presumption being that they would demand the complete restoration of Catholicism. They probably also had in mind the decrees of Trent, another of Lorraine's objectives. The document proclaimed a struggle to the death against all who refused to join the association, and all who might seek to withdraw from it. All Catholics of the "corps des villes et villages" were to be secretly informed by the *gouverneurs*, requested to enter into the association, and to raise men and arms to perform its purposes. All members were required to swear a corporeal oath of loyalty and obedience "au chef qui sera député."

16. Francois, *Lettres de Henri III*, vol. ii, 443–44, 8 June 1576, Henry to d'Humières, 445–46, 14 June 1576, Henry to Bellièvre; 445, n. 1.

Since this was clearly not the king, the tone and content of this document is gravely derogatory to the royal authority, to which it pays lip service. It has never been doubted that the unnamed leader was to be the duc de Guise. Louis de Maimbourg said that it was actually Guise who compiled this manifesto and sent it to d'Humières to be propagated in the provinces.[17] D'Humières, it must be recognized, was not of a rank to command the league himself, though his age and greater experience may well have been esteemed. Such a league could, initially, have been purely national and self-supporting, and it is not clear whether any help was sought from the Papacy or from Spain. Evidence relating to Catholic negotiations in Rome is neither conclusive in itself, nor precisely connected with the Picardy league. But, whether true or fabricated, this evidence gravely affected the climate of opinion and must be presumed to have influenced the king.

The evidence from Rome concerned one, David, a Parisian advocate, who vociferously maintained on the street corner that the crown belonged by right to the house of Lorraine. He is said to have gone to Rome in the suite of the bishop of Paris, who left on 22 June 1576 to obtain authorization for the alienation of Church property.[18] David is said to have been well received by Cardinal Pellevé—an agent of the Guises—who arranged an audience with the pope. It is not known what passed between them. David died on the return journey and his possessions fell into Protestant hands. Thereupon they published a document, said to have been part of a "plus ample discours des choses dessignées au consistoire Romain . . . ." This meeting is likely to have been—if it occurred at all—in the second half of July 1576.[19]

The so-called memoir of David was a highly subversive document. Its chief purpose was to overthrow the Valois dynasty and annul the Capetian succession in favor of the duc de Guise. It

---

17. Maimbourg, *Histoire de la Ligue*, 24–29.

18. François, *Lettres de Henri III*, vol. ii, 450, 20 June 1576, Henry to Gregory XIII; de l'Estoile, *Journal de Henri III*, vol. i, 135.

19. Goulart, *Mémoires de la Ligue*, i, 1–7; Capefigue, *Histoire de la Réforme*, iv, 45 seq; Forneron, *Les Ducs de Guise*, ii, 232–34; Brémond d'Ars, *Jean de Vivonne*, 72–75.

went on to outline how this should be achieved. The king would be advised to "remettre secrettement toute la charge au seigneur de Guise, lequel... pratiquera les ligues envers la noblesse et les habitans des villes, lesquelles il obligera par serment... de telle sorte qu'ils ne pourront reconnoistre autre chef que son excellence." Guise would order the *curés* of the towns and villages to prepare muster rolls. Then the king would summon the estates general, "fosse faite aux Hérétiques en laquelle ils tomberont." The estates would declare the duc de Guise lieutenant general of the kingdom. The local forces previously raised would, together with other regular forces, converge on the estates in order to arraign and arrest the king. At the same time captains, who had retained some of the local forces, would take the field and fall upon the Protestants everywhere. Anjou was to suffer some "pugnition exemplaire"; as heir apparent his removal was essential to the overthrow of the dynasty.[20] Finally, according to the David memoir, with the permission of the pope, the king and Catherine were to be imprisoned in a monastery. It should not be supposed that such permission had been granted. The proposal was unrealistic to the point of absurdity, and evaded the issue. Regicide, however, the only real solution, was not a proposition to ventilate. These things being accomplished, Guise would proceed to the extinction of "l'erreur des privileges de l'eglise gallicane," and the reception of the decrees of Trent. Probably this also implied the establishment of the Inquisition, thwarted in 1558. Not only Anjou, but also Navarre and Condé, were to be persuaded to attend the estates general. Obviously their removal was equally necessary if the overthrow of the Valois dynasty were not to inaugurate that of the Protestant Bourbons. But it was not crediting the princes with much discernment to suppose that they would gallop into the same trap as their respective fathers,

20. It is interesting to note that on 27 December 1576, when the estates were in session, Anjou complained of an attempt to murder him by poison in his wine. He had been violently ill, but recovered. This is not necessarily either significant or true, but it does show that the idea of his destruction was indeed consciously formulated. *CSPF., 1575–77,* p. 453, 27 December 1576, Monsieur to Henry III.

Antoine and Louis, who were arrested at Orléans in October 1560, having been commanded to attend the estates general. Condé, it will be remembered, was condemned to death.

Clearly the David memoir did not represent a formulated plot, but rather heads of proposals to be presented to the pope, whose sanction—and probably also money—would have been needed to establish a new dynasty. These proposals were no more flamboyant than those of the Triumvirate and should not be discredited because of their theatrical nature. Indeed, a most arresting thing about the David document is that its proposals would have formed a French counterpart to the English projects of Don John to overthrow Queen Elizabeth in favor of Mary Stuart. This is not without significance since there was always a French counterpart to Spanish plans for the invasion of England.

The David document is too close to past and future Catholic thinking to assume, as Guise maintained, that it was a libelous Huguenot forgery.[21] But there is no concrete reason for believing that Guise, the beneficiary, was responsible for it. Forneron maintained that it was Guise who sent David to Rome.[22] This is a doubtful assumption, since Guise would hardly have needed to employ an hysterical crackpot—for such was David's reputation. The bishop of Paris, however, was a much more likely intermediary for the Catholics in France. He was Pierre de Gondi, brother of Albert de Gondi, comte de Retz, the extreme political Catholic who was widely believed to have been deeply implicated in the massacre. This likelihood is enhanced by the fact that a few months later Gondi went to the duke of Savoy "to practice with Damville"; in other words, to solicit the duke to persuade Damville to support the Catholic cause in his *gouvernement* of Languedoc.[23] This was a desirable objective of which Spain was not unmindful. Damville's affiliations in that key province were of crucial significance, but his family and the Guises were long-standing adversaries. David, however, might conceivably have been useful to Guise or to Gondi in testing the pope's reactions to

21. Brémond d'Ars, *Jean de Vivonne*, 74–75.
22. Forneron, *Les Ducs de Guise*, ii, 232.
23. *CSPF.*, *1575–77*, p. 538, 4 March 1577, Paulet to Burghley.

more extreme proposals than they could otherwise safely advance. Henri Martin believed that David revealed "la pensée la plus secrète de Guise."[24] This may be so, but we do not know, and the opinion of Brémond d'Ars seems more judicious. He believed that David did genuinely meet the pope, but without commission, and that the pope was noncommittal. David then inflated the result, while the pope simply reported the discussion.[25] According to de Thou, Saint-Gouard, a Gondi kinsman and French ambassador in Spain, obtained a copy of the pope's report, which was sent from Rome to Philip II. Via Saint-Gouard, it was communicated to Henry III.[26] L'Estoile reported that about November 1576 the David memoir "commencèrent à courir."[27] In other words it became notorious in Paris, and it is said to have been shown to the king.

Since several accounts of the memoir have survived—varying only in detail—it seems most probable that some such document genuinely existed, and also that it was made known to the king. But even if it were a forgery, its implications would still have been disturbing. Henry, having matured under the aegis of Lorraine, would rather have been frightened than astonished by the memoir. To anyone like himself, familiar with the past, the proposals were alarmingly reminiscent of a mysterious plot which occurred in the autumn of 1571. This appears to have been a Guise/Spanish conspiracy in favor of Henry himself, then the duc d'Anjou, to be openly supported as Catholic leader in France, in defiance of the king. The conspiracy would have averted the intended marriage between Henry and Queen Elizabeth, which the Catholics opposed, and should have coincided with the Ridolfi plot to murder her.[28] Then, as also in 1576, Elizabeth was to have been replaced by Mary Stuart, cousin of Guise. It is not, how-

24. Quoted by Brémond d'Ars, *Jean de Vivonne*, 76, n. 1. from Martin, *Histoire de France*, ix, 441.

25. Brémond d'Ars, *Jean de Vivonne*, 73–74.

26. De Thou claimed to have heard this from Saint-Gouard himself, whose correspondence is missing for this time. Brémond d'Ars, *Jean de Vivonne*, 75.

27. L'Estoile, *Journal de Henri III*, vol. i, 144.

28. Sutherland, *The Massacre of St. Bartholomew*, chap. xi.

ever, certain whether Henry was aware of the intentions and instructions of Don John, who passed through France to the Netherlands shortly before Henry is said to have learnt of the David affair. However this may be, the David memoir must have cast a lurid light upon the manifesto of Péronne and augmented Henry's reasons for distrusting the duc de Guise.

Early in August 1576 Guise was reported to be inciting opposition to various articles of the edict in Picardy, Normandy, Champagne and Burgundy—all provinces under Guisard influence—and obstructing the introduction of royal garrisons. In many places the edict was never published, and the *chambres mi-parties* were not established. In the words of one English agent, "it is as if the edict had never been made."[29] Soon after the estates general had been convoked, on 6 August, the Guises withdrew to Joinville[30] and began to raise forces, presumably to dominate the estates. This is precisely what they had done—and for comparable reasons—before the estates of Orléans, held in the same months of December to January 1560–61, when they planned to ensnare the princes, Navarre and Condé.

On the last day of August 1576, Henry complained to the duc de Montpensier, *gouverneur* of Brittany, who was leaving to attend the estates in his province, that he had heard of "quelques ligues et associations," and of "certain menées et practiques secrettes qui s'y faisoient avec amas d'armes et chevaux." It is significant that he went on to defend the necessity of the recent peace, made with "peine, travail et soin," and for which there were precedents, if the State were not to be destroyed. This indeed was the stake, and Henry knew it, in spite of his devious propensity for avoiding issues. He added, and this was very much to the point, that with the peace, Alençon had been reconciled. There was, the king concluded, no justification for these leagues; their existence constituted *lèse-majesté*, and they must be dis-

29. Desjardins, *Négs. Tosc.*, iv, 77, 5 August 1576; B. N., Mss. Italien, 1729, f. 813, 8 August 1576; *CSPF.*, *1575–77*, pp. 471–72, 1576. According to this report, the edict had been published only in the *parlement* of Paris.

30. Charleville, *Les États Généraux de 1576*, p. 21.

solved.[31] This was his initial policy, but he was powerless to implement it.

It is apparent from Henry's letter to Montpensier that as a deeply Catholic king, he was dangerously vulnerable as a result of the liberal terms of the peace of Monsieur. In essence, this was the predicament and the tragedy of his reign. Henry's awareness of this problem and danger is indicated by the care with which he explained to the pope, among others, that the peace had been a matter of duress.[32] While there is no evidence that the pope agreed to support a French Catholic league in 1576, the danger of his doing so was obvious, and his attitude was not reassuring. Early in 1577, during the estates, there was to be no misinterpreting the clamor of his envoys. The cardinal d'Este, no less, was expressly instructed to "blow the coals of this quarrel of religion."[33] This was certainly playing into the hands of the Catholic league, whether or not the pope was a party to it. He had little interest, political or religious, in supporting the compromised Valois, whose Christian mission could have been better and more advantageously performed by Philip II, or by the Guises under Spanish tutelage. Nor can this be dismissed as an exaggerated fancy, since Lorraine had actually proposed something of the kind in 1567.[34] Henry's deposition would have furthered the known papal purpose, adopted by Don John, to dispose of Queen Elizabeth and restore her kingdom to Rome, under Mary Stuart.

Thus, in spite of his ostentatious piety, Henry III received no support from Rome. Caught, as he was, between the Catholic hammer and the Protestant anvil, his ambivalent infirmity of purpose is hardly surprising. In the summer of 1576 he may have wanted peace at all costs, since he was unable to make war. He

31. Gomberville, *Mémoires de Nevers*, i, 110–14, 31 August 1576, Henry to Montpensier.

32. François, *Lettres de Henri III*, vol. iii, 136, 15 January 1577, Henry to d'Abain, ambassador in Rome.

33. *CSPF.*, *1575–77*, pp. 482–83, January 1577, occurrents. In March 1577 Paulet referred to a "strait intelligence between France and Spain and the Pope." France, of course, meant the Catholics, by whom the king was politically ensnared. Ibid., 536–38, 4 March 1577, Paulet to Burghley.

34. Sutherland, *The Massacre of St. Bartholomew*, 61–62.

may have wanted to revenge himself against those who had placed him in a well-nigh insoluble dilemma. He almost certainly wanted justification in the eyes of Catholics, and especially the pope, for what he had been obliged to concede. Perhaps most of all, he wanted to thwart and neutralize the Catholics, now forming into associations, whether by superseding them or setting the Huguenots against them. Like Philip II in the Netherlands, Henry III could neither conquer his dissidents nor yet impose on them a political settlement. All the evidence suggests that he quickly became more afraid of the Catholics than of the Huguenots. In this he was right: it was the Catholics who would make any peace impossible; it was they who might call on the power of Spain, and they who were shortly to threaten his crown.

In these circumstances the forthcoming meeting of the estates general offered both opportunities and dangers to all parties. The Huguenots, who had originally demanded the estates, presumably hoped that their edict would thereby be sanctioned. They may also have hoped, through the estates, to influence the composition of the council. On the other hand, it is possible, perhaps because of the non-implementation of the edict, that they had abandoned hope in the estates by the time of the elections, since they were not to be fully represented. La Rochelle and certain *bailliages* or *sénéchaussées* in the Midi failed to send deputies.[35] The Catholics not only hoped, but fully intended, the exact opposite, that the edict would be rescinded and the cult prohibited. As for the king, could he so maneuver as to obtain some support for whatever policy he found himself obliged to pursue—for there was little prospect of his being a free agent? Could he use the estates to overcome the league? According to the manifesto of Péronne, the king was to be presented with articles recalling him to the duty of his coronation oath. The implied intention was to use the estates to flout the king's authority and to frustrate the edict. The outcome of the estates general was therefore to be of maximum importance in the Huguenot struggle for recognition; thus everything would depend on the composition of the assembly.

35. Charleville, *Les États Généraux de 1576*, p. 32.

Although little is known about the crucial elections to the estates general of 1576–77,[36] the assumption is that they were managed by the Catholics, who succeeded, if not precisely in packing, at least in dominating, the assembly. This, however, is not clearly so, in the case of the *tiers*. The three estates, which sat separately were, however, far from servile. It was extremely difficult to control their proceedings, especially since they were evidently more concerned to score off each other, than to achieve anything constructive. Condé subsequently complained that they had not been convoked in the usual, solemn manner, and that "messengers had been sent through the country to practise the election of the deputies."[37] He denied their authority, and denounced them as being merely "the tool of others, who desired the ruin of the state"—a thinly veiled reference to the Guises.[38] The Protestants also maintained that at the time of the elections not many of them had yet been restored to their houses, property and positions—in other words that the edict had not been implemented. They were therefore unable to take part in the elections, from which they had also been excluded by the use of arms, intimidation and menaces.[39]

The deputies to the estates general had gathered at Blois by 24 November, although it was not until 6 December that Henry opened the assembly. Both he and the deputies had preparatory work to do. It may well have been then that Henry reached decisions which could no longer be avoided. Sometime between the summer and the meeting of the estates he was obliged to modify his regal attitude to the Catholics, as expressed in his letter of 31 August to Montpensier, in order to play along with the Catholic associations he was powerless to destroy. How this came about is not clear but, at the end of November, the Catholic leaders were trying to further their purposes in Blois by canvass-

36. Picot, *Histoire des états généraux*, ii, 305–7; he suggests that the Catholics used a variety of tricks, such as announcing the elections during mass, from which the Protestants were absent.

37. *CSPF.*, *1575–77*, p. 493, 28 January 1577.

38. Idem.

39. PRO/SP/70/142/1060, a supplication to the king. Such a supplication was submitted on 21 December 1576. *CSPF.*, *1575–77*, p. 452.

ing the deputies. Thus, on 29 November Monsieur de Blanchefort, and other members of the *noblesse*, were summoned to a
private meeting in the lodgings of a certain anonymous prelate,
together with several more "de sa qualité." Someone then proposed to these deputies "un certain formulaire d'association,"
tending to destroy the edict of pacification and rekindle war
between the king and the Protestants—extremist objectives.[40]
Blanchefort, however, held the moderates' point of view, that the
king should not be obliged to make war, and that it was impossible
to defeat the Protestants in France. The articles contained certain
clauses reminiscent of the June manifesto of Péronne, derogatory
to the king's authority, and Blanchefort refused to sign it, on
grounds of loyalty.[41]

While the Catholics were trying to persuade the estates to
adopt their articles of association[42] and force the king to impose
one religion, by means of war, it is absolutely incontestable, from
abundant documentation, that what Henry really wanted was
peace. But the treaty of Monsieur, which had cost him so much,
had not brought peace; it had merely changed the quarter from
which trouble arose—hence the Catholic leagues. Throughout
the period of the estates, Henry's conduct and utterances demonstrate that he was seeking, above all, to reestablish his authority.
He expressed this, for example, quite clearly in a letter to
d'Humières, one of the first to defy him.[43] Since the estates had
been summoned, obviously Henry must try to manipulate them
in such a way as to procure some generally accepted and *enforce-
able* solution. No one could easily challenge the authority of the
estates or, on that account, insolently remind the king of any
embarrassing aspect of his duty. Henry might, in this way, shift
the responsibility to the estates for whatever proved to be un-

40. Gomberville, *Mémoires de Nevers*, i, 458–61.
41. Ibid., 437–39.
42. It looks as though the Catholics in question may have been deputies
of the first estate.
43. François, *Lettres de Henri III*, vol. iii, 95–96, 9 December 1576,
Henry to d'Humières; 130, 9 January 1577, Henry to Villars; 107, 21
December 1576, Henry to Damville; 159, 13 February 1577, Henry to
Mandelot.

avoidable. Finally, Henry counted, if unwisely, on obtaining money from them.[44] Curiously enough, there is no record of anyone's having doubted that money would be forthcoming, although Catherine had no liberal memories of the estates of Orléans.

A demand for only one religion must have featured in the original articles, which, according to the treaty of Péronne, were to be presented by the (packed) estates to the king—recalling him to the duties of his coronation oath. It is not clear how this original, subversive treaty was superseded, but the same principle was implicit in the more moderate—if not entirely innocuous—articles of association propounded to members of the *noblesse* on 29 November. The *leagueurs* must, presumably, have been among those who intended to make this demand. Not having obtained the peace he desired by making concessions to the Huguenots, Henry also would have preferred only one religion, but he wanted it without war. Above all, if the demand were to come from the bellicose *leagueurs,* whom he believed he could not resist,[45] then he was determined that they should not be allowed to deprive him of the credit for restoring religion in France. Henry was particularly anxious that the pope should understand that the determination to restore religion arose from his *own* initiative— "ce que j'en ay faict a esté de moy mesme induict de ma seule volunté." He could not afford to lose this advantage. Similarly, he also wished to persuade the pope that the reprehensible treaty had been made under duress—which was true—in order to reconcile Alençon and avert an invasion by foreign troops.[46]

Henry therefore held a council meeting on 2 December to consider how to obtain only one religion, before it could be alleged that it was the estates which had incited him to "une telle louable entreprise." It was then decided to bring pressure to bear on the deputies, to induce them to petition for one religion. In this way, Henry tried to obtain the best of both worlds: to claim

---

44. Ibid., 97, 10 December 1576, Henry to Villars.
45. Ibid., 107, 21 December 1576, Henri to Damville.
46. Ibid., 136, 15 January 1577, Henry to d'Abain, ambassador in Rome.

the credit for this initiative, before the assembly opened, while sheltering behind the petition in respect of the consequences. Catherine later referred to the strenuous efforts, "pratiques et menées" which she had made, upon the king's command, to induce the deputies to this resolution. They would not, she declared, otherwise have agreed, because most of them claimed that they had no such mandate.[47] They probably feared its concomitant, a demand for money. Evidently the estates had been less than completely packed by the Catholics; perhaps because there had been insufficient time. Henry himself declared that he had "brigué, s'il faut ainsi dire, les gens des trois estats, qui n'alloient que d'une fesse, pour les pousser à demander une seule religion."[48] In the light of these remarkable revelations, one is tempted to wonder whether Henry might, on the contrary, have been able to use the estates to resist the *leagueurs*, who wanted war. The difficulty was that their power lay outside the estates, through which Henry sought to remove the wind from their sails. Henry's only possible alternative, since the estates were not to be relied upon, was some sort of agreement with the Catholic leaders, in order himself to control and command this league and its offshoots, which his extreme displeasure had failed to destroy. On the same day, therefore, as deciding to require the deputies to demand only one religion, Henry himself approved and adopted a set of articles of association to be sent to all the provinces. The *leagueurs'* articles, discussed on 29 November, provided for the election of a "chef" other than the king, and referred to the crown itself as elective. Furthermore, they placed upon him the burden of financing the league's activities. It would be interesting to know whether the Catholics had already tried to force their articles upon the king, or whether he pre-empted this. The *leagueurs* could not publicly reject Henry's alternative articles without disclosing their subversive intentions and discarding the cloak of religion. Quite a few of the articles of 2 December were identical to those of the Catholics, and they subscribed to the same objectives. But, as well as excluding all the subversive and revolutionary elements,

47. Gomberville, *Mémoires de Nevers*, i, 175.
48. Ibid., 176.

they also positively stressed the duty of obedience and service to Henry, reigning by God's will, as their sovereign king and *seigneur*, "et qui est legitimement à la succession... par la loy du royaume et apres luy à toute la posterité de la maison de Valloy." This left no room for challenging the dynasty, and seemed to refer more to the previous manifesto of Péronne than to the Catholics' current articles of association. Furthermore, all members were specifically bound to expend their lives and property in the maintenance of Henry's State and authority, and in the execution of *his* commands. Clauses relating to provincial preparations for the defense of Catholicism were much the same as in the treaty of Péronne, but the provinces themselves were to contribute substantially. The articles clearly stated that Henry did not intend any harm to Protestants who remained quiet, provided they did not contravene any regulations made by the king after the estates; in other words, provided they submitted to the suppression of their religion. This, of course, was a royal interpolation. Henry did, in this way neutralize the revolutionary danger of a powerful league operating not only without, but also against, his authority, and which might even have sought to depose him. In order to obtain peace, he would have to subdue one of the two factions, and it might, in this way, have been possible to mobilize sufficient support to impose his will on the Protestants. After 1577 he knew that this could never be done.

Insistence in the articles that peaceful Protestants should be protected, and repeated announcements to this effect, was one way in which Henry hoped to diminish the adverse repercussions of his new policy. How to handle the consequences of the decision to tolerate only one religion and to establish Catholic associations everywhere, became the principle problem. It was hoped that by being overwhelmingly strong on the royal and Catholic side (and Henry made real attempts to achieve this), by detaching Damville, conciliating Navarre and isolating Condé, the Protestants might be forced to submit. These were not, in themselves and at that time, entirely foolish ideas, but there was never any real likelihood that if they were accomplished, they would have the desired effect. The Huguenots were too well organized and strongly entrenched. Navarre, also, was a moderate and loyal prince. While he would do nothing deliberately to ruin the king, he would not lightly abandon the Huguenots.

Henry proceeded one step at a time, though not, as he discovered too late, in the right order. At the same time as approving the articles of association on 2 December, he prepared a covering letter to the provincial *gouverneurs* requiring them to execute the articles, each in his own province, within four to six weeks.[49] It seems likely, however, that in the first place the articles were only sent to Catholic-controlled provinces. It was not until three weeks later that Henry informed Damville in Languedoc.

In the meanwhile, Henry reiterated previous letters to Damville and other *gouverneurs* that he wished absolutely to maintain peace.[50] He even went so far as to write to Damville about the establishment at Montpellier of the *chambres mi-parties* accorded in the peace of Monsieur, presumably because it was not yet time, early in December, to disclose his intention to supersede the treaty.[51] These exhortations to peace accorded well with his speech inaugurating the estates on 6 December. Henry emphasized his past efforts for reconciliation and peace, and his present hope of finding means "de mettre ce Royaume en repos et . . . donner remède aux maux dont le corps de cet etat est tellement viceré qu'il n'a membre sain et entière." This was fairly strong language. Clearly Henry was not unmindful of his kingdom, but he happened not to be a warrior king, and only force could then succeed. Finally Henry appealed to the deputies to help him root out divisions, reform abuses and "repurger les mauvaises humeurs." He made no reference either to religion or to finance. In the case of finance, this omission later helped the estates to avoid granting subsidies.[52]

49. François, *Lettres de Henri III*, vol. iii, 86–88, 2 December 1576, Henry to ———— [?].

50. Ibid., 77–78, 26 November 1576, Henry to Damville, Mandelot and Rambouillet; 80, 30 November 1576, Henry to La Trémoille; 90, 4 December 1576, Henry to Damville; 98–99, 13 December 1576, Henry to Damville.

51. Ibid., 91, 5 December 1576, Henry to Damville.

52. Gomberville, *Mémoires de Nevers*, i, 440–43.

Four days later, emphasizing that he had summoned the estates in order to establish a durable peace, Henry requested the Protestant leaders to call a small assembly of the Protestants and *catholiques unis*. He intended to send a gentleman to this assembly to request them to name their own Protestant deputation to the estates "afin que . . . nous puissions en ceste assemblée generalle des estatz, prendre une bonne resolution pour parvenir a ce que dessus"—namely a durable peace.[53] This suggests that the king hoped to make his divided subjects sort things out for themselves, and arrive at a peaceful solution for which he could not be blamed, either politically or morally.

At this stage, in mid-December, the question of one religion and war or peace was being hotly debated. Certain "deputies of the religion" had already gone to Blois to protest the nullity of the estates, for which audacity they narrowly escaped with their lives.[54] On 15 December the *tiers* finally agreed to demand one religion, but not without violent altercation in the assembly. Jean Bodin, deputy for Vermandois, came out clearly with the real problem, that to demand one religion would entail war. He therefore supported the edict. Others decided to demand only one religion, but without war. This was an expedient for evading the issue, since everyone knew that the Huguenots would never accept this passively. They were strong and they were bound to defend their edict. Indeed, they began to do so without delay.[55] The same day, or the one after,[56] two deputies from Navarre and Condé arrived to assure the king that no hostilities had occurred in Guyenne, as was alleged at court, and to plead for the edict. They may well have brought with them a remonstrance of this time from the churches of Languedoc, Provence and Dauphiné,

---

53. François, *Lettres de Henri III*, vol. iii, 96–97, 10 December 1576, Henry to Damville. In the event, this assembly never took place.

54. *CSPF.*, *1575–77*, p. 441, 8 December 1576, occurrents; 448, 17 December 1576, Laurence Jonson to Daniel Rogers.

55. Mayer, *Des États Généraux*, xiii, 223–24, Mayer prints Jean Bodin's journal of the estates.

56. Ibid., 226–27; *CSPF.*, *1575–77*, p. 452, 24 December 1576, events in France.

protesting against the activities of the Catholic leagues and infractions of the edict.[57] On 19 December "certain of the nobility propounded to break the edict, to establish one only religion, to banish all [Protestant] ministers... within six weeks, giving liberty of conscience... until other order might be taken by a general and national Council." Deputies from Provence and Guyenne resisted this and "contention grew to be very hot."[58] All the *cahiers*, then in preparation, included this demand, and that same day the king showed Nevers an exhortation which he addressed to the deputies "pour faire tenir bon pour la religion."[59] On 21 December the deputies of the reformed churches presented the king with a "supplication." It protested that the estates had no power to discuss religion because this was not specified in the election commissions. Nor had the king himself, in his opening speech, directed the assembly to deal in the matter. They therefore begged the king to preserve the edict, to prohibit the estates from discussing religion, and to expunge from the records anything already said, done or proposed.[60] In making this request, they appear to have been unaware that the king himself had required the estates to demand one religion, which entailed abrogation of the edict. Henry evaded this issue and replied that he "could not do so without breach of their liberty, a thing they did especially challenge, but that his meaning was to conserve his subjects in peace."[61]

By 21 December it was too late to save the edict, let alone to prohibit the discussion of religion. Henry already knew that the

57. Devic and Vaisseté, *Histoire générale de Languedoc*, xii, 1173–78.
58. *CSPF.*, *1575-77*, p. 451, 24 December 1576, events in France.
59. Gomberville, *Mémoires de Nevers*, i, 167.
60. PRO/SP/70/142/1060.
61. *CSPF.*, *1575-77*, p. 452, 24 December 1576, events in France; 461–62, the "supplication"—inadequately calendared. The king could of course forbid what he liked. Catherine de Medici had forbidden the estates of Orléans to discuss the government in 1561. But Henry could not *prevent* them from discussing religion. It is tempting to wonder whether Queen Elizabeth ever heard of Henry's comment on prerogative and freedom of speech.

estates were going to include in their *cahiers* the demand he wanted for only one religion. Thus supported, he was now ready to come out publicly in favor of this himself. The time had therefore come to dispatch the articles of association to the remaining provinces. These included the duc de Montmorency in the Île-de-France, and his brother Damville in Languedoc. It is not clear whether there were any others not previously notified. It was in this letter to Damville that Henry clearly stated his position in relation to the leagues, and why he was adopting this new policy. He appealed to Damville as a Catholic (unlike Navarre and Condé) to understand his desire for one religion, and required him to form a Catholic association in Languedoc within a month.[62] Henry had sought to prepare the way for this, and the detachment of Damville from the Protestants, by assurances of his royal favor, and of his trust in Damville if he would cooperate in restoring peace in the kingdom.[63] Talk of only one religion was, however, rapidly leading to war, and news was already coming in of widespread Protestant resistance. The *tiers* were therefore becoming alarmed and, on 28 December, they quarreled over the issue of war or peace. All three estates requested the king to deal with the Protestant disturbances. This could only be done in arms and could only lead to war. Nevertheless the king asked them to elect deputies to be sent to Navarre, Condé and Damville, presumably hoping thereby to escape responsibility for whatever transpired.[64] As the question of war or peace hung in the balance, Henry again wrote to Damville, increasing his blandishments.[65]

Having sent the articles of association to all the provinces, Henry then came to the climax of this drama: he prepared a

62. François, *Lettres de Henri III*, vol. iii, 107–8, 21 December 1576, Henry to Damville.

63. Ibid., 81, undated, Henry to Damville.

64. Mayer, *Des États Généraux*, xiii, 228–30; Gomberville, *Mémoires de Nevers*, i, 167–69; François, *Lettres de Henri III*, vol. iii, 123–24 [1 January 1577], Henry to Oignon.

65. François, *Lettres de Henri III*, vol. iii, 122–23, 1 January 1577, Henry to Damville.

declaration in favor of one religion in order to make known his royal will throughout the kingdom.[66] This declaration was intended to justify both the peace of Monsieur in the first place, and its subsequent abrogation, and therefore to explain his policy. It began by stating that the king, having attained his majority, wished to maintain and "conserve" (the Catholic) religion and that the (Protestant) ministers should depart. He did not intend to employ any Protestant in the administration of justice or in his household. He wished them to be "maintenuz et conservez en toute seurete en leurs maisons soubs la garde d'aulcuns qui seront deputez en chascune province." The edict of pacification had been made under duress in order to recall Anjou (to his allegiance) and to expel the foreign troops in the service of (Damville's) *catholiques unis* and the *RPR* (Huguenots). This declaration was to be sent to Navarre, Condé and Damville. If, in consequence, anyone took up arms, the king was resolved to employ all his means and his friends against them and to impose his authority (se faire recognoistre) sparing nothing, to the last drop of his blood, and without any hope that he might incline to peace. To this he added the obligation of his coronation oath to live and die, come what come might, in the Catholic faith, in respect of which the crown had been placed upon his head by the peers of France.

The declaration was placed before the council on 22 December and discussed in Catherine's cabinet two days later.[67] It is difficult to imagine how such an extraordinary document was agreed upon. There must surely have been some unrecorded row. Although, like his articles of association, it emphasized Henry's authority, it was still injudicious to the point of lunacy, and presumably strongly influenced by the Catholic extremists. They appear to have obtained, in this way, some of the subversive clauses expressly excluded from the articles of association. It was one thing to declare that Henry would fight, if necessary, for the imposition of his authority. But why did he publicly proclaim that he would never compromise, when everyone knew that he

66. PRO/SP/70/142/1003, 3 January 1577. This document is incorrectly rendered in the *CSPF.*, *1575–77*, p. 474.
67. Gomberville, *Mémoires de Nevers*, i, 167–69.

would have to? To fight to the death was not only contrary to his nature, but totally beyond his capabilities. Why, also, should he gratuitously declare that he owed his crown to the peers of France, thereby inferring that they might equally withdraw it, if he (ever again) transgressed his coronation oath? Certainly the oath had become a thorny problem; nevertheless, the hereditary king of France was no probationer. Catherine and Bellièvre, doubtless among others, deplored these unnecessarily damaging statements. They echo the tone of the manifesto of Péronne, and one is bound to suspect that Henry was somehow constrained to make them. Henry's determination that an apparently inevitable war should be *his* war, might account for the tone of the declaration, but this would not explain its more derogatory items.

It was probably in view of Henry's proposed declaration that, in the first days of January 1577, members of the council all made a written submission on the burning issue of war or peace.[68] These submissions are too long to analyze in detail. They revealed a general preference for peace, as well as a general belief in the inevitability of war, since the Protestants were already in arms. Most of the depositions were therefore devoted to practical matters. This involved, above all, the raising of money, the exploitation of the new Catholic associations, and the mobilization of forces. Catherine de Medici—whose deposition was by far the most intelligent and interesting—as well as the marshals, all discussed in some detail how the king's forces should be deployed. Catherine wanted Henry to go in person to Guyenne, preceded by Montpensier, a prince of the blood. Only Bellièvre pronounced on the impossibility of imposing one religion, and no one expressed any fear that the estates might refuse the necessary money to execute their demands. It is interesting that the duc de Guise coyly evaded making his deposition on the specious grounds of his youth and inexperience. There is no mention at this stage of any extremist opinions.

The largely pacific and cautious advice of his council did not cause Henry to change his mind. His declaration, which, in the circumstances, would commit him to war, was dated 3 January

68. Ibid., 227–88.

1577 and sent to the Huguenot leaders.[69] Thus Biron went to Navarre, Camille Feré to Condé, and Oignon to Damville.[70] To Navarre Henry wrote on 3 January that the declaration, to be brought by Biron, represented his "resolue vollonté," emphasizing his sovereign authority, to which obedience was due.[71] Biron's instructions, dated 6 January, were in fact a rather pathetic complaint together with reassurances of a general nature. Henry would do everything that he reasonably could to content Navarre. But he complained that the estates had been summoned on the insistence of the Huguenots. Their deputies then "protested as to the nullity of the proceedings," while others wanted him to forbid the assembly to discuss religion or the edicts. He now demanded to "understand of such requests as they may make, so that he may be the better able to order what will tend to that he so much desires, his subjects in peace."[72] It was reported that Biron had to treat with Navarre about a marriage between his sister Catherine and Monsieur (Anjou).[73] Considering his own matrimonial experience, Navarre was unlikely to find the proposal attractive. But, when he was creating Catholic associations in all the provinces, there was little for Henry to say to Navarre, whose intransigent Huguenots would fight in spite of him, if not at his command.[74] Neither king was free to go far enough to meet the other half way.

The purpose behind Biron's mission was to seek to detach Navarre who, as first prince of the blood, had a vested interest in the preservation of the monarchy. Oignon's mission (two days earlier) was similarly to detach Damville. Henry himself warmly assured Damville of his good will in respect of "ce qui touche vostre particulier." For this purpose, Henry said, he was sending

69. François, *Lettres de Henri III*, vol. iii, 129, 3 January 1577, Henry to Navarre.

70. Ibid., 128, 2 January 1577, Henry to Mauvissière.

71. Ibid., 129, 3 January 1577, Henry to Navarre.

72. *CSPF.*, *1575-77*, p. 483, 6 January 1577, instructions to Biron.

73. Ibid., 482 [15? January] 1577, occurrents in France.

74. Idem.

Oignon, to whom Damville might "parler ouvertement de ce que vous desirez de moy," and promised him satisfaction.[75] Henry had already dismissed Saint-Vidal from an appointment in Languedoc in order to humor Damville, who wanted none but Joyeuse to share his command.[76] Oignon was to countermand the Protestant assembly that Henry had commanded in December, because the estates were now sending their own deputies "qui devront chercher avec lui les modalités du rétablissement de la situation," a masterpiece of imprecision. Damville was to be asked, as an earnest of good faith, to join Navarre, to whom the king was sending Montpensier, an elderly Bourbon prince of wisdom and experience. Oignon was also to rehearse Henry's reasons for making and breaking the peace, his confidence in Damville, and his intention that the Protestants should be protected, provided they submitted to whatever the king determined after the conclusion of the estates. Then, in a typically magisterial tone, the instructions continued: Henry "n'entend plus souffrir mettre en compromis ny dispute ce qui sera par luy ordonné...." For both these reasons Damville was commanded to establish the league in Languedoc according to the articles of association.[77]

By a further letter of 2 January 1577, Henry insisted that Damville should maintain peace in Languedoc. Similar letters went to several other *gouverneurs*.[78] To Villars on 9 January he explicitly declared his extreme desire for peace for the reestablishment of his authority. The inference was that in case of war he would be controlled by the Catholic extremists.[79]

To Condé, who was aggressive in tone and belligerent in conduct, there was little that Henry could usefully say through Camille Feré. But, provided Navarre and Damville were won, Condé would not be considered important. Feré's instructions

75. François, *Lettres de Henri III*, vol. iii, 122, 1 January 1577, Henry to Damville.

76. Ibid., 127, 2 January 1577, Henry to Mandelot.

77. Ibid., 123–24 [1 January 1577], Henry to Oignon, and 124, n. 1.

78. Ibid., 125 seq.

79. Ibid., 130, 9 January 1577, Henry to Villars.

contained the same arguments as the others. Perhaps most important of all was the mission of Montpensier to Navarre.[80] Montpensier's instructions were a curious mixture of self-defense, cajolery and threats—candid and lacking in dignity. They began by stating the desire of the estates and of the king for only one religion, to which the king was committed by his coronation oath. The last edict had not brought the desired pacification and had led to the Catholic leagues. Although the king had been annoyed about the associations, he had come to appreciate the necessity for them and "s'en rendre chef et les commander." Thus the king also wished Navarre to join. Henry, however, did not want Navarre to think that he meant to reopen war, "mais elle [sa majesté] ne peut estre blasmé de voulour conserver le septre que Dieu luy a mis en main." This accords with the wording of Henry's declaration of 3 January in favor of one religion, and would appear to hint that if Henry did not satisfy the Catholics, he might be deposed. The most interesting and significant clause in Montpensier's instructions is that Henry then urged Navarre to abjure. To this were added reminders of his unlawful conduct in negotiating with foreign princes, leading a faction, and other transgressions. It was futile for Henry to threaten Navarre, to whom he had nothing to offer. Navarre was almost certainly stronger than the crown, and had every reason to distrust the king. It is difficult to see what Henry really hoped for or expected from him. Even his abjuration, which was unthinkable in those circumstances, would almost certainly have precipitated trouble from Anjou, who was quite as dangerous as either faction, and less predictable.

The instructions for the deputies of the estates to visit the Protestant leaders were the subject of some dispute. They are said to have been "penned by some of the Privy Council with sharp and bitter words, denouncing war if they should refuse to unite

---

80. B. N., Mss. Fr., 3323, ff. 7–9, undated, instructions for Camille Feré; 15534, ff. 302v–11, undated, instructions for Montpensier. I am indebted to Dr. A. Soman for having transcribed these documents for me.

themselves with the king for the maintenance of the Romish religion." This, again, is in keeping with the wording of the royal declaration. But the estates, which did not want war, "thought good to set them down in mild terms."[81] Navarre and Condé are said to have been threatened with deprivation of their rights to the succession, if they did not yield all in return for freedom of conscience. Damville was to be threatened on the one hand with disinheritance and, on the other, offered bribes to abandon the Huguenot alliance and return to his allegiance. The draft instructions were conveyed to the *tiers* by the clergy. When the *tiers* persisted in opposing the "paroles aigres et piquantes," the clergy disclosed that it was the king who wished them so. Here, again, Henry was trying to shift onto the estates responsibility for the impending hostilities, which he was also counting on them to finance. But it was the extremists, not the majority of the estates, who wanted war, and the *tiers* prevailed. The instructions were completed on 5 January and the deputies departed on 6 and 7 January 1577.[82]

Consequently the instructions for the deputies to Navarre were conceived in "mild terms," neither provocative of war, nor yet containing constructive proposals. They began, like those for Biron, by emphasizing the king's authority. They expressed the intention to restore peace, which toleration prevented. As the edict had not ensured peace and was impossible to enforce, Navarre was invited to join the estates and the king in ordaining one religion. If Navarre were to plead that the king had pledged his word, the answer was that he could make no pledge contrary to the interests of the State. Nor could he contravene the fundamental laws, of which the Catholicity of France was one. The estates alone could alter fundamental law—a clause which did nothing to enhance the authority of the crown and which was unlikely to commend itself to Navarre. Navarre was guilty of not having restored Catholicism in his lands, and contravention of the

81. *CSPF.*, *1575–77*, pp. 481–83, undated, placed under 15 January 1577, occurrents in France.
82. Mayer, *Des États Généraux*, xiii, 231–37.

edict justified its withdrawal. This was a wholly specious argument, ignoring all breaches on the Catholic side. The edict had, in any case, been extorted. Navarre was reminded of his proximity to the crown, and invited to attend the estates. The only concession contained in the instructions was that the Huguenots should not be persecuted.[83]

Henry's protestations and assurances that he wanted peace were heartfelt and genuine. Whatever the realities of the situation, he continued to issue peaceful instructions. On various dates from 25 January, he distributed a declaration to the nobility in each province on the subject of maintaining peace. Again on 2 February he addressed to the *parlement* of Paris a memoir distributed to all the *baillis* and *sénéchaux* on the maintenance of peace. The *gouverneurs* had already received repeated instructions on the subject.[84] Although Henry meant to fight if necessary, he also meant to avoid it if he could. Henry must have realized that Bellièvre was right when he advised that Protestantism could never be eradicated. But he had to demonstrate that he was in earnest about religion, and presumably hoped that eventual concessions could be royally conceded, as of grace, and not again extorted in arms. Thus, if he were ever going to fight the Huguenots again, this was the time to do so. Indeed, matters were in any case moving towards war. Thus he wrote to Mauvissière, ambassador in England, that the estates had unanimously demanded one religion. He hoped the Protestants would incline but, if necessary, he would not hesitate to use force. He had already given orders for the arrest of Condé, which was hardly conciliatory.[85] Henry therefore began to prepare for war, and on

83. Gomberville, *Mémoires de Nevers*, i, 445–52, instructions for the deputies of the estates sent to Navarre, 4 January 1577. According to the report on the return of the deputies, these instructions had also contained some personal gratification for Navarre. Mayer, *Des États Généraux*, xiii, 284.

84. François, *Lettres de Henri III*, vol. iii, 142–43, 21 January 1577, Henry to Mandelot; 143, n. 1.

85. Ibid., 152, 3 February 1577, Henry to Mauvissière; 147, 31 January 1577, Henry to Mandelot.

a large scale, hoping at the same time that it would never happen.[86]

The first essential was obviously to raise money, and for this the king turned to the pope and to the estates general. Having argued his innocence in the matter of the peace of Monsieur and its abrogation, and having claimed the credit in seeking to establish only one religion, he asked the pope for 50,000 *écus* per month for six months, towards the expenses of three large armies. It was not, however, until June that the pope acceded to this Catholic plea.[87] Apart from the pope, who surely had some duty in the matter, Henry's principal hope of extraordinary revenue lay with the estates. In this, however, they failed him completely. On 11 January the king was already complaining that they did not proceed with the matter of money.[88] When, in a plenary session of the estates on 17 January, Henry formally accepted their demand for only one religion, he was reasonably expecting them to help finance the consequences. This, no doubt, was partly because Versoris, deputy for Paris, who spoke for the third estate, was an extremist. He therefore omitted to say, as he was instructed to do, that the *tiers'* demand was for one religion, but without war.[89] This omission led to an uproar when, in the following days, Henry made known his urgent need for money.[90] Money to finance war against the Huguenots was not an item that Henry could have included in the commissions for the elections to the estates. Besides, he had not, at that time, been forced to adopt his *leagueur* position. Nevertheless, this omission enabled the deputies to evade the issue by pleading no mandate. This they did whenever it suited them, otherwise forgetting the principle. By

---

86. Letters patent of 10 January 1577 called for the survey of the military potential of each province. Ibid., 133, n. 1, and passim.

87. Ibid., 135–38, 15 January 1577, Henry to d'Abain; 139, 15 January 1577, Henry to the pope; 303, 26 June 1577, Henry to d'Abain.

88. Mayer, *Des États Généraux*, xiii, 244–45.

89. Ibid., 348–53.

90. 23 and 26 January 1577. Ibid., 256–63; Gomberville, *Mémoires de Nevers*, i, 171–72.

31 January the request for money had been flatly refused. To Villeroy, his favorite secretary and confidant, Henry expressed his resentment against the estates which, "en lui prêtant l'intention de recommencer la guerre font le jeu des réformées." In refusing the subsidies he requested, they favored the extension of the religion they claimed to oppose.[91] Henry was therefore left in a dangerous, as well as an embarrassing position, which, as he said, favored the Huguenots' resistance. Already on 29 January Henry had expressed his anxiety over a gathering in arms around Clermont d'Amboise, but felt that he could not take action before receiving replies from the deputies sent by the estates to Navarre and Condé.[92]

The deputies to Condé were the first to return, on 8 February. There was, however, little to be hoped from their mission, since Condé had previously made himself clear. On 23 January, upon news of events at Blois, he had issued a violent "protestation" against the "unjust and hateful resolution taken by the perjured and corrupted estates.... " He denounced the "wicked counsellors of the king, destroyers of the crown, pensioners of Spain,[93] authors of the massacres, [who had] decided to abolish the reformed religion. They had excited the fury of the leagues, endeavouring also to ruin by arms and assassination the Bourbons and Montmorencys, and to deprive the better and more faithful Catholics [moderates] of the honours due to them, seeking to give them to the most unworthy of their party."[94] Clearly, for him, the Catholic conspiracy was a continuing state, and no uncertain hypothesis, whatever its current form. It was therefore not surprising that Condé had refused even to receive the delegates of the estates, whose authority he denied. Indeed, he declared that he

91. François, *Lettres de Henri III*, vol. iii, 150 [January 1577], Henry to Villeroy.

92. Ibid., 146, 29 January 1577, Henry to Rambouillet.

93. In a general sense this was true, though Henri duc de Guise does not appear to have received money from Spain before 1579. Martin, *Henry III and the Jesuit Politicians*, 65.

94. *CSPF.*, *1575-77*, pp. 488–89, 23 January 1577, protestation of the prince de Condé.

and the nobility with him would "spare nothing to subvert their designs."[95]

At this stage, early in February, Catherine de Medici began to strive, as she always did, to avert the war that was gathering pace. On 8 February she proposed a truce for one month, and the day after argued the necessity of some measure of toleration, pending a council.[96] This was an empty formula. She knew from long experience that there must eventually be concessions, and she deplored the king's mistaken priorities which caused him to publish an intransigent declaration that he was quite unable to implement.[97]

A week later, on 15 February, the deputies returned from Navarre. His reply was serious, responsible and sad. Its principal burden was a desperate, reiterated plea for greater realism. His whole desire—like Henry's—was for peace, but the demand for one religion would bring worse trouble than ever before. It had been, and it was still, impossible to eradicate Protestantism, "tant de fois accordé." As king of Poland, Henry had sworn to preserve it, in order not to disturb the State. Even if their religion *were* heresy, it was only for a council, and not for the estates to alter it; they had no competence in matters of religion. Navarre was astutely careful not to exclude the possibility of his own abjuration. Eventually this became necessary, and he doubtless foresaw the contingency. He declared that if his religion were false, then let his opponents show and convince him of the right way, and he would follow it. This judicious statement was erased by Protestant ministers, but Navarre had it restored. His interests, whether as first prince, heir apparent or king, never fully coincided with those of the Protestant party, and this was already apparent. Finally, Navarre implored the estates to think and think again, and to consider not only what was intrinsically good, but also what was good for the kingdom.[98] The estates were, by

95. Ibid., 493, 28 January 1577.
96. Gomberville, *Mémoires de Nevers*, i, 172.
97. Ibid., 176.
98. Mayer, *Des États Généraux*, xiii, 284–91; Gomberville, *Mémoires de Nevers*, i, 452–57, Navarre's reply, 1 February 1577, Agen.

then, anxious to depart, partly perhaps to avoid any further demands for money. They elected to ignore Navarre's reply. Standing on a technicality, they declared themselves powerless to debate it after the presentation of their *cahiers*. [99]

The last to arrive, on 26 February, were the deputies from Damville. Damville was anxious for self-justification, and to proclaim his unshakable Catholicism. Nevertheless, it was untrue, he said, that the two religions were incompatible. He had compelling reasons for saying so, since the estates of Languedoc had sworn to observe the edict. If, therefore, Damville inclined to the demands of the estates general, he would bring terrible suffering to Languedoc. He was careful, however, to leave the matter open, hiding behind his need to consult Navarre and Condé. Like Navarre, Damville "prayed" the estates "well to consider" what advice they gave the king. [100]

All the deputies having returned, there was a further heated debate about the issue of war or peace. The war desired by the extremists seemed virtually to have begun. Condé was in the field and, on 27 February, Henry called out the *gendarmerie*. [101] Earlier in the month the estates had attempted to purge the council of several of its leading moderates and supporters of Catherine—Limoges, Bellièvre and Morvillier, a man of peace who died soon after. [102] It is not, however, clear that the Catholics succeeded in this attempt, since the councilors were all present at the beginning of March. Both Bellièvre and Morvillier tried to persuade the *tiers* to sanction some alienation of the royal domain, if they would not otherwise provide money for "la guerre qui se presentoit." But they were not to be shamed into compliance, and obstinately declined both requests. This was their final refusal of financial aid. [103]

The day after their deputies had returned from Damville, the

99. Mayer, *Des Etats Généraux*, xiii, 292–95.

100. *CSPF.*, *1575-77*, pp. 512–13, 8 February 1577, Damville to the deputies of the estates.

101. Ibid., 526–27, 27 February 1577, proclamation.

102. Morvillier died in October 1577. Desjardins, *Négs. Tosc.*, iv, 132, 31 October 1577.

103. Mayer, *Des États Généraux*, xiii, 297–302.

clergy and the nobles invited representatives of the *tiers* to debate his reply, as well as the rumors of peace which had spread since the return of Biron from Navarre. Some of the *tiers* wished to ask the king for peace. The estates and the council were therefore already heading for the final showdown when, on 28 February, Montpensier returned from Navarre. It was the sobering advice of this elderly prince which tipped the balance. To each of the estates in turn, Montpensier made an earnest plea for peace. He declared that he had been impressed by Navarre's sincerity. Sixteen years of war had altered nothing, and the king had no means of waging it. Charles V had found no other solution in the Empire, and even Philip II had had to make concessions in the Netherlands. Montpensier was therefore obliged to advise the king to modify his declaration (of 3 January), to avail himself of Navarre's willingness to compromise ("retrancher et diminuer l'edit"), and so to renegotiate the peace. This Montpensier regarded as the only expedient solution, albeit provisional.[104] The *tiers* finally decided to request the king to reunite his subjects in one religion, without war, though some still wished to omit the qualifying phrase.

Similar discussions naturally occurred in the council, where a debate arose on 1 March about the demand for one religion in the *cahier* of the clergy. Various compromise formulae were suggested, and Catherine "fit merveille de bien dire pour la paix." She was supported by Biron, Cossé (a marshal), Montpensier, Morvillier and Bellièvre, but opposed by Guise, Cardinal Guise, Mayenne and Nevers—all of them *leagueurs*.[105] Nevers advised Henry to make war, declaring that the king could not again change his opinion "sans avoir aucune nouvelle occassion." But there was in fact a "nouvelle occasion": namely, the refusal of the estates to finance the war. Catherine is said to have heard Nevers with impatience. She supported the principle of one religion, but said that the king should defer his resolution until he could ensure its accomplishment. She herself had advised and assisted the king to make use of the estates. Had they failed to do so, the estates

104. Ibid., 308–13.
105. Ibid., 314.

might easily have misused him. But, Catherine continued, Henry had been too precipitate in declaring his resolution. She also pointed out that religion had come to be tolerated in every country in which it could not effectively be suppressed. There was hardly enough money for ordinary living, let alone for war; and Catherine explicitly dissociated herself from those who wished to profit from war. This was a clear statement of the policy she had held since 1560, and was always to hold, because it was the only realistic one. But, as she had declared, there were always those who wished to profit from renewed war.

Henry's own statement is interesting. He had, he said, made it perfectly clear how much he wanted only one religion, and he had himself procured this demand from the estates. But as they had refused him the necessary means, he had no hope of succeeding in his intention. But, he asserted, effectively reversing Nevers's argument, it was permissible to change one's mind if occasion arose. For his part, he said, "je ne pense point faillir si je ne declare pas *maintenant* que je veuille entretenir une seule religion dans mon Royaume, puis que je n'ay pas les moyens de le faire."[106] It was Catherine who carried the day, in support of Montpensier. Consequently Biron left on 3 March to reopen peace negotiations with Navarre, followed once again by Montpensier, on 20 March.[107]

Thus the king had wanted only one religion, and the credit for this policy in Catholic estimation. But when he found that it could not be achieved without war, which the estates declined to finance, he changed his mind and inverted his arguments. One could say that he was mistaken not to have secured the money before committing himself. This would nevertheless be a gross oversimplification of a highly complex problem, not least in its timing. The estates were wayward and dilatory, and jealous of each other. They were also disinclined to vote any money at all. Henry could not afford to wait upon their leisure while the league

106. Gomberville, *Mémoires de Nevers*, i, 176–77; Mayer, *Des États Généraux*, xiii, 314.

107. Desjardins, *Négs. Tosc.*, iv, 114, 7 March 1577; 117, 20 March 1577; B. N., Mss. Italien, 1730, f. 4, 7 March 1577. Others involved were Biron, Descars, Saint-Sulpice, La Mothe-Fénelon and Villeroy, all highly experienced negotiators.

situation developed beyond his control and the Huguenots had time to prepare for any eventuality.

To Henry III the estates general had had nothing positive to offer; but they were potentially very dangerous. Indeed they bluntly frustrated his declared policy by their refusal to provide the money. Nevertheless, Henry had succeeded in using them to affirm his Catholic will. In this he was largely sincere, at least in thought, and he probably helped to erase the moral defeat of the peace of Monsieur. But he manifestly could not, unaided, revoke the disastrous treaty. It was therefore not unskillful to have burdened the estates with what would, in any other circumstances, have been his sole responsibility. But this was not all. Henry also succeeded in exploiting the existence of the estates to cover his humiliating need to supersede and command the Catholic league and associations. This was the means by which he publicly proposed to implement the estates' demand for one religion. If this decision entailed the danger of religious war, it at least removed the greater danger that the Catholics might have made war without him, and even, perhaps, the danger of his deposition. Certainly his fear of deposition is inherent in his own articles of association, and possibly points to the effect of the David memoir. While Henry strongly resented the refusal of the estates to finance the war which insistence on one religion entailed, this was not without its benefits: the rejection of war frustrated the Catholic league, which could not otherwise prosper, and therefore released the king from the danger of its tyranny.

It was only offensive war, however, which could be avoided by a council decision, and the kingdom was already in a state of combustion.[108] Both sides had forces in the field, and more forces under preparation; furthermore, neither wanted to negotiate from a military disadvantage. Few of the Huguenots were as moderate as Navarre. The Catholic leaders, for their part, left court early in March to continue their preparations. This was always a danger signal; but momentarily it eased the task of the moderates. About the same time, Damville, who was ceded the marquisate of

---

108. François, *Lettres de Henri III*, vol. iii, 185–87, 13 March 1577, Henry to d'Abain; 204–5, 28 March 1577, Henry to d'Abain.

Saluces, declared against the Huguenots.[109] Once again, throughout the summer, hostilities and peace negotiations continued simultaneously. By mid-summer, when the Huguenots began to receive help from Queen Elizabeth, the situation had become really dangerous.

Forces were also expected from Germany. Furthermore, the Flemish were pressing Anjou to go to the Netherlands which, if not positively helpful to the Protestants, was immensely dangerous for the king. Early in August the Protestants had even begun to invest Poitiers, where the court was in residence.[110] Late in August they took Brouage, opposite the Île d'Oléran, intending to cede it to England as security for a loan. This was reminiscent of the cession of Le Havre—which the crown had had to recapture in 1563—and the surrender of territory would enable Elizabeth to reopen the question of Calais, a Channel port on the Netherlands' frontier. Navarre insisted that if peace were not quickly made, it would elude them altogether. The Catholics had no monopoly of intransigent hotheads and, like the king, Navarre could barely contain the pressures behind him. Having previously accepted the Protestants' requirements in 1576, notwithstanding his protests about duress, the king had little room for maneuver. Yet now he could hardly agree to the very terms he had so recently been forced to abrogate. Still, it is doubtful if Navarre wished so to mortify the king, who did, after all, stand between him and the Catholics, and whose throne he might well inherit.

Thus the peace which Henry always desired had again become both imperative and urgent. It is significant that it was only achieved by working outside the council. The king, Catherine, Anjou, Villeroy, Biron and some say Bellièvre, ended by transacting the negotiations privily, and granting Navarre certain secret articles, in order to circumvent the Catholic opposition.[111]

---

109. Desjardins, *Négs. Tosc.*, iv, 109–10, 13 February 1577; 111, 24 February 1577; 114, 7 March 1577; 117, March 1577; 118–19, May–June 1577.

110. B. N., Mss. Italien, 1730, ff. 105–6, 4 August 1577.

111. Desjardins, *Négs. Tosc.*, iv, 124, 1 September 1577; B. N., Mss. Italien, 1730, f. 130, 2 September 1577; Sutherland, *The French Secretaries of State*, 197–200. Biron was made a marshal for his long and patient labors in constructing the peace together with Villeroy.

This was an expedient which Navarre assimilated and later successfully employed. Even after the conclusion of peace, on 17 September 1577,[112] there was a hitch when Condé intercepted a letter to the Guisard duc de Nemours explaining that the king was only deceiving the enemy and playing for time.[113] The allegation may be discounted, though the letter probably existed; such was Henry's nutcracker predicament. Indeed his greater need for agreement was with the Catholic extremists, who, by whatever name—Guisards, Triumvirate, Holy League or Catholic League—never conceded the *principle* of accommodation with the Huguenots, even though they could not always escape formal consent to the edicts if they wished to participate in council business.

The agreement of September 1577 is known as the peace of Bergerac, where it was negotiated, and also as the edict of Poitiers, where the king was resident. It has been described by J.-A. de Thou as achieving a just balance—referring, presumably, to the toleration clauses. This was another long edict of sixty-four articles, plus forty-eight secret articles concluded with and for Navarre and Condé. It was of course inevitable, according to the basis of negotiation, that the edict should have resembled that of 1576. Thus, except for the principal items concerning the toleration clauses, justice, the *places de sûreté*, and certain minor matters, Poitiers was a repetition, frequently word for word, of the peace of Monsieur. The items do not recur in the same order, but nothing of any significance was omitted. Poitiers therefore represented another, or renewed Huguenot charter, and was destined, like the others, to the same fate. It did not, any more than Monsieur before it (but unlike the final edict of Nantes), make any reference to the Protestant "state." Navarre had not been a party to its creation, nor did he ever manage to control it; indeed, as Henry IV, he had virtually to conquer it. Apart from special privileges for the nobles and gentry, which had featured in all the edicts since 1563, the cult was permitted in the *faubourgs* of one town per *bailliage* or *sénéchaussée*. To this was added—which

112. This date is sometimes given as 16 September. One or other must be a copyist's error.
113. B. N., Mss. Italien, 1730, f. 143, 20 September 1577.

may have been considerable—all the towns where it was publicly held on 17 September when the agreement was concluded, except for those in Protestant hands, but actually belonging to Catholic *seigneurs* who had not permitted it before the recent hostilities. One town per *bailliage* or *sénéchaussée* was a return to the first post-war agreement of Amboise, 1563, restored by Longjumeau in 1568. This was more favorable than the peace of Saint-Germain, accepted by Coligny, which had allowed only two towns per *gouvernement*.

By the edict of Poitiers the *chambres de justice* were not *mi-parties*—equal numbers of Catholics and Protestants, as in 1576—which had never been implemented, but their composition for each of the *parlements* was precisely specified, and the appointments were to be made by the king. This was a device by which the Catholics appeared to be favored, while the Huguenots effectively could be. This interpretation is fairly clearly indicated by number 10 of the secret articles, which stipulated that these royal appointments should be approved by the Protestants. The king undertook to replace whomsoever they impugned. Like the peace of Monsieur, Poitiers allowed eight *places de sûreté* for six years, in Languedoc, Dauphiné, Provence and Guyenne. The *places* must certainly have been one of the difficulties, which protracted the negotiations, since Navarre demanded more like sixty, while his intransigent party aspired to possession of the entire province of Guyenne.

The secret articles did, however, greatly elucidate the judicial arrangements, augment the toleration clauses, especially in respect of Navarre's duchy of Vendôme, and concede two places near La Rochelle—as well as Saint-Jean-d'Angély in Poitou—for Condé. The king further agreed to finance a garrison of 800 men for the *places de sûreté*, to pay off Casimir of the Palatinate and the German forces (an item which had caused excruciating difficulties in 1576), and to rehabilitate the prince of Orange.[114]

Strong in this more moderate peace of Bergerac, Henry was then able to destroy the Catholic league.[115] This success reversed

114. Sutherland, *The French Secretaries of State*, 195, and nn. 3, 4.
115. Article 56 of the peace of Poitiers prohibited all leagues.

his servitude of the previous summer and, for the moment, restored his authority. On the one hand, therefore, the league was dissolved and, on the other, the Protestant alliance with Damville's *catholiques unis*. Damville, as well as Anjou, had now been detached, and this lessened the dangers in Languedoc. In this way, Henry was liberated both from the stigma of the peace of Monsieur, and from the menace of the league which opposed it. He may also have learnt, in the process, that Navarre was not a dangerous enemy, in any treacherous sense. He would, like Coligny before him, insist upon an adequate edict, but he would not deliberately threaten the crown. Since total success had never been possible against either party, Henry had cause for some ephemeral satisfaction with the edict of Poitiers. However, this was only the conclusion of one more round. The Catholics had finally understood that lack of money and preparation had repeatedly impeded their destruction of the Protestants; also, perhaps, that this would never be achieved under the command of Henry III. Nor was he ever again to hold the command. It seems, in retrospect, as though he had been exhausted by the struggle. He turned, increasingly, away from affairs of state, leaving Catherine de Medici to resume the burden.

There were to be two further edicts—Nérac, 28 February 1579, and Fleix, 26 November 1580—both explanatory and supplementary to that of Poitiers, indicating the problems which either remained or arose. But once again the precise timing of these arrangements related, as in the case of Monsieur and Poitiers, to immediate political and military conditions.

Following the conclusion of the peace of Bergerac, the king and Navarre both sought to implement the edict, although attention was focused on Anjou. He was determined to campaign in the Netherlands, and was preparing to do so, while the king and Catherine struggled to prevent him because of the gravity of the implications. Not the least of the inherent dangers was that of war with Spain, for whom the Guises were recruiting forces released in France by the peace of Bergerac. Constant troop movements, together with this atmosphere of simmering crisis, were hardly conducive to the complex and contentious business of implementing internal peace; from the start, it was regarded as insecure.

This situation was alarmingly reminiscent of the spring and summer of 1572, which had not ended happily. It was also feared that Anjou might engineer some league between himself, the Netherlands' estates, Casimir of the Palatinate, England and Navarre. It was therefore doubly important to satisfy Navarre and to settle the Huguenots in France, since they would otherwise be a dangerously exploitable force.

For these reasons, once Anjou had for the moment irretrievably departed, entering Mons in July 1578, Catherine turned her attention to the problems of the edict. She therefore left Ollainville on 2 August on what proved to be a long and arduous struggle through the southern provinces, from which she did not return to Paris until November 1579.

The problems of peace were still what they had always been, except that article 56 of the edict of Poitiers had most expressly dissolved all leagues and associations; a benefit which had, nevertheless, to be accounted for to the pope. For the moment, therefore, there was less organized Catholic opposition than usual. The problem of Anjou, however, fully counterbalanced that improvement. In February 1579 he created a fresh crisis when, dissatisfied with the Netherlands' estates, he stormed back into France prepared to champion any *malcontents*. Whether he was more dangerous at home or abroad was becoming difficult to determine. It was fear that he might then instigate a new rebellion—another 1576 situation—that accounts for the timing of the articles of Nérac, 28 February 1579. A number of the twenty-seven articles, some of which are very long, elucidated specific administrative problems. In a wider sense, the major difficulties of a general pacification emerge as demands for the free exercise of religion everywhere—the lost benefit of Monsieur—for the impartial administration of justice, which had been a problem ever since the Reformation began; for fifty-nine *places de sûreté* for six years, and a general amnesty for everything which had occurred since the publication of the edict of Poitiers. Its violation is thereby acknowledged, and formulated in the very long article 11. Catherine is said to have insisted that to grant all these requests would merely encourage "evil men and assassins to persist in their iniquities," and to have reminded Navarre of all the evils of the continuance of war.[116] She was right, and Navarre himself was mindful of these arguments when he came to wear the crown and bear the burden of an almost ungovernable country.

The articles of Nérac were intended to restore peace where this had been violated since Poitiers, and where it had never been accepted. Apart from the modifications of Nérac, therefore, Poitiers was reaffirmed. Without going into administrative details, there were certain major points which should be noted. Article 2 permitted the purchase or construction of *temples* in the cult towns. This is said to have been included in the terms of the peace of Bergerac but inadvertently omitted from the edict of Poitiers, and therefore subsequently sanctioned by letters patent of 13 November 1577. When the cult towns proved to be inconvenient, they might be changed; and certain additional rights were granted to *seigneurs*. Further items related to the necessity of raising money for the payment of pastors and the administration of the churches, which was presumably to facilitate observance of the prohibition against raising taxes.[117] Nine articles (17–25) dealt with the problem of towns and their administration. Poitiers had allowed Navarre eight *places de sûreté* for six years; Nérac stipulated the surrender of all "villes et places gardées" by the Protestants, but allowed Navarre to hold three in Guyenne until 31 August, and four in Languedoc until 1 October 1579. This represented six months in each province from the agreed date of execution of the edict. Superficially, it appears that Navarre would therefore only hold seven towns for six months each. But a careful reading of the articles suggests, more plausibly, that these towns were additional to those previously granted for six years. No doubt it was hoped that few Catholics would read the agreement with studied care. Finally, among the more important matters, five articles dealt with problems relating to the administration of justice.

116. *CSPF.*, *1575–77*, p. 465 [February 1579], pacification of Guyenne and Languedoc. This document is placed in error under 1576.

117. The Venetian ambassador reported that Navarre was to receive 36,000 francs. B. N., Mss. Italien, 1731, f. 7, 17 March 1579. The report in the *CSPF* also recorded this item, which was not in the articles.

The articles of Nérac, so it appears, covered the problems relating to Guyenne and Languedoc, though the document does not say so, and the indomitable Catherine traveled on to Provence and Dauphiné. In the summer of 1579 these provinces were still in arms.[118] Indeed, nothing permanent had been achieved in any of these provinces, and, at the end of the stipulated six months, the Huguenots refused to restore the seven *places de sûreté* in Languedoc and Guyenne on the grounds that the peace had not been enforced.[119] A decision to keep what they held had, in fact, been taken by an assembly at Montauban chiefly, it would seem, from fear and as a bargaining counter. Navarre was certainly not in a position to dictate the conduct of his followers. This is borne out by the Protestants' revision of their *règlement* in 1579, which disclosed some lack of confidence in Navarre—whose powers were carefully defined—as he himself later averred.[120] In May 1580 the Tuscan ambassador had reported that intrigues in France were such that whoever saw clearest saw least. No one's position, whether personal or military, was clear.[121] All parties were arming for their separate reasons, and much of France was in a state of anarchy. The nature of this anarchy and its possible solution was analyzed by Villeroy, whose *département* included Languedoc. Three months later, when plague was prevalent and war ubiquitous, the Venetian wrote wearily of another return to simultaneous war and negotiations.[122] A new chapter in the old story of Anjou, the Netherlands, and Spain opened up in September 1580, and relations between Anjou and Navarre were once again dangerously close.[123]

118. Desjardins, *Négs. Tosc.*, iv, 258, 21 June 1579; B. N., Mss. Italien, 1731, ff. 1-4, 10 March 1579; ff. 81, 86-87, two letters of 28 January 1579.
119. B. N., Mss. Italien, 1731, f. 371-74, 5 August 1580.
120. Ibid., f. 114, 3 August 1579.
121. Desjardins, *Négs. Tosc.*, iv, 316, 9 May 1580.
122. "Le cose in questo regno stanno nelli soliti termini. Si tratta la pace et si continua la guerra." B. N., Mss. Italien, 1731, f. 382, 25 August 1580; Sutherland, *The French Secretaries of State*, 216 seq.
123. This was held to be through Navarre's wife, Marguerite, who was devoted to her brother, Anjou. B. N., Mss. Italien, 1731, f. 222, 18 October 1579; f. 392, 11 September 1580.

There were, therefore, no new principles involved in the treaty of Fleix—only a fresh crisis. The treaty was concluded by Villeroy and Bellièvre on 26 November 1580, and confirmed by the king on 26 December. The fact was that France had never been more than partially and spasmodically at peace since the massacre of 1572; nor was she ever to be so, until her firm subjection at the hands of Henry IV. This therefore places the entire reign of Henry III in a period of anarchy, and thereby accounts for its obscurity. The treaty of Fleix necessarily confirmed those of Poitiers and Nérac, as article 1 declared, and the principal difficulties were, still, yet and again, those of the *places de sûreté*, and the administration of justice—the civil face of security.

The forty-seven articles of Fleix therefore refer in detailed explanation to those of the preceding edicts. By this time there was little which could be added to the edicts of pacification, and nothing of substance that could safely be subtracted. From the point of view of the Huguenot struggle for recognition, what would happen in the future depended more than ever on the strength or weakness of the king and the pressure of Catholic opposition. But, ill and neglectful of his duties, the king was incapable of restoring the royal administration and protecting the Protestants, though he defended the policy implicit in the edicts to an assembly of notables at Saint-Germain in November 1583. Villeroy, who was largely left with the burden of government, was constantly anxious about conditions in the south, where his own province of Languedoc was undefended and open to Spain; he was also apprehensive that the Protestants would never recover from their "maudite maladie de deffiance."[124] The restoration of confidence was to be another achievement of Navarre, as Henry IV.

During the years 1581–84 the pressure of Catholic opposition was gradually increased. The king of Spain had been temporarily diverted by the annexation of Portugal in 1580 but, since the dissolution of the Catholic leagues in 1577, he had been loosely in touch with Guise through his ambassador Vargas, and had not forgotten the potential utility of Damville. By September 1581 it

124. Sutherland, *The French Secretaries of State*, 236.

was reported that Damville was in league with Spain.[125] A year later Guise is known to have received Spanish money, and it was Navarre himself who warned the king of this connection.[126] Guise attention at the time, however, was primarily focused on the "enterprise of England," in conjunction with the pope.[127]

It was therefore not until after the death of Anjou in June, and the murder of William of Orange in July 1584, that the Catholic League in France was formally constituted. The death of Anjou left Navarre heir presumptive to the throne, and that of Orange precipitated a crisis in the Netherlands which was to lead to the open intervention of England.[128] It was therefore in the mutual interest of Spain and the Guises to rekindle war in France in order to protect the Netherlands by occupying Navarre and opposing the Protestants. Not unnaturally, the Huguenots refused to relinquish their *places de sûreté*. The new Catholic League was embodied in the treaty of Joinville of 31 December 1584, between the Guises and Spain.[129] Philip undertook to pay the Guises 50,000 *écus* per month so long as they made war in France to exterminate the Protestant religion and to place the cardinal of Bourbon on the throne.[130] This proposal is held to have stimulated more ambition than piety in the Guises, since Bourbon was an elderly nonentity whom they could easily control.[131] These were the dramatic circumstances which led, yet again, to the destruction by the Catholics of the current edict or—since Nérac and Fleix—edicts of pacification, by which alone the Huguenot minority could be contained.

In conformity with the treaty of Joinville, the Guises prepared a rising, timed for 6 April 1585. As the Huguenots would also take up arms, Villeroy observed, the king would now have to

125. Desjardins, *Négs. Tosc.*, iv, 397, 7 September 1581; Törne, "Philippe II et Henri de Guise, 1578," *Revue historique*, clxvii, 1931.

126. Törne, "Philippe II et Henri de Guise, 1578," *Revue historique*, clxvii, 1931, p. 333; Sutherland, *The French Secretaries of State*, app. v, p. 323.

127. Martin, *Henry III and the Jesuit Politicians*, chap. viii.

128. Parker, *The Dutch Revolt*, 217.

129. B. N., Mss. Fr., 3363, f. 9, 31 December 1584, original.

130. Bourbon was Navarre's uncle, but ineligible as a prelate.

131. He died in 1590.

defend himself against them both[132]—the very situation he had adroitly averted in 1576–77. Had Henry turned upon the Guises, whose intentions were to descend upon Paris (as they did, originally, in March 1562), he might have received considerable loyalist support. But he was totally unprepared for war, and concentrated on trying to preserve peace. So, with very little time in hand, Catherine went to Epernay on 30 March to bargain with the Guises.[133] That she kept them talking for three months, mostly from her sickbed, was no mean achievement. Guise, however, stubbornly refused to negotiate except on the basis of the revocation of the edicts—of Poitiers, Nérac, and Fleix—and agreement to make war on the Huguenots. This time, the Guises were already prepared for war and, paid by Spain, could act independently of the crown—an advantage Lorraine had never enjoyed. Thus, whereas in 1577 Henry had managed if not exactly to control, at least to frustrate, the nascent league, in 1585 it was the well-organized Catholics who dominated him. On 7 July, by the treaty of Nemours, they obtained for themselves and for Spain the consent of the defeated king to disrupt his kingdom.

The treaty of Nemours strongly resembled Lorraine's edict of Saint-Maur, 1568, but without its long preamble. Because it was also imposed on the crown, Nemours was the only other exclusively Catholic edict, and necessarily corresponded closely to the objectives of the former Catholic league of 1576–77. It was not a "treaty" of peace, except insofar as it reprieved the king from immediate liquidation, but rather a virtual declaration of war— the very last thing that Henry wanted. In June 1585, he had written to Villeroy, in whom he had more confidence than in Catherine herself: "si vous pourriez tant guaigner . . . que le faict de la religion ne se fist si rigoureux et trouver moyen de ne nous metre à la guerre, mais je le tiens impossible."[134] This plea is typical of Henry's despondent way of flickering out, as if his attention had strayed, and with scant regard for syntax. His de-

132. Sutherland, *The French Secretaries of State*, 255–56.

133. These negotiations are very fully documented. Ibid., 275 seq., and notes.

134. B. N., Mss. N. A. F., 1244, no. 60, f. 157 [June 1585], Henry to Villeroy.

spondency was understandable, because he had passed that way before and knew the alternatives.

The treaty, which contains no separate articles, began by prohibiting the cult, and proceeded to an explicit revocation of the edicts of pacification, which was more than the Catholics had achieved in 1576–77. Pastors were to leave the country within a month, and everyone else was to abjure within six months, and live as Catholics, or else incur the penalty of exile. Permission for Protestants to sell their property was the only concession. Not content with a general abrogation of the edicts, it was further specified that no Protestant was to be eligible for offices; the *chambres de justice* were dissolved and the *places de sûreté* withdrawn. Offices, *chambres* and *places* were among the basic requirements of the petition of 25 August 1573. They had been dearly won and were—during another terrible thirteen years—to be dearly won again and ultimately incorporated into the edict of Nantes in 1598. Finally, the Guises insolently secured for themselves exoneration for all their activities, including, in less explicit terms, their alliance with the king of Spain. The treaty of Nemours did not actually specify an agreement to make war on the Huguenots, an omission or form of words which Catherine or Villeroy may have regarded as a potential loophole. If so, it was rapidly closed. The treaty was followed in September 1585 by the papal excommunication of Navarre and Condé—surely not a coincidence—which disqualified them in the eyes of Catholics from succession to the throne.[135] This may be evidence that the Guises, in council, had been behind the deputies of the estates of Blois, who, in January 1577, threatened the princes with disqualification. Similarly, the same bull of Sixtus V menacingly reminded the king of his coronation oath. In view of his now advanced religious mania, one must suppose that the awful specter of excommunication preyed upon his mind, and weighed in his considerations. It could hardly be otherwise. Thus the Catholic extremists would seem to have achieved all that had eluded them in 1576–77. At this stage, the David memoir no longer appears so hyperbolic.

Having won virtual control of the king, the Catholics began to

135. Haag, *La France protestante*, x, 187–91, 9 September 1585.

squeeze him. Thus, in October 1585, Henry declared that the time he had allowed for the Protestants to abjure the faith or to sell their property had been abused for the purpose of preparing for war. They were therefore commanded to lay down arms or else be condemned to the confiscation of their property in order to finance the war against them.[136] It is difficult to imagine whether there were any cases in which this was feasible. Consequently they were allowed not three final months, but only two more weeks in which to make their decisions and arrangements. Navarre reacted vigorously, not without a touch of sour humor. He formally and angrily rejected the excommunication and disqualification of "Monsieur sixte, soi disant pape (sauve sa sainteté)," who had thus overstepped the limits of his vocation, confounding the temporal with the spiritual. Furthermore, he swore vengeance and "guerre perpetuelle et irréconciliable," calling on the help of all truly Christian princes, kings, towns and communities to assist him. This was an uncharacteristically intransigent declaration, no doubt a measure of his outrage and frustration. Navarre also called on all allies of France to oppose with him "la tyrannie et usurpation du pape et des Ligués conjurateurs en France, ennemis de Dieu, de l'Estat et de leur Roi et du repos général de toute la chrétienté."[137] Although Queen Elizabeth's agreement with the estates general of the Netherlands preceded the excommunication of the French princes by some three weeks,[138] this multiple crisis in France—now dynastic as well as religious—had much to do with the European war which is probably best known in terms of the Spanish armada. Certainly it was no coincidence that England—where the Babington plot was hatching—openly invaded the Netherlands at the end of December—in mid-winter.[139]

136. Ibid., 191–94, declaration de Henri III sur son édit de juillet 1585.

137. Ibid., 191, 6 November 1585, response of Navarre and Condé to their excommunication; 194–95, 30 November 1585, Declaration du roi de Navarre.

138. The treaty of Nonsuch, 20 August 1585.

139. The reconquests of Parma in the Netherlands were, by this time, impressive, and there was now no one else to fight Elizabeth's battles for her. In March 1585 Henry III declined to help the estates general, and

A few weeks later Philip II began preparations for the great armada.[140] If he could conquer England and restore her to Catholicism, that would alter her foreign policy. If this was barely realistic, he might, at the least, gain control of the Channel in order more easily to suppress the Netherlands. Guise, it should be noted, was not to command the enterprise of England. By the terms of the treaty of Joinville he was to be fully—and from the Spanish point of view, more safely—employed in France, both destroying Protestantism and also subverting the succession. This was something that Navarre could not be expected to tolerate and he was no feeble opponent. In this way the Huguenot struggle became, once again, an intrinsic part of the great European drama, and their danger was extreme. So was that of Henry III, whose almost monastic piety was simply an embarrassment to his Catholic enemies.

The years 1586–88 followed the now familiar pattern of simultaneous hostilities and negotiations. They did not notably alter the fortunes of the Huguenots until, in December 1588, Henry III murdered the overmighty duc de Guise, by whom his throne was certainly endangered. In the violent aftermath of this event, Henry could only turn to Navarre for help against their common enemy, the Catholic League. One way or another, there was clearly much fighting to be done, and it seems unlikely that Henry III could ever again have emerged supreme. In the event, he too was to be murdered, in August 1589. For the Huguenots, the accession of their "protector" as Henry IV broke the oft-repeated deadlock, but it could not quickly solve their long-term problems. Thus, for the Huguenots and for Henry IV began the long, hard struggle towards Nantes, both to the same destination, but not always from the same camp.

Antwerp fell on 17 August. It was Leicester who arrived in December, English intervention having occurred in stages. Parker, *The Dutch Revolt*, 217–18.

140. Ibid., 218–19.

9

The "Protestant State" and the Edict of Nantes, 1589–1598

THE EDICT OF NANTES was signed by Henry IV and four deputies on behalf of the Protestants in April 1598. As a landmark in the history of religion and civil war, and as a symbol of the constructive work of Henry IV, the edict is very well known. But it is generally treated in isolation—even as an apparent inspiration on the part of the king—while its complex origins, its real nature and historical setting remain largely unfamiliar.

The struggle for the edict of Nantes, which formed an integral part of the final phase of the civil wars of the sixteenth century, essentially represented a prolonged crisis of confidence on the part of the Protestants which, though a legacy from the past, became acute and intolerable as a result of their changed attitude to the king—their erstwhile "protector"—after his abjuration in July 1593. This basically religious struggle, however, was exploited on account of the private passions of a number of extremists, in particular the duc de Bouillon, and frustrated by the public pressure of political events, notably the declaration of war on Spain in January 1595, and the fall and recapture of the strategically vital city of Amiens in 1597. These were interrelated forces and they nearly resulted in the victory of Spain, which would have been fatal for the king and the Protestants alike.

The active determination of the Protestants to achieve the edict dates from the abjuration of Henry IV. Their efforts found expression in the proceedings of a series of Protestant assemblies whose fortunes, and those of the war with Spain and the Catholic League, interacted upon each other. But, in order to understand the nature and complexity of this struggle for the edict, it is necessary first of all to consider the relations of Henry of Navarre with the independent Protestant "state," to account for the influence on the Protestants of the duc de Bouillon and, finally, to examine the Huguenots' juridical position.

The Protestant organization was basically an ad hoc union for the purpose of defense, whose origins can be traced from about 1560, when the churches in the south and west had begun to seek local protectors among the nobles and gentry.[1] This resulted in the growth of what has been called a fatal "feudal" hierarchy, and hence in the cleavage which developed between those who became Protestants for social and political reasons—who later included most of the extremists—and those who were known as the "zelés de religion," together with the ecclesiastical element or "consistoriaux," who were mainly moderates. It was not, however, until after the massacre of St. Bartholomew in 1572, that the Protestants had developed their independent organization within the State. Not only did the massacre deprive them of many of their *seigneurs;* it also destroyed their confidence in the protection of the crown and engendered a deep suspicion of the princes of the blood who, nevertheless, remained their natural leaders. This distrust was to be one of the major difficulties confronting Henry of Navarre, both before and after his accession.

It has been seen how the problem of the partial peace of La Rochelle, most acute in the Midi, led to the drafting at Montauban of the Protestant petition of August 1573. It has also been seen how the assembly at Montauban and two others at Millau,[2] in December 1573 and July 1574, produced *règlements* for the government of the Protestants under an elected leader, Henry de Bourbon, prince de Condé, who was curiously styled "chef, gouverneur général et protecteur au nom lieu et autorité du

---

1. These origins are still obscure. See Romier, "Les protestants français à la veille des guerres de religion," *Revue historique*, cxxiv, 1917, pp. 257–58; Léonard, *Histoire générale du protestantisme*, ii, 128 seq.

2. Millau in the Aveyron. This formed part of the Rouergue in the Bourbon appanage of Henry of Navarre.

roi de France et de Pologne."[3] This nascent organization, which began with the province of Languedoc, was completed by the *règlement* of Nîmes in February 1575.

Since this Huguenot "state within the State" included persons of widely different aims and outlook, the Protestant conception of its theoretical nature was variable and inconsistent. There were occasional attempts to justify its existence by some formal deference to the authority of the king,[4] but the fact remains that for many years it gravely threatened his authority, its very existence reproaching the weakness of the crown which failed to govern. Thus, in a sense, the Protestant organization was as much a result of the incompetence of the monarchy and of the revolutionary situation, as a product of religious strife. Furthermore, it offered a solution—from their own point of view—to the problem of the nobility, by creating a need for their social, political and military leadership. This was what finally made the religious movement so dangerous, since it was not the *zelés de religion*, but the nobility in arms, exploiting the protestants, who threatened to destroy the monarchy of Henry IV. The same was, of course, true of the Catholic nobility, who similarly opposed the crown, but on different pretexts. In 1597 the Protestants observed that the king himself compared them to the *ligueurs*. The result of this noble disaffection could easily have been the fragmentation of France.

It might have been supposed that Navarre's accession to the throne in August 1589 would greatly improve the Huguenot prospects and terminate their struggle for recognition: this was their own expectation. But, after the treaty of Nemours between the king and the Guises in July 1585, France had been plunged into renewed civil war by the highly organized Catholic League, in alliance with the king of Spain. In these circumstances, Navarre's accession merely created different problems, both for himself

---

3. Anquez, *Histoire des assemblées*, 4–15. Charles IX died on 30 May 1574, and his brother Henry III returned to France from his kingdom of Poland, arriving at Lyons on 6 September 1574.

4. Their oath of union, May 1581, was unobjectionable. Ibid., 452–53.

and for the party. As king of France, his first task was to impose his own authority and not, any longer, to promote the Protestant cause before all others. By the accession of their protector, the "Protestant state" was merged—as Henry quickly pointed out—in the royal State of France.[5] As the king, he was bound to oppose the existence of a second state within his own, potentially no less menacing than the rebellious Catholic League. He was equally bound to deny that there was any need for guarantees and capitulations. The protection of the king of France was, in theory, all that the Protestants could desire. But, so long as his royal authority remained in abeyance through the perpetuation of civil war, they were deprived of their former guarantees, under the edicts of pacification, without obtaining alternative protection or a clearly-defined juridical status. Because their long-awaited acceptance into society was a juridical and administrative problem, entirely dependent on the hitherto failing power of the crown, it could not, by its very nature, be solved during the course of a civil war in which the king was deeply engaged against precisely those intensely hostile Catholics who were determined not to tolerate their Protestant opponents. The problem was exacerbated because Henry IV came near to defeat. The Protestants were consequently required to wait for nine long years during which their patience and hope expired. Meanwhile their worsening plight was exploited by the unscrupulous extremists who claimed to be their leaders but who could—had they not been more concerned with their own ambitions—have assisted the king to a speedier victory and an earlier settlement for the Protestants.

Henry's predominant need to impose his authority and to gain the submission of the Catholic League and the obedience of the *parlements* inevitably suggested the probability of his abjuration, a factor which greatly complicated his relations with the Protestants at the time of his accession. These relations, which had never really been harmonious, had recently been strained to the point of conflict.

When Navarre became "protector" in 1576, he was the most

5. Duplessis-Mornay, *Mémoires et correspondance*, iv, 428, 7 November 1589, Henry to Duplessis-Mornay; Anquez, *Histoire des assemblées*, 52.

distinguished leader the Protestants could have, but his advent was not, even so, without opposition. As first prince of the blood, and therefore associated with the crown, Navarre—together with the prince de Condé and the comte de Soissons—was considered suspect. He could not be expected to endorse the advanced republican notions of those *seigneurs* who lived by the "Protestant state," or to approve their fractious jockeying for power and precedence.[6] In 1581 the relations between the "protector" and the churches were further defined by a *règlement* which gave expression to a certain distrust inspired by Navarre's past changes of religion.[7] There was a strong tendency to resist his authority, and his powers were curbed by a council of four, possibly at the instigation of a few *seigneurs* who, since the massacre, had become influential in the party. The most important of these was the comte de Turenne, better known as the duc de Bouillon, who was seconded by his kinsman, the young Claude de La Trémoille.[8] The princes apart, Turenne, for rank, ability and wealth was, perhaps, the Protestants' most obvious leader, and he was skillful and ruthless in promoting his own interests. He had been in the service of the duc d'Alençon[9]—a regrettable training for any young man—and became a kind of professional *malcontent*, such as the civil wars produced, who readily embraced whatever project of the moment offered the maximum hope of profit. He was by no means always precisely in opposition, but nevertheless vouchsafed, at best, a kind of negative cooperation, constantly prepared to withdraw his service or otherwise betray a cause. "J'avisay," he wrote in his memoirs, "en servant le public, de

6. Anquez, *Histoire des assemblées*, 50. There was clearly a considerable—albeit unidentified—group of extremists.

7. Ibid., 31–32. Brought up a Protestant, Navarre was forced to abjure at the time of the massacre and returned to his original faith on his escape in 1576.

8. Henri de la Tour d'Auvergne, vicomte de Turenne, duc de Bouillon 1591, marshal 1592. Claude duc de La Trémoille, duc de Thouars, brother-in-law of Henri prince de Condé. Bouillon (secondly) and La Trémoille married the sisters Elizabeth and Charlotte, daughters of William the Silent.

9. François duc d'Alençon, younger brother of Henry III; duc d'Anjou 1576.

servir à mon particulier."[10] He brought to his exploits the scrupulous care required of his unscrupulous conduct, seldom committing himself on paper and speaking in terms of prevarications, "d'une manière si obscure et si embarrassée qu'il y pouvoit donner le sens qui lui plaisoit."[11] Turenne's influence was therefore to be reckoned with, and Henry, according to his way, sought to attach him to his service by giving him honorable employment.[12] In spite of this, for about twenty years Turenne remained one of his most dangerous enemies.[13]

The dangers which beset the Protestants with the renewal of war in 1585 found the party gravely divided. This was largely because of the jealous rivalry between the leaders, who were primarily concerned with their own power and influence or, as Turenne said, their "particulier."[14] The prince de Condé was inordinately jealous of Navarre's position as protector, which he had previously held himself, and his brother the comte de Soissons—who was refused the hand of Navarre's sister, Catherine—quit his service in 1588.[15] This disharmony among the princes was fostered by Turenne and by his supporter, La Trémoille. Turenne's prospects in the party and his bid for leadership became a personal contest between himself and Navarre. This was a result of the death of Turenne's rivals, Bouillon and Condé. The duc de Bouillon—whose sister and heiress Turenne was to marry—died in January 1588. Condé died the following

10. Petitot, série i, vol. xxxv, *Mémoires du duc de Bouillon*, 216; Ouvré, *Aubéry du Maurier*, 26.

11. Marsollier, *Bouillon*, 217–18.

12. Henry made Turenne his lieutenant in Guyenne, later *gouverneur* of Languedoc and, just before the outbreak of war with the League, in December 1584, honored him personally with the post of first gentleman of his chamber. Marsollier, *Bouillon*, 208–9; Ouvré, *Aubéry du Maurier*, 25–26.

13. He later took part in the Biron and other conspiracies and only submitted in 1606, when he was pardoned, after the king had laid siege to his town of Sedan.

14. Ouvré, *Aubéry du Maurier*, 26–27; Michaud, série ii, vol. ii, Sully, *Oeconomies royales*, i, 60, seq.

15. Michaud, série ii, vol. ii, Sully, *Oeconomies royales*, i, 64–66. Condé and Soissons were first cousins of Navarre.

March.[16] About this time, La Trémoille was inciting Turenne to assert himself and seize absolute power in the Protestant-controlled provinces of Anjou, Poitou, Aunis, Saintonge and Angoumois.[17] In other words, Turenne and La Trémoille sought to divide the party and dismember the State in order to establish themselves independently in the west of France. Turenne was not only agreeable to the proposal, but also considered mastering all the strong places in the Limousin and Périgord, where some of his estates were situated.[18]

Thus, at this time of crisis in 1588, when the survival of Protestantism was at stake and Henry's right to the succession was contested, the Protestant party, which should have united in self-defense, was threatened with disintegration. It was in an effort to remedy this desperate situation that Henry summoned an assembly to La Rochelle in December.[19] He was immediately faced with a barrage of opposition and his relative lack of authority was all too apparent. Already, after the battle of Coutras against a royal army in October 1587, he had been attacked for his allegedly negligent conduct of the war, and accused of being more heir to the throne than protector of the churches. This was a meaningless distinction, albeit reflecting the truth that—religion apart—Navarre had more in common with the king than with the turbulent nobility by whom they were both threatened.[20] Now, in the assembly, Navarre was also reproached by the *consistoriaux*, who were apt to invite him to reform his morals; and he was also accused of afflicting the party with his "tyrannie protectorale."

16. Condé was allegedly poisoned by his wife, Charlotte-Catherine de La Trémoille, sister of Claude. Her son, Henri II de Condé, became heir apparent to Navarre, but his legitimacy was disputed.

17. These areas belonged to three Protestant provinces at this date, but were united in June 1594. D'Aubigné, *Histoire universelle*, ix, 87, 98.

18. Michaud, série ii, vol. ii, Sully, *Oeconomies royales*, i, 64. Sully made the point, ibid., 636, that Turenne was no different from the nobles of the League who coveted independent provinces.

19. Henry was there from 8 to 22 December 1588; Berger de Xivrey, *Lettres de Henri IV*, vol. ii, 611.

20. This is thoroughly attested, but see, for example, Duplessis-Mornay, *Mémoires et correspondance*, iii, 141–45, July 1585, Navarre to the king; Ouvré, *Aubéry du Maurier*, 27.

On these grounds, the Huguenot provinces[21] threatened to choose their own leaders, or to provide the party with a different protector. As a result, Navarre had to submit to the increase of his "conseil de surveillance" from four members to ten.[22] Afterwards, returning to the field of battle with evident relief, he commented: ". . . vraiment, s'il se faisoit encore une assemblée, je deviendrois fou."[23] Not only had Turenne—according to Sully[24]—"noué ces intrigues,"[25] but he also came clean out, on this occasion, with his bid for absolute power in certain western provinces.[26] His future secretary, Aubéry du Maurier, recorded that a permanent rupture occurred between Turenne and Philippe Duplessis-Mornay,[27] Navarre's own right hand, on account of "various things" and because they had "des fins bien dissemblables." Thereafter, their necessary relations were confined to those "à la mode de la cour, c'est-à-dire fort superficielle."[28]

The nature and extent of Turenne's provincial backing is, unfortunately, one of the really important unknown factors. It is clear that the extremists mostly came from the western provinces[29] where, incidentally, La Trémoille was established. But

---

21. Ouvré, *Aubéry du Maurier*, 28, mentions eighteen Protestant provinces at this time. In June 1584, there were only ten. D'Aubigné, *Histoire universelle*, ix, 87, 88.

22. Ouvré, *Aubéry du Maurier*, 28; Anquez, *Histoire des assemblées*, 41.

23. Berger de Xivrey, *Lettres de Henri IV*, vol. ii, 411-12, 22 December 1588, Henry to Madame de Gramont.

24. Maximilien de Béthune, marquis de Rosny, duc de Sully 1606. His better-known title is used for the sake of clarity.

25. Ouvré, *Aubéry du Maurier*, 28.

26. Michaud, série ii, vol. ii, Sully *Oeconomies royales*, i, 64, 66–67; Henry, however, later referred to what had been "brassoit soubs main" on this occasion; Duplessis-Mornay, *Mémoires et correspondance*, iv, 427, 7 November 1589; ibid., i, *Mémoires de madame Duplessis-Mornay*, 166 and n. 1; Anquez, *Histoire des assemblées*, 38-51.

27. Philippe Duplessis-Marly, *dit* Duplessis-Mornay, 1549-1623, *gouverneur* of Saumur; entered Navarre's service in 1576.

28. Ouvré, *Aubéry du Maurier*, 28.

29. Some of these provinces were particularly exposed to *leagueur* incursions from Brittany.

we know nothing of Turenne's relations with the local nobility or with the agencies through which he elicited sufficient support to challenge not only the king of Navarre but subsequently also the king of France. At the time of Henry's accession, Turenne was away on his estates, "retenu... par le dépit autant que par les suites d'une blessure."[30] The inference was that he had disapproved and declined to support the truce, known as the "traité de la trève,"[31] concluded in April 1589 between Navarre and Henry III in order to join forces against their common enemy, the Catholic League. This truce had only served to enhance the impression of those who chose to see things that way, that Navarre was more interested in the crown than in the Protestant churches. Immediately after Navarre's accession, Duplessis penned one of his eloquent appeals, imploring Turenne to conduct his forces to the king's assistance: "... il est necessaire que chacung mette la main à cette couronne d'espines, si on veult qu'elle se tourne en fleurs de lis," he wrote felicitously.[32] But the truth was that Turenne preferred the thorns, and witheld his services until the end of August 1590, when he joined the king with 1,000 horse and 4,000 foot.[33]

It is impossible to establish—either in 1588 or later on—the precise nature or extent of Henry's relations with the moderate majority of the Protestant party. Their interests now appear to have been periodically submerged by the power and influence of this largely unidentified group of extremists, whenever the general situation was amenable to exploitation. Henry himself frequently referred to the existence of this faction and alleged as early as November 1589, that these extremists were trying to separate him from "ceulx avec lesquels j'ai si longuement conversé." He himself sought to remain in touch with the churches

30. Ouvré, *Aubéry du Maurier*, 29.
31. Duplessis-Mornay, *Mémoires et correspondance*, iv, 351–55, 3 April 1589.
32. Ibid., 402, 18 August 1589, Duplessis-Mornay to Turenne. He also did his best to restrain La Trémoille; ibid., 442–43, 23 December 1589.
33. Ouvré, *Aubéry du Maurier*, 29.

and the rest of the party, particularly through the services of his moderate and statesmanlike supporter, Duplessis-Mornay, who, from 1589 to 1598 performed the office of honest broker.[34]

These difficult relations between Navarre and the Protestants did nothing to ease his sudden transition from protector to king, and nothing to allay their suspicions, calm their fears, or remove the demoralizing sense of insecurity arising from the extreme confusion of their position, both juridical and actual. The edicts of pacification had been revoked by those of July 1585 and July 1588. In the face of these edicts of annihilation, the "traité de la trève," arranged between the two Henrys in April 1589, represented an appreciable improvement. During the year for which the truce was to run, from 3 April "toutes choses demeureront es lieux teneus d'une part et d'aultre, en l'estat qu'elles sont à present."[35] Thus the status quo, which was the result of war, was legalized, though probably no one ever knew precisely what this meant in civil, military or religious terms. Navarre was authorized to retain, for his own purposes, and in trust for the repayment of his expenses, one recaptured town in each *bailliage* or *sénéchaussée*, and the Protestants were so far recognized as to be restored to the enjoyment of their property. This much was signed by the king and a secretary, but underneath appears the phrase "oultre ce dessus, feut conveneu à part," followed by more specific concessions. The Protestants were not to be persecuted; the cult might be publicly celebrated in the army, wherever Navarre happened to be, and in each of the towns which he was permitted to retain.

It is not clear what happened to this document or how widely it was publicized, with or without its appendage. But Henry III, in his embarrassment, drafted a second document, entitled "lettres d'armistice avec le Roi de Navarre comme chef huguenot," which was registered by the *parlement* of Paris, then at Tours, on 26 April 1589. This document was fanatically Catholic in tone and represented the truce—which it defended on the grounds of the

34. Duplessis-Mornay, *Mémoires et correspondance*, iv, 426–30, 7 November 1589, Henry to Duplessis-Mornay.
35. Ibid., 351.

illicit and offensive activities of the League—as a means of arresting Protestant progress. This pernicious custom of drafting different versions of the same law, greatly contributed to the juridical and administrative chaos which underlay much of the trouble of this period.[36]

When Henry IV came to the throne, therefore, he himself was legally barred from the succession, and the Protestants were legally subjected to the terms of the two repressive Catholic edicts, duly registered by the *parlements*. On the other hand, the existence of the Protestants—though not their right to exist, except as good Catholics—had been implicitly recognized by the "lettres d'armistice," and their property had, technically, been restored. Although the terms of the Catholic edicts were, to some extent, remitted by those of the "traité de la trève," concluded on the king's incontestable authority, these terms were certainly unknown to the majority of Catholic France. Nor did the truce come within the cognizance of the *parlements*, for which the Catholic edicts alone were valid.

Thus, from the beginning of Henry's reign, the legislative position of the Protestants was chaotic and their actual position unfavorable. They appear to have expected—with a total disregard for the exigencies of war and politics—that Henry would forthwith convert the truce into an advantageous treaty and resolve the existing confusion. They were therefore alarmed and dismayed when, on 4 August 1589, he signed a declaration[37] which, in fact, was imposed on him by the Catholics of the royal camp.[38] Their loyalty and support were indispensable if he were not to be

36. Appended clauses enabled the crown and the beneficiaries to claim that they existed, and equally enabled hostile officials to ignore them. Furthermore, such clauses were frequently, if not always, secret, and it is impossible to say whether those responsible for their execution were ever informed of their existence.

37. Isambert, *Recueil général*, xv, 3–5, 4 August 1589; de Thou, *Histoire universelle*, xi, *livre* xcvii.

38. "... après plusieurs contestations." They were mostly royal officials and Henry did this to retain their obedience and "l'estat tout ensemble." Duplessis-Mornay, *Mémoires et correspondance*, iv, 427, 7 November 1589, Henry to Duplessis-Mornay.

forthwith seized and disarmed.[39] This curious document, which was either very subtle or very badly worded, would appear to mean virtually nothing more than the maintenance, for six months, of the status quo including, in fact, concessions to the Protestants, embodied in the "traité de la trève." But, as the declaration was intended to reassure the new king's Catholic entourage, its superficially Catholic bias made the Protestants afraid that Henry would neither protect the cult nor restore their eligibility to public offices, of which they expected a goodly share at his hands. They consistently saw this claim not only as intrinsically desirable, but also as one of the best means of protecting their interests in the country. Worse still, they feared that Henry was already preparing to become a Catholic, because of an evasively worded clause by which he undertook to receive instruction from a "bon légitime et libre concile général et national pour en suivre et observer ce qui y en sera conclu et arrêté."[40]

The reaction of the "Protestant state" was swift and hostile. Early in September, a month after Henry's accession, they promptly held a synod at Saint-Jean-d'Angély, which condemned the declaration as contrary to the honor of God and the reputation of his majesty, and threatened to elect a new protector.[41] Henry censured this initiative and blamed it on "des malcontents qui se servent de tous les artifices qu'ils peuvent," and declared that those who had been plotting in the assembly at La Rochelle in 1588 now saw an occasion "tout à propos" for the realization of their designs.[42] He therefore appealed to Duplessis-Mornay to represent the immediate difficulties of his position to the "gens de

39. Navarre was in the field at Saint-Cloud at the time of Henry's murder and not in a position to withstand the combination of royalist Catholics with those of the League. Many persons of both religions deserted him at this time, including Épernon. Patry, *Duplessis-Mornay*, 179, n. 34.

40. Isambert, *Recueil général*, xv, 3.

41. Patry, *Duplessis-Mornay*, 183, and n. 49, procès verbal 12 September 1589; Duplessis-Mornay, *Mémoires et correspondance*, iv, 426–30, 7 November 1589, Henry to Duplessis-Mornay; Anquez, *Histoire des assemblées*, 51–52; Léonard, *Histoire générale du protestantisme*, ii, 139.

42. Duplessis-Mornay, *Mémoires et correspondance*, iv, 427. There is no precise mention of Turenne, but the reference appears to be to him.

bien," who would believe him.[43] He had been constantly detained in the field without leisure to attend to civil matters and was therefore incensed against these exigent troublemakers "qui ne voyent ni considerent mes actions, qui vouldroient que je bandasse l'arc de mes affaires à la corde de leur passions, ou bien que je leur rendisse compte de mes conseils, et qui vouldroient encore me donner loi en ce qui despend de l'administration"—an excellent summary of the king's point of view.[44]

It appears that in deference to the king's wishes, the "Protestant state" was partially disbanded at this time, and the Huguenots did begin to wait, without active opposition, for what they held to be their rights. Thus the struggle for the edict might not have developed had not the length of the war with the League—during which the Protestants suffered increasingly from the implacable hatred of the *parlements*—and the abjuration crisis together rendered it inevitable.

An intermediate crisis occurred, however, before the king's abjuration, in the summer of 1591, when, after eighteen months of strenuous campaigning, it was clear that Henry had little hope of conquering the Catholic League, now strongly supported by Spain and the pope.[45] One result of pressure from the League was that Henry had to issue certain letters patent of 4 July 1591, which included a reaffirmation of the desire expressed in the declaration of 1589, for a "saint et libre concile, ou quelque assemblée notable" for the settlement of religion, and for his own instruction. Both documents were interpreted as an expression of his willingness to abjure, even though their virtually meaningless

43. Duplessis-Mornay proposed to assemble "les principaux des Eglises," but Henry was too busy with war to attend to this advice. Patry, *Duplessis-Mornay*, 184.

44. Duplessis-Mornay, *Mémoires et correspondance*, iv, 430, 7 November 1589, Henry to Duplessis.

45. Henry began by campaigning in Normandy and in the region of Paris: May–August 1590, the unsuccessful siege of Paris; February–April 1591, the siege and capture of Chartres. On 12 February 1591 a Spanish garrison entered Paris. About this time the League began to discuss who to elect as a Catholic king. Poirson, *Histoire du règne de Henry IV*, i, *livre* ii, ch. iii recounts the king's relations with the pope, Gregory XIV.

wording provided for the pious hope or diplomatic fiction of religious agreement and reconciliation.[46] If this declaration had produced a menacing Protestant reaction in 1589, it was certain to be even more dangerous in 1591. Henry therefore wasted no time in forcing through the council the edict of Mantes, revoking those of 1585 and 1588 and reenacting the edicts of pacification. This concession, though basically reasonable and as much as the king could possibly attempt, did not satisfy the Protestants, initially because the Edict of Mantes was only registered by the *parlements* of Paris and Rouen so that, over large areas, and particularly in the strongly Protestant south and west, the *leagueur* edicts remained in force.[47] This was the measure of the king's inability to coerce the *parlements*, which defiantly obstructed the execution of the law and his declared intentions in relation to the Protestants. Thus the quarrel, at least of the moderate Protestants, was far more with the *parlements* and other Catholic officials who defied his authority, than it was with the king himself. But, if their rejection of the edict of Mantes was originally based on its nonexecution, the Protestants generally, of whatever complexion, were soon asserting the right to better conditions than those imposed by Henry III, and supporting a claim to guarantees against the malice of their adversaries.

It was not, however, until two years later, in the summer of 1593, when the king's abjuration appeared to be imminent, that the Protestants showed any signs of activity. Then Turenne—or the duc de Bouillon as he had become in 1591—employed his influence to avert this seeming catastrophe. After their estrangement at the assembly of La Rochelle in 1588, Bouillon had even-

---

46. A few moderate souls, including Duplessis-Mornay, would have liked to promote this, within an established, Gallican framework, perhaps because they saw in it a hope of reconciliation between the Protestants and the *parlements*, several of which resisted the pope's attacks on the king. The *parlement* of Paris declared his condemnatory bulls null and void, and ordered the arrest of the nuncio. Isambert, *Recueil général*, xv, 27–28, 5 August 1591.

47. The registration was with reservations. Duplessis-Mornay, *Mémoires et correspondance*, vii, *Discours*, 276–77; Faurey, *Henri IV et l'édit de Nantes*, 14.

tually rejoined the king at the end of the siege of Paris in August 1590; thereafter Henry did his best to retain the duke in his service.[48] But Bouillon was never satisfied and is said to have become "fort pressant et assez peu respectueux"[49] at the time of the conference of Suresnes, between the loyal Catholics and the League.[50] He was then among those who insisted that Henry should impose a declaration on his commissioners, undertaking not to conclude anything contrary to the edicts of pacification or to the prejudice of the Protestant cause, before the meeting of an assembly, to be summoned at Mantes for 20 July. This was a maneuver by which the Protestants played for time in order to bring contrary pressures to bear on the king.[51]

The summonses for this assembly at Mantes, which proved to be the first of seven Protestant assemblies, were sent out forthwith, late in May 1593, when the king's abjuration was in the air but not publicly determined.[52] Bishops and pastors were invited, among others, presumably to give the impression of preparing for a national council, and Duplessis-Mornay, not wanting to be caught unawares, sought to arrange for the attendance of ambassadors and deputies from friendly Protestant countries, accom-

48. In October 1591, Henry married Turenne to Charlotte de La Mark, in whose right he received the dukedom of Bouillon, as well as the principalities of Sedan, Jametz and Raucourt, and a sizeable income. In March 1592 he became a marshal of France, but he quarreled, nonetheless, with other commanders. Ouvré, *Aubéry du Maurier*, 29–30; Duplessis-Mornay, *Mémoires et correspondance*, v, 262, 30 March 1592.

49. Ouvré, *Aubéry du Maurier*, 34–35.

50. This conference opened on 29 April 1593.

51. Isambert, *Recueil général*, xv, 65, and n. 1, 18 May 1593; Ouvré, *Aubéry du Maurier*, 35; de Thou, *Histoire universelle*, xi, livre cvi.

52. In the middle of June the king sent one Vicose to Guyenne, and Beauchamp to Languedoc and Dauphiné, apparently with letters addressed to Protestant notables summoning them "pour adviser à l'etablissement des affaires, et nommement au contentement de ceulx de la religion." Other provinces were also contacted and, according to d'Aubigné, the envoys conducted a propaganda campaign, "la cadence de toutes choses tombant tousjours à destruire parmi les réformez tout ordre et police différent de l'estat." Duplessis-Mornay, *Mémoires et correspondance*, v, 451, 9 June 1593; 455–56 [June 1593]; 457, 14 June 1593; d'Aubigné, *Histoire universelle*, ix, 80–81.

panied by skilled theologians against the eventuality of a learned disputation.[53] Nevertheless, he did not believe that this was what the king intended, but rather that he summoned ministers from each province "pour asseurer du desir qu'il continuera à conserver les Eglises, afin qu'à leur retour ils en puissent emporter asseurance aulx peuples."[54] Even if the assembly were not to be a council, Duplessis-Mornay still hoped that it might serve to clarify the position of the Protestants, "qui a tousjours flotté depuis son avènement."[55] He therefore ensured that the deputies came well instructed and provided some with a suitable memoir advising them to press for certain specific points relating to religion, justice and security.[56] They were to seek greater facilities for the celebration of the cult, especially in the armies and at court,[57] the establishment of special *chambres de justice* permitted by the edicts of pacification, and the admission of Protestants to a proportion of public offices. As for their security, the deputies were to request the provision of properly paid garrisons because Catholic officials undermined their position by intercepting the money for them. Finally, they were to call for the payment of ministers from public funds specifically assigned for the purpose, a requirement which, from first to last, was one of the most explosive of all the Protestant demands. These were the principal points upon which the Protestants sought a "règlement certain et asseuré."[58] While these arrangements were under way—for 20 July had never been a realistic date—without awaiting those he had supposedly summoned to advise him, Henry was swiftly instructed by the bishops, and abjured at Saint-Denis on 25 July 1593.[59] By means of this "saut périlleux," Henry could hope first

53. Duplessis-Mornay, *Mémoires et correspondance*, v, 458–59, 18 June 1593.

54. Ibid., 450, 9 June 1593; 455 [June 1593].

55. Ibid., 457–58, 14 June 1593.

56. Ibid., 450–53, 9 June 1593, "mémoire envoyé par M. de Vicose."

57. These were two of the concessions in the "traité de la trève" which were not being enforced.

58. Duplessis-Mornay, *Mémoires et correspondance*, v, 458, 14 June 1593. All these demands were eventually included in the edict of Nantes.

59. Henry announced his abjuration to the pope, and also his inten-

to divide and then to destroy his enemies, who were only united in a negative purpose through a temporary conjunction of dissimilar interests. They were, therefore, predictably incapable of constructive agreement on the election of a Catholic king. Five days after his abjuration, Henry concluded a truce with the League.

The manner and timing of the king's abjuration—for which he had compelling, if not pious, reasons—came as a terrible shock to the Protestants. After four years of reasonable patience, and just as they were about to be consulted, it seemed like a deliberate betrayal and very ominous for the future.[60] Protestant confidence in the king's intentions was always an unstable factor, but the basic, overriding fear was of the degree of control which the forces of Catholicism might succeed in establishing over the king, whether through successful persuasion or by gradual coercion against his will. Although sometimes clothed in irrational argument,[61] this was, at the start, a valid fear, and found expression in such phrases as "le monopole du roi," or "les maulvais desseigns de ceulx qui vous possedent."[62] This "possession" took the form, among others, of surrounding Henry with Catholic officials and advisers, thereby ousting the Protestants from positions of influence and, above all, from proximity to his person.

After the abjuration, the Protestants were particularly concerned about the king's desire for papal absolution, which, it was claimed, would only be granted on conditions certain to be damaging to the Protestants. Similarly, they were afraid that an extension of the truce into peace with the League would only be conceded at their expense, recalling the "traité de l'union" in

---

tion of sending a solemn embassy to the Holy See on 9 August 1593. Berger de Xivrey, *Lettres de Henri IV*, vol. iv, 10–11, 11–12. The duc de Nevers was later sent to Rome to seek the king's absolution. He arrived on 21 November 1593 and had five audiences between then and 10 January 1594. Poirson, *Histoire du règne de Henry IV*, i, 564, 566.

60. For Duplessis-Mornay's reactions see Duplessis-Mornay, *Mémoires et correspondance*, v, 510–11, 11 August 1593; 512, 11 August 1593. He was deeply grieved and did not even believe in the political wisdom of the abjuration.

61. Ibid., 535–44 [September 1593], Duplessis-Mornay to the king.

62. Ibid., 485, 500, 528, 535–44.

1588, which was forced on Henry III by the duc de Guise. They were also alarmed by the publication by the League of the decrees of the council of Trent,[63] and by the implications, for a Catholic king, of the coronation oath enjoining the extirpation of heresy.

The desire, however, for an edict "certain et asseuré," as Duplessis had said, prevailed among the Protestants for a few years after the abjuration, and in their first three assemblies of Mantes, Sainte-Foy and Saumur. There were signs, however, of growing exasperation, and, in the provinces, there was evidently an increasing amount of extremist activity. The failure of the assemblies to obtain satisfaction gradually exposed them to more extreme influences which, in turn, exposed the whole movement to exploitation by the nobility. Already, in 1593, the provincial situation had become alarming.[64] The Protestants, Duplessis wrote to the king, had been told to wait until the times were more propitious, "et le temps est perdu. Les affaires sont pourris en meurissant. Cependant ne peuvent vous celer que les esprits sont agités, passent de l'espoir du bien à l'attente du mal; de la longue et inutile patience en la recherche du remede. Et vous sire, nous le savons bien, n'en estes sans allarme; vous ne prendrés plaisir de voir un protecteur; vous seriés jaloux s'ils s'adressoient ailleurs qu'à vous."[65] Yet, his abjuration now accomplished, the king was disinclined to face an assembly. The original summons had been withdrawn and Bouillon, for one, advised him against it.[66] But Duplessis had taken the matter in hand; he was determined to see it through, and, if possible, with Bouillon's help.[67] To dismiss the deputies at such a juncture would be to reject their cooperation, greatly increase their sense of grievance, and encourage extremist agitation. An assembly, on the other hand, would offer hope of

63. Ibid., 562, 18 September 1593.
64. D'Aubigné, *Histoire universelle*, ix, 83–84, gives an interesting account of Protestant activity in Poitou.
65. Duplessis-Mornay, *Mémoires et correspondance*, v, 535–44 [September 1593], Duplessis to the king.
66. Ibid., 558, 14 September 1593, Montigny to Duplessis.
67. Ibid., 560–64, 18 September 1593, Duplessis-Mornay to Bouillon. He gave Bouillon a skillfully adapted version of his reasons for insisting on holding an assembly.

legal redress, provide a focus for Protestant attention, serve to reunite the churches, and contain their activity within proper limits.

Duplessis-Mornay won his point, and the deputies assembled at Mantes on 8 October 1593, although the king was called away to the field in Normandy and did not see them until 12 December.[68] The assembly of Mantes clearly illustrates the king's position and his attitude towards the Protestants. The commission appointed to examine the *cahiers* informed the deputies that although their contents were intrinsically reasonable, they were hopelessly inopportune, but that "lors que sa Majeste seroit mieux establie et obeye elle pourvoirroit mieux et plus amplement a ceulx de la Religion."[69] Meanwhile they must rest content with the edicts of pacification, together with certain amplifications. The basis of discussion was thereby shifted from the *cahiers* to the edicts. The deputies protested, and, as a result, certain verbal concessions were read out to only three of them, which they memorized as best they could or noted down "en leurs tablettes."[70] These concessions, conceived as a series of secret articles or a "règlement provisionnel," in fact constituted a draft edict of considerable liberality which went far towards meeting the Protestant demands. It also offered an assurance that neither the coronation oath nor anything else would oblige the king to make war on them. But the draft was retained by the chancellor Bellièvre, and the secretaries of state "pour se regler selon iceluy les expeditions." The king was to instruct the *gouverneurs* and other royal officials to act according to its terms,[71] but nothing was given to

68. While they were waiting they prepared their *cahiers*, one general, comprising at least ninety-eight articles, and one particular. B. N., Mss. N. A. F., 7191, ff. 170v-74; Duplessis-Mornay, *Mémoires et correspondance*, v, 561; ibid., i, *Mémoires de madame Duplessis-Mornay*, 262-63; Anquez, *Histoire des assemblées*, 58-59.

69. Six deputies were named to work with the commission. B. N., Mss. N. A. F., 7191, ff. 174v-76; Duplessis-Mornay, *Mémoires et correspondance*, vii, *Discours*, 280.

70. B. N., Mss. N. A. F., 7191, ff. 177v-79v; Duplessis-Mornay, *Mémoires et correspondance*, vii, *Discours*, 281.

71. Duplessis-Mornay, *Mémoires et correspondance*, i, *Mémoires de madame Duplessis-Mornay*, 265-67, 288, records the articles.

the deputies in writing, "pour ne scandaliser ... le roy vers ceulx de la Ligue."[72] He was awaiting news from Rome, and the submission of the League had just begun with the city of Meaux on Christmas day.[73]

The king had done his best to make it clear that he would suffer the Protestants to do what they liked and to hold what they could, provided they acted discreetly, and it was reasonable that he should have regarded the articles as a substantial token of good will for the future, since he was thereby committed. The Protestants, however, regarded them as useless, since there was no means of ensuring their execution. Their state of mind rendered them unable or unwilling to appreciate that this was basically the king's own point: he would make no new laws unless or until he could enforce them. Beyond this, he was never prepared to go, until, in July 1597, he was forced, under duress, to accept certain concessions made in his name. Even so, by an odd blend of management and circumstance, there was no question of their completion or implementation until peace had been restored at home and abroad. The assembly expressed its dissatisfaction in remonstrances to the king, without either accepting or rejecting the articles.[74] These they resolved to enforce wherever they could and, meanwhile, to report home to the provinces. Before dispersing, about 23 January, they obtained permission to hold provincial assemblies, a national synod and another general assembly, which was to meet at Sainte-Foy in five or six months' time.[75] Finally, in the very proximity of the court, they solemnly renewed their oath of union and, apparently, also took other steps "pour entretenir les intelligences entre les églises réformées."[76]

72. Ibid., vii, *Discours*, 281.

73. Berger de Xivrey, *Lettres de Henri IV*, vol. iv, introd., p. vi.

74. B. N., Mss. N. A. F., 7191, ff. 179v-91v; Duplessis-Mornay, *Mémoires et correspondance*, i, *Mémoires de madame Duplessis-Mornay*, 267; ibid., vii, *Discours*, 281.

75. Sainte-Foy, Lot-et-Garonne. Duplessis-Mornay, *Mémoires et correspondance*, vii, *Discours*, 282, says 15 July, which may be an error for June. D'Aubigné, *Histoire universelle*, ix, 85, gives mid-May as the original date. The deputies did not usually arrive all at once, but at least a quorum assembled in June. Ibid., ix, 98.

76. This is indicated in article 27 of the assembly of Sainte-Foy; d'Aubigné, *Histoire universelle*, ix, 95; B. N., Mss. N. A. F., 7191, f.

It therefore already appeared inevitable that the "Protestant state" would be revived; this was done by the assembly of Sainte-Foy. If Mantes had, in a sense, been little more than a large deputation, meeting under the eye of the court, Sainte-Foy, far away in the Protestant south, rather recalled the defensive gatherings which harassed the reign of Henry III. The assembly, composed of some thirty deputies, met in June 1594 and at once received a collection of complaints about the "fascheuse condition" of the Protestants in the provinces, many of whom were very restive.[77] "Il n'y a pas peu de peine," Duplessis had already reported in February, "à retenir nos hommes impatiens de souffrir ce dur traictement soubs celui qui a este leur protecteur."[78] Their continued insecurity induced a fractious attitude to the king and to the edicts, which they began to condemn as insufficient. The Huguenots were dissatisfied partly because the edicts pertained to the previous reign, and partly because they were resisted by the *parlements*. Furthermore, the religious clauses had been partially abrogated by the terms of the various *leagueur* edicts, granted to towns and prominent members as they made their submission.[79] This represented a new problem, which had to be resolved in the edict of Nantes. The assembly, at first uncertain what course to take, received three memoirs containing suggestions, and it may have been one of these which proposed the election of a new protector, a plan allegedly promoted by Bouillon, whose candidate was the elector Palatine, to be assisted by several French lieutenants.[80]

181v; Anquez, *Histoire des assemblées*, 58; Duplessis-Mornay, *Mémoires et correspondance*, vii, *Discours*, 281–82; ibid., i, *Mémoires de madame Duplessis-Mornay*, 268.

77. D'Aubigné, *Histoire universelle*, ix, 85; Anquez, *Histoire des assemblées*, 61.

78. Duplessis-Mornay, *Mémoires et correspondance*, vi, 10, 19 February 1594.

79. The towns of Meaux, Lyons, Orléans, Bourges, Rouen, Troyes, Rions and Abbéville had submitted. In March 1594, the king entered Paris and the comte de Brissac submitted. The ducs de Guise and Lorraine submitted later in the year. Ibid., 67; Berger de Xivrey, *Lettres de Henri IV*, vol. iv, introd., p. vii.

80. Anquez, *Histoire des assemblées*, 61.

Bouillon himself was not present at Sainte-Foy. He had been at court at the time of the assembly at Mantes and had then gone to campaign in the region of Hainault, evidently under some sort of cloud, since Duplessis-Mornay twice made anxious inquiries as to the terms on which he had taken leave of the king.[81] He did not attend the coronation at Chartres in February 1594; he took no part in the recovery of Paris in March, and in April he was rumored to be "fort mal avec le roy."[82] In June, when the deputies were assembling at Sainte-Foy, Bouillon was embroiled in disputes over the inheritance of his wife, who had died in May, and made this a pretext to excuse his absence from the siege of Laon. Later, when the king agreed to his wishes in the matter of the inheritance, Bouillon joined him in the field, and in August followed him to Paris. This was partly to be received by the *parlement* as a marshal of France[83] and partly, perhaps, because he was seeking in marriage Elizabeth, daughter of William of Orange.[84] By this marriage, celebrated on 16 February 1595, Bouillon became a kinsman of Maurice of Nassau and Frederick, elector Palatine.[85]

It is therefore highly probable, if not actually proven, that Bouillon sought to associate the valuable foreign support of these princes with his own designs for the Protestant party. It appears, however, that the plan to revive the protectorate was thwarted in the assembly of Sainte-Foy by the opposition of the *consistoriaux*, who were still averse from "la tyrannie protectorale."[86] This refusal to accept a protector reveals the basic moderation of the *consistoriaux*, and the cleavage which existed between their objectives and those of the Protestant nobility. Because they remained in a majority, Bouillon never found in the Protestant party a

81. Duplessis-Mornay, *Mémoires et correspondance*, vi, 13, 27 February 1594; 17, 4 March 1594.

82. Ibid., 43–44, 4 April 1594.

83. Ibid., 92–93, 28 September 1594.

84. Elizabeth was in Paris at least by the end of September 1594. Ibid., 92–93.

85. Elizabeth was a half sister of Maurice of Nassau.

86. Anquez, *Histoire des assemblées*, 61; Benoist, *Histoire de l'édit de Nantes*, 123.

really suitable instrument for his purposes. But, if the assembly rejected the idea of a protector, it nevertheless desired the security of the former Protestant organization, which, after three weeks of "débats et d'oppositions,"[87] was reconstituted in twenty-eight articles and eight secret articles. The articles substituted corporate control for any form of presidency by providing for the holding of regular assemblies, once or twice a year, each announcing the time and place of the next. Thus the deputies agreed to meet again at Saumur, on the Loire, on 1 December 1594. Owing to the great importance they attached to the report to be delivered by the representatives they were sending to the king, it was decided to double the size of the assembly.[88] The *cahier* which they entrusted to two of their members, de Chouppes and Tixier,[89] was undoubtedly a moderate one, probably based partly on their articles and partly on a memoir prepared by Duplessis-Mornay and submitted through de Chouppes, one of the deputies for his province.[90] The memoir was strictly loyal and respectful and emphasized, in particular, the results of the refusal of the *parlements* to register the edicts—really the Protestants' most intractable problem[91]—the non-implementation of the king's

87. This was largely on the part of Languedoc, where conditions were said to be better. The Protestants of the Île-de-France had agreed to accept the edicts of pacification and were disavowed on this account by the synod of Montauban, June 1594. Thus, there were also divisions among the moderates. D'Aubigné, *Histoire universelle*, ix, 86; Faurey, *Henri IV et l'édit de Nantes*, 15.

88. Article 1, and the fourth secret article. D'Aubigné, *Histoire universelle*, ix, 87, 97.

89. Pierre de Chouppes, seigneur de Chouppes et Availles, *gouverneur* of Loudun, deputy for Anjou and the associated provinces. He was no hot-headed youngster, but an old man of sixty-three. Tixier represented Haut-Languedoc and Haute-Guyenne at the assembly of Loudun in 1596. Their instructions were dated 31 July 1594, B. N., Mss. N. A. F., 7191, f. 202v; Duplessis-Mornay, *Mémoires et correspondance*, i, *Mémoires de madame Duplessis-Mornay*, 279, mentions a third deputy, a minister called Feugueray.

90. Ibid., vi, 66–72, 11 June 1594.

91. This opposition constantly increased, and, in 1596 for example, the *parlement* of Aix imposed the death penalty for the exercise of the cult. Benoist, *Histoire de l'édit de Nantes*, i, 167.

will as expressed in his answers to the *cahier* of Mantes. Duplessis-Mornay stressed the importance of the articles relating to security, owing to the malign hatred of their enemies.

Thus, when the deputies de Chouppes and Tixier went to court on behalf of the assembly, they had the whole weight of the revived "Protestant state" behind them. The organization was purely defensive in intention, but the very fact of its existence naturally made the movement easier to exploit. There was evidently no lack of agitators anxious to do so, and Henry had been receiving written reports of disquieting rumors which led him to fear the occurrence of "quelque nouveauté."[92] He sent for Duplessis to discuss with him this and other matters, and it may have been one of the reasons why he sought to accommodate the duc de Bouillon and draw him back to his presence at the siege of Laon. Henry was detained at Laon from June to August,[93] and thereafter distracted by "une maladie si compliquee,"[94] so that it was not until the beginning of November, after three months of waiting, that the deputies were finally received at Saint-Germain.[95]

The king's mind was on other matters because, as Duplessis-Mornay wrote from Paris, "nous ne sommes pas sans affaires."[96] It was apparent that Spain, in conjunction with the duc de Mayenne—whose dispatches were intercepted—was planning a dangerous new offensive against the north of France and, in particular, an invasion of Picardy from the Netherlands. Henry, for his part, was contemplating a declaration of war. Bouillon was

92. Duplessis-Mornay wrote on 4 October 1594 that he had been in Paris for a month and that de Chouppes had arrived at the same time. Elsewhere he recorded that the deputies had to wait for three months. Duplessis-Mornay, *Mémoires et correspondance*, vi, 94, 4 October 1594; ibid., vii, *Discours*, 282–83; ibid., i, *Mémoires de madame Duplessis-Mornay*, 277.

93. Laon had capitulated by 24 July, but the king was there at least until 29 August. Ibid., vi, 81, 24 July 1594, Henry to Duplessis-Mornay; Berger de Xivrey, *Lettres de Henri IV*, vol. iv, 1032–33.

94. Duplessis-Mornay, *Mémoires et correspondance*, vi, 92, 28 September 1594. The king suffered from kidney, stomach and liver trouble.

95. Ibid., 99–100, 5 November 1594.

96. Ibid., 94, 4 October 1594; 96, 16 October 1594.

destined to command a mixed force of French and foreign troops to create a powerful diversion on the frontier, a plan described by Duplessis as "traversé de grandes envies," and he commented enigmatically, "j'espere que sa majesté en sera bien servie."[97] The defense of Brittany had also to be provided for, and the nobility of Languedoc, Dauphiné and Provence were at each others' throats. The duke of Savoy and the *leagueur* duc de Nemours also had large and menacing forces on the southeastern frontiers, where the king's personal presence was urgently required.[98] At the same time, the king was engaged in negotiating the submission of the duc de Lorraine, and the duc de Guise, who received the *gouvernement* of Provence in return for his services against the rebel duc d'Épernon.[99] "Voila," Duplessis-Mornay himself summed up the situation, "comme nous sommes tirés en diverses parts." Thus, while the king was bound to be concerned by any threat of further trouble from the Protestant south and west of France, especially if it involved the danger of treachery from Bouillon on the frontiers of Picardy, it is understandable that he should have regarded a petition for the redress of civil wrongs as a matter of secondary importance.[100] By the same token, however, the Protestants—or some of them—were becoming aware that only the threat of force could effectively compel the king's attention.

Henry still refused to break new ground with de Chouppes and Tixier, but, as a result of their mission, he undertook to have the edicts registered by all the *parlements* and the articles of Mantes enforced. For this reason, on 15 November 1594 he issued an

97. Ibid., 93, 28 September 1594; 94, 4 October 1594.

98. The king had been planning to go to Lyons at least since the beginning of August 1594, but appears not to have been able to move towards the east of France until the end of May 1595. Ibid., 85–86, 2 August 1594, Henry to Duplessis-Mornay; Berger de Xivrey, *Lettres de Henri IV*, vol. iv, 1039.

99. Lorraine and Guise submitted in November 1594. Épernon, in Provence, was also in league with Spain, but on his own account, seeking to possess the province himself.

100. On the state of public affairs see Duplessis-Mornay, *Mémoires et correspondance*, vi, 90–101, 28 September, 4, 16 October, 5 November 1594.

edict in the form of a declaration solemnly reaffirming the edicts of pacification in their entirety and "nonobstant... tous autres edits et declarations faictes depuis... qui y peuvent porter contrarieté invention ou d'ambiguité."[101] Five days later he sent for members of the *parlement* of Paris and subjected them to an eloquent harangue which, however, failed to produce the desired registration.[102] This was not finally obtained until 6 February 1595 and no other *parlement* followed suit. Nothing therefore had been achieved, and Duplessis commented that the year 1594 had passed uselessly.[103] According to the secretary Villeroy, the king attributed this evil disposition of the *parlement* to the workings of "les factieux" who sought to "bastir ung nouveau remuement sur le faict de la relligion," and he hoped that Duplessis-Mornay would prevail, in the forthcoming assembly, over deputies of this complexion.[104] The question of registration was important to the king because it might have reassured the Protestants and provided a modicum of security at home on the eve of his declaration of war with Spain.[105]

The declaration of war was a highly controversial decision, and

101. Fontanon, *Les Édits et ordonnances*, iv, 360. Henry was now wading in juridical confusion, since this invalidated certain aspects of the *leagueur* edicts, which themselves contravened the edicts of pacification.

102. La Grange, *Mémoires de La Force*, i, 253, 22 November 1594.

103. Even the declaration was registered with certain reservations. Compare the form of assent of the edict of Mantes, July 1591, with that of 15 November 1594. Fontanon, *Les Édits et ordonnances*, iv, 360. See also Petitot, série i, vol. xxxvii, J.-A. de Thou, *Mémoires*, 501; de Thou, *Histoire universelle*, xii, *livre* cxi; Duplessis-Mornay, *Mémoires et correspondance*, vii, *Discours*, 284. The *parlement* of Normandy registered the edict, with reservations, on 5 February 1597, which was too late to be of any use. Floquet, *Histoire du parlement de Normandie*, iv, 94–96.

104. Duplessis-Mornay, *Mémoires et correspondance*, vi, 126–28, 26 December 1594, Villeroy to Duplessis-Mornay. Duplessis-Mornay had already promised de Lomenie to do his best. Ibid., vi, 104–5, 6 December 1594.

105. Isambert, *Recueil général*, xv, 94–97, 16 January 1595, an extraordinarily interesting document on Franco-Spanish relations. Ouvré, *Aubéry du Maurier*, 40.

one which the duc de Bouillon strongly urged on the king.[106] Bouillon might have been influenced in this advice by his recent failure to reestablish the Protestant protectorate, or by the growing unrest in the provinces. He could also have been encouraged by his foreign kinsmen, or simply have seen in the war an opportunity to harass the king. The Venetian ambassador later reported that England had been a principal cause of the declaration of war, "acting through the huguenots who have weight with his Majesty."[107] If this is true, then it must be concluded that Bouillon and others were in touch with England. Whatever the truth may be, the war with Spain became a cardinal factor in the story of the "Protestant state" and the edict of Nantes from the time of the assembly of Saumur.

This assembly opened on 24 February 1595, not 1 December 1594 as arranged. Considering the unsatisfactory mission of de Chouppes and Tixier and the growing ferment in the provinces, this assembly was surprisingly insignificant.[108] It belongs, in category, to those of Mantes and Sainte-Foy, and sent deputies to the king with comparable requests,[109] though it was at this time that the demand arose for a completely new edict, incorporating the neglected *cahiers* of Mantes and Sainte-Foy.[110] The deputies

106. Marsollier, *Bouillon*, 176–78; Michaud, série ii, vol. ii, Sully, *Oeconomies royales*, i, 190, opposed the war and says that the king was swayed against his better judgment.

107. *CSPVen.*, *1592–1603*, p. 170, 28 October 1595, Duodo to the doge. Duodo suggests that Elizabeth regulated her assistance to ensure the continuation of the war.

108. It is possible that some of the more turbulent elements may have joined Bouillon in the field in Luxembourg.

109. Duplessis-Mornay, *Mémoires et correspondance*, i, *Mémoires de madame Duplessis-Mornay*, 287. The assembly was not the large one that had been intended, but consisted of only eleven members at the start, some provinces having excused themselves. B. N., Mss. N. A. F., 7191, ff. 198–99, actes de l'assemblée de Saumur, 24 février–23 mars 1595.

110. B. N., Mss. N. A. F., 7191, f. 203; de Thou, *Histoire universelle*, xii, *livre* cxiii; Duplessis-Mornay, *Mémoires et correspondance*, vi, 247–48, 27 March 1595. Duplessis-Mornay made the interesting observation that "... en debattant la rell[gion], les relligieux se gastent."

to Saumur did, however, show some signs of becoming tough, by deciding to seize royal revenues, if necessary, for the payment of garrisons, and to have all their documents and *cahiers* signed by the "plus grands et principaux gouverneurs gentilhommes et autres plus notables," in order to give them greater authority.[111] It seems likely, however, that this had the effect of forcing dissenters and extremists to show their hand, and thus of emphasizing the cleavage in their ranks.[112]

The deputies sent to the king by the assembly of Saumur—La Noue, their president, and La Primaudaye—had no better success than their predecessors.[113] The timing of their mission is rather uncertain, but they appear to have seen the king at Lyons in September[114] when he was deeply preoccupied. He was awaiting his absolution at the hands of the pope, which would destroy any remaining pretext for the rebellion of the League;[115] he was also negotiating for the submission of Mayenne, its leader[116]— two good reasons for not making concessions to the Protestants just then.[117] Added to this, the war with Spain was causing grave anxiety. The towns of Ham and Doullens had fallen during the summer, and, in September, the king hurried north, calling out all the nobility, in the hope of saving Cambrai, where Bouillon's conduct aroused suspicion.[118] After the fall of Cambrai, for which, whether rightly or wrongly, Bouillon was blamed after a

---

111. B. N., Mss. N. A. F., 7191, ff. 203v–4v, 206v.

112. B. N., Mss. Fr., 15815, f. 47.

113. Odet de la Noue, seigneur de Téligny, son of François, the famous Huguenot captain; Jacques de la Primaudaye.

114. Duplessis-Mornay, *Mémoires et correspondance*, vii, *Discours*, 285; ibid., vi, 352, 15 September 1595.

115. Henry's absolution was granted in Rome on 30 August and celebrated there on 17 September 1595. Berger de Xivrey, *Lettres de Henri IV*, vol. iv, introd., p. xiii.

116. Mayenne submitted in October 1595, but this was not made public until January 1597. Ibid., p. xiv.

117. All they obtained was a promise to send commissioners to supervise the execution of the edicts, which was normal procedure. Duplessis-Mornay, *Mémoires et correspondance*, vii, *Discours*, 285.

118. The king was too late and Cambrai fell on 9 October. Berger de Xivrey, *Lettres de Henri IV*, vol. iv, introd., pp. xiii–xiv.

record of failures and quarrels in the north,[119] he went into open and menacing opposition. Both he and La Trémoille withdrew their service and their forces for the long, exacting siege of La Fère in Picardy, which occupied the king for the next seven months.[120] With tactful forbearance, the king dealt with this situation by sending Bouillon on diplomatic missions to England and Holland, countries from which the king was seeking help. This was honorable employment, potentially useful to Bouillon, which kept him occupied for about a year.[121] What he made of this is not known, but, with or without his help, Queen Elizabeth certainly exploited, even if she did not actively manipulate, the growing Protestant crisis.

The siege of La Fère was not yet over and the fall of Calais already threatened[122] when, on 1 April 1596, the Protestant deputies met at Loudun, determined to obtain a hearing and not to be dismissed for yet another year. For this reason, the assembly remained almost constantly in session though it moved to Vendôme, Saumur and to Châtellerault, and the character of the struggle changed from this time. The assembly was soon attended and swayed, if not actually controlled, by the nobles and extremists who had hitherto remained aloof, and who regulated the pressure they exerted on the crown according to the fortunes of the war with Spain. The king was therefore unable to evade their importunate and untimely demands, even in the shadow of military defeat, and was forced to the only remaining solution of

119. Ouvré, *Aubéry du Maurier*, 40-41; Marsollier, *Bouillon*, 181 seq.; Duplessis-Mornay, *Mémoires et correspondance*, vi, 332-50, 7 September 1595, declaration of Nevers against Bouillon.

120. The siege of La Fère lasted from November 1595 to 22 May 1596. *CSPVen.*, *1592-1603*, p. 205, 25 May 1596.

121. Ouvré, *Aubéry du Maurier*, 42; Marsollier, *Bouillon*, 88 seq.; *CSPVen.*, *1592-1603*, pp. 197-98, 3 May 1596; 203-4, 18 May 1596; 205-6, 25 May 1596; 209, 25 June 1596; 223, 27 July 1596; 235-36, 26 October 1596; 236, 2 November 1596; *CSPD.*, *1595-97*, p. 276, 9 September 1596, Thomas Fane to Lord Cobham; Birch, *An Historical View*, 45.

122. The siege of La Fère ended on 22 May 1596 and Ardres was lost on the twenty-third. Calais fell to Spain on 16 April, a serious loss which complicated Henry's relations with England.

appointing commissioners to treat with the assembly. This amounted to a tacit recognition of the reconstructed "Protestant state," which soon obliged the royal commissioners to abandon the old, discredited edicts, and the king to concede the principle of a new one.[123] These developments were a partial admission of royal defeat, and later resulted in certain concessions which the king would not have chosen to make, not because he did not care for the Protestants—though he failed to inspire this belief[124]—but for two significant reasons of state. Henry had always intended to provide for the Protestants, and no one was better equipped to do so than he. But he had planned to grant and enforce the conditions of civil peace himself, through the legitimate authority of the crown. Now the "Protestant state" had reemerged within the royal State of France. Subjects sought to dictate and enforce the law in their own interests and through their own sanctions. In 1597 their conditions became the price of peace, and were something the king could no longer avoid. This was why the edict of Nantes partially accepted the "Protestant state." Thus the royal authority, not religion, was the real issue in this final stage of the struggle which culminated in the edict; the Protestants' survival was never threatened by Henry IV.[125] But in two important respects the king managed to prevail: in spite of the concessions he was forced to make, the timing and the form of the edicts were his.

The deputies to the next assembly at Loudun were angry about the king's absolution, angry that he had obtained possession of the young prince de Condé, heir apparent, to have him brought up a Catholic; and the report submitted by La Noue and La Primaudaye was described as "gere approuvé."[126] The deputies were not, according to Duplessis, troublemakers, but he was re-

123. Anquez, *Histoire des assemblées*, 71.

124. See, for example, B. N., Mss. Fr., 4047, f. 256, 13 June 1596, Henry to d'Emery; Berger de Xivrey, *Lettres de Henri IV*, vol. iv, 826, 11 August 1597, Henry to the duc de Piney-Luxembourg.

125. One could say that the royal authority had been the principal issue in France since about 1576, when the crown was isolated in the presence of two fully organized armed factions.

126. B. N., Mss. Fr., 15815, f. 46v.

ferring only to the ten who opened the assembly.[127] It was in vain, Duplessis said, to preach patience, which they had practiced for seven years, and he had already warned the king that "ces cures palliatives de paroles, de remises, de promesses" would no longer suffice.[128] Nevertheless, their single emissary, Vulson,[129] did not receive an auspicious hearing when he sought the king on the field of battle at the siege of La Fère. He returned towards the end of May with the usual assurances, but also with orders to require the assembly to disperse. This was a tactical error which precipitated a crisis and very nearly a civil war, for had they gone home in those circumstances "en intention de chercher les remedes... se feust infailliblement ensuyvi ung trouble." According to Madame Duplessis-Mornay, it was entirely due to her husband's influence that the king was persuaded to retract the order.[130] Duplessis-Mornay at once sought to exert his influence on La Noue, again president of the assembly, "de ne prendre resolution qui nous puisse engager en une guerre," which would not only be infinitely damaging, but also "feroit paroistre

127. The ten deputies met in the lodgings of the *gouverneur*, de Chouppes. Ibid., ff. 44-45; Duplessis-Mornay, *Mémoires et correspondance*, vi, 464, 8 April 1596, Duplessis-Mornay to the king; 467, 3 May 1596.

128. Duplessis-Mornay, *Mémoires et correspondance*, vi, 467-68, 3 May 1596. The deputies declared that they could neither subsist nor escape "une entière ruine" under the old edicts, and agreed to defend themselves on the basis of the "traité de la trève" which implied, presumably, under a protector. It is hard to say whether this resolution should be related to the appeal to Bouillon, made by the assembly at Vendôme a little under a year later.

129. Pierre Vulson, *conseiller* in the *parlement* of Grenoble, deputy for Dauphiné. Vulson must have left on or after 17 April 1596, when he received his traveling allowance. He was ordered to remain at court for a fortnight only, and to return to Loudun with or without an answer. B. N., Mss. Fr., 15815, ff. 49v-50, 53v.

130. Duplessis-Mornay, *Mémoires et correspondance*, i, *Mémoires de madame Duplessis-Mornay*, 301; de Thou, *Histoire universelle*, xiii, *livre* cxvii; Duplessis-Mornay, *Mémoires et correspondance*, vii, *Discours*, 287; the secretary de Lomenie criticized his colleague Fresne Forget for the tactless way in which Vulson's reply had been drafted. Ibid., vi, 492, 9 June 1596, de Lomenie to Duplessis-Mornay.

de la division en nous mesmes." He suggested instead the preparation of specific articles to seek compensation for ways in which the edicts had been contravened.[131] This, he hoped, would support the urgent request which he sent to the king for the appointment of a commissioner to treat with the deputies.[132]

The king, who hardly knew which way to turn, did not hesitate to take Duplessis-Mornay's advice.[133] But the crisis deepened with the inevitable delay before the arrival of the commissioners, and, when Duplessis-Mornay informed the assembly of their appointment, he found not only that their attitude was hardening, but also that the small, original gathering had been "fortifiés de tous les gouverneurs et principaulx gentilshommes de Poictou et Xaintonge, par eulx pryé de s'y trouver," so that he commented, "par des actions qui ne les y semblent pas mener tout droict, se trouveront avoir passé le rubicon for gaiement."[134] This, in other words, was the moment at which the assembly delivered itself into the hands of extremist elements, including La Trémoille.[135] The Protestant gentry, moreover, were not anxious to sit and talk, and it was largely thanks to Duplessis-Mornay that the assembly was still there to receive the king's commissioners when they arrived about 20 or 22 July.[136] But the king's position remained

131. Duplessis-Mornay, *Mémoires et correspondance*, vi, 483–87, 28 May 1596, Duplessis-Mornay to La Noue.

132. Ibid., 488–90, 2 June 1596, Duplessis-Mornay to the king. It was not the first time that Duplessis-Mornay had made this request and it was typical of his statesmanship that he took care to indicate how this could be done without royal loss of face.

133. Ibid., 488, 2 June 1596, Henry to Duplessis-Mornay; 491–93, 9 June 1596, de Lomenie to Duplessis-Mornay.

134. Ibid., 502–3, 19 June 1596, Duplessis-Mornay to the king; 504, 19 June 1596, Duplessis-Mornay to Bouillon.

135. The king was highly suspicious of La Trémoille at this time, also of Jean de Bandeau de Parabère, his lieutenant general in Poitou. La Grange, *Mémoires de la Force*, 274–76, 6 October 1596.

136. Emery de Vic, seigneur d'Ermenonville, president in the *parlement* of Toulouse, *conseiller d'état, garde des sceaux* 1621; Soffrey de Calignon, chancellor of Navarre. De Vic was a Catholic and Calignon a Protestant. B. N., Mss. Fr., 4047, f. 256, 13 June 1596, Henry to d'Emery; f. 258, June 1596, Villeroy to d'Emery; Duplessis-Mornay, *Mémoires et correspondance*, vii, *Discours*, 288; d'Aubigné, *Histoire universelle*, ix, 276, n.6.

unchanged and their mission was not to commence negotiations, but to charm the deputies into accepting Henry's assurances; an impossible undertaking. Their instructions[137] were a masterly composition, designed at once to reproach and conciliate; eminently gracious, condescending and explanatory, yet sternly warning recalcitrant extremists. Basically, however, they only offered the former edicts with a few minor concessions. Nothing, therefore, was achieved, and, after only a matter of days, the assembly broke up for a couple of months to go home and renew contact with the provinces.[138] Duplessis-Mornay, wise and constructive as ever, took this opportunity to appeal to the churches of Languedoc and to convey directly to them the substance of the king's message. Soon after, he advised Calignon, who had returned to court, to urge the king to appoint a committee of the council to negotiate with a number of deputies.[139] This, in fact, is what was done and, in October, when they had all reassembled,[140] six deputies were chosen to join the court and the assembly of notables which was meeting at Rouen. The principle was now established that the Protestants should negotiate on their own demands. The deputies left Loudun on 4 November and on the sixteenth, at the king's request, the assembly moved to Vendôme, albeit reluctant to depart from "les provinces qui lui faisoit épaule."[141] Vendôme belonged to the king.

137. B. N., Mss. Fr., 3463, ff. 60–69v, [9] July 1596, drafted by Villeroy.

138. This was proposed in the commissioners' instructions. At the end of July, de Vic and Calignon returned to court with two deputies, des Rioux and La Motte. B. N., Mss. N. A. F., 7191, ff. 278–79.

139. Duplessis-Mornay, *Mémoires et correspondance*, vii, 2, 28 July 1596, Duplessis-Mornay to all the churches of Languedoc. Bas-Languedoc had not been represented, at least at the opening of the assembly. Ibid., 5–6, 11 August 1596, Duplessis-Mornay to Calignon; 9, 15 September 1596, Henry to Duplessis-Mornay.

140. All the deputies reassembled at Loudun at the end of September. De Vic arrived on 11 October and Calignon on or before that date. B. N., Mss. N. A. F., 7191, f. 278v; Duplessis-Mornay, *Mémoires et correspondance*, vii, 12, 13, two letters of 11 October 1596.

141. B. N., Mss. N. A. F., 7191, ff. 235–37v, 11 September 1596, second instructions for de Vic and Calignon; B. N., Mss. Fr., 3550, f. 107, 18 October 1596, the assembly to the constable. La Noue, de

The brief assembly at Vendôme marks the beginning of a grave deterioration in the Protestants' relations with the king. When the deputies returned from the court on 16 January 1597, the secretary, Forget, warned Duplessis-Mornay that both sides were baring their teeth. This was because the discussions were no longer on the basis of the edicts and the king found cause to complain of "les esprits . . . qui se licentient par trop contre ce qui est de mon auctorité."[142] The deputies, for their part, observed with bitterness that the king believed there was "en leurs poursuittes plus de faction que de religion, qu'ils importunoient hors temps et retardoient comme par plaisir le cours de ses affaires jusques a les comparer quelques fois a ceux de la ligue." This impression was no doubt enhanced by the Protestants' seizure of royal revenues, their raising of illegal levies and by Schomberg's[143] solemn warning that the war with Spain and the struggle with Mercoeur in Brittany were "secondés de plusieurs dangereux desseins dedans du royaume."[144] The deputies also returned with the impression that their enemies were urging the king to make peace with Spain, which would be detrimental to their interests—a concern with the impact of foreign affairs which points to the influence of the nobility—and they interpreted the delays in the return of the commissioners, both to Loudun and to Vendôme, as an indication of some "mauvais desseign" on the part of the king.[145] This was true, and it was generally known

---

Chouppes, La Motte, de Fonds, Brunier and Tixier were chosen; Mss. N. A. F., 7191, ff. 279v–81; Duplessis-Mornay, *Mémoires et correspondance*, vii, *Discours*, 290.

142. Duplessis-Mornay, *Mémoires et correspondance*, vii, 111–12, 15 January 1597, Forget to Duplessis-Mornay; 133, 26 January 1597, Henry to Duplessis-Mornay.

143. Gaspard de Schomberg, born in Saxony, naturalized French, comte de Nanteuil, *gouverneur* of La Marche. He first served the Protestants and later became a Catholic, abandoning his military profession on account of bad health. He served as councilor and diplomat.

144. B. N., Mss. N. A. F., 7191, ff. 242–44v, 18 January 1597, instructions for de Vic and Calignon; 251–52v, 13 February 1597, Schomberg to the king; 281.

145. The deputies at Loudun feared that if treaties were made with Spain and Mercoeur, "on vouldroit mesurer leur condition, non plus à la

that he was working for peace with the duc de Mercoeur, the last of the *leagueurs*. It was also true in January 1597, if not before, that he was deeply involved in secret negotiations for peace with Spain through the mediation of the pope;[146] but not for the purpose of enabling him to destroy the Protestants. Peace before an edict had always been his clearly stated order of priorities, for the old edicts had already given trouble enough without heaping more fuel on to such a fire. In the absence of Huguenot support, he was, after all, dependent on the Catholics for his army.

De Vic and Calignon, who arrived at Vendôme on 3 February, nearly three weeks after the deputies, stayed until 8 February before returning to court with a fresh set of "repliques" and a request that they should be joined by de Thou[147] and Schomberg to conclude the negotiation. Having expressed its discontent, the assembly told the commissioners that "l'oppression où on faisait vivre les Réformés les obligerait enfin à chercher quelque soulagement en eux mesmes,"[148] whereupon they despatched one d'Aurival—apparently a pseudonym for no less a person than Agrippa d'Aubigné—to the duc de Bouillon, to invite him to Vendôme and to seek his advice.[149] Bouillon proceeded with typical caution, wanting both to assume the leadership of the Calvinists and also "se ménager avec la court."[150] He excused himself from attending the assembly on the grounds that he had to escort

---

justice de leurs demandes, mais à la discretion de leurs malveillans." Duplessis-Mornay, *Mémoires et correspondance*, vii, 156, 4 February 1597, Schomberg to Duplessis-Mornay; ibid., vii, *Discours*, 289. De Vic and Calignon returned to Vendôme on 3 February 1597. One simple reason for the delay was that Calignon did not want to go. Douglas, *Documents inédits pour servir à l'histoire du Dauphiné*, i, 349–50, 18 January 1597, Henry to Calignon.

146. Birch, *An Historical View*, 49.

147. B. N., Mss. N. A. F., 7191, f. 248v, 7 February 1597, de Vic and Calignon to Henry; ff. 282v–83. Jacques-Auguste de Thou, baron de Meslay, historian, diplomat, *conseiller au parlement de Paris, maître des requêtes* 1586, *conseiller d'état* 1588; a Catholic.

148. Faurey, *Henry IV et l'édit de Nantes*, 20.

149. Soulier, *Histoire du calvinisme*, 278–79; d'Aubigné, *Histoire universelle*, iv, 38, n. 5, gives Dorival.

150. Marsollier, *Bouillon*, 217.

his wife to Turenne, but intimated that he would come later. He advised them not to disperse before receiving satisfaction and only to hold their assemblies in towns which they controlled.[151] Most important of all, he stated that he wished the negotiations with the court to be spun out, for the "plus grands du party" to join the assembly, and for this to remain in session for another two or three years, until the edict they were seeking had been fully executed. In other words, the edict was to be both dictated and applied at the point of a Protestant sword. It is recorded that the king learnt of this *démarche* and concluded that Bouillon was the principal author of all his troubles with the assembly, and also that at this time, "il s'en prit ouvertement au ducs de Bouillon et La Trémoille."[152]

The assembly followed in every particular the advice they received from Bouillon. Thus they returned to Saumur at the beginning of March[153] and became a large gathering of seventy to eighty persons[154]—including La Trémoille[155]—as opposed to some thirty at Vendôme. This hostile assembly was awaiting the return of de Vic and Calignon when, on 16 March, Montglas arrived with letters from the king announcing the shattering news of the loss of Amiens, the strategic key to Paris and indeed to all France north of the Loire. This calamity threw everything into disorder and suspense, superseding all other concerns; many people panicked and it was widely believed that France was lost.[156] In the assembly, the news "partagea diversement les es-

---

151. Henry IV was the duc de Vendôme.

152. Bouillon is said to have refused to send his reply in writing but caused d'Aurival to make a copy and himself withdrew the original. Soulier, *Histoire du calvinisme*, 279; Marsollier, *Bouillon*, 217–18; Faurey, *Henri IV et l'édit de Nantes*, 21; Benoist, *Histoire de l'édit de Nantes*, i, 182.

153. B. N., Mss. N. A. F., 7191, f. 283, gives 1 March; Anquez, *Histoire des assemblées*, 72, 5 March; d'Aubigné, *Histoire universelle*, ix, 276, claims that they were driven out of Vendôme by "quelque épidémie."

154. B. N., Mss. N. A. F., 7191, ff. 247–48, 7 February 1597, de Vic and Calignon to the king; d'Aubigné, *Histoire universelle*, ix, 277–78.

155. D'Aubigné, *Histoire universelle*, ix, 277.

156. Amiens fell on 11 March 1597, containing much of the king's equipment and ammunition. B. N., Mss. N. A. F., 7191, ff. 295v–298, 12 March 1597, Henry to the assembly; Duplessis-Mornay, *Mémoires et*

prits" between those who were genuinely dismayed and "ceux qui . . . fondaient là-dessus de grandes espérances."[157] Two days later, in the midst of this confusion, the commissioners arrived—de Vic, Calignon, Schomberg and de Thou—and the burden of their message, like that of Montglas, was to implore the assembly to sink, or at least to postpone, all other considerations and hasten to the king's assistance. Henry had every reason to command such support from the nobility—especially from those who had all but forced him into the war—and to point out that thereafter their demands would come with "plus de faveur et de recommendation." Such timely assistance would have strengthened his hand in making concessions, but the extremists who now swayed the assembly rather sought to embarrass the king than to defend the kingdom or provide for the Protestants, though to obtain an edict was still, ostensibly, their primary purpose. Their initial antagonism was greatly increased by the firmness of the commissioners' instructions—drafted before the fall of Amiens—and by the king's complaint that in constantly increasing their demands, they were rendering a settlement impossible.[158] Such intransigence again points to the influence of the nobility. The assembly therefore not only refused to assist the king, but sent back an insolent reply protesting that they trembled to think of the hazards he must face, and, in effect, that they yearned to lay their lives at his feet, only by his denials he prevented them from doing so. For the rest, ignoring the fate of the kingdom, they returned to their complaints and demands.[159]

This combination of Spanish and Protestant pressure came very

---

correspondance, vii, 172, 17 March 1597, Duplessis-Mornay to Schomberg; Anquez, *Histoire des assemblées*, 73; Faurey, *Henri IV et l'édit de Nantes*, 21.

157. De Thou, *Histoire universelle*, xiii, *livre*, cxviii; Duplessis-Mornay, *Mémoires et correspondance*, i, *Mémoires de madame Duplessis-Mornay*, 303.

158. B. N., Mss. N. A. F., 7191, ff. 265–71, 4 March 1597, instructions for commissioners. The king commented that he could not and did not see that he should grant any more. B. N., Mss. Fr., 4047, f. 271, 4 March 1597, Henry to de Thou.

159. B. N., Mss. N. A. F., 7191, ff. 296v–300v, 25 March 1597, the assembly to the king; Anquez, *Histoire des assemblées*, 73.

near to crushing the king. This was the only time at which his normally buoyant nature almost gave way to despair, and, partly perhaps because he was ill and in pain, he could see no hope for the future. He regretted the war as a cardinal error, exposing him, as it did, to the exploitation of the nobles, and of England, and lamented to Schomberg that if the Protestants persisted in demanding things he could not grant without dividing his subjects even more than ever, "ils m'accableront... et m'osteront tout le moyen de remedier au mal qui nous consomme."[160] But even in this despair, Henry declined to purchase the service of his subjects—offered at a price—against his judgment and proper conception of his office. He chose rather to face the danger—regarded as honorable—of total disaster on the field of battle, where he fully expected to die. He did, however, send back his commissioners a second time,[161] and also Montglas and La Force, with an impassioned appeal to help save the country from Spain;[162] he received a second insolent reply lamenting the Protestants' inability to serve.[163] A state of deadlock had therefore been reached in which the assembly broke up at the beginning of May. The commissioners and La Motte returned to court, and the deputies to the provinces. They had called for an even larger assembly, "fortifiées de plus grand nombre que faire se pourroit des plus notables de tous les ordres," to meet at Châtellerault on 15 June.[164]

160. Berger de Xivrey, *Lettres de Henri IV*, vol. iv, 725–27, 31 March 1597, Henry to Schomberg; 730, 4 April 1597, Henry to Duplessis-Mornay; 743, 19 April 1597, Henry to the *parlement*; *CSPVen.*, *1592–1603*, pp. 266–67, 23 April 1597.

161. De Vic and Montglas returned to the court at the end of March 1597. Protestant affairs were debated in Paris between 4 and 13 April. De Vic rejoined the assembly on 24 April. La Grange, *Mémoires de La Force*, i, 284–86, 286–87, 4 and 13 April 1597; B. N., Mss. Fr., 15814, ff. 48v–50v, 20 April 1597, instructions brought by de Vic for the commissioners; Duplessis-Mornay, *Mémoires et correspondance*, vii, 189, 24 April 1597.

162. B. N., Mss. N. A. F., 7191, ff. 301–2, 19 April 1597, Henry to the assembly.

163. B. N., Mss. Fr., 15815, ff. 67–68v, 1 May 1597, the assembly to the king.

164. B. N., Mss. N. A. F., 7191, ff. 286–v.

What would happen in the interlude was unpredictable. There was no lack of "gens irritez"[165] inciting the Protestants to take up arms, and there appear to have been, as Schomberg said, several designs afoot. The comte d'Auvergne,[166] for instance, quit the king's service in Picardy and went to Auvergne, where he was devising some sedition, "par le moyen des intelligences quil a avec quelques perturbateurs du repos publique," presumably Bouillon, among others, who was skulking there with troops raised at the king's expense which he steadily refused to conduct to Amiens.[167] La Trémoille, for his part, had troops in Poitou, and there were some who urged him to establish a base at Tours from which he and his followers—d'Aubigné mentioned a force of 3,500—should advance to present a petition in arms or, in other words, an ultimatum. He added, "les plus de voix et les plus saines reduisirent les autres à la patience."[168] It is hard to say why civil war did not recur at this time, except that the extremists were evidently of several minds, and the perpetual remonstrances of the king's moderate servants may have contributed to a fatal hesitancy of the nobility arising from the uncertainty of their real objectives.[169]

This was a situation which could not stagnate. Everything therefore depended on the outcome of the next assembly at Châtellerault, which punctiliously followed Bouillon's advice, conveyed by d'Aurival to Vendôme. The assembly, which opened on 16

165. D'Aubigné, *Histoire universelle*, ix, 279.

166. The comte d'Auvergne was the illegitimate son of Charles IX by Marie Touchet. As a possible claimant to the succession, he was doubly dangerous. He took part with Bouillon in the Biron and other conspiracies later in the reign, and was condemned to death by the *parlement* of Paris in 1605. Henry commuted the sentence to one of life imprisonment.

167. Berger de Xivrey, *Lettres de Henri IV*, vol. iv, 767–68, 26 May 1597, Henry to La Chastre; Duplessis-Mornay, *Mémoires et correspondance*, vii, 228–29, 30 June 1597, Duplessis-Mornay to La Trémoille; Petitot, série i, vol. xxxvii, de Thou, *Mémoires*, 509.

168. Petitot, série i, vol. xxxvii, de Thou, *Mémoires*, 509; d'Aubigné, *Histoire universelle*, ix, 279–80.

169. De Thou did his utmost to persuade them to serve at Amiens, but they refused. Petitot, série i, vol. xxxvii, de Thou, *Mémoires*, 510; Ouvré, *Aubéry du Maurier*, 49.

June 1597,[170] was a large gathering of over two hundred, reinforced by "personnes de qualité" from all the provinces. Bouillon
arrived on 26 June,[171] and, while awaiting the king's commissioners, the leaders created a major crisis on their discovery in July that
Henry was engaged in negotiations with Spain.[172] They promptly
sent a deputy to court[173] with what was, in effect, a traitorous
announcement threatening action if his conduct of affairs did not
meet with their approval.[174] They were already assured of the
support of the gentry, who were bound by oath, and they sought
the cooperation of Lesdiguières, who could have assisted them by
exposing the frontier of Dauphiné to the Catholic, pro-Spanish
duke of Savoy.[175]

This was perhaps the most critical moment of the king's long
years of strife. The immediate crisis, however, was skillfully
turned by the courage and sense of Schomberg, when he arrived
from Brittany.[176] Without awaiting his colleagues or any instructions, Schomberg assumed authority and promptly concluded with
a committee of the assembly, which was dominated by the ex-

---

170. Duplessis-Mornay, *Mémoires et correspondance*, i, *Mémoires de
madame Duplessis-Mornay*, 302; Petitot, série i, vol. xliii, Cayet, *Chronologie
nouvenaire*, *livre* viii, 398; Marsollier, *Bouillon*, 218; Soulier, *Histoire du
calvinisme*, 296–97; Anquez, *Histoire des assemblées*, 73–74.

171. Duplessis-Mornay, *Mémoires et correspondance*, vii, 222, 26 June
1597; Marsollier, *Bouillon*, 218, gives 27 June.

172. B. N., Mss. N. A. F., 7191, f. 305v gives the date of this discovery as 18 July, but Duplessis-Mornay, *Mémoires et correspondance*, vii, 250,
referred to the matter in a letter of 11 July. The previous negotiation had
been disrupted by the capture of Amiens.

173. Augustin Constant, *gouverneur* of Marans, close friend of d'Aubigné. He had served Navarre after his escape from court in 1576. Constant left on or after 18 July.

174. Soulier, *Histoire du calvinisme*, 302–3, "ils se munissent contre le
mal."

175. François de Bonne, duc de Lesdiguières, marshal, and constable
1626, lieutenant general of Dauphiné 1597. Bouillon had in fact been
trying for some months to obtain his cooperation in order to involve the
king in war on two fronts, but, though a Calvinist, he was loyal. Marsollier, *Bouillon*, 217; Soulier, *Histoire du calvinisme*, 278, 303–4.

176. Soulier, *Histoire du calvinisme*, 304.

tremists,[177] a number of articles on the major Protestant claims, which formed the basis of the future edict of Nantes.[178] This was a triumph for the "Protestant state" in arms.

Henry was possibly expecting this, or something like it, for Sully recalls a visit to Amiens during which the king disclosed his despair because the assembly was resolved to demand such an edict as the courts would never register, or, if he refused them as heretofore, to take up arms.[179] This ugly predicament was in fact resolved by the recent determination of the Protestant extremists— unknown to Schomberg and the king—to obstruct an agreement and prolong the assembly for several years.[180] They did so because they were not primarily concerned with the Protestants, but with opposing the king; but in this respect they played into his hands. Since they did not mean to conclude the matter, the agreement with Schomberg was no sooner made than the Protestants began submitting other demands.[181] While awaiting the king's replies, they looked abroad for support from England and Holland,[182]

177. Marsollier, *Bouillon*, 219, gives Bouillon, La Trémoille, d'Aubigné, Parabère, Duplessis-Mornay, La Motte and La Noue; Soulier, *Histoire du calvinisme*, 304, omits Duplessis-Mornay. Schomberg mentioned them all, and added Clermont and Montgomery. B. N., Mss. N. A. F., 7191, ff. 289-90, 28 July 1597, Schomberg to the king.

178. These consisted of at least nineteen articles. Schomberg sent Constant, Montmartin and Rignac with a memoir to the king, and returned to Brittany on or after 28 July. B. N., Mss. N. A. F., 7191, f. 331v; Berger de Xivrey, *Lettres de Henri IV*, vol. iv, 819-20, 4 August 1597, Henry to La Force.

179. Michaud, série ii, vol. ii, Sully, *Oeconomies royales*, i, 252-53, no date. He wrote a remarkable letter seeking to restrain La Trémoille, of whose intentions he was evidently informed.

180. This later became the subject of much negotiation when they demanded permission to remain in session until the edict was fully executed, that is to say indefinitely. In this way the nobles could have instigated trouble and planted the blame. B. N., Mss. N. A. F., 7191, f. 333v, 18 September 1597; Soulier, *Histoire du calvinisme*, 302, 306.

181. Soulier, *Histoire du calvinisme*, 305.

182. Constant returned on 12 August with general reassurances about the Spanish treaty. Next day the assembly decided to send to England and Holland. B. N., Mss. N. A. F., 7191, ff. 322 seq., 20 August 1597,

since England, in particular, could be relied upon to do all in her power to sabotage a treaty with Spain. The envoy's instructions were cautiously worded, but the general idea seems to have been that Elizabeth should guarantee the execution of their edict or, according to the circumstances, assist them in "une guerre domestique." Elizabeth, of course, replied noncommittally, but the overture strengthened her hand in menacing the king for, although England and France were technically allies, they had little in common but the enmity of Spain.[183]

This disloyal initiative, taken in the very presence of the royal commissioners,[184] indicates sufficiently clearly that the dukes did not mean to honor their agreement—part of the arrangement made with Schomberg—to join the king at the siege of Amiens.[185] Bouillon, when it came to the point, explained to Schomberg with intolerable effrontery that originally his health had kept him away. Thereafter, the king's service had required his presence at Châtellerault, since there were "d'etranges esprits et qui iroient bien loin s'ils n'estoient retenues par des personnes d'autorité." Soon after,

---

instructions for Saint-Germain going to England and La Forest going to Holland. These were virtually identical.

183. *CSPVen.*, *1592–1603*, p. 277, 5 July 1597; 301, 9 December 1597; Birch, *An Historical View*, 64–66, 29 November 1597, Naunton to the earl of Essex.

184. De Thou, de Vic and Calignon arrived at Saumur on 15 August, and probably at Châtellerault on 16 August 1597; Schomberg was expected on 19 August. B. N., Mss. N. A. F., 7191, f. 321; Duplessis-Mornay, *Mémoires et correspondance*, vii, 318–19, 16 August; 319–20, 18 August 1597; B. N., Mss. Fr., 4047, ff. 272 seq.; their instructions were dated 19 July and supplemented by others of 4 August 1597.

185. Schomberg had said in his letter of 28 July that Henry must attract the dukes to court immediately "et a quelque prix que ce puisse estre car la moindre longueur ou accroche fera un mouvement dans vostre estat." B. N., Mss. N. A. F., 7191, ff. 289–90, 28 July 1597, Schomberg to the king. Henry sent for Bouillon by the seigneur de Rignac and others. He expected him by 25 August and sent blank commissions for him to raise fifteen companies of foot. La Trémoille was also to have gone. B. N., Mss. Fr., 4047, f. 282v, 2 August 1597, Henry to Schomberg.

he departed for Turenne.[186] The pretext for this may well have been that the commissioners brought certain amendments to Schomberg's agreement, which the king had declined to ratify as it stood. He had indeed been constrained, as he said, "de lascher quelques graces aux huguenots pour oster le moyen aux chefs de party et factieux de les esmouvoir,"[187] but the changes he had made were more in the form than in the substance, "pour rendre les choses plus faciles et recevables," namely by the *parlements*.[188]

From this point onwards, therefore, the basis of an agreement existed, the king having been forced to commit himself in the midst of war. Yet, at the same time, he was ironically saved by the action of the extremists from his former embarrassment of having to refuse an edict. All the wrangling was thus over the form and detail of these concessions, together with a series of new demands, raised to gain as much as possible and to delay agreement.[189] Under extremist influence, the assembly expressed its dissatisfaction with the king's amendments and sent two of its members—Clairville and La Motte—back to the court again, together with the king's commissioners.[190]

This fractious and undisguised opposition was not in the interests of the *consistoriaux* and probably deepened the rift, which the king exploited as much as he could, between the moderates and the

186. Marsollier, *Bouillon*, 220. He probably left late in August and returned on 6 January 1598.

187. Berger de Xivrey, *Lettres de Henri IV*, vol. iv, 825–26, 11 August 1597, Henry to the duc de Piney-Luxembourg.

188. Ibid., 819–20, 4 August 1597, Henry to La Force; 820–21, 5 August 1597, Henry to Duplessis-Mornay. Montmartin returned with this letter.

189. Henry specifically referred, a little later, to the difficulties and delays created "à l'apetit de quelques-uns exprès pour faire durer ladite assemblée et s'en prévaloir au préjudice du repos de mes sujets de la R. P. R." Soulier, *Histoire du calvinisme*, 317–18, 22 February 1598, Henry to Calignon and de Thou.

190. B. N., Mss. N. A. F., 7191, ff. 330v–33v, 18 September 1597, instructions for Clairville; Soulier, *Histoire du calvinisme*, 312–13. Clairville's mission related to security, the appointment of *gouverneurs* and the form of the edict. He was a pastor from Loudun.

extremist leaders. Indeed, it was held to be largely their disunity which kept the party from arms, since neither section could fight without the other. In particular, the nobles wanted to control the money raised for war, whereas the ministers and *anciens*—said to have represented two-thirds of the assembly—wished the finances to be entrusted to a committee. These disagreements, so it was said, opened their eyes to their real situation and "plusieurs virent le precipice ou quelques remuans les vouloient jetter en prenans les armes."[191] The king's changes in the form of the articles of agreement had not antagonized the moderates, who were now largely satisfied. All the subsequent difficulties were raised by the nobles, partly to menace the king's position, and partly, when the final settlement came, to enhance their position in the provinces within the framework of the "Protestant state," and at the expense of the royal authority.[192] But although the nobles maintained their menacing attitude, in a sense the crisis was already over because they were left without a cause. On the other hand, they were still a danger so long as the war with Spain continued, which was why they sought to oppose its conclusion.

Thus, the king's triumphant recovery of the city of Amiens on 19 September—even before the deputies and commissioners had reached the court—virtually disarmed the dukes, for it implied the defeat of Spain in France and the establishment of the royal authority. Amiens was a military and moral victory which made it clear that the king would prevail in France. But the opposition did not collapse, for the situation was still confused and the treaty of peace had yet to be made. So the nobles refused to cooperate with the royal commissioners, who returned to Saumur (not Châtellerault) at Christmas.[193] The nobles manipulated the points at issue so as to

191. Petitot, série i, vol. xliii, Cayet, *Chronologie novenaire, livre* viii, 398–99.

192. B. N., Mss. Fr., 4047, f. 300v, 17 January 1598, Henry to de Thou and Calignon.

193. Clairville arrived on 20 December 1597, with a letter from the king. The commissioners reached Saumur on 26 December expecting to meet Schomberg. B. N., Mss. N. A. F., 7191, ff. 335v seq., 20 December 1597; f. 311, 6 December 1597, Henry to the assembly; f. 390, 7 January 1598, La Trémoille to de Thou; B. N., Mss. Fr., 4047, ff.

create opposition in the assembly, and they dispatched two more deputies—Cazes and Courtaumer—to court with a highly disrespectful message.[194] One can see what was behind the mission from the complaint, written into their instructions, that the dukes were being wronged by the king's council, which blackened them, in spite of their constant loyalty, in order to keep them in disfavor.[195] They also complained that the replies to Clairville's mission refused them adequate security on the grounds that it offended the king's authority. To this they retorted with arrogant presumption that in the kingdom of France there was no such thing: "a nostre très grand regret... l'estat du Royaume est telle qu'elle [the royal authority] n'est point recogneue ny ses commandements receus comme ceux de la Religion desirent et en font tous les jours prières à Dieu."[196]

In fact they were wrong: the days were over when Henry IV could be safely defied. The time was approaching when he had always meant to provide for the Protestants and, at that point, the discussions would cease. He allowed them to continue until he was ready to march to Brittany to eject Mercoeur; then the Protestants were also expected to become "plus traictables."[197] His intensions were perfectly clear, but his approach, in force, was nonetheless impressive: "il n'est pas à croire," d'Aubigné wrote, "l'aprehension qu'ils en prindrent."[198] So, when the king sent for Bouillon and La

---

289–90v, 6 December 1597, instructions for de Vic and Calignon; Duplessis-Mornay, *Mémoires et correspondance*, vii, 475, 25 December 1597; 491–92, 7 January 1598, the assembly to Duplessis-Mornay; 492–96, 3 January 1598, memoir to the king.

194. Jean de Cazes; Jean-Antoine de Saint-Simon, marquis de Courtaumer. B. N., Mss. N. A. F., 7191, ff. 338v–44, 28 January 1598, instructions.

195. Ibid., f. 342; Birch, *An Historical View*, 82, 16 December 1597, Naunton to the earl of Essex, referred to "the king's late capital spleen against the duke of Bouillon."

196. B. N., Mss. N. A. F., 7191, f. 341.

197. Ibid., f. 400v, 19 January 1598, Forget to de Thou and Calignon; Berger de Xivrey, *Lettres de Henri IV*, vol. iv, 896, 11 January 1598, Henry to La Chastre; Anquez, *Histoire des assemblées*, 78; Soulier, *Histoire du calvinisme*, 317–18.

198. D'Aubigné, *Histoire universelle*, ix, 280.

Trémoille to join him at Angers, they obeyed.[199] This sign of submission marked the end—in Henry's reign—of the exploitation of the religious movement by the rebellious nobility.[200] All obstacles having finally been removed, the edict followed a few weeks later, after the peace with Spain[201] and while the king was at Nantes in Brittany, "triomphant et se voyant sans ennemis."[202] This was the timing that Henry had intended. Only then was he free to enforce the law and to avert the possible consequences, for he claimed that he alone was holding the two factions apart.[203] Certainly nothing but his unhampered authority could enforce such a regulation; to this the civil wars themselves bear witness.

The edict of Nantes which emerged from these years of strife was not one document, but four. It consisted of ninety-two general articles, fifty-six secret articles, also described as *particuliers*, and two royal *brevets*.[204] The two sets of articles formed the edict proper, registered together by the *parlements*. The two separate *brevets*, issued on different dates, depended on the sole authority of the crown and were neither sealed in the chancellery nor registered by the sovereign courts.[205] The French historian, Georges Pagès, called these documents an "ensemble complexe d'actes de valeur inégale," a just description but one which suggests abstruse juridical arguments, whereas the explanation of this curious form was strictly practical.[206] It had been thrashed out between the king and

199. Soulier, *Histoire du calvinisme*, 318.

200. Religious pretexts were necessarily abandoned and Biron and Bouillon, *leagueur* and Huguenot, later made common cause.

201. The edict of Nantes was signed on 13 April and the treaty of Vervins on 2 May 1598, but the treaty was already basically concluded.

202. D'Aubigné, *Histoire universelle*, ix, 280-81.

203. Berger de Xivrey, *Lettres de Henri IV*, vol. iv, 825, 11 August 1597, Henry to the duc de Piney-Luxembourg.

204. A *brevet* is defined as an "acte par lequel le roi concède une grace quelconque."

205. Isambert *Recueil général*, xv, 170-210, prints the two sets of articles; Fontanon, *Les Édits et ordonnances*, iv, 361-73, gives only the general articles; Benoist, *Histoire de l'édit de Nantes*, i, 62-98, prints all four documents; so do Anquez, *Histoire des assemblées*, 456-502, and Mousnier, *L'Assassinat de Henri IV*, 294-334.

206. Pagès believed that Henry put into the edict proper those clauses which were intended to be permanent and into the *brevets* those which

the Protestant deputies, mostly since the summer of 1597. It reflected, on the one hand, the struggle between the king and the
nobles—he to preserve and to wield his own authority and they for
power and sanctions in the guise of security. On the other hand, it
illustrated the fundamental problem of how to enforce a necessary
law to which much of the country was opposed and which the
parlements resisted; for the king had either to win their cooperation
or to circumvent their opposition.

The Protestants wanted the entire document drafted in the form
of an edict—which they described as being "en forme
authentique"—and, consequently, registered by the *parlements*,
whereas the king favored a prerogative form of law, except for the
clauses relating to justice which affected the *parlements* themselves.[207] The use of *brevets* was, as much as anything, in order to
avoid undesirable publicity, contention and opposition. The Protestant demand for an edict was not so much an expression of their
opinion on the relative juridical value of different forms of law, as a
reflection, at best, of lack of confidence in the crown and, at worst,
of hostility to the king. The result, therefore, was a compromise.

The edict—taken to mean the four documents together—was not
simply one more regulation in favour of the Protestants; neither
was it another peace treaty in the form of an edict. Its purpose, as
stated in the preamble, was to provide one general law regulating all
differences between those of the two religions, for the establishment of a durable peace, and so that the worship of God might be
at least with one common intention, if not yet "en une même forme
de religion." The main body of ninety-two articles—signed on 13
April—comprised all the religious and civil clauses, beginning with
the restoration of mass to all places whence it had been abolished,

---

were intended to be temporary. This is a misconception and easily disproved by Henry's negotiations with the assemblies. Only the security
clauses were intended to be temporary, and this was expressed in the
text, not in the form of the document. B. N., Mss. N. A. F., 7191, ff.
242–44v, 330v–33v, 336v; Mss. Fr., 4047, ff. 302–v; Pagès, "Les Paix de
Religion et l'Édit de Nantes," *Revue d'histoire moderne et contemporaine*,
n.s., v, 1936.

207. B. N., Mss. N. A. F., 7191, f. 244, 18 January 1597.

and the return of all Church property. The principal clauses relating to the Protestants are very well known. Besides complete liberty of conscience, Protestants were granted the exercise of the cult in all places where it pertained in 1596 and up to August 1597—following earlier precedents—and in all places where it was established under the edicts of pacification. To this was added one more town per *bailliage*, making two in all. The cult was also to be permitted in the *châteaux* of certain *seigneurs*, amounting to some 3,500. The privileges of the nobility, first established in 1563, were therefore retained. The Protestants again received full civil rights, equally with the Catholics, and eligibility to all posts and offices, as well as renewed judicial protection by means of the *chambres de l'édit* or *chambres mi-parties* in the *parlements*.

The articles in the second group of fifty-six were roughly of three kinds: those which, referring to articles in the first group, were explanatory; those dealing with exceptions and covering possible gaps in the law; and those dealing with the exercise of the cult in places comprised within the *leagueur* edicts, in order to reconcile contradictions in the law.

The first of the two *brevets*, dated 3 April 1598, was a very brief document providing for the payment to a specified agent of 45,000 *écus* per annum for certain secret affairs of the Protestants. This was simply to overcome the problem of Catholic opposition to the public payment of pastors. The Protestants had always attached great importance to this item, particularly since they had to contribute to the expenses of the Catholic Church.

The second *brevet*, dated 30 April 1598, was much longer. It contained the celebrated and controversial guarantee clauses, tenaciously disputed, detail by detail, between the king and the deputies, together with certain other clauses not clearly distinguishable from those in the secret group. The Protestants were permitted to retain for eight years from the publication of the edict (15 February 1599) all the towns which they held in August 1597. These amounted to some 200 (excluding those in Dauphiné, which were dealt with separately) of which about half were garrison towns, for whose upkeep the king agreed to pay 180,000 *écus* per annum. These two major concessions, together with the time limit,

had been part of Schomberg's capitulation.[208] Both, though necessary at the time, were damaging to the king's authority, and he had
therefore been firm with the deputies about a number of significant
details. The Protestants claimed, for instance, not only the garrisons but also the right to apportion them. The *brevet*, however,
reserved to the king the right to "dresser l'état," while agreeing to
consult their opinion. They also demanded the right to seize royal
revenues if the garrisons were not fully paid for, an unthinkable
precedent explicitly refused in the *brevet*. Similarly, the deputies
had wished the king to appoint Protestant *gouverneurs* upon their
nomination. The king undertook to appoint Protestants agreeable
to the *colloque*, but declined to accept nominees.

The *brevet* also contained two other controversial clauses,
though not ones which were contested by the king. In one he
undertook actually to appoint Protestants to offices, thus going
materially further than a mere admission of their eligibility; in the
second he permitted persons of rank to celebrate the cult at court,
provided they did so privately and silently, "sans psalmodier à
haute voix." A study of the *brevets*, therefore, makes it perfectly
clear that the king placed in these documents, and granted purely
as of grace, those concessions which impinged on his authority,
together with clauses which there would be no hope of forcing
through the *parlements*.

The ecclesiastical organization of the Protestants was recognized
by the secret article 34, which permitted the holding of consistories, *colloques* and provincial and national synods. But the general
article 82[209] expressly forbade the imposition of taxes, the construction of fortifications, the raising of troops and the holding of
any meetings or assemblies other than those explicitly permitted by
the edict. These activities were an essential part of the existence of
the "Protestant state" as an independent organization, which was
thereby condemned. It was not, otherwise, directly referred to,
except by article 21 of the second *brevet*, which dealt with the

208. B. N., Mss. N. A. F., 7191, f. 331v, articles 18, 19.
209. Poirson, *Histoire du règne de Henry IV*, ii, 515, maintained that
article 82 preserved the political assemblies, but he was mistaken.

pretension of the nobility to prolong the existence of the last assembly. The king thereby permitted ten deputies to remain in session at Saumur until the edict had been registered by the *parlement* of Paris, "nonobstant qu'il leur soit enjoint par ledit edit de se separer promptement." This temporary concession clearly underlined the king's intentions in relation to the "Protestant state."

The abolition of political assemblies was not necessarily more than an inconvenience, so long as religious ones were permitted, since a synod could easily be made to serve political purposes. The *parlement*, for this reason, inserted into the secret article 34, which allowed for the holding of religious assemblies, the modification "by permission of his Majesty."[210] This was undoubtedly a judicious decision, for the impulse to maintain the political organization was strong. The assembly at Saumur, for instance, was still in session at the end of 1599, and the king had to apply his authority to oblige the deputies to disperse.[211] In fact, an ecclesiastical and military organization had been maintained, and ways round the edict were devised, so that it cannot be regarded as having satisfactorily terminated the existence of the "Protestant state." The edict was not, indeed, regarded as satisfactory at all, either by the Protestants, the king or the *parlements*. Nevertheless, it was a sane and reasonable compromise. In an eloquent and powerful harangue to the *parlement* of Paris, which delayed registration for ten dangerous months, the king maintained not that the edict was good, but that it was necessary. He did not ask his Catholic courts to endorse a principle of toleration—nowhere does the edict so much as hint at such a thing—for Henry was not concerned with toleration; he was concerned with peace. He could not legislate for the one, but he could provide for the other, and so he declared: "ceux qui ne desirent que mon edict passe me veulent la guerre"; and this, he made it clear, was something he would on no account endure.[212]

210. Benoist prints the article with this modification, and Anquez without.

211. Soulier, *Histoire du calvinisme*, 333.

212. Berger de Xivrey, *Lettres de Henri IV*, vol. v, 90–94, 7 February 1599, Henry's speech to the *parlement*.

Appendix
The Edicts of Religion, 1525–1598

Abbreviations for References Used in the Appendix

Cat. *Catalogue des Actes de François Ier*

Ord. *Ordonnances des rois de France. Règne de François Ier*

Haag Haag, *La France Protestante*

Isambert Isambert, *Recueil général des anciennes lois françaises*

Fontanon Fontanon, *Les Édits et ordonnances des rois de France*

Michaud Michaud et Poujoulat, *Nouvelle collection des mémoires pour servir à l'histoire de France*, série i

Duplessis-Mornay Duplessis-Mornay, *Mémoires et correspondance*

The following code is used so that it may be quickly seen, for purposes of reference, which edicts dealt with certain topics of importance.

A	Arms	O	Offices
C	Censorship	P	Property
D	Death penalty	PS	*Places de sûreté*
Inq.	Inquisition	T	*Temples*
J	Justice		

10 June 1525, Letters Patent
Cat. i, 408, no. 2170; Haag, x, 1.   Inq.

These letters patent implemented a bull of pope Clement VII, 17 May 1525, against the Lutherans (*Cat.* i, 405, no. 2154). The pope appointed Jacques de la Varde, André Verjus, Nicolas le Clerc, *conseillers* of the *parlement* of Paris, and Guillaume du Chesne, *curé* of Saint-Jean-en-Grève, to assist the inquisitor, according to the usual procedure in heresy cases. The function of inquisitor had, since the thirteenth century, been vested in the prior of the Dominicans. Le Clerc and du Chesne were both masters of theology and scholars of the University of Paris. This regulation applied only to the jurisdiction of the *parlement* of Paris. It is the first sign of an inclination, which can be traced through much of the sixteenth century, to revive the papal Inquisition.

29 December 1530, Saint-Germain, Letters Patent
Cat. vi (supplement, 1527–47), 240, no. 20120; *Ord.* vi
   (i), 135–36, no. 553.   Inq.

These letters patent required the *parlements, baillis, sénéchaux* and other officials of royal justice to aid and assist those appointed by Antoine du Prat, cardinal legate, archbishop of Sens and chancellor of France, in proceeding against the Lutherans in conjunction with the inquisitors ("d'avoir à prêter main-forte, aide et prisons aux juges délégués par Antoine Du Prat"); *juges délégués* was a technical term for those appointed to inquisitorial duties. Those for the *parlement* of Paris were Jacques Mesnager, Jean Chanderon, Jean Lécuyer and Quélain.

Unlike the regulation of 1525, this one applied to the whole kingdom. It was the first to require the royal officials both of the administration and the judiciary to assist those specially appointed to proceed against heretics as well as the *inquisiteurs de la foi*, which included the prelates.

10 December 1533, Lyons, Royal letters addressed to the *parlement* of Paris
Cat. ii, 579, no. 6584.   Inq.

These royal letters commanded the *parlement* to register two papal bulls, of 30 August and 10 November 1533, concerning the extirpation of Lutheranism (*Cat.* ii, 497, no. 6194; 522, no. 6450).

The first of these invited the king to attend to the extirpation of heresy and to reestablish in France the tribunal of the Inquisition.

The second related to the defrocking of heretic priests.

Francis I had just married his second son Henry to Catherine de Medici, niece of Clement VII, whose alliance he needed.

While this is not strictly an edict, the importance and relevance of the document warrant its inclusion.

13 January 1535, Letters Patent
Cat. iii, 3, no. 7461.   C

These were letters patent prohibiting the printing in France of any new book, until further notice.

There had previously been censorship regulations of the *parlement* of Paris. This was the first regulation to be issued by the crown and should probably be related to the incident known as the *placards*, in October 1534.

29 January 1535, Edict of Paris
Cat. iii, 8, no. 7486; *Ord.* vii (ii), 183–84, no. 678;
    Fontanon, iv, 245–46; Haag, x, 6.   P

This is known as the edict against harboring Protestants. It imposed the penalties of heresy on those who harbored or concealed heretics to save them from being brought to justice. Those who denounced either heretics or their protectors were to be rewarded with one quarter of the confiscations of property or fines imposed.

This edict should be related to the repercussions of the affair of the *placards*.

23 February 1535, Saint-Germain, Letters Patent
Cat. iii, 23–24, no. 7559.   C

These letters patent commissioned the *parlement* of Paris to elect twenty-four persons "bien califfiez et cautionnez." Of these, twelve were to be appointed to the sole right to print (i.e., reprint) in Paris, books approved and necessary for the public good ("pour imprimer à Paris seulement les livres approuvés et necessaires pour le bien de la chose publique"). No mention was made of the prohibition against the printing of any *new* works because it complemented the letters patent of 13 January 1535. Together they imposed a rigid control over printing within the jurisdiction of the *parlement* of Paris. Both were aimed at suppressing heretical works.

16 July 1535, Edict of Coucy
Cat. iii, 109, no. 7990; *Ord.* vii (3), 248–51, no. 701;
    Haag, x, 7–8; Isambert, xii, 405–7.   C D Inq. P

The edict of Coucy is usually described as an act of clemency because it declared that those who had been accused of heresy, and those who were suspect but not charged, should not be proceeded against. Those who had been imprisoned were to be released, and those who had suffered confiscations were to have their property restored; those who had fled might return if they abjured within six months before the bishop or his vicar-general together with the *inquisiteur de la foy*. But the edict excluded both recidivists and *sacramentaires*. Furthermore, it was forbidden, under penalty of the gallows, to read, assert, translate, compose, or print, in public or private, any doctrine contrary to the (Catholic) Christian faith.

The apparent clemency of this edict was intended to placate the king's German Protestant allies, while the exclusion clauses covered virtually all the potential beneficiaries.

This was the first regulation to introduce the death penalty for the propagation of heresy by any spoken or written means.

30 May 1536, Lyons, Letters Patent
Cat. iii, 208–9, no. 8472; *Ord.* viii (1), 90–92, no. 740;
Isambert, xii, 503. **Inq.**

These letters patent approved the replacement of the deceased Valentin Lievin by Mathieu Ory as prior of the Dominicans in Paris, and confirmed his traditional office of *inquisiteur de la foy*. The significance of this document is that Ory's powers were extended to the whole kingdom. He was empowered to proceed to the cognizance and punishment of cases concerning the Inquisition, together with the civil and ecclesiastical judges, according to the law. These specifications are not self-explanatory.

31 May 1536, Lyons, Letters Patent
Cat. iii, 209–10, no. 8476; *Ord.* viii (1), 93–96, no. 741.

This was a reissue of the edict of Coucy, 16 July 1535, for similar, diplomatic reasons.

16 December 1538, Edict of Paris
Cat. iii, 660, no. 10534. **C**

This edict was addressed to the *parlement* of Toulouse on the request of the *procureur général*. It authorized the *parlement* itself to proceed against heretics and those who trafficked in or concealed heretical books. The *parlement* was also to exhort the prelates to perform their duties in this respect.

This edict reflected the fact that Languedoc was a strongly Protestant area. This was the first time a lay authority was empowered to take the initiative in heresy cases.

24 June 1539, Edict of Paris
Cat. iv, 14, no. 11072. **P**

Previous measures to eradicate heresy, and the appointment of papal *juges délégués*, had not been effective, and the king was informed that those who spread heresy were assisted and protected by persons of rank. Thus the king, for his part, in respect of his own authority, also desired to rectify the matter; "ayans de nostre part en ce qui deppend et touche nostre puyssance et auctorité, désir et affection d'y mectre tel ordre que se doit. . . ." He therefore now required the *parlements, baillis* and *sénéchaux* to take cognizance of heresy as well as assisting the bishops, their vicarsgeneral, and the *inquisiteurs de la foy*, and to dispose of such cases without appeal, unless the *parlement* wished to increase the penalty. In certain circumstances they were authorized to apply torture. A quarter of the confiscated property and fines were to be awarded to the informers. The prelates were to pay the costs of heresy cases, and the *procureurs* of the *parlements* were to report to the king every six months.

This edict extended to all the *parlements* the power first granted to that of Toulouse to take the initiative in heresy cases. The *baillis* and *sénéchaux* were also similarly empowered. This, therefore, was when the king stepped in, and the royal administration began to take a direct part in the prosecution of heresy all over France.

This was the first edict to mention the use of torture in heresy cases, and the first to refer to the role of the nobility ("gros personnaiges") in the spread of heresy.

1 June 1540, Edict of Fontainebleau
Cat. iv, 111, no. 11509; Fontanon, iv, 246–48; Haag, x, 8–11.   Inq.

Because previous efforts to suppress heresy had been ineffective, the king himself also wished to assist in the matter. For this reason, and because he was informed that those who spread the infection were encouraged by persons of rank, it was decreed that the *parlements, baillis* and *sénéchaux* were all to have cognizance of, and to give priority to, heresy cases. The prisoner and the case were to be sent without delay for immediate judgment in the *chambre criminelle* of the *parlement. Seigneurs haut justiciers* were also to have cognizance of heresy cases, which they had to pass to the *baillis, sénéchaux,* or other royal judges. It was forbidden to receive or assist heretics because the profession of false doctrine "contiennent en soy crime de lèze-majesté divine et humaine, sédition de peuple et perturbation de nostre estat et repos public." Article 9 specifically declared that it was not the intention of the edict that the ecclesiastical authorities and *inquisiteurs de la foy* should cease to act against those within their jurisdiction, but they were to cooperate with secular officials. The *procureurs* were to keep the king informed, every six months, of their progress in the extirpation of heresy. This edict repeats the main provisions of that of 24 June 1539, presumably because the latter had not been registered by the *parlement* of Paris. It therefore demonstrates the beginning of a conflict of jurisdiction in heresy cases. The *parlement* will have resented the sovereign powers granted to the *baillis* and *sénéchaux* in 1539. In 1540 they were revoked, and these officials were enjoined to send their heresy cases to the *parlements* for judgment. Cognizance of heresy cases was now extended to all courts, and, in defining false doctrine as sedition, this edict rendered heresy a criminal as well as a canonical offense.

30 August 1542, Edict of Lyons
Cat. iv, 364, no. 12709.

This was a confirmatory edict addressed to the *parlements* of Paris, Bordeaux, Dijon, Grenoble and Rouen, exhorting them to execute the laws against heresy.

23 July 1543, Edict of Paris
Cat. iv, 473–74, no. 13224.

This edict published and erected into law twenty-five articles prepared by the Sorbonne in March 1543 (Fontanon, iv, 230–34). This was an attempt to define the Catholic faith—before the council of Trent—and rejection of these articles was declared to be heresy. This stipulation had the effect of being anti-Protestant because it made heresy easier to define. One of the obligatory tenets was the doctrine of transubstantiation, rejected by all branches of Protestantism.

23 July 1543, Edict of Paris
Cat. iv, 474, no. 13225; Fontanon, iv, 225–26.

This confused edict appears to have been in response to complaints by the clergy that the edict of 1 June 1540 had diminished their powers, although these were defined in article 9. The edict

purports to be interpretative, but in fact modifies the previous one
by attributing the judgment of heresy to the Church, and sedition
to the State, although both might initiate proceedings in such
cases. It seems likely that this should be related to the edict of the
same day which, by adopting certain articles of faith, made simple heresy easier to define. This edict might be seen as adumbrat-
ing that of Romorantin, May 1560, often alleged to be the first to
distinguish clearly between heresy and sedition, which was intended to protect Protestants from the Guise extremists who
dominated the council. In 1543, this fumbling distinction was not
helpful, since, by the edict of 1 June 1540, heresy itself was
declared sedition. The edict of 23 July 1543 made one other
important change: cases were no longer to be sent to the *parlements* for judgment, but had only to be reported to them within
two months. This change therefore marked a return to the sen-
tencing provisions of the edict of 24 June 1539, which the *parlement* of Paris had not registered. It would appear that there was
not only a conflict of jurisdiction between the sovereign courts
and the royal judiciary, but also between civil and ecclesiastical
authorities.

By 1543 the heresy laws were in a state of confusion.

5 April 1545, Letters Patent
Bulletin de la Société de l'histoire du protestantisme français,
    xxxiv, 1885, 26–27.   Inq.

These letters were a commission to five *conseillers* of the *parlement*
of Paris to perform the function of inquisitors in five areas under
the jurisdiction of the *parlement* of Paris: Claude des Asses to
Anjou and Touraine; Jacques de Roux to the *bailliage* of Sens;
Nicole Sanguin to the *bailliages* of Meaux and Provins; Guillaume
Bourgoing to the duché de Bourbonnais; and Louis Gayant to the
duché d'Orléans and the comté de Blois.

The particular reason—if there was one—for this commission is
not clear, but it could have been to enforce the regulations relating to the Sorbonne Index, first issued in March and completed in
August 1544.

11 December 1547, Edict of Fontainebleau
Fontanon, iv, 373–74. C

This was the first of the religious edicts of the reign of Henry II, in which he declared his intention to extirpate heresy. A principal means of doing this, the edict stated, was by the control of printed matter. It provided for control by the Sorbonne of the dissemination of any work on the scriptures, including those imported from abroad. It was also illegal to display or to sell any commentary on the scriptures without the name of the author, the printer and the printer's address. Finally, it was forbidden to possess—as well as to sell—any book proscribed by the Sorbonne. This clause referred to an Index produced by the Sorbonne in March 1544 and completed in August 1544, reissued in July 1545 and supplemented in December 1546. It included Calvin's *Institution Chrétienne*.

The Sorbonne had always been active in the matter of censorship. This edict extended censorship regulations to the whole country.

19 November 1549, Edict of Paris
Fontanon, iv, 249–50; Haag, x, 14–17.

This edict is sometimes said to be of 29 November 1549. It returned to the problem of jurisdiction in heresy cases, which had existed since the edict of 24 June 1539, and had aroused objections since that of 1 June 1540. The complaint still obtained that this edict had diminished the powers of the clergy by granting cognizance of heresy cases to the royal judiciary. This edict of 1549 therefore reiterated the declaration of 1543 that simple heresy pertained to the Church alone, and also extended clerical jurisdiction in heresy cases beyond the confines of the diocese. Where derivative offenses were involved, ecclesiastical and lay authorities should cooperate. Royal officials were not required to refer cases to the *parlements* for judgment, but the sovereignty of the *parlements* was restored in the case of appeals. Previously there had been no appeal. It was partly because of this problem of jurisdiction that, according to the preamble, Henry II had instituted, at the time of his accession, *une chambre particulière* in the *parlement* of Paris. This became known as the *chambre ardente*, and dealt exclusively with heresy cases until January 1550.

This edict would appear to be an attempt to resolve conflicts of jurisdiction, while maintaining the distinction between heresy and sedition, at the same time as repeating—in precisely the same words—the 1540 definition of heresy as sedition. It therefore achieved a partial clarification of the law.

11 February 1550, Edict of Fontainebleau
Fontanon, iv, 251.

This edict was largely confirmatory and made provision for cases of negligence in the pursuit of heretics.

22 June 1550, Letters Patent
Fontanon, iv, 226–27; Isambert, xiii, 173.   Inq.

The purpose of these letters was to bring the powers of Mathieu Ory, *inquisiteur général de la foy*, already confirmed on 16 November 1547, into line with the edict of 19 November 1549. The edict was not meant to detract in any way from Ory's powers, as he had apparently feared, and he was not required to report his activities to anyone but the bishops, who were also to keep him informed. Ory was to travel, as necessary, throughout the country "pour revoquer les errans... recevoir les penitens... et poursuivre les obstinez."

27 June 1551, Edict of Châteaubriant
Fontanon, iv, 252–57; Haag, x, 17–29.   C J O

The edict of Châteaubriant consists of a preamble and forty-six articles. It was the first comprehensive religious edict, described as "un vrai code de persécution." This phrase registers a shift in emphasis from prohibitions and control to positive persecution. This was because all the previous measures, which are inaccurately rehearsed in the preamble, had been ineffective. At least one of the reasons for this was the unreliability of the judiciary, which was partially Protestant. Thus the first article embodied yet another change in the juridical regulations. Now only the *parlements* and the presidial judges were to proceed against disorders arising from heresy in laymen and were to pronounce judgment without appeal. But simple heresy was the province of the Church. Articles 2 to 22 codified the stringent censorship regulations. One new provision was that the libraries of deceased persons had to be examined before sale. In Lyons, a big printing center, there were to be three special inspectors. This section also contained an injunction (article 18) against the defacing and smashing of images; the age of iconoclasm had begun. Apart from the control of printed works, it was made illegal to correspond with religious exiles in Protestant places and, in the case of "illiterate persons and foreigners," even to discuss religion. This suggests an element of near hysteria. The edict of Châteaubriant was the first to refer to what became the vexed question of offices and eligibility (articles 24 to 26). No one was to be appointed to a judicial or administrative office without a certificate of Catholicity. Furthermore, teachers in all schools, academies and universities, and even private tutors, had to be Catholic. This was also the first edict to render mandatory the duty of informing (articles 27 to 33). As a corollary to this, heretics and forbidden books were to be tracked down in private houses. Heretics were therefore no longer safe on condition of good conduct. This seeking out was an essential element of the Inquisition. The property of religious exiles, present and future, was to be confiscated (article 29). This clause would tend to obviate the development of a group of dangerously wealthy exiles. Another new aspect of this edict was the inclusion of certain obligatory religious observances. Church attendance and good conduct were compulsory, and the clergy were enjoined to read out the Sorbonne articles of faith of 1543 in every church on Sundays. With the edict of Châteaubriant, the religious persecution was beginning to move towards its climax.

This edict was not published by the *parlement* of Paris until 3 September 1551.

Isnard, *Actes royaux*, i, 179, no. 1014, gives the date of this edict as 21 June 1551. The difference is not significant.

24 July 1557, Letters Patent
Fontanon, iv, 228–29.   Inq.

These immensely important letters patent, described as a declaration on the papal brief of 26 April 1557, represent the principal
attempt to reestablish the Inquisition in France. Considering that
the popes had previously established "estats d'inquisiteurs de
la foy" and that "la voye de l'inquisition générale estoit grande-
ment utile," the king had requested the pope to delegate persons
of authority, virtue and probity. In response to this, his brief of
26 April 1557 had appointed the cardinals of Lorraine, Bourbon
and Châtillon "inquisiteurs généraux en nostre royaume." This
provision was accepted by the king on condition that they would
only delegate their powers to churchmen or others of proven
quality, who would swear an oath of fidelity before the privy
council. They were also to be obliged to cooperate with the
bishop in whose diocese they operated. The cardinals themselves
were to establish appeals tribunals in the *parlement* towns consisting of ten "bons et notables personnages," of whom at least six
were to be *conseillers* of the *parlement*. Decisions on the appeals
had to be executed by the royal officials. It is clear that the king
feared the opposition of the *parlement* in partly removing a latter-
day Inquisition from the control which they had obtained during
the later Middle Ages. Henry was right: the letters patent were
not registered until 15 January 1558—together with the edict of
Compiègne—and the *parlement* obstructed their implementation.
The letters patent and the papal commission of 26 April 1557 to
the cardinals were apparently rescinded in June 1558.

24 July 1557, Edict of Compiègne
Fontanon, iv, 258–59; Haag, x, 29–31.   D P

It should be noted that the edict of Compiègne bore the same date
as the letters patent confirming the papal appointment of three
cardinal inquisitors. It was the most savage of all the religious
edicts because it fulfilled the king's undertaking to support the
newly-decreed Inquisition with all the power of his secular arm.
The preamble refers to six previous edicts, which were clearly
meeting with different forms of opposition. This rather badly

drafted edict is of supreme importance in considering the religious causes of the civil wars. Its principal purpose was to impose the death penalty, without appeal, on all *sacramentaires* (who denied the doctrine of the Real Presence); all who preached in public or in private; who offended against the Sacrament, images, the Virgin and saints and who, in the furtherance of these things, raised seditions and popular assemblies; those who went to Geneva and the bearers of condemned books. The confiscated property of heretics was no longer to be appropriated or awarded to informers, but to be used for charitable purposes after the payment of expenses. The death penalty, however severe, was still a form of justice. But the document contained an even greater threat. It stated, in article 1: "... nous, considerans que telles emotions [religious disorders] sont autant à chastier et reprimer par armes que par voye de justice, et qu'à nous seul... appartient la correction et punition de telles seditions et troubles...." This article, together with the appointment of the cardinal inquisitors, could only be interpreted as a declaration of war by the king against his Protestant subjects. It is therefore not surprising that they prepared to defend themselves.

The edict of Compiègne was not registered in Paris until 15 January 1558.

2 June 1559, Letters Patent
Romier, *Les Origines politiques des guerres de religion*, ii, 362-64.

These letters patent, of Écouen, were issued two months after the peace of Cateau-Cambrésis, which terminated the so-called Italian wars. The king declared that he had been unable to proceed against the Protestants because of his preoccupations with foreign war. In the meanwhile—since 1557—the problem had worsened. Now the king intended to meet force with force. The revocation of the nascent Inquisition had therefore not changed Henry's disposition. If there had been any doubt about his intention in 1557 to take up arms against the Protestants, there could be none in 1559, more especially since the intention to extirpate heresy had been expressed in the peace treaty.

4 September 1559, Edict of Villers-Cotterêts
Fontanon, iv, 259–60.

The purpose of this Guisard edict, in the new reign of Francis II, was to prevent the continuation of illegal meetings, assemblies and conventicles by night. It declared that it was necessary to inflict "peine sur peine." Houses used for such meetings were to be razed to the ground. Presumably it was supposed that house owners would be more careful, and meetings become more difficult to organize.

This provision was resisted by the *parlement* of Paris except in cases in which the owner participated in the illegal activities. This proviso would, of course, make it possible to hold meetings without risking the house.

November 1559, Letters Patent, Blois
Fontanon, iv, 260.   D

This document appears to register the mounting anxiety of the Guises, who controlled the council of the young Francis II. Assemblies and conventicles had not only continued but even increased and were attended by "tant de diversites d'hommes," in other words, persons of all classes, including the nobility. Now it was feared that these meetings were not exclusively for religious purposes: "ils sement et divulguent plusieurs vilains, infames et injurieux propos contre nostre personne, et pour inciter nostre peuple à mutinerie et sedition." Thus, everyone holding or attending illicit meetings for religion or any other purpose, by day or by night, was to die. Houses used for meetings were to be razed. This regulation, therefore, extended the death penalty imposed by the edict of Compiègne, and confirmed that of Villers-Cotterêts, 4 September 1559. One may surmise that it was prompted by the first rumors of a conspiracy which materialized as the tumult of Amboise in March 1560.

This edict was registered on 23 November 1559. It is not clear whether it preceded or followed that of 13 November 1559.

13 November 1559, Letters Patent, Blois
Fontanon, iv, 260.

A second document of November 1559 (with the same page reference), contained the same statement about the increase in illicit assemblies and their attendance by all sorts and conditions of men. It made it obligatory to denounce meetings, on pain of punishment for heresy. An informant who had himself been involved would be pardoned, and, for one denunciation only, there was a reward of 100 *écus*. Informers were to be protected.

February 1560, Letters Patent, Amboise
Fontanon, iv, 261.

This document was issued on the first betrayal of the impending conspiracy of Amboise. It therefore repeated the statement in the letters of November 1559 that meetings were not only held for religion, but "s'y font plusieurs conspirations contre la chose publique tendans à la subversion . . . [du] Royaume." The purpose of the letters was to deprive of their office or jurisdiction anyone who ought to have prosecuted Protestants but did not. In order to check on their promptitude and efficiency, all such cases were to be reported to the *parlements* within a month. Those who failed in these two duties were themselves to be prosecuted by the *parlements*. This is the first document in the series to refer to the *seigneurs* who were protecting Protestants, and indicated the Guise fear of the country gentry, who were then involved in the conspiracy of Amboise.

From this time on, the current political situation and control of the council is reflected in the religious edicts.

March 1560, Edict of Amboise
Fontanon, iv, 261–63; Haag, x, 42–43.

This is the first edict both to mention and to show the influence of the queen mother, Catherine de Medici. It is expressly stated that her advice was sought, and from this time the edicts move away from the extreme repression of Henry II towards the edict of

January 1562, when limited toleration was granted. Thus it is stated that, various punishments having been tried, the king did not wish to sully the first year of his reign by a bloodbath—a reference to the conspiracy of Amboise then about to break—but hoped for greater success "par la misericorde." The purpose of the edict was therefore to offer a pardon for all past crimes of religion on condition of abjuration. Pastors, however, were excepted from the pardon, as were conspirators against the royal family, the State, and the king's ministers; also those who released prisoners and obstructed couriers. This edict, therefore, carried a limited pardon, calculated to detach the leadership from the rank and file. It was the first edict to mention the influence of pastors from Geneva. It also openly stated that the number of Protestants was so great that the situation was out of hand. From this time on, Catherine acted in the realization that Protestantism could not be extirpated from France.

This edict was followed by a pardon, about 18 March, for all who came in arms—to Amboise—provided they withdrew in twos or threes within forty-eight hours. Those who persisted, however, and many did, were to be hanged and strangled there and then, without trial, and by any person. The king, however, would receive their petition.

The Guises would never have issued such a pardon. It was the work of Catherine de Medici and the chancellor L'Hospital—possibly also of Coligny, but for this there is no evidence.

This edict was issued about 2 March, and registered on the eleventh.

March 1560, *"Ampliation de l'Édit du Roy"*
Isnard, *Actes royaux*, i, 251, no. 1487; B. N., Mss. Fr., 47022 (16).

The edict and pardon of Amboise was followed, on the advice of Catherine de Medici, by this "ampliation." Many of those who had approached Amboise in arms with a petition to the king were discovered, upon interrogation, to be simple souls, ignorant of the implications of their actions. This further, specific pardon gave them an opportunity to withdraw. The exemplary punishment of everyone who was captured would, in any case, have presented even the angry Guises with practical difficulties.

This pardon was published in Amboise on 17 March and in Tours on 22 March 1559/60.*

May 1560, Edict of Romorantin
Fontanon, iv, 229–30; Haag, x, 43–45.   C

The preamble to this edict is important, both in itself and as a clear statement of the policy of Catherine de Medici, to whom it refers. It states that the king's predecessors had been obliged to "prendre en main la cognoissance et punition de tels crimes." In other words, the judiciary had been empowered to act in heresy cases. But now the king wished—and this was Catherine's policy—"de mettre les choses à l'ancien forme et estat." The edict therefore returned to the position which obtained before 1530, and no civil court or authority, including the *parlements*, was to have competence in heresy cases, "ne s'en mesler aucunement." Thus, "l'entière cognoissance de tout crime d'heresie" was left to the prelates. This presumably included those canonical offenses listed in the edict of Compiègne, 24 July 1557, as sedition, and subject to the death penalty. As the Church did not impose capital punishment, this was a relatively unobtrusive way of departing from the extreme persecution of Henry II. The bishops were commanded to reside in their dioceses and attend to the problem of heresy. Royal officials were to report on absentees. Similarly, the removal of heresy from the cognizance of civil authorities eliminated the odious inquisitorial clauses of the edict of Châteaubriant, 27 June 1551, by which people could be persecuted in their homes. Thus the situation was restored in which Protestants could survive if they behaved discreetly, though naturally no such intention was expressed.

The purpose of this edict was not, however, to distinguish between heresy and sedition, as has often been alleged. If not,

*I am indebted to Dr. J. Bergin for having read this document for me.

perhaps, quite so sharply, this distinction had existed in the edicts since 1543. The edict of Romorantin was issued during the aftermath of the conspiracy of Amboise the previous March. Its purpose was to provide more specifically for the maintenance of law and order, at the same time as alleviating the judicial—not the religious—position of sincere Protestants. Thus the edict not only again prohibited all illicit assemblies (sic), but also "forces publiques," without, however, any reference to the purpose of the gathering. The inference was that this referred to groups assembling in arms, as at Amboise. Anyone who held or attended any such assembly or gathering was declared an enemy and a rebel and subject to the penalties of *lèse-majesté*. The *gouverneurs, lieutenants, baillis, sénéchaux, prévôts des marchands* and all judges were to obviate and prevent all such assemblies and, where they occurred, to act immediately, and to prepare the case for the prosecution. These cases were to be submitted to the sovereign jurisdiction of a tribunal of ten in the presidial courts. These were the newest of the royal courts and therefore presumably the most easily controlled by the crown. It was obligatory to inform on illicit assemblies; informers who had attended were pardoned, and innocent informers were rewarded with 500 *livres*. Preachers and makers of placards, cartels and libels, their printers, vendors and distributors were also subject to the same penalties as for holding illicit assemblies. Thus the most important aspect of this significant edict, which marks a turning point in Protestant affairs, was its preoccupation with law and order rather than with religion. While clamping down severely on all acts of public disorder it implied, though it did not declare, liberty of conscience and an end to *persecution* on purely religious grounds; though heretics were still subject to *prosecution* by the Church. Finally, its removal of jurisdiction in heresy cases from the then violently Catholic *parlements* was a fundamental change, to the advantage of the Protestants.

The *parlement* of Paris refused to register this edict until 16 July and complained that the position of the *parlements* was unclear. A declaration of 6 August 1560 (Fontanon, iv, 230) stated that it had not been intended to deprive the *parlements* of cognizance in cases of illicit assemblies and "forces publiques." This would appear to be a modification, possibly to appease the *parlements;* but it could be an omission.

May 1560, Edict of Loches
Condé, *Mémoires*, i, 539.

This was an edict of amnesty for all past religious offenses. It may 'have been issued because the pardon following the edict of Amboise, March 1560, had not been honored by Catholic extremists. It could also have been an attempt to obviate further repercussions. It clearly demonstrated the influence of Catherine de Medici and her moderate advisers.

28 January 1561, *Lettres de cachet*
Michaud, *série* i, vol. vi, *Mémoires du prince de Condé*, 570–71.

This was a personal measure of Catherine de Medici, then queen regent, because it was she who possessed the royal *cachet*, the personal seal of her ten-year-old son, Charles IX. It was, therefore, what would be called in English, a prerogative form of law, not requiring registration by the *parlements*. It specifically confirmed—in the new reign—the edict of Romorantin, and was described as an act of clemency upon the king's accession (5 December 1560). Thus all prisoners for religion were to be released and all heresy cases suspended, even those against persons who had assembled in arms or provided money. Catherine therefore used her new position to issue a final amnesty for those involved in the conspiracy of Amboise, except for the "aucteurs et chefs des séditions." It is interesting to note that pastors were not excluded from the amnesty. This was the first edict to mention Antoine de Bourbon, king of Navarre, who was associated with Catherine de Medici in the regency. The timing can be related to events in the estates general, then in session, which were inclined to challenge the regency on which they had not been consulted. It was declared that the *lettres de cachet* were to be regarded as letters patent, which would have been subject to registration by the *parlements*. The *parlement* of Paris predictably resisted this stipulation. Thus it was ordered, by letters patent of 22 February 1561 (ibid., 571) to implement the letters of 28 January. As a sop, the *parlements* were required to decree, on pain of the gallows, the exile of any released prisoner who refused to abjure. This clause therefore modified the *lettres de cachet*, and illustrates the implacable conflict between the crown and the *parlement* over the treatment of Protestants, which existed from May 1560 until the edict of Nantes in 1598.

19 April 1561, Edict of Fontainebleau
Condé, *Mémoires*, ii, 334–35.   P

This edict related to the increase in public disturbances, of which many occurred over Easter in 1561. It also confirmed existing regulations which were being resisted. The edict prohibited mutual abuse and provocations and the use of epithets such as "Huguenot" and "papist"; also all forms of iconoclasm, offenses against property, and the detention of persons. Anyone in prison, who should have been freed after the *lettres de cachet* of 28 January, was to be released. Persons exiled for religion since the previous reign might return and recover their property if they abjured, or, refusing abjuration, they might sell it. It was now specified that nobody was to be persecuted in his house, thereby repealing that clause of the edict of Châteaubriant, 27 June 1551. Here again one can see Catherine de Medici working for the protection of those who behaved discreetly. This last clause, however, was interpreted as permission to hold private assemblies. It is clear from the Protestant petition of 11 June 1561 (Condé, *Mémoires*, ii, 370–72) that this edict was not implemented.

11 July 1561, Edict of Saint-Germain
Condé, *Mémoires*, i, 42–45; Fontanon, iv, 264–65;
    Haag, x, 47–48; Isambert, xiv, 109–11.   A D

This edict followed what were called the "pourparlers de Paris," which considered the Protestant petition of 11 June 1561. The document actually states that the king had assembled the council in the *parlement*. Estienne Pasquier described this as a neutral edict. This is because it reflected the difference of opinion on the problem of religion, and the struggle for power in the council. Because there was no agreement upon what the edict should contain, it was very ambiguously drafted. It confirmed the edict of Romorantin, May 1560, in respect of heresy, specifically confirming the attribution of religious sedition to the presidial courts, thereby ignoring the declaration of 6 August 1560, which had again included the *parlements*. It also reaffirmed the provisions of the edict of Fontainebleau, 19 April 1561, against provocations, incendiary preaching and the violation of persons and property. It was, however, specified that no religious assemblies were to be held, in public or in private, thereby closing the loophole in the edict of Fontainebleau. Banishment was to be the maximum penalty for heresy, and the edict pardoned all religious offenses, including sedition, since the death of Henry II. It therefore rehabilitated those responsible for the conspiracy of Amboise. This was probably in favor of the prince de Condé, who was popularly believed to have been behind the conspiracy, although this is impossible to demonstrate. It was further stipulated that authorities were not to pursue persons indiscreetly—"n'abuser de l'execution du contenu." This would appear to have restored the loophole of Fontainebleau for holding assemblies in private. Finally, it was prohibited, for the first time in this series of edicts, to carry arms, on pain of death. This severity reflected the government's grave preoccupation with the mounting problem of law and order and the new menace of firearms.

20 October 1561, Edict of Saint-Germain

Fontanon, iv, 265–67; Condé, *Mémoires*, ii, 520, gives 18 October.   A D

This edict followed the failure of the *colloque* of Poissy, and the preamble stated that neither justice—i.e., severity—nor clemency had been effective in appeasing the religious troubles. This is a severe edict, because of the government's anxiety at the ever-increasing disorders (preamble). The king had received complaints against persons who had seized churches and committed other offenses against Church property. All seized churches were to be relinquished, and all property restored and returned immediately; any further offenses in this category were to be punished by death. The prohibition against mutual provocations was again repeated, and those guilty of any form of iconoclasm were to be hanged. The prohibition against carrying arms was similarly repeated, and the penalty was death. No hotellier was to lodge anyone carrying arms without reporting it, and in towns and villages arms were to be surrendered under supervision of the *gouverneur*. The *baillis* and *sénéchaux* were censured for negligence and absence and, together with the *gouverneurs* and their *lieutenants*, were ordered to their posts in the provinces to maintain order and enforce justice.

The explanation of the extreme penalty for offenses against the Church, Church property and revenues is that the government hoped, thereby, to obtain money from the clergy, then assembled.

The edict described the king of Navarre as lieutenant general throughout the kingdom. This office conferred vice-regal powers and the position of commander-in-chief. Slipping it into a religious edict was a way of legally confirming the appointment, so that it could not be challenged. Since it was unwelcome to Catholics, this was important.

17 January 1562, Edict of Saint-Germain
Fontanon, iv, 267–69; Haag, x, 48–52.   A C D

This edict—which was influenced by the Protestant petition of 11 June 1561—is generally known as the edict of January. As the first to grant a measure of limited toleration, it is one of the most important of the whole series. Its purpose was "d'appaiser les troubles et seditions pour le fait de la religion." The preamble stated both the problem and the difficulties experienced since the *pourparlers de Paris* the previous June. Consequently, a similar meeting of the council in the *parlement* had been summoned to Saint-Germain in January 1562. The edict of January repeated the prohibitions of 20 October 1561 relating to Church property, and maintained the death penalty. It was expressly forbidden to meet in the towns, by day or night, for preaching. However, it was provisionally permitted to meet outside the towns, unarmed, by day to celebrate the cult. It should be noted that in making this arrangement the government still had in mind the problem of public order. While purely religious meetings were not to be prevented, all sedition was to be prosecuted. Only persons of good life were to be admitted to meetings. No synods or consistories were to be held without permission from, or in the presence of, some royal official. Any necessary rules for the exercise of religion were to be submitted for authorization. All charities were to be voluntary, and no money or men were to be raised. It was obligatory to observe Church holidays (for commercial reasons) and the prohibited degrees in marriage. Ministers were to swear to obey the edict, and to observe certain rules about preaching. Printers and distributors of placards and libels incurred the death penalty for a second offense. The clause in the edict of 20 October 1561 ordering officials to their posts was repeated because, it is stated (article 14), the regulation was made for the preservation of general peace. In the provinces, officials were to deal promptly with any sedition, using the tribunals of ten in the presidial courts, from which there was no appeal. It should be noted that the Protestants were still forbidden to possess churches.

In several ways this edict was strongly Catholic, making only minimum concessions. Thus, apart from permission to celebrate the cult, outside the towns, unarmed, and by day, it was specified that previous edicts should "en toutes autres choses sortir leur plain et entier effet, et demeurer en leur force et vertu." This edict of January was a last resort in the hope of avoiding war. On the Protestant side, it probably would have averted war, because Calvin forbade them to take up arms in the cause of religion. But it failed, like all the edicts which followed, because it was implacably opposed by the extreme Catholics. Thus it helped to precipitate the war it was intended to obviate.

The edict of January was followed, on 14 February, by a "declaration" (Fontanon, iv, 269–70) clarifying certain points and specifying that the edict was not to be taken as implying approval of two religions in the kingdom. This was because of the opposition of the *parlement*, which refused to register the edict until 6 March, after having received two *lettres de jussion*. Not only did the *parlement* oppose any degree of toleration, but the edict of January once again denied them jurisdiction in cases arising from heresy.

11 April 1562, Declaration on the edict of January
Fontanon, iv, 271. D

The refusal of the *parlement* to register the edict of January had resulted in a Protestant rising at Orléans. The rebels were afraid of being deprived of the benefit and protection of the edict. The declaration therefore expressly confirmed the edict, so that those who were sincerely concerned for religious liberties should have no cause to rise, and those who were not would be exposed. Quarrels and provocations on the subject of religion were now prohibited on pain of death—a clause which was probably aimed at the nobility.

It should be noted that this declaration was issued on the same day as the manifesto of the prince de Condé. The purpose of the declaration was to bring about the laying down of arms, under the protection of the king and, for the Protestants, to secure the edict of January.

It is possible to see the influence of Catherine de Medici in the express confirmation of the edict, in spite of the Guisard control of the council. On the other hand, since the Protestants could hardly lay down arms unilaterally, it could have been a Catholic device for placing the Protestants in the wrong.

19 March 1563, Edict of Amboise
Fontanon, iv, 272-74. A D O P

This was the first of the "edicts of pacification," so-called because they terminated civil wars. The preamble referred to the miseries of war, in particular the entry of foreign mercenaries and the danger from foreign neighbors (line 19). The reference was to Spain, and to the presence of the English in Le Havre. It was hoped that time, a good, holy, free general or national council, and the majority of the king would bring peace. This was the first edict to allow the nobility (who alone knew how to make war) certain privileges in respect of religion. Thus *seigneurs haut jus-ticiers* might hold the cult in their own houses in which they were resident, each with his own family and vassals. Others holding fiefs might celebrate the cult at home for their families only. This edict modified the toleration clause of the edict of January, which, for all its inconvenience, had been relatively liberal and, far more important, free of administrative problems. The cult was now permitted in the subrubs of only one town per *bailliage* or *sénéchaussée;* also in one or two places in each town where it had been exercised up to 7 March 1563. All Church property, goods and revenues seized during the war were to be restored. Everyone was to be restored to his property, status, honors and offices. Condé and his followers were pardoned and rehabilitated. The edict declared a total amnesty for all injurious acts committed during the war, and prohibited the pursuit of quarrels arising from them on pain of death. Religious prisoners and prisoners of war were to be released. Article 15 prohibited the formation of any associa-tions, within or without the kingdom, and the raising of money and men. The first Catholic leagues dated from about this time, and the moderate Catherine had reason to fear them.

This edict was heavily weighted in favor of the nobility, whereas the real religious problem lay in the towns. It raised almost insu-perable administrative problems, and was never satisfactorily im-plemented. On 18 June the king issued commissions to *conseillers* of the *parlements* to travel the provinces with powers to enforce the edict (Fontanon, iv, 274-76). There was no appeal against their decisions except to the royal council. A declaration of 14 June 1563 (Fontanon, iv, 276-79) details the complexity of the administrative problem. Another declaration of 4 August 1564 (Fontanon, iv, 279-81) reintroduced the death penalty for acts of provocation and of iconoclasm and repeated the prohibition against carrying arms. The edict of Amboise was unwisely con-ceived, in view of the pre-war difficulties.

23 March 1568, Edict of Longjumeau
Fontanon, iv, 289–91; Haag, x, 83–87.   O P

The edict of Longjumeau which terminated the second civil war restored, without any of its subsequent modifications, the previous peace of Amboise, 19 March 1563. This would appear to have destroyed an immense amount of subsequent work on its execution. The edict of Longjumeau was to be sent direct to the *gouverneurs* for publication and implementation, without awaiting registration by the *parlements*. They were ordered to drop all other business and to register it forthwith. The appointment of the duc d'Anjou as lieutenant general in December 1567 was formally confirmed in this edict, like that of Navarre in the edict of 20 October 1561. Anjou's appointment was made in order to avoid replacing the constable of France after the death in November 1567 of the old duc de Montmorency. In theory this expedient retained the function of commander-in-chief for the crown.

[28] September 1568, Edict of Saint-Maur
Fontanon, iv, 292–94.

This remarkable edict was prepared by the cardinal of Lorraine largely to precipitate the third civil war, which he desired. It mostly consisted of a long preamble, representing a highly partisan account of the extreme Catholic point of view since the reign of Henry II, when Lorraine and the duc de Guise were powerful. Apart from the Catholic statement, the purpose of the edict was to prohibit the exercise of any but the Catholic religion, and to banish the Protestant pastors.

8 August 1570, Edict of Saint-Germain
Fontanon, iv, 300–4; Haag, x, 91–99.   J O P PS

This is an important, seminal edict. It was negotiated over a long period of time during which the Huguenots were militarily strong enough to obtain an edict of rehabilitation. Its purpose was to restore peace. Article 1 imposed an amnesty, and article 2 forbade attacks, injuries and reproaches. This was the first edict to require the restoration of mass (article 3) wherever it had been discontinued. There were slight modifications in the toleration clauses: the nobility retained religious privileges, and the cult was permitted in the suburbs of two towns per *gouvernement* and not, as previously, per *bailliage* or *sénéchaussée*. These towns were named in the edict, thereby obviating the difficulties which had arisen in 1563. The cult was also permitted in places where it was publicly held on 1 August 1570. It was not permitted within two leagues of the court, or nearer to Paris than Senlis, Meaux and Melun. The *baillis* and *sénéchaux* were to provide for Protestant burials, by night. The edict contained exoneration clauses, similar to those of Amboise and Longjumeau, and prohibitions against associations and the raising of men and money. It also specified the restoration of all property and offices. All documents and title deeds were to be restored, and Anjou, the lieutenant general, and the marshals of France were constituted as a special tribunal for cases arising from the wars. It was the first edict to embody civil and judicial rights for Protestants. There was to be no religious discrimination in admission to schools, universities, hospitals, and the like, and they were expressly declared eligible for appointment to all offices (article 22). Nor were they to be taxed more than Catholics. All judgments passed against Protestants since the reign of Henry II were to be suspended, and the records erased from all courts. Cases between persons of different religions were to be heard before the *baillis* and *sénénchaux*. In the *parlements* Protestants had the right to impugn four judges in any one case. The edict of Saint-Germain reflected the Protestants' mounting preoccupation with security because previous edicts had been ill-enforced and violently opposed by the Catholics. Thus they obtained four *places de sûreté* for two years: La Rochelle, Montauban, Cognac, and La Charité on the Loire. The problem of enforcement, which had frustrated the purpose of three previous edicts, was tackled in article 32, which required all royal officials and municipal officers to swear to observe the edict; similarly the *parlements*, who were also ordered to register it forthwith. Anyone who obstructed its publication and enactment by arms, force or violence was subject to the death penalty; non-violent obstruction was subject to other punishments such as banishment, fines, whipping and penance. In order to avoid any confusion or tergiversation, article 43 declared this edict to supersede all others. For this reason it had in itself to be comprehensive. Thenceforth the Huguenots persistently claimed these new advantages.

[2] July 1573, Peace of La Rochelle (Edict of Boulogne, Paris)

Haag, x, 110–14.   J O P PS

The peace of La Rochelle was intended to end the fourth civil war, which began with the massacre of St. Bartholomew in August 1572. On the national level, it had consisted of the siege of La Rochelle. In most respects this edict was very similar to that of Saint-Germain, except for the vital toleration clauses. For this reason it was the cause of still worse trouble. Articles 1 to 3 on amnesty, recriminations and the restoration of mass corresponded to those of Saint-Germain. But, apart from freedom of conscience, there was little religious liberty. The privileges of the nobility were curtailed (article 5), and only the inhabitants of La Rochelle, Montauban and Nîmes were allowed to exercise the cult privately. Except that the *baillis* and *sénéchaux* were—as under Saint-Germain—to provide for burials, this was all. The articles of Saint-Germain relating to civil rights and offices were repeated. Similarly, property was to be restored. It was now also permitted to sell property and go into exile, or to enjoy property revenue abroad (article 9). In case of death, Protestant heirs were assured the right of inheritance (article 16). Everyone was to recover his house; moveable property was to be restored or paid for, and—as under Saint-Germain—all documents and title deeds were to be returned. As previously, cases between Catholics and Protestants were to be heard in the first instance by the *baillis*, *sénéchaux* and *juges ordinaires*. But in cases of appeal to the *parlement*, the king would, within one year, provide impartial judges, except for the *parlement* of Toulouse (article 18). Various articles related to the three privileged towns. The enforcement clause (article 25) was not nearly as comprehensive as that of Saint-Germain. Only the *baillis* and *sénéchaux* were to have the principal inhabitants of their towns swear to observe the edict. This was a disastrous edict, rashly concluded and crudely drafted; its real purpose was to extricate the duc d'Anjou from La Rochelle. He was held to be in danger and had been elected to the throne of Poland.

6 May 1576, Peace of Monsieur (Edict of Beaulieu)
Haag, x, 127–41.   C J O PS T

The peace of Monsieur belongs in importance with those of January 1562 and Saint-Germain, 8 August 1570. The peace of Monsieur should be related to the terms of the Protestant petition of 25 August 1573, which specified their minimum requirements. This was the most liberal edict they ever achieved, and its timing and content were closely related to the political and military situation. Its vast concessions were virtually dictated in arms.

Like the peace of La Rochelle, it reiterated the first three articles of Saint-Germain, to which it bears a close resemblance. The principal new achievement in 1576 was the free, general and public exercise of the cult in all Protestant places and elsewhere by consent. This excluded Paris and a circumference of two leagues. As in the edict of January 1562, synods and consistories were authorized in the presence of royal officials. Furthermore the possession of churches (*temples*) was permitted for the first time. Protestant burials were again provided for; they were required to observe Church holidays and the degrees of consanguinity. The clauses of Saint-Germain on eligibility were retained (articles 11, 17, 22, 23, and 46), and those unable to take an oath of office might affirm. Furthermore, the king undertook actually to make Protestant appointments. Similarly, previous clauses about the restoration of property, including that of the Church, were repeated. In respect of justice (articles 18 to 22), this edict went beyond that of Saint-Germain, creating the *chambres mi-parties*, namely tribunals of equal numbers of Catholics and Protestants. Their composition, in each *parlement*, was specified. Those cases pertaining to the sovereign tribunals of the presidial courts were to have the right of appeal—temporarily—to the new *chambres*, unless the presidial tribunals could themselves be *mi-parties*.

The peace of Monsieur rehabilitated all those involved in the massacre of St. Bartholomew, and restored rights of inheritance to relatives of the deceased. It also exonerated all acts of hostility which had followed and stemmed from the massacre, every aspect of which was amnestied. No one was to be pursued for non-payment of taxes since the massacre, and Protestants—now referred to as *RPR, religion prétendue réformée*—were not to be taxed more than Catholics. Similarly, all those involved in acts of hostility and the arrangements necessary for war since 1573 were pardoned and rehabilitated. Associations were again prohibited, although the catholics immediately proceeded to form leagues and associations to resist the peace. The king declared his intention to summon an estates general at Blois in six months' time. Certain censorship regulations were revived (article 5). The problem of security had rather increased than diminished. Thus, besides various military arrangements, eight *places de sûreté* were permitted, two each in Languedoc, Guyenne, Provence and Dauphiné. The enforcement regulations of the edict of Saint-Germain were reiterated and extended, and the marshals—hinting at force—were to attend to its implementation. It was to be published and enforced immediately, and, as under Saint-Germain, its obstruction in arms was subject to the death penalty. These were the main clauses of the peace of Monsieur, which superseded all others.

17 September 1577, Edict of Poitiers (Peace of Bergerac)

Fontanon, iv, 318–26; Haag, x, 142–56; Isambert, xiv, 330–41.   C J O PS

The peace of Bergerac was concluded on 14 September and the edict of Poitiers (where the king was resident) was signed on 17 September. It represented the modification of the peace of Monsieur, 6 May 1576, which resulted from the Catholic opposition to the peace, the demand of the estates general, 1576–77, for only one religion, and the hostilities which that demand provoked. After the liberal terms of the peace of Monsieur, the Huguenots would never again submit to a total denial of their religion, and they were too strong to be coerced.

The edict consisted of sixty-four articles, plus forty-eight secret ones concluded with Navarre and Condé, comprising certain privileges for them. The king also undertook to pay for 800 men to guard the *places de sûreté,* and to pay the Protestants' German mercenaries—*reistres.* Apart from minor details, the sixty-four articles of the main treaty followed the peace of Monsieur, most of which was safely retained, except for the clauses relating to toleration, justice and the *places de sûreté.* Certain religious privileges were restored for the nobility and the cult was permitted— as under the edict of Amboise, 19 March 1563—in the suburbs of one town per *baillage* or *sénéchaussée,* as well as in all towns where it was publicly held on 17 September, except those which belonged to Catholic *seigneurs* and had not been Protestant before the war. The *chambres de justice* were no longer to be *mi-parties.* Their composition in each *parlement* was specified in the edict and all members were to be appointed by the king. The Protestants were again permitted eight *places de sûreté* in the same four southern provinces, but this time for six years. This edict is held to have restored a reasonable compromise after the peace of Monsieur and its later abrogation by the estates general.

28 February 1579, Treaty of Nérac
Haag, x, 159–67.   J PS T

The articles of Nérac interpreted and added to those of Poitiers, 17 September 1577, illustrating the difficulties which had arisen. They were intended to restore peace where this had been broken. The religious privileges of the nobility were extended; article 11 of Poitiers was interpreted to include permission to acquire churches (first allowed in the peace of Monsieur); arrangements were made for the raising of money—otherwise forbidden—for the payment of pastors—although they were indirectly designated. Most of the articles consist of detailed administrative matters and further efforts to enforce articles of Poitiers, which had been ignored.

26 November 1580, Treaty of Fleix
Haag, x, 171–78.

Since the peace of Nérac, further troubles had ensued. The treaty of Fleix confirmed the articles of Poitiers, 17 September 1577, plus its secret articles, and the treaty of Nérac, 28 February

1579. The king was to be asked (sic, article 38) to supply a further 45,000 *livres* to pay the Protestants' mercenaries. The agreement was confirmed by the king at Blois, on 26 December 1580.

7 July 1585, Treaty of Nemours
Haag, x, 184–87.   J O P PS

The treaty of Nemours was imposed on Henry III by the duc de Guise and his Catholic League and, like the edict of Saint-Maur, September 1568, destroyed all the laboriously won edicts of pacification. The Catholics, with the help of Spain, now succeeded where they had failed in 1576. Thus the edicts of pacification were formally revoked, and the exercise of the *RPR* was forbidden. Pastors were to be banished within a month and Protestants were to abjure within six months or be exiled, but they might either sell their property or receive their income. The *chambres de justice* were revoked and Protestants were declared ineligible for offices. Anyone who took any sort of action because of the prohibition of the cult, was subject to the death penalty. The *places de sûreté* were to be evacuated and garrisons withdrawn. Finally, the Guises built into this treaty with the king exoneration for their rising, and for having negotiated abroad (with Spain). This treaty was followed, on 9 September (Haag, x, 187–91), by a papal bull barring Navarre, heir apparent, and Condé from the succession, and all other inheritances.

Thus the treaty of Nemours heralded the final years of tragedy in the reign of Henry III, and the Huguenot struggle for a guarantee of religious and civil rights had to begin all over again.

7 October 1585, Declaration of Henry III on the Treaty of Nemours
Haag, x, 191–94.   P

The king had allowed the Protestants six months in which to abjure, or else to dispose of their property and leave France. According to the declaration, this period had been abused to support an armed rising in Guyenne, Languedoc and Dauphiné.

Protestants were therefore commanded to lay down arms on pain of confiscation of property to pay for war against them. No one was to sell them anything or disburse money owed to them. The Protestants now had only two more weeks in which to abjure or make their arrangements, except for women, who might have the remainder of the original six months.

30 November 1585, Declaration of the King of Navarre
Haag, x, 194–95.

On 6 November 1585 Navarre replied in angry and irreverent terms to the papal bull of 9 September 1585, by which he was excommunicated and barred from the throne. Then, on 30 November, he reluctantly declared war. He protested that he had used the greatest moderation, and deferred action as long as he could. Now he was obliged to oppose "une si extrême et injuste violence."

July 1588, Édit d'Union
Haag, x, 201–3.   O

By July 1588 Henry was no more than a puppet of the League. He was now forced to subscribe to terms he had evaded in 1577. Thus he reaffirmed his coronation oath to extirpate heresy, "sans faire jamais aucune paix ou trève avec les hérétiques ni aucun édit en leur faveur." He summoned all Catholics to join him in a similar oath, and not to obey a heretic prince—Navarre—if he, Henry III, died childless. He promised to give no military post to a non-Catholic and to admit no one to financial or judicial office without an oath of Catholicity. He announced his union to the Catholic League, and all Catholics were to devote themselves to "la conservation de nous et de notre autorité." Those who refused to sign this act of union and those who subsequently contravened it were declared rebels. In some respects this document resembled Henry's articles of association, 2 December 1576 (François, *Lettres de Henri III*, vol. iii, 85–88), but he could not overmaster the Catholic confederates a second time, with Philip II and the pope behind them. Again, as in the treaty of Nemours, the Guises incorporated a total exoneration for all their acts of treason, including the events of 12–13 May, the barricades in Paris, when the king escaped with his life by fleeing to Chartres.

Thus Henry's capitulation was complete; five months later, in December 1588, he executed against Guise an act of summary jurisdiction.

3 April 1589, *Traité de la Trève* Duplessis-Mornay, iv, 351–55.

The death of the duc de Guise, slain in the *château* of Blois in December 1588, opened the way for an agreement between the king and Navarre. Navarre agreed to serve the king against those "qui violent l'auctorité de sa majesté et troublent son estat." For this purpose they agreed on an immediate cease-fire and a truce for one year in order to join forces against their common enemy. During this time the status quo should be frozen. The meaning of this is obscure. Navarre was to receive Les Ponts-de-Cé—to provide a crossing over the Loire—but in fact Saumur was substituted. Navarre's task was to march immediately against the duc de Mayenne, brother of the late duc de Guise, and now leader of the Catholic League. He was not to interfere with the Catholic religion or Church property. Any captured *places* were to be ceded to the king. But Navarre might, for his safety and financial security, keep one town per *bailliage* or *sénéchaussée*, without molesting the Catholics. Neither were Protestants to be molested. The cult was authorized in Saumur, in the army, wherever Navarre was present, and in the town that he held in each *bailliage* and *sénéchaussée*. There was a clause to cover the restoration, on both sides, of all sequestered property.

This, therefore, was a hasty working agreement between Henry and Navarre permitting him to oppose Mayenne without delay. Just as Guise was to die a few months after the *édit d'union* so, one may suspect, the *traité de la trève* may have had something to do with the murder of Henry III four months later. The king and Navarre together might well have vanquished the League.

24 April 1589, Declaration of Navarre on the *Traité de la Trève*

Haag, x, 203–5.

The purpose of this declaration was to justify the truce with the king. It was well-known that Navarre had been forced to take up arms against the enemies of the kingdom, and wished, in this respect, to serve the king. "Il est evident," he declared, "que cette guerre commencée sous ombre de religion s'est trouvée tout à coup pure guerre d'etat." In these circumstances Navarre's duty was to serve the king, and from this he hoped for "une bonne paix à l'avenir." Thus Navarre issued his orders for the observance of the truce.

26 April 1589, Declaration of the king on the *Traité de la Trève*

Haag, x, 205–8; Isambert, xiv, 645–50.

Like Navarre, Henry was also obliged to justify his truce with the Protestants. He declared that his Catholicism had been clearly demonstrated, but the impediment in this had not come from the Protestants, but from others who had "practised a league" for the usurpation of the kingdom. They had rebelled against the king, publicly threatened his life, and planned with foreign princes to partition the kingdom. All these activities had enabled the Protestants to strengthen themselves, because the king could not oppose them both at once. The king was obliged to couch his apology in anti-Protestant terms, and to affirm his continuing support for Catholicism; it was essential propaganda—not intended to worry Navarre.

4 August 1589, *Declaration et serment du roi à son avènement à la courrone*

Isambert, xv, 3–5.

From the religious point of view, his accession to the throne placed Henry IV in a fearful predicament. Clearly, as king, he had to support Catholicism; equally clearly, he was committed to the Protestants. Thus, from his camp at Saint-Cloud, he declared his support for Catholicism and his own willingness to receive instruction from a "bon, légitime et libre concile général et national," whatever that might be, which he would convoke within six months or as soon as possible. Meanwhile he confirmed the "traité de la trève," 3 April 1589, which had allowed the Protestants the same religious liberties as the edicts of Amboise, 19 March 1563, and Poitiers, 17 September 1577, although naturally this was not alluded to. These arrangements should stand until they might be otherwise determined by a general peace or by the estates general, which the king would also summon within six months. This document is ably drafted. Its tone was as pro-Catholic as it had to be, yet it deprived the Protestants of nothing.

4 July 1591, Letters Patent
Isambert, xv, 22–27.

Since his accession Henry IV had been too desperately involved in war to attend to other matters. The purpose of these letters was therefore to reaffirm his undertakings of 4 August 1589. He declared his life-long desire for peace, and denounced at some length the continuing rebellion of the Catholic League for purely political purposes. The League had also libeled him to Sixtus V, the late pope, falsely persuading him that the king opposed religion and refused instruction. Meanwhile it was the Catholics themselves, by prolonging the war against him, who had prevented him from assembling the council he had promised. These letters were, therefore, an interim declaration of intent.

4 July 1591, Edict of Mantes
Haag, x, 209–10.

Having, in his letters patent of the same date, made clear his proper Catholic intentions, Henry then ventured to issue this edict reenacting the edicts of pacification, which Henry III had been forced to revoke. Thus he reestablished the position obtaining after the peace of Fleix, 26 November 1580, until such time as peace was restored and he could "pourvoir au fait de la Religion suivant la promesse que nous avons faite à l'avènement à la couronne." Henry's "promesse" referred to his proposal to summon a council and receive instruction, and was intended to mollify the Catholics. But he had never made any declaration of intent that prejudiced the promulgation of a satisfactory edict for the Protestants.

December 1593, Edict of Mantes
Duplessis-Mornay, *Mémoires*, i, *Mémoires de madame Duplessis-Mornay*, 265–67.

The very pressing demand for this edict, which remained provisional, secret, and unsatisfactory to the Huguenots, should be related to the king's abjuration on 25 July 1593, followed by his truce with the Catholic League five days later. Naturally these events incensed and alarmed the Protestants, who pressed the king for better terms, though, in theory at least, they enjoyed all the concessions of the edicts of pacification. They were now allowed a few additional secret articles, which remained in the hands of the chancellor and the secretaries of State. The cult was also permitted—but discreetly—in towns which acknowledged the king, with some local variations according to circumstances. It should also be allowed at court, and in the houses of certain persons of rank. One very important clause was that the king should not be obliged by any oath to persecute the Protestants. This was, of course, a reference to the coronation oath. Since the king's abjuration, and his impending reconciliation with the pope, the oath may have been what worried the Protestants most of all. This draft agreement also provided for a fund to pay for the pastors, a problem which was later reflected in the first royal *brevet*, 3 April 1598, of the edict of Nantes. The deputies departed, however, without having either accepted or refused these articles. It is impossible to estimate whether this edict had any practical effect, but it was a demonstration of the king's continued good will towards the Protestants and may have served as guidance for the conduct of loyal servants.

13 April 1598, Edict of Nantes
Haag, x, 226–57; Mousnier, *L'Assassinat d'Henri IV*, 294–334.   C J O P PS T

The final edict, of Nantes, was naturally based on the previous edicts of pacification, which embodied most of the Huguenots' demands; but it contained much more detail than previous edicts. Little, if anything, was left to chance or to be subsequently worked out. The edict of Nantes was in fact an ensemble of four documents comprising ninety-two general articles, fifty-six secret articles, and two royal *brevets*, both of a later date. The purpose of the edict, as described in the preamble, was to provide all the king's subjects with "une loy générale, claire, nette et absolue, par laquelle ils soyent réglez sur tous les différens qui sont cy-devant survenus entr'eux... et établir entr'eux une bonne et perjurable paix." This, basically, had been the purpose of the edict of January 1562. The difference was that Henry IV had conquered the Catholic extremists and excluded Spain. These achievements enabled him to enforce the edict, at least to a sufficient extent. The first three articles, on amnesty, recriminations, and the restoration of the mass corresponded to those of Saint-Germain, 1570, La Rochelle, 1573, Monsieur, 1576, and Poitiers, 1577. The toleration clauses (articles 6 to 12) were more extensive than ever before, except for the peace of Monsieur. The religious privileges of the nobility were restored. The cult was permitted in all places where it was established, or ought to have been established, according to the edict of Poitiers, 1577, and the treaties of Nérac, 1579, and Fleix, 1580; also in one additional town per *bailliage* or *sénéchaussée*. The construction of churches was permitted in the cult towns (article 16). Protestant burials were to be suitably provided for (articles 28 and 29). Protestants were expected to observe Church holidays, the degrees of consanguinity, and to pay Church dues. There was a new turn to the censorship laws, which had lost much of their importance. Protestant works might only be printed and publicly sold in the cult towns. Elsewhere religious works were subject to censorship (article 21). Protestants were restored to full eligibility for schools, academies, hospitals etc., and for all posts and offices (articles 22 and 27). The justice clauses were similar to those of the peace of Monsieur, which created the *chambres mi-parties*. The edict of Nantes constituted new *chambres de l'édit*, as they were now called, to hear and determine cases in which Protestants were principally involved. The *chambre* in the *parlement* of Paris, which provisionally also covered Normandy and Brittany, is not specified as being equally composed of Catholics and Protestants. The *chambres* for Grenoble and Bordeaux, however, were *mi-parties*. In Toulouse an unspecified existing arrangement was confirmed. Grenoble was also to cover Provence, and Burgundy could apply either to Grenoble or to Paris. These were to be sovereign courts, established within six months. The edict of Nantes, like others before it, provided for the restoration of property and documents; for equality of taxation and the release of prisoners. It also comprised the most comprehensive exoneration clauses for all political and military offenses. It has been frequently stated that the edict of Nantes, with its liberal toleration and guarantee clauses, established the Protestants' "state within the State." In fact, this was established in 1575, and article 82 of Nantes decreed its abolition: "Lesdites assemblées et conseils établis dans les provinces se sépareront promptement, et seront toutes ligues et associations . . . cassées." Furthermore, it was stipulated that there should be no assemblies "autres que celles qui leur sont permises par nostre présent édit, et sans armes." The reference is to article 34 of the second series.

The fifty-six secret articles dealt with executive matters rather than ones of principle. They tended to amplify the first set, often in terms favorable to the Protestants, which might have attracted unnecessary Catholic opposition, particularly from the *parlements* whose registration was required. Article 34 authorized consistories, synods and *colloques* in the cult towns, with royal permission. This set of articles also covered omissions and obfuscations. The royal *brevet* of 3 April 1598 provided, in veiled terms, for a royal grant of 45,000 *écus* per annum for the payment of pastors. This was a new concession. Under the terms of Nérac, 28 February 1579, the Protestants had been allowed to raise money for this purpose. The concession was considered reasonable because the Protestants had to pay ecclesiastical dues.

The second royal *brevet* of 30 April 1598 was more important. It contained the guarantee clauses. These were temporary. They were also contrary to the wishes and authority of the king, who therefore did not want them registered as an edict. The *parlements*, in any case, would probably have refused registration, and this would have sabotaged the whole peace. As *places de sûreté*, the Protestants were permitted to retain for eight years from 1599, all the towns they held in August 1597. This was estimated to comprise about 100 garrison towns, for the upkeep of which the king agreed to pay 180,000 *écus* per annum, and 100 other towns. The king retained the right to appoint their *gouverneurs*, but agreed that such appointments should be acceptable. Henry also undertook to make Protestant appointments to offices—mere eligibility being no guarantee. Finally, he agreed to permit persons of rank to hold the cult at court, provided it was privately done. This had sometimes happened, but had never before been permitted in law. He also allowed the celebration of the cult in any Protestant place in which he was present for more than three days.

Bibliography

Manuscript Sources

PARIS

Bibliothèque Nationale

    Fonds Français (B. N., Mss. Fr.)
    Nouvelles Acquisitions Françaises (B. N., Mss. N. A. F.)
    Cinq Cents Colbert
    Fonds Italien

Institut de France

    Fonds Godefroy

CHANTILLY

Musée Condé

    Archives de Chantilly
    Papiers Condé

GENEVA

    Archives d'État de Genève
    Pièces historiques
    Régistres du Conseil

LONDON

Public Record Office

    State Papers (PRO/SP)

HATFIELD

Cecil Papers, by courtesy of the marquess of Salisbury

Works Cited in the Text

Acta Nuntiaturae Gallicae, ix, *Correspondance du nonce en France, Prospero Santa-Croce, 1552–1554*. Ed. J. Lestocquoy. Rome, Paris, 1972.

Acta Nuntiaturae Gallicae, xii, xiii, *Correspondance du nonce en France, Antonio Maria Salviati*, i, 1572–1574, ii, 1574–1578. Eds. Pierre Hurtubise and R. Toupin. Rome, 1975.

Acta Nuntiaturae Gallicae, xiv, *Correspondance des nonces en France, Lenzi et Gualtiero, légation du cardinal Trivultio, 1557–1561*. Ed. J. Lestocquoy. Rome, 1977.

Amirault, Moyse. *La Vie de François de la Noue*. Leiden, 1661.

Ancel, René. *Nonciatures de France. Archives de l'histoire religieuse de la France*, i, parts i and ii (1909, 1911). *Nonciatures de Paul IV.*

Anquez, Léonce. *Histoire des assemblées politiques de la France, 1573–1622*. Paris, 1859. *(Histoire des assemblées.)*

Archivo documental Español, *Francia, 1559–1566*. 9 vols. Real Academia de Historia. Madrid, 1950–54.

Atkinson, E. G. *The Cardinal of Châtillon in England, 1568–1571*. London, 1890.

Aubigné, A. d'. *Histoire universelle*. Ed. A. de Ruble. 10 vols. Paris, 1886–1909.

Aumale, *Histoire des Princes de Condé pendant les XVIe et XVIIe siècles*. 8 vols. Paris, 1863–96.

Aymon, Jean. *Tous les Synodes nationaux des églises réformées de France*. 2 vols. The Hague, 1710.

Baguenault de Puchesse. *Lettres de Catherine de Médicis*. Vols. vi–ix. Paris, 1897–1905.

Bastard d'Estang, L. de. *Vie de Jean de Ferrières vidame de Chartres seigneur de Maligny*. Auxerre, 1858.

Baum, G., and Cunitz, E., eds. *Histoire ecclésiastique des Églises réformées au royaume de France*. 3 vols. Paris, 1883–89.

Benoist, Élie. *Histoire de l'édit de Nantes*. 3 vols. Delft, 1693–95.

Berger de Xivrey, Jules. *Recueil des lettres missives de Henri IV.* 7 vols. Paris, 1843–58.

Berthoux, Gabrielle. *Antoine Marcourt. Du Livre des marchands au placards de 1534.* Geneva, 1973.

Birch, T. *An Historical View of the Negotiations between the Courts of England, France and Brussels.* London, 1749.

Bonnet, Jules. "L'Église réformée de Paris sous Henri II, ministère de François de Morel." *Bulletin de la société de l'histoire du protestantisme français,* xxvii, 1878.

––––––. *Lettres de Jean Calvin.* 2 vols. Paris, 1854.

Boscheron Desportes, C. *Histoire du parlement de Bordeaux.* 2 vols. Bordeaux, 1877.

Bourrilly, V.-L. *Guillaume du Bellay, seigneur de Langey, 1491–1543.* Paris, 1905.

Brambilla, M. E. *Ludovico Gonzaga, duca di Nevers.* Udine, 1905.

Brantôme, Pierre de. *Oeuvres complètes.* 11 vols. Ed. Ludovic Lalanne. Paris, 1864–82.

Bref discours de tout ce qui a este negocié pour la querelle qui est entre les maisons de Guyse et de Chatillon. 1564. (Attributed by D. Thickett to Estienne Pasquier.)

Brémond d'Ars, Guy de. *Jean de Vivonne sa vie et ses ambassades près de Philippe II et à la couronne de Rome.* Paris, 1884.

Bulletin de la société de l'histoire du protestantisme français. (Bull. Prot.)

Cabié, Edmond. *Ambassade en Espagne de Jean Ébrard de Saint-Sulpice, 1562–1565.* Albi, 1903.

Calendar of State Papers Domestic (CSPD).

Calendar of State Papers Foreign (CSPF).

Calendar of State Papers Rome (CSPRome).

Calendar of State Papers Spanish (CSPSp).

Calendar of State Papers Venetian (CSPVen).

Calvini Opera, Corpus Reformatorum, vols. 29–87. Ed. G. Baum, E. Cunitz, E. Reuss. Brunswick, Berlin, 1863–1900. *(Cal. Op.)*

Capefigue, J. B. H. R. *Histoire de la Réforme de la Ligue et du règne de Henri IV.* 8 vols. Paris, 1834–35.

Catalogue des Actes de François Ier. 10 vols. Paris, 1887–1908.

Cayet, Palma. *Chronologie novenaire.* See Petitot, série i, vol. xliii.

Champion, Pierre. *Charles IX, la France et le contrôle de l'Espagne.* 2 vols. Paris, 1939.

Charleville, Edmond. *Les États Généraux de 1576.* Paris, 1901.

Charrière, E. *Négociations de la France dans le Levant.* 4 vols. Paris, 1848–60.

Cimber et Danjou. *Archives curieuses de l'histoire de France depuis Louis XI jusqu'à Louis XVIII.* 27 vols. Paris, 1834–40.

Concilium Tridentinum. Vols. i–iii. *Diariorum.* Fribourg. 1963–64.

Condé, Louis Ier, prince de. *Mémoires.* 6 vols. Ed. London, 1743.

Coquerel, A. J. *Précis de l'histoire de l'Église Réformée de Paris, 1512–1594.* Paris, 1862. (Coquerel.)

Darest, R. "François Hotman, sa vie et sa correspondance." *Revue historique,* ii, 1876.

De Caprariis, V. *Propaganda et Pensiero Politico in Francia durante le guerre di religione,* i, 1559–1572. Naples, 1959.

Delaborde, Jules. *Gaspard de Coligny amiral de France.* 3 vols. Paris, 1879–82.

——. *Les Protestants à la cour de Saint-Germain lors du colloque de Poissy.* Paris, 1874.

De Potter, Joseph. *Lettres de Saint Pie V.* Brussels, 1827.

Desjardins, Abel. *Négociations diplomatiques de la France avec la Toscane.* 6 vols. Paris, 1859–86. *(Négs. Tosc.)*

Devic, C., and Vaisseté, J. *Histoire générale de Languedoc.* 18 vols. Paris, 1872–1904.

Digges, Dudley. *The Compleat Ambassador.* Ed. London, 1655.

Douais, C. *Lettres de Charles IX à M. de Fourquevaulx ambassadeur en Espagne, 1565–1572.* Paris, 1897.

Douais, M. J. C. *L'Inquisition, ses origines, sa procédure.* Paris, 1906.

Douglas, L. A. *Documents historiques pour servir à l'histoire du Dauphiné.* 4 vols. Grenoble, 1874–84.

Du Bouchet. *Preuves de l'histoire de l'illustre maison de Coligny.* Paris, 1662.

Dufey, P. J. S. *Massacres de la Saint-Barthélemy.* In *Paris révolutionnaire,* vol. iii. Paris, 1838.

Duplessis-Mornay, Philippe. *Mémoires et correspondance.* 12 vols. Paris, 1824–25.

Dureng, J. "La Complicité de l'Angleterre dans le complot d'Amboise." *Revue d'histoire moderne et contemporaine,* vi, 1904–5.

Duruy, Georges. *Le Cardinal Carlo Carafa, 1519–1561.* Paris, 1882.

Ellis, Henry. *Original Letters Illustrative of English History.* 11 vols. London, 1824–46.

Este, Hyppolite d'. *Négociations ou lettres d'affaires ecclésiastiques et politiques écrites au pape Pie IV.* Ed. Paris, 1658.

Evennett, H. O. *The Cardinal of Lorraine and the Council of Trent.* Cambridge, 1930.

Faurey, J. *Henri IV et l'édit de Nantes.* Bordeaux, 1903.

Floquet, P. A. *Histoire du parlement de Normandie.* 7 vols. Rouen, 1840–43.

Fontanon, A. *Les Édits et ordonnances des rois de France.* 4 vols. Paris, 1611.

Forbes, Patrick. *A Full View of the Public Transactions in the Reign of Queen Elizabeth.* 2 vols. London, 1740–41.

Forneron, H. *Les Ducs de Guise et leur époque.* 2 vols. Paris, 1877.

François, Michel. *Le Cardinal François de Tournon, 1489–1562.* Bibliothèque des Écoles françaises d'Athènes et de Rome, fasc. 73, 1951.

————. *Lettres de Henri III.* 3 vols. Paris, 1959–72. In progress.

Frémy, Edouard. *Essai sur les diplomates du temps de la Ligue.* Paris, 1873.

Gachard, L. P. *Correspondance de Guillaume le Taciturne.* 6 vols. Brussels, 1850–57.

————. *Correspondance de Philippe II sur les affaires des Pays-Bas.* 5 vols. Brussels, 1848–79.

————. *La Bibliothèque nationale à Paris, Notices et extraits des manuscrits qui concernent l'histoire de Belgique.* 2 vols. Brussels, 1875, 1877. (Gachard, *Notices et extraits.*)

Gautier, J. A. *Histoire de Genève.* 8 vols. Geneva, 1896–1911.

Geisendorf, Paul-F. *Théodore de Bèze.* Geneva, 1967.

Gomberville, Marin Le Roy, seigneur de. *Les Mémoires de Monsieur le duc de Nevers.* 2 vols. Paris, 1665.

Goulard, S. *Les Mémoires de la Ligue.* 6 vols. Amsterdam, 1758.

Haag, E. *La France Protestante.* 10 vols. Paris, 1846–59. 2nd ed. incomplete, 6 vols. Paris, 1877–88. First edition reprinted in 10 vols. Geneva, 1966.

Haynes, S. *A Collection of State Papers Relating to Affairs in the Reigns of Henry VIII, Edward VI, Queen Mary and Queen Elizabeth.* London, 1740.

Hérelle, Georges. *La Réforme et la Ligue en Champagne, documents.* 2 vols. Paris, 1887, 1892.

Historical Manuscripts Commission. *Calendar of the Manuscripts of the Marquis of Salisbury, at Hatfield House.* 23 vols. London, 1883–1973. (HMC Hatfield.)

Hurtubise, Pierre. See *Acta Nuntiaturae Gallicae.*

Imbart de la Tour, Pierre. *Les Origines de la Réforme.* 4 vols. Paris, 1905–35.

Isambert, F. A. *Recueil général des anciennes lois françaises.* 29 vols. Paris, 1829–33.

Isnard, Albert, and Honoré, S. *Catalogue général des livres imprimés de la Bibliothèque Nationale, Actes royaux.* 7 vols. Paris, 1910–60.

Kingdon, Robert M. *Geneva and the Coming of the Wars of Religion in France, 1555–1563.* Geneva, 1956.

La Ferrière, H. de. *Catherine de Médicis, Lettres.* Vols. i–iv. Paris, 1880–95.

————. "La Troisième guerre civile et la paix de Saint-Germain." *Revue des questions historiques,* xlii, 1887.

————. "Les Dernières conspirations du règne de Charles IX." *Revue des questions historiques,* xlviii, 1890.

La Grange. *Mémoires de Jacques de Caumont, duc de la Force.* 4 vols. Paris, 1843.

La Huguerye, Michel de. *Mémoires.* Ed. Alphonse de Ruble. 3 vols. Paris, 1877–80.

Lalourcé et Duval. *Recueil de pièces originales et authentiques, concernant la tenue des états généraux.* 9 vols. Paris, 1789.

La Mothe-Fénelon, Bertrand de Salignac de. *Correspondance diplomatique.* Ed. J. B. A. T. Teulet. 7 vols. Paris, London, 1838, 1840.

La Planche, Regnier de. *Histoire de l'Estat de France sous le règne de François II.* Ed. Buchon. Paris, 1836.

Léonard, E. G. *Histoire générale du protestantisme.* 3 vols. Paris, 1961–64.

Le Plat, J. *Monumentorum ad Historiam Concilii Tridentini.* 7 vols. Louvain, 1781–87.

Lestocquoy, J. See *Acta Nuntiaturae Gallicae.*

L'Estoile, Pierre de. *Journal de Henri III.* See Petitot, série i, vol. xlv.

Le Tocsain contre les autheurs du massacre de France. Rheims, 1578.

Lettenhove, Kervyn de. *Documents inédits relatifs à l'histoire du XVIe siècle.* Brussels, 1883. (Lettenhove, *Documents inédits.*)

———. *Les Huguenots et les gueux, 1560–1585.* 6 vols. Bruges, 1883–85.

———. *Relations politiques des Pays-Bas et de l'Angleterre sous le règne de Philippe II.* 11 vols. Brussels, 1882–1900.

L'Hospital, Michel de. *Oeuvres complètes.* 3 vols. Ed. P. J. S. Dufey. Paris, 1824–25.

Luçinge, René de. *Lettres sur les débuts de la Ligue.* Ed. Alain Dufour. Paris, Geneva, 1964.

Lutteroth, Henri. *La Réformation en France.* Paris, 1859.

Maimbourg, Louis de. *Histoire de la Ligue.* Paris, 1684.

———. *The History of the League.* Translated by John Dryden. London, 1684.

Mansi, G. D. *Sacrorum Conciliorum.* 1759.

Marlet, Léon. *Correspondance d'Odet de Coligny cardinal de Châtillon.* Société historique et archéologique du Gâtinais, documents, i. Paris, 1885.

———. *Le Comte de Montgomery.* Paris, 1890.

Marsollier, J. *Histoire de Henry de la Tour d'Auvergne, duc de Bouillon.* Paris, 1719.

Martin, A. Lynn. *Henry III and the Jesuit Politicians.* Geneva, 1973.

Martin, Henri. *Histoire de France.* 15 vols. Paris, 1834–36.

Mayer, C.-A. *La Religion de Marot.* Travaux d'Humanisme et Renaissance, xxxix. Geneva, 1960.

Mayer, C. J. *Des États généraux et autres assemblées nationales.* 18 vols. The Hague, 1788–89.

Mergey, Jean de. *Mémoires.* See Michaud et Poujoulat.

Mesnard, L. *Histoire civile, ecclésiastique et littéraire de la ville de Nismes.* 8 vols. 1750–58.

Mesnard, Pierre. *L'Essor de la philosophie politique au XVIe siècle.* Paris, 1936.

Michaud et Poujoulat. *Nouvelle collection des mémoires pour servir à l'histoire de France.* Série i, 12 vols. Paris, 1819–26. Vol. vi, *Mémoires-journaux du duc de Guise;* vol. ix, *Mémoires de La Noue, Mémoires de Jean de Mergey.*

Mignet, F. A. M. "Lettres de Jean Calvin." *Journal des Savants,* July 1857.

Monter, E. William. *Calvin's Geneva.* New York, 1967.

Mours, Samuel. *Le Protestantisme en France au XVIe siècle.* Paris, 1959.

———. *Les Églises réformées en France.* Paris, Strasbourg, 1958.

Mousnier, Roland. *L'Assassinat de Henri IV.* Paris, 1964.

Naef, Henri. *La Conjuration d'Amboise et Genève.* Geneva, 1922.

Navarrete, M. F. *Colección de documentos ineditos para la historia de España.* Vols. i–iv. Madrid, 1842.

Nugent, Donald. *Ecumenism in the Age of the Reformation: The Colloque of Poissy.* Cambridge, Mass., 1974.

Ordonnances des rois de France. Règne de François Ier. 8 vols. Paris, 1902–72. *(Ordonnances.)*

Ouvré, H. *Aubéry du Maurier.* Paris, 1853.

Pagès, G. "Les Paix de religion et l'édit de Nantes." *Revue d'histoire moderne et contemporaine,* n. s., vol. v, 1936.

Paillard, C. "Additions critiques à l'histoire de la conjuration d'Amboise." *Revue historique,* xiv, 1880.

Paris, A. L. *Négociations, lettres et pièces diverses relatives au règne de François II.* Paris, 1841.

Parker, Geoffrey. *The Dutch Revolt.* London, 1977.

Pasquier, Estienne. *Lettres historiques.* Ed. D. Thickett. Geneva, 1966.

Pastor, Ludwig. *Histoire des papes.* 16 vols. Paris, 1888–1934.

Patry, R. *Philippe Duplessis-Mornay, 1549–1623.* Paris, 1933.

Petitot, C. B. *Collection complète des mémoires relatifs à l'histoire de France.* Série i, 52 vols. Paris, 1819–26. Vol. xliii, Palma Cayet, *Chronologie novenaire;* vol. xlv, Pierre de L'Estoile, *Journal de Henri III;* vol. xxxvii, J.-A. de Thou, *Mémoires.*

Picot, Georges. *Histoire des états généraux.* 4 vols. Paris, 1872.

Piot, Charles. *Correspondance du cardinal de Granvelle, 1565–1586.* 12 vols. Paris, 1877–96.

Poirson, A. *Histoire du règne de Henry IV.* 4 vols. Ed. Paris, 1862–67.

Pommerol, M. H. de. *Albert de Gondi, maréchal de Retz.* Geneva, 1953.

Potter, G. R. *Zwingli.* Cambridge, 1976.

Prinsterer, Groen van. *Archives ou correspondance inédites de la maison d'Orange-Nassau.* Série i, 8 vols. Leiden, 1835–96.

Ribier, G. *Lettres et mémoires d'estat.* 2 vols. Blois, 1666.

Rochambeau, Achille Lacroix de Vimeux, marquis de. *Lettres d'Antoine de Bourbon et de Jehanne d'Albret.* Paris, 1877.

Roelker, N. L. *Queen of Navarre, Jeanne d'Albret, 1528–1572.* Cambridge, Mass., 1968.

Romier, Lucien. *La Conjuration d'Amboise.* Paris, 1923.

———. *Les Origines politiques des guerres de religion.* 2 vols. Paris, 1913–14.

———. "Les Protestants français à la veille des guerres de religion." *Revue historique,* cxxiv, 1917.

Ruble, Alphonse de. *Antoine de Bourbon et Jeanne d'Albret.* 4 vols. Paris, 1881–86.

———. *L'Assassinat de François duc de Guise.* Paris, 1897.

———. *Le Colloque de Poissy.* Mémoires de la Société de l'histoire de Paris, xvi. Paris, 1890.

Sainte-Croix, Prosper de. *Lettres adressées au cardinal Borromée.* See Cimber et Danjou, série i, vol. vi, 1885.

Serrano, Luciano. *Correspondencia diplomatica entre España y la Santa Sede durante el Pontificado de S. Pio V.* 4 vols. Madrid, 1914. (Serrano, *Correspondencia diplomatica.*)

———. *La Liga de Lepanto entre España, Venecia y la Santa Sede, 1570–1573.* 2 vols. Madrid, 1918–19. (Serrano, *Lepanto.*)

Soulier. *Histoire du calvinisme.* Paris, 1686.

Sutherland, N. M. "Antoine de Bourbon, King of Navarre and the French Crisis of Authority, 1559–1562," in *French Government and Society, 1500–1850.* Ed. J. F. Bosher. London, 1973.

———. "The Cardinal of Lorraine and the *colloque* of Poissy, 1561: A Reassessment." *The Journal of Ecclesiastical History,* July 1977.

———. *The French Secretaries of State in the Age of Catherine de Medici.* London, 1962.

———. *The Massacre of St. Bartholomew and the European Conflict 1559–1572.* London, 1973.

Theiner, A. *Annales Ecclesiastici.* 3 vols. Rome, 1856.

Thou, J.-A. de. *Histoire universelle.* 11 vols. Ed. The Hague, 1740.

Törne, P. O. von. *Don Juan d'Autriche et les projets de conquête de l'Angleterre, 1568–1578.* 2 vols. Helsinki, 1915, 1928.

———. "Philippe II et Henri de Guise, 1578." *Revue historique,* clxvii, 1931.

Vaissière, P. de. *De Quelques assassins.* Paris, 1912.

Valois, N. "Projet d'enlèvement d'un enfant de France." *Bibliothèque de l'École des Chartes,* lxxv, 1914.

Viénot, John. *Histoire de la réforme française des origines à l'édit de Nantes.* Paris, 1926–34.

Weiss, Charles. *Papiers d'État du cardinal de Granvelle.* 9 vols. Paris, 1841–52.

Weiss, Nathanael. *La Chambre ardente.* Ed. Geneva, 1970.

Index

Alava, Don Francés de (Spanish ambassador in France), 171, 193

Alençon, François, duc d' (duc d'Anjou, *1576*), 161*n*82, 190; proposed marriage to Queen Elizabeth, 185, 200; hostility to Charles IX, 212; adversary of the Guises, 212, 220, 225–26, 233, 234; solicited by the Flemish, 219; conspired at court, 219, 220, 221–22; relations with the Huguenots, 219, 225, 233, 273; promised the lieutenancy general, 221; detained at court, 221, 222, 223; leader of the malcontents, 221, 225, 226; and the Netherlands, 221, 233, 236*n*8, 270, 273, 274; league with the elector Palatine and Condé, 225; escaped from court (*1575*), 225, 226; anti-Guise declaration, 226; pardoned in the peace of Monsieur, 230, 244; proposed marriage to Catherine de Bourbon, 258; furthered the peace of Bergerac, 270; death, 278

Alessandrino, cardinal (legate in France), 195

Alva, Fernando Alvarez de Toledo y Pimentel, duke of: stood proxy for Philip II, 58; at Bayonne, 148–49; planned to "eliminate" Protestants, 149, 150, 151, 160; governor of the Netherlands, 151, 153, 160, 163, 164, 179, 188, 191, 197–209 passim; obstructed peace in France, 172

Amboise, conspiracy of (*1560*), 61, 102–16 passim, 346–53 passim

Amboise, edict of (*1560*), 104–5, 110, 111, 112, 121

Amboise, peace and edict of (*1563*), 142–57 passim, 176, 214, 272, 347–48, 351, 356–57, 358, 359, 363, 368

Amiens, 283, 318, 323, 324, 326

Andelot, François d' (colonel general of the infantry): arrested, 56, 69; attended psalm singing, 65; expelled from the council, 135; life threatened, 150, 163, 171; suspicious death, 170–71

Anduse, Protestant assembly at, 217

Angers, Calvinist church of, 38

Anjou, François, duc d'. *See* Alençon, François, duc d'

Anjou, Henri, duc d'. *See* Henry III (king of France)

Aubigné, Agrippa d', 317, 321, 327

Augsburg, religious peace of, 50, 52

Aumale, Claude de Lorraine, duc d', 146, 150, 155, 158, 190, 192

Auvergne, comte d' (natural son of Charles IX), 321, 321*n*166

Avanson, Guillaume d' (French ambassador in Rome), 50

Bas-Languedoc, estates of, 217

Bayonne, conference at (*1565*), 148–49, 150, 151, 170

383

A